# Revisiting The Chinese Learner
## Changing Contexts, Changing Education

## CERC Studies in Comparative Education

25. Carol K.K. Chan & Nirmala Rao (eds.) (2009): *Revisiting the Chinese Learner: Changing Contexts, Changing Education.* ISBN 978-962-8093-16-8. 360pp. HK$250/US$38.

24. Donald B. Holsinger & W. James Jacob (eds.) (2008): *Inequality in Education: Comparative and International Perspectives.* ISBN 978-962-8093-14-4. 584pp. HK$300/US$45.

23. Nancy Law, Willem J Pelgrum & Tjeerd Plomp (eds.) (2008): *Pedagogy and ICT Use in Schools around the World: Findings from the IEA SITES 2006 Study.* ISBN 978-962-8093-65-6. 296pp. HK$250/US$38.

22. David L. Grossman, Wing On Lee & Kerry J. Kennedy (eds.) (2008): *Citizenship Curriculum in Asia and the Pacific.* ISBN 978-962-8093-69-4. 268pp. HK$200/US$32.

21. Vandra Masemann, Mark Bray & Maria Manzon (eds.) (2007): *Common Interests, Uncommon Goals: Histories of the World Council of Comparative Education Societies and its Members.* ISBN 13: 978-962-8093-10-6. 384pp. HK$250/US$38.

20. Peter D. Hershock, Mark Mason & John N. Hawkins (eds.) (2007): *Changing Education: Leadership, Innovation and Development in a Globalizing Asia Pacific.* ISBN 13: 978-962-8093-54-0. 348pp. HK$200/US$32.

19. Mark Bray, Bob Adamson & Mark Mason (eds.) (2007): *Comparative Education Research: Approaches and Methods.* ISBN 10: 962-8093-53-3; ISBN 13: 978-962-8093-53-3. 444pp. HK$250/US$38.

18. Aaron Benavot & Cecilia Braslavsky (eds.) (2006): *School Knowledge in Comparative and Historical Perspective: Changing Curricula in Primary and Secondary Education.* ISBN 10: 962-8093-52-5; ISBN 13: 978-962-8093-52-6. 315pp. HK$200/US$32.

17. Ruth Hayhoe (2006): *Portraits of Influential Chinese Educators.* ISBN 10: 962-8093-40-1; ISBN 13: 978-962-8093-40-3. 398pp. HK$250/US$38.

16. Peter Ninnes & Meeri Hellstén (eds.) (2005): *Internationalizing Higher Education: Critical Explorations of Pedagogy and Policy.* ISBN 962-8093-37-1. 231pp. HK$200/US$32.

15. Alan Rogers (2004): *Non-Formal Education: Flexible Schooling or Participatory Education?* ISBN 962-8093-30-4. 316pp. HK$200/US$32.

14. W.O. Lee, David L. Grossman, Kerry J. Kennedy & Gregory P. Fairbrother (eds.) (2004): *Citizenship Education in Asia and the Pacific: Concepts and Issues.* ISBN 962-8093-59-2. 313pp. HK$200/US$32.

13. Mok Ka-Ho (ed.) (2003): *Centralization and Decentralization: Educational Reforms and Changing Governance in Chinese Societies.* ISBN 962-8093-58-4. 230pp. HK$200/US$32.

12. Robert A. LeVine (2003): *Childhood Socialization: Comparative Studies of Parenting, Learning and Educational Change.* ISBN 962-8093-61-4. 299pp. HK$200/US$32. [Out of print]

11. Ruth Hayhoe & Julia Pan (eds.) (2001): *Knowledge Across Cultures: A Contribution to Dialogue Among Civilizations.* ISBN 962-8093-73-8. 391pp. HK$250/US$38. [Out of print]

10. William K. Cummings, Maria Teresa Tatto & John Hawkins (eds.) (2001): *Values Education for Dynamic Societies: Individualism or Collectivism.* ISBN 962-8093-71-1. 312pp. HK$200/US$32.

9. Gu Mingyuan (2001): *Education in China and Abroad: Perspectives from a Lifetime in Comparative Education.* ISBN 962-8093-70-3. 252pp. HK$200/US$32.

8. Thomas Clayton (2000): *Education and the Politics of Language: Hegemony and Pragmatism in Cambodia, 1979-1989.* ISBN 962-8093-83-5. 243pp. HK$200/US$32.

7. Mark Bray & Ramsey Koo (eds.) (2004): *Education and Society in Hong Kong and Macao: Comparative Perspectives on Continuity and Change.* Second edition. ISBN 962-8093-34-7. 323pp. HK$200/US$32.

6. T. Neville Postlethwaite (1999): *International Studies of Educational Achievement: Methodological Issues.* ISBN 962-8093-86-X. 86pp. HK$100/US$20.

5. Harold Noah & Max A. Eckstein (1998): *Doing Comparative Education: Three Decades of Collaboration.* ISBN 962-8093-87-8. 356pp. HK$250/US$38.

4. Zhang Weiyuan (1998): *Young People and Careers: A Comparative Study of Careers Guidance in Hong Kong, Shanghai and Edinburgh.* ISBN 962-8093-89-4. 160pp. HK$180/US$30.

3. Philip G. Altbach (1998): *Comparative Higher Education: Knowledge, the University, and Development.* ISBN 962-8093-88-6. 312pp. HK$180/US$30.

2. Mark Bray & W.O. Lee (eds.) (1997): *Education and Political Transition: Implications of Hong Kong's Change of Sovereignty.* ISBN 962-8093-90-8. 169pp. [Out of print]

1. Mark Bray & W.O. Lee (eds.) (2001): *Education and Political Transition: Themes and Experiences in East Asia.* Second edition. ISBN 962-8093-84-3. 228pp. HK$200/US$32.

Order through bookstores or from:

Comparative Education Research Centre
Faculty of Education, The University of Hong Kong, Pokfulam Road, Hong Kong, China.
Fax: (852) 2517 4737; E-mail: cerc@hkusub.hku.hk; Website: www.hku.hk/cerc

The list prices above are applicable for order from CERC, and include sea mail postage. For air mail postage costs, please contact CERC.

No. 7 in the series and Nos. 13-15 are co-published with Kluwer Academic Publishers and the Comparative Education Research Centre of the University of Hong Kong. Books from No. 16 onwards are co-published with Springer. Springer publishes hardback versions.

CERC Studies in Comparative Education 25

# Revisiting The Chinese Learner
## Changing Contexts, Changing Education

### Edited by
## Carol K.K. Chan & Nirmala Rao

Springer　**Comparative Education Research Centre**
**The University of Hong Kong**

# Contents

## CONCLUSION

# List of Tables

# List of Figures

# Abbreviations

| | |
|---|---|
| CHC | Confucian-heritage culture |
| D&T | Design and Technology |
| EDB | Education Bureau |
| ISM | Inventory of School Motivation |
| LPG | Lesson Preparation Group |
| MANOVA | Multivariate Analysis of Variance |
| PIRLS | Progress in International Reading Literacy Study |
| PPCLS | Preschool and Primary Chinese Literacy Scale |
| PPVT | Peabody Picture Vocabulary Test |
| PRC | People's Republic of China |
| QKT | Qualified Kindergarten Teacher |
| SD | Standard Deviation |
| TPD | Teacher Professional Development |
| TRG | Teaching and Research Group |
| TRO | Teaching Research Office |
| TSLN | Thinking Schools, Learning Nation |
| WRAT | Wide Range Achievement Test |

# Foreword

It is seventeen years since I first formulated 'The paradox of the Chinese learner' in a conference in Kathmandu, Nepal. My original formulation of the paradox was that westerners saw Chinese students as rote learning massive amounts of information in fierce exam-dominated classrooms – yet in international comparisons, students in the Confucian heritage classrooms greatly outperformed western students learning in 'progressive' western classrooms. This seeming paradox raised all sorts of questions to which many others have contributed important answers, especially that by Ference Marton on how Chinese learners construed the roles of memory and understanding in ways that were foreign to typical western educators. Much of this work was brought together in *The Chinese Learner* (1996), edited by David Watkins and myself. That work raised more questions still, especially about educational contexts, beliefs and practices, which were investigated in contributions to *Teaching the Chinese Learner* (2001). And now we have *Revisiting the Chinese Learner*, which is a very timely collection of excellent contributions that take into account the many changes that have taken place since 2001, changes such as:

1.  The globalisation of education especially through educational technology, and enormous socio-economic changes, especially in China itself.
2.  Changes in educational policy, aims, curriculum and organisation, and decentralisation of educational decision-making in many Confucian heritage cultures.
3.  Changing theories of learning and teaching, with increasing emphasis on knowledge construction rather than knowledge transmission, and the view of learning and teaching as situated. Thus, rather than talking about *the* Chinese learner, we should talk about Chinese learners in their various contexts and systems.

In the present book, the focus is on how these changes impact: on learners and their beliefs about and conceptions of learning; on teachers' beliefs and conceptions and on their educational practices; and on how teachers are themselves learning to deal with changing policies and practices.

Learning virtues rather than content, especially learning to self-perfect, has long been a traditional Chinese value – and still is, as Li Jin explains, albeit modified to the new context. In Hong Kong, the Education Commission brought about changes designed to reduce the baneful effect of competition in schools, but they pulled their punches. Instead of eliminating banding, a practice very dear to the Hong Kong heart, they reduced the number of bands from five to three. The change, as Watkins' data demonstrates, was no change. Law *et al.* demonstrate a finding that is to recur in this book: in response to changing policies and aims, especially for lifelong learning, the status quo bends but remains. Students and teachers develop a 'new' epistemology of knowledge construction through collaborative learning that sits alongside the traditional conception of absorbing knowledge through didactic instruction for the purpose of sitting exams. Carol Chan sees this occurring in actual teaching practice: a high structure, almost didactic, constructivism that 'forces' students to think. Despite a policy of decentralisation, Rao *et al.* found that the teaching of mathematics is different from traditional 'force-feeding', students now being more actively involved, but apart from resources, teaching is much the same in urban and rural schools. Teaching English by immersion Siegel *at al.* found to be highly effective; while Rao found that in Hong Kong preschools traditional conceptions prevailed: students were expected to be obedient, quiet and to complete all assigned tasks – yet the tasks are now different, requiring more activity and interactivity between teachers and students.

This recurring theme of traditional beliefs sitting alongside changing aims and practices suggests that teachers, and students, are having a hard time grappling with the new ideas and policies. Tsui and Wong try to work out what this means for teacher development in the new China. Again, we find the old and new co-existing. Two traditional notions of enacting theories in practice, and guidance by mentors, are built upon to help teachers through the transition from traditional to more student-centred, constructivist notions of teaching. An important point here is that this transition is contextual. It cannot be ordered top-down but must be worked through by teachers in the context in which they are currently

teaching. Chan and Rao provide an excellent and comprehensive summary of what these contributions mean for easing learners and teachers
into the twenty-first century.

The work presented here should be of interest to educators everywhere. The present focus might be on Chinese systems, but the central
theme, of coping with educational change in a fast changing world, is a
universal concern. It would be too easy for western educators to dismiss
this work as irrelevant to them, but it is not. I am reminded of where I
stood twenty years ago when I came to Hong Kong. The challenges of
integrating what western educational theory saw as good teaching and
learning with what was going on in Hong Kong schools – let alone what
was happening across the border – seemed overwhelming, a paradox
indeed. But differences between systems, in this case Chinese and
western, only overwhelm when we focus on the etic practices and beliefs,
those that are culture-specific. There are, however, universals of human
learning that can only work when contextualised in the particular. As we
see here, Chinese educational systems, wherever they are located, are
embracing global aims and practices of education, while striking an
interacting balance with Chinese beliefs about teaching and learning.
This is an evolutionary process that takes place anywhere, if change is to
be successfully implemented at all.

*John B. Biggs*
*Hobart, Tasmania*

# Preface

This volume is a sequel to two acclaimed volumes, *The Chinese Learner* (Watkins & Biggs, 1996) and *Teaching the Chinese Learner* (Watkins & Biggs, 2001). The pioneering research on Chinese learners, which began in the 1990s, has continued to generate burgeoning research interest. What or who is the 'Chinese learner'? How do Chinese students learn? How can Chinese learners be both rote and successful learners? How are they different from learners in other parts of the world? Is there a distinct Chinese pedagogy? What makes Chinese teachers effective in teaching their students despite what are considered unfavourable conditions (e.g., large class sizes)? Although these questions focus on Chinese learners, they have marked implications for understanding psychological, cultural and contextual influences on learning and development.

Since the publication of the first volume on the Chinese learner, major advances in research have been made, primarily debunking the myth that Chinese learners are rote and passive learners. Many Western educators now look to Asian classrooms for 'secrets' that could possibly improve education in Western contexts. Interestingly, new paradoxes and pendulum shifts have been observed. The once commonly held view that Chinese students are passive rote learners has been replaced with a somewhat glamorized view of Chinese students as successful and competent learners. Accordingly, the usefulness of adopting new teaching approaches, developed mostly in the West, has been questioned by educators, given the view that Chinese learners are apparently better students. When the focus is placed on learners in general, rather than on learners in different contexts and systems, there can be other biases and new questions continue to emerge.

The title of this volume, *Revisiting the Chinese Learner: Changing Contexts, Changing Education,* highlights two related themes that motivated our work. First, there is a need to revisit the notion of the Chinese learner because of wide-ranging socioeconomic changes, technological advances, and educational policy changes all over the world. Chinese students and their teachers now live in a yet faster-changing world with new educational demands for productive citizenship in the so-called knowledge era. Second, it is through examining the Chinese learner in different contexts that we will be able to move beyond dichotomies and understand better the Chinese learner. This book, in particular, responds to the need to understand how Chinese teachers and students face the challenge of educational change and reform. The editors of the volume are Asian by upbringing, but completed their higher education in the West, thereby bringing both insider and outsider perspectives to examining and understanding the Chinese learner.

The volume assembles research by a group of renowned scholars from different backgrounds and disciplines in education who have examined teaching and learning in Chinese societies. The first chapter provides a rationale for revisiting the Chinese learner. The following chapters examine how Chinese cultural beliefs and contemporary changes influence student beliefs and pedagogical practice, and consider how Chinese learners and teachers respond to new educational goals while interweaving new and traditional beliefs and practices. Contributors focus on both continuity and change in analysing student learning, pedagogical practice, teacher learning and professional development in Chinese classrooms and societies. The concluding chapter synthesizes research to provide a framework for addressing the paradoxes and illuminating the educational process for Chinese learners in the 21st century. Although the volume focuses on Chinese learners, it raises questions for scholars examining learning, culture and change and has broad implications for educators around the world faced with educational change and reform.

The book is intended for scholars from a broad range of disciplines, including educational psychology, developmental psychology, learning sciences, curriculum studies, comparative education and educational policy. We hope that the chapters in the book will be useful readings in graduate courses in psychology and education which explore topics of learning and development, curriculum and instruction, culture and learning, and educational change and innovation, and in specialized courses on Chinese learners.

We are indebted to the authors for their willingness to collaborate with us through the long process of this project and for their excellent contributions to the volume. We are also particularly grateful to the following people. First, we must express our thanks to our former colleagues, John Biggs and David Watkins, for their pioneering research on the Chinese learner that inspired us to continue their seminal work. We owe our gratitude to Mark Bray, former director of the Comparative Education Research Centre (CERC) in the Faculty of Education at the University of Hong Kong, who invited us to edit this volume. We continued to receive much support and encouragement from Mark Mason, the CERC director when the volume was written. There are many others who provided different ideas and we have benefited much from their insightful comments. We thank Ference Marton, Linda Siegel and Mark Constas, who had inspiring discussions with us and provided us with valuable feedback. We also thank various anonymous reviewers for their constructive criticisms and suggestions for the chapters. We are grateful for the editorial input provided by Veronica Peterson and Mike Poole, which has improved the chapters.

Our thanks go to W. Y. Bo and Vincent Lee for the cover design, with its illuminating images of Chinese learners in traditional and contemporary settings and with the Chinese characters of 'learning' [xuexi, 學習] in classical form. We thank Yvonne Becher, Diana Lee, Christina Pang, Jin Sun, Abbie To and Coco Zhao for their assistance. Tracy H. Y. Lee deserves special thanks for her meticulous work in checking and putting the manuscript in order. We also thank Emily Mang for her dedication as production editor. We would also like to acknowledge the funding support from the Strategic Research Themes of Comparative Education and the Sciences of Learning, the former supporting the launching of the book project through an author workshop and subsequent editorial input, and the latter the final production of the volume.

We thank those colleagues who have taken an interest in understanding the Chinese learner. We hope that through *Revisiting the Chinese Learner*, we can collectively continue to raise new questions and contribute to the understanding of learning for improving the quality of education in different cultural contexts.

*Carol K.K. Chan & Nirmala Rao*
*May, 2009*

# INTRODUCTION

# 1

# Moving Beyond Paradoxes: Understanding Chinese Learners and Their Teachers

*Nirmala RAO and Carol K.K. CHAN*

## Introduction

Over the past two decades, researchers have accorded increasing attention to understanding Chinese students. This interest has been spurred by many factors, including the consistently high performance of East Asian students in cross-national studies of achievement (e.g., Mullis, Martin, Gonzalez, & Chrostowski, 2004a, 2004b; Organization for Economic Co-operation and Development [OECD], 2007), pioneering research that has sought to explain this superior performance (Stevenson, Chen, & Lee, 1993; Stevenson & Lee, 1990; Stevenson, Lee, & Stigler, 1986), the large numbers of Chinese students studying overseas (Rastall, 2006), and, more recently, the marked expansion and influence of the Chinese economy.

This volume is concerned with understanding the learning and teaching of Chinese students and extends the ground-breaking work discussed by our colleagues, David Watkins and John Biggs, in *The Chinese Learner: Cultural, Psychological and Contextual Influences* (Watkins & Biggs, 1996) and in *Teaching the Chinese Learner: Psychological and Pedagogical Perspectives* (Watkins & Biggs, 2001). This chapter first reviews the major contributions of these two earlier volumes, and then elucidates the rationale for *Revisiting the Chinese Learner*. Finally, we outline the conceptual framework for this volume and provide a brief introduction to the ensuing chapters.

# Contributions of Earlier Volumes

## *The Chinese Learner*

Earlier volumes in this series significantly advanced our understanding of learning as experienced by Chinese students. Watkins and Biggs (1996) coined the term "Chinese learner" to refer to Chinese students in Confucian-heritage culture (CHC)[1] classrooms who are influenced by Chinese belief systems, and particularly by Confucian values that emphasize academic achievement, diligence in academic pursuits, the belief that all children regardless of innate ability can do well through the exertion of effort, and the significance of education for personal improvement and moral self-cultivation (Lee, 1996; Li, 2003). These Confucian values are evident in Chinese families residing in societies with very different political structures, such as mainland China, Hong Kong, Singapore, and Taiwan, and are also manifest in overseas Chinese families. The latter are likely to maintain some culturally determined beliefs and values. Chinese-American parents have been shown to be more similar to their counterparts residing in Chinese societies than to European-American parents (Hess, Chang, & McDevitt, 1987), and the beliefs, values, and attitudes of Asian-American students regarding education are more similar to those held by Chinese students than to the beliefs of European-American students (Chen & Stevenson, 1995). This suggests that Chinese cultural values are transmitted through the expectations and behavior of parents, which means that Confucian notions about learning and education will continue to influence contemporary learning and instruction in Chinese societies.

The first and second volumes introduced the phrases, the "paradox of the Chinese learner" and the "paradox of the Chinese teacher", respectively, and proceeded to explain them. Before we explicate what is meant by the term "paradox of the Chinese learner", it is useful to consider what is meant by student approaches to learning. Three decades of qualitative and quantitative research studies have identified two contrasting approaches to learning known as the "surface" and "deep" approaches. In a pioneering qualitative study, Marton and Säljö (1976) asked students to read an academic text and told them that they would later be asked questions about it. The results indicated that the students either took a surface approach to the task wherein they focused on remembering facts in the text on which they thought they would be tested, or deployed a deep approach to learning that focused on meaning. Using a quantitative research approach, Biggs (1987, 1993) and other researchers (Entwistle, 1981, 2007; Kember, 2000; Ramsden, 1992; Watkins, 1996) investigated the deep and surface approaches to learning adopted by thousands of students from different countries. Deep learning necessitates a critical analysis of new facts and concepts, the linking of new knowledge to prior knowledge, and a focus on meaning, and enables problem-solving in novel contexts. In contrast, when a surface learning approach is deployed, new information is memorized as isolated facts and there is no attempt to link them to existing concepts and knowledge. This approach is considered analogous to rote learning, and promotes the superficial retention of material for assessment rather than long-term retention, understanding, or problem-solving in unfamiliar contexts.

What then is the paradox of the Chinese learner? Simply stated, Chinese students are traditionally considered rote learners, which would predispose them to a surface approach to learning, and are assumed to experience what Western educators would deem a less favorable educational environment (large class sizes, expository instructional styles, and considerable norm-referenced assessment), yet they score higher on measures of a deep approach to learning, display good subject-matter understanding, and show strong academic performance (Watkins & Biggs, 1996, 2001). Indeed, as has been stated, Chinese students have consistently outperformed their counterparts in other countries in cross-national studies of mathematics and science achievement (Mullis et al., 2004a, 2004b[2]; OECD, 2007[3]), and the results from the 2006 Progress in International Reading Literacy Study (PIRLS 2006) show Russia, Hong Kong, and Singapore to be the three best performing countries in terms of Grade 4 reading achievement (Mullis, Martin, Kennedy, & Foy, 2007).

In *The Chinese Learner*, Biggs (1996) and Biggs and Watkins (1996) explained this paradox by highlighting Western misperceptions of CHC.

> Despite large classes, external examinations, seemingly (to Westerners) cold classroom climates, and expository teaching, there are things going on in the fine-grain which are clearly adaptive: predispositions to put in effort and seek meaning; to persist in the event of boredom or failure; and to foster the kind of interaction between teacher and student, and student and student, that engages higher rather than lower cognitive processes. Thus, gross charac-

teristics, such as class size or even heavy external examinations, take on a different meaning in the CHC context to those in the Western context (Biggs, 1996, p. 63).

Biggs and Watkins (1996) argued that earlier research may have used a "Western" lens to interpret learning and teaching in Chinese cultures, and that the dichotomies employed to explain the factors that contribute to student learning and attainment in Western contexts are less distinct in CHC. They suggested that the distinctions between memorization and understanding and the differences among other constructs related to achievement motivation are less clearcut in Chinese students. We consider the perspectives of Biggs and Watkins and some recent research on these dichotomies in the following sections.

## *Dichotomies Used to Understand Student Learning.*

*Memorization versus understanding.* The research presented in *The Chinese Learner* indicates that many Chinese students who use memorization are not rote learners, but memorize with understanding. Marton and his colleagues (1996) argued that memorization can lead to understanding for Chinese students, and that repetition can contribute to higher-level learning outcomes (Dahlin & Watkins, 2000; Marton, Dall'Alba, & Tse, 1996; Watkins, 1996). Research published after *The Chinese Learner* (in *Teaching the Chinese Learner* and elsewhere) also suggests that memorization among secondary and university students in Hong Kong and China involves more than rote or mechanical memorization, as it is integrated with understanding (Gow, Balla, Kember, & Hau, 1996; Marton, Watkins, & Tang, 1997) and shows a distinct trajectory (Marton, Wen & Wong, 2005). Indeed memorization and understanding are seen to be complementary in leading to higher cognitive outcomes (Dahlin & Watkins, 2000). Factor analysis of the Chinese Version of the Motivated Strategies for Learning Questionnaire (see Pintrich, Smith, Garcia, & McKeachie, 1993) as completed by secondary school students in Hong Kong showed that items that tapped rehearsal fell on the same scale as items that tapped higher-order metacognitive skills and involved the understanding and transformation of information (Rao & Sachs, 1999).

It should be noted that in the Confucian tradition, memorization is placed alongside understanding, reflecting, and questioning as basic components of learning (Lee, 1996). Understanding can facilitate memori-zation, and memorization is seen as a precursor to deep understanding (Marton et al., 1996). The distinction between memorization and under-standing continues to garner research interest, and there is evidence to suggest that the use of memorization as a route to understanding is not unique to Chinese contexts, but is also common among Japanese (Hess & Azuma, 1991) and Indian students (Clarke, 2001). This volume presents research that considers how changes in instructional paradigms and the integration of technology into pedagogy have affected the relationship between memorization and understanding among Chinese students.

*Effort versus ability attributions*. The dichotomy used to distinguish the attributions of academic performance in Western contexts may not be relevant in Chinese contexts. Students tend to attribute success or failure in a task to their own ability and effort, luck, their mood at the time, or task difficulty. Western psychologists tend to consider the effort and ability attributions to be at odds with each other, but Chinese students in Hong Kong believe that effort is more important for success than ability, and that ability itself can be improved by working hard (Hau & Salili, 1996; Salili, 1996).

*Extrinsic, intrinsic, and achievement motivation in the Chinese tradition*. Intrinsic motivation is seen as desirable and a prerequisite to deep learning. However, Biggs and Watkins (1996) contended that the distinc-tion between the two constructs is not as clear cut among Chinese learners, and argued that Chinese learners may deploy a variety of strategies that reflect extrinsic (external) motivation to achieve deep and meaningful learning outcomes.

Lee (1996) explained how the Confucian ideology emphasizes the intrinsic significance and the pragmatic utility of education at the same time.

> The fact that a person should seek perfection (pursue sagehood) within and a government office without has thereby become an ideal of the Confucian tradition, which is typified in the notion of "sage within and king without" (*neisheng waiwang*) [內聖外王] (Chang, 1976, p. 293). The process of building sagehood has much to do with education. Likewise, to be able to obtain a government office (i.e., to become king without) is also seen as the product of

education. Education is in this sense seen as an important means to obtain a government office. Of course, a government office can also be an extrinsic reward associated with fame, wealth, a beautiful wife, and upward social mobility, which have nothing to do with internal sagehood. (Lee, 1996, p. 37)

Yu (1996) considered the meaning and nature of achievement motivation among Chinese students from an indigenous perspective. Confucian values, transmitted during the socialization process, influence the nature and form of achievement motivation in Chinese societies. Using empirical research among students and young adults as a basis, Yu argued that achievement motivation among the Chinese is socially oriented, and is directed to perfection of the moral and familial self. For the Chinese, achievement motivation is based on group or collectivist values. Thus, whereas Western students tend to want to do well to meet individual goals, Chinese learners want to do well to please their families as well as themselves. They assume that their success and failure affects those close to them, and feel more pressure to do well in school (Salili, 1996). This is in contrast to Western societies where achievement motivation tends to be individually oriented.

Achievement motivation is held by Western psychologists to be based on individualist, ego-enhancing values (McClelland, 1961). Ego- and task-oriented forms of motivation are considered to be mutually exclusive among Western students (Nicholls, 1984), yet significantly positive correlations between the two variables have been reported among Chinese students (Rao, Moely, & Sachs, 2000; Whang & Hancock, 1994).

The research to date clearly suggests that motivational constructs developed in Western contexts do not adequately describe the achievement motivation of Chinese learners.

*Individual and collective orientations.* The constructs of individualism and collectivism (Hofstede, 1983) have been used to contrast the behaviors of individuals from Chinese collectivist cultures and those from Western individualist societies. Individualist cultures emphasize personal goals and boundaries between self and other, whereas collectivist cultures emphasize group goals and connectedness and ways of behavior that promote harmony among in-group members by helping each other. However, more recently Oyserman, Coon, and Kemmelmeier (2002) highlighted the limitations of the individualism-collectivism model for the measurement of ethnic and cultural differences, especially in cross-cultural studies.

In short, the thesis of *The Chinese Learner* is that psychological attributes, cultural values, and contexts such as educational systems interact to influence student learning, and unless these factors are taken into account and examined from within the culture, Chinese students' approaches to learning and motivation cannot be fully understood.

## *Teaching the Chinese Learner*

Whereas the first volume considered the paradox of the Chinese learner, the second volume focused on the paradox of the Chinese teacher, and sought to explain the following.

> Given that teachers in Confucian-heritage cultures operate under substandard classroom conditions in terms of Western standards, and that CHC students perform so well, how do these teachers do it? How can teachers engage students in productive learning activities when they teach large numbers at a time, in an expository manner, in which the students' role is essentially passive? (Watkins & Biggs, 2001, p. 3)

The second volume is premised on the notion that the way in which teachers think about (conceptualize) learning influences their conceptions about teaching, which in turn affects their approach to teaching. The main objectives and themes of the first two volumes are shown in Table 1.1. The research presented in *Teaching the Chinese Learner* illustrates that Chinese teachers are able to produce positive learning outcomes in their students even though they operate in conditions that Western researchers do not consider conducive to good learning, and explores teacher thinking, classroom practices, and changing teaching through professional development programs.

The findings from the various studies presented in the volume indicate commonalities and distinctions between Chinese and Western teachers in their notions about teaching. For example, although both Chinese and Western teachers feel that they have to promote academic development, Chinese teachers believe that they are also responsible for "cultivating students" and promoting development in non-academic areas. Chinese teachers regard teaching and learning as being more holistic than their Western counterparts, and see themselves as "moral educators" who help students to understand their roles in society.

Biggs and Watkins (2001) showed how the categorizations about teaching espoused by Western researchers are not completely relevant in the Chinese context. Teaching is conceptualized as being either "teacher centered and content oriented" or "student centered and learning oriented" by Western researchers. However, Biggs and Watkins argued that teaching in the Chinese classroom is both "teacher centered" and "student centered." Research on Chinese pedagogy also shows that although classroom teaching seems to the outsider to be "teacher centered," Chinese teachers craft the teaching process with sophistication (Paine, 1990), orchestrate student involvement in large classes (Cortazzi & Jin, 2001), and deploy variation to obtain meaningful understanding (Marton & Tsui, 2004; Mok et al., 2001).

The relationship between culture and pedagogy has been documented in various large-scale observational studies of teaching and learning across countries. The TIMSS Video study (Stigler, Gonzales, Kawanaka, Knoll, & Serrano, 1999; Stigler & Hiebert, 1999) was the first rigorous comparison of actual teaching practices across cultures. Eighth-grade mathematics lessons classes in Germany, Japan, and the United States were compared using video and cross-cultural analyses, and it was concluded that teaching is a cultural activity, as each country had a particular way of teaching mathematics. Alexander (2000) conducted a thorough comparison of primary education in five countries and illustrated how teaching is reflective both of the broader culture in which it is embedded and the cultural universals of pedagogy.

Along these lines, there appears to be a distinct Chinese pedagogy, and research has highlighted the unique way that teaching is orchestrated in the Chinese classroom (Cortazzi & Jin, 2001; Leung, 2005, 2006; Mok et. al., 2001; Paine, 1990). Ma's (1999) interviews with primary school mathematics teachers in China and the United States also illustrate the relationship between culture and teaching. In the interviews, teachers were asked to explain how they would teach four problems covered in the primary curriculum, and Ma found that compared with American teachers, Chinese teachers had a "profound understanding of fundamental mathematics."

Bronfenbrenner's (1979, 1989) influential ecological systems theory initially described four nested environmental systems (micro-, meso- exo-, and macro-systems) that influence the developing child. He posited that there are mutual influences across and within the elements of each system, and that an understanding of the relationships between them engenders a better understanding of the factors that influence child development. Similarly, Biggs and Watkins (2001) contended that to understand learning in context we should not focus on the teacher per se, but should study teaching and learning from a systems perspective, with a focus on the bi-directional relationships between the different elements of the educational system.

Biggs and Watkins further argued that to be able to explain the paradox of the Chinese teacher, we must not focus only on the individual characteristics of a Chinese teacher, but must consider the process of teaching the Chinese learner and its relationship with contextual factors. For example, there is a tendency in the West to focus on expert teachers, whereas the Chinese and Japanese systems, although recognizing master teachers, also emphasize teachers working together to improve teaching through lesson studies, rather than through individual efforts only.

As shown in Table 1.1, *Teaching the Chinese Learner* posits that teacher conceptions affect classroom instruction. A corollary to this is that by changing teacher conceptions about learning one can change teacher practice, which has traditionally been considered hard to modify. Indeed, several of the chapters in the volume showed that it is possible to do so through the introduction of Western-based pedagogical approaches or through professional teacher development programs.

Biggs and Watkins (2001) discussed the issue of identifying the Chinese learner, as well as aspects of the Hong Kong and mainland Chinese educational systems, and the conditions necessary for educational reforms to be successful. We follow similar themes in this volume. They espoused a systems model that emphasizes the interaction among different components to explain the paradoxes of the Chinese learner and the Chinese teacher. Taken together, the earlier volumes advanced the view that Western assumptions about learning and teaching do not necessarily apply in Chinese contexts because of the distinct cultural beliefs of the Chinese about learning and their different education systems.

This volume is also premised on the theses advanced in the earlier volumes, and further discusses empirical research that considers the distinct features of education in the changing Chinese context. We now consider the wide-ranging changes that have provided the impetus for *Revisiting the Chinese Learner*.

# Why Revisit the Chinese Learner?

The earlier volumes advanced our knowledge about learners and teachers in Chinese contexts. It should be noted that volumes such as *The Psychology of the Chinese People* (Bond, 1986) and *The Handbook of Chinese Psychology* (Bond, 1996) and research on filial piety and Chinese sociali- zation (Ho, 1986, 1994, 1996) have also contributed much to the under- standing of psychological processes among the Chinese. However, al- though this volume addresses the application of some psychological processes in the Chinese context, our focus is on understanding the Chinese learner, the Chinese teacher, and the potent influence of changes in sociocultural context on learning and education. Table 1.1 highlights how each successive volume is a natural extension of that preceding it.

Since the pioneering work on the Chinese learner (Watkins & Biggs, 1996, 2001), a burgeoning body of research has developed on the learning and teaching of Chinese students in different parts of the world. Some of this work has continued to advance the ideas proposed in the earlier volumes, and has debunked the myth that Chinese students are rote learners (e.g., Chalmers & Volet, 1997; Dahlin & Watkins, 2000; Kember, 2000; Watkins, 2000). Other important publications include a book volume on *How Chinese Learn Mathematics* (Fan, Wong, Cai, & Li, 2004) and special issues of journals on Chinese Learners in Higher Education (Rastall, 2006) and Construction and Deconstruction of the Chinese Learner (Lee & Mok, 2008). Other authors have focused on the Chinese conceptualization of learning (Li, 2001, 2002), memorization and under- standing (Marton et al., 1997; Marton et al., 2005), the Chinese pedagogy of mathematics (Leung, 2006; Ma, 1999), and the intellectual styles of Chinese students (Zhang, 2008; Zhang & Sternberg, 2006).

Since the publication of the first two volumes on the Chinese learner, many changes have occurred. In addition to the growing empiri- cal literature on Chinese students, the advent of the knowledge era has influenced learning and teaching in Chinese contexts. However, despite tremendous interest in understanding Chinese learners, there is no systematic work to date that examines the influence of the changing educational context on the Chinese learner. Given the pivotal role of context on learning and teaching, there is a need to revisit the Chinese Learner to enrich our understanding of them as they move into the 21st century.

**Table 1.1**

*Rationale and Tenets of the Three Volumes about the Chinese Learner*

|  | Goals | Main theses | Guiding Principles |
|---|---|---|---|
| Volume 1<br><br>*The Chinese Learner: Cultural, Psychological and Contextual Influences* | To explain the paradox of the Chinese learner | Western dichotomies relevant to student learning do not adequately capture learning in Chinese contexts.<br><br>Memorization is intertwined with understanding. | Understanding student approaches to learning using a systems perspective. |
| Volume 2<br><br>*Teaching the Chinese Learner: Psychological and Pedagogical Perspectives* | To explain the paradox of the Chinese teacher | Must move beyond understanding "teachers" to a focus on understanding "teaching."<br><br>The conceptions of Chinese teachers influence their approaches to teaching and learning. | Understanding teacher conceptions and practices using a systems perspective. |
| Volume 3<br><br>*Revisiting the Chinese Learner: Changing Contexts, Changing Education* | To explain the paradoxes and to examine contemporary and future Chinese learners | Wide-ranging societal changes and tensions of old and new views have brought about changes in conceptions and practice of Chinese learners and teachers.<br><br>Contemporary Chinese learners transcend Western dicohotomies developing new epistemology and Chinese teachers transform Western-based pedagogy in teaching Chinese learners of tomorrow. | Understanding both student and teacher conceptions and teacher practices (against the background of changes) using a systems perspective. |

## Changing Socioeconomic and Global Contexts

China has experienced phenomenal economic growth, globalization has occurred, the world has entered a knowledge-based era, and the influence of technology on education is pervasive. Further, both foreign- and Chinese-born researchers are now conducting research on teaching and learning in the Chinese mainland. These macro-level changes have significantly influenced education, and, along with the marked increase in professional knowledge about teaching and learning, have affected educational policies and practices, as illustrated in Figure 1.1. A discussion of the specific ways in which education has been affected is beyond the scope of this chapter, but a useful review is given in Hershock, Mason, and Hawkins' (2007) book *Changing Education: Leadership, Innovation and Development in a Globalizing Asia Pacific*.

## Changing Paradigms Guiding Learning and Instruction

Over the past two decades, there has been a major shift from viewing learning as an individual activity to seeing it as a social, situated, and distributed pursuit (see Bereiter, 2002; Bransford, Brown, & Cocking, 1999; Bransford et al., 2006; Brown, Collins, & Duguid, 1989; Lave & Wenger, 1991; Salomon, 1993). The individualist model of learning has been replaced by a model that considers learning as a sociocultural process and that accords considerable weight to the context in which learning takes place (Bransford et al., 2006; Brown et al., 1989). Learning is seen as being "situated", that is, embedded in a social and physical environment. This focus on the individual, social, and community dimensions of learning has engendered a variety of metaphors to conceptualize learning, including "knowledge acquisition," "participation," and "knowledge creation" (Paavola, Lipponen, & Hakkarainen, 2004; Sfard, 1998).

Changes in the theoretical view of learning have led to the emerging field of learning sciences (Sawyer, 2006), which focuses on the intersection of cognition, technology, and context. Since the 1990s, researchers in learning sciences have examined learning in complex educational settings (Collins, Joseph, & Bielaczyc, 2004). Research on learning and instruction has led to innovative models of pedagogy supported by technology, such as problem-based learning (Evensen & Hmelo, 2000), argumentation (Andriessen, 2006), scientific inquiry (Linn, Lee, Tinker, Husic, & Chiu, 2006), and knowledge building (Bereiter & Scardamalia, 2006; Scardamalia & Bereiter, 2003).

It has also been argued that classrooms should become communities of learning in which students learn how to learn (Bielaczyc & Collins, 1999) and the teacher is no longer seen as merely a source of content and discipline information but as the person responsible for designing the learning environment to support the construction of shared understanding and knowledge.

The systems model taken in *The Chinese Learner* (Biggs & Watkins, 1996) aligns well with the changing conceptions of learning in the fields of educational psychology and learning sciences. We posit that learning is situated, and that it needs to be examined in context if its nature and complexity are to be understood. Emerging research and advances in pedagogy and technology-enhanced learning have provided the impetus for understanding how learning and teaching has developed in contemporary Chinese classrooms and will change over time.

## Educational Policy and Reforms

Over the past decade, there have been major educational reforms all over the world that have influenced pre-primary, primary, secondary, and tertiary education. In some Confucian-heritage culture (CHC) systems, these reforms have involved decentralization, school-based development, the redefinition of educational goals, and an emphasis on lifelong learning.

The promotion of lifelong learning is now etched in educational policy in many CHC systems, including Hong Kong and mainland China, a process in part driven by rapid advances in the scientific and technological domains. These continual changes in information (and society) mean that students will not have the professional knowledge and skills to cope with future changes that will occur in their profession during their working lives if they have only received initial profession training. Other factors such as globalization and the advent of a knowledge-based economy have also contributed to the increased need for life-long education. Further, secondary school graduates today will frequently change their jobs and even careers, further fuelling the need for on-the-job, on-demand, and lifelong learning (Cheng, 2007). Lifelong education is often associated with e-learning or blended learning, pedagogical practices currently being introduced at the school and tertiary levels in CHC systems.

## New Understandings about Confucian Beliefs

As noted earlier, previous volumes in this series have considered the important role of cultural beliefs, including Confucianism, in explaining the paradox of the Chinese learner (Lee, 1996). Although the Chinese learner has been identified as having roots in Confucian-heritage culture, there is much controversy about the nature and interpretation of Confucianism (Fan et al., 2004) as the philosophy has evolved over time. Some researchers argue that Confucianism as it was originally conceived actually encouraged active participation among learners and did not subscribe to the notion of the passive learner. Others have also discussed the possible congruence between Confucianism and new ways of thinking that emphasize reflection and understanding (Lee, 1996; Shi, 2006). Watkins and Biggs (1996) highlighted a particular aspect of the paradox of the Chinese learner that Chang (2000) has termed "vernacular Confucian," or the way in which Confucianism is interpreted and implemented by the lay Chinese person today. Gieve and Clark (2005) further criticized the general view that Confucian beliefs have led to obedient and reticent Chinese students and the adoption of a "deficit" model.

Teaching and learning are culturally embedded activities, but the cultural context is constantly changing. To adequately understand the Chinese learner, the influence of traditional Chinese beliefs and "vernacular" Confucianism on the ethnotheories held by teachers and parents about learning and student achievement must be considered. These include the value of education for family development, an emphasis on the accumulation of knowledge through memorization, the importance accorded to effort, and beliefs related to achievement motivation and collectivist values. In short, the potency of the sociocultural context in beliefs about learning must be adequately considered.

This volume focuses on the influence of recent changes in context on the Chinese learner, as change cannot be successfully effected without taking into account the context in which it is to occur. Sociocultural theory (Vygotsky, 1986; Wertsch, 1991, 1998) has contributed significantly to our understanding of the importance of social context and related implications for attempts to reform education or to import educational ideologies that do not fit local cultures (Serpell, 2002). Here, we continue to explore the influences of culturally-based views on notions of learning.

Changes in socioeconomic and global contexts, learning and instructional paradigms, educational reforms, and long-held ethno-theories about learning affect school organization, curriculum, and assessment methods, which in turn affect teachers, students, and classroom practices.

## Conceptual Framework

We argue that given the recent contextual changes, including the paradigm shift from knowledge transmission to knowledge construction, extant research on the Chinese learner, and wide-ranging social, economic, technological and educational policy changes, there is an important need to *revisit* the existing notions of the Chinese learner and the Chinese teacher. The earlier volumes in the series focused on the paradoxes associated with the Chinese learner and considered how Chinese cultural beliefs and other contextual influences affect teaching and learning. This volume follows the latter tradition to consider how traditional Chinese beliefs, changing educational goals and pedagogy, educational reforms, and wide-ranging socioeconomic factors interact with each other and impinge upon notions of teaching and learning processes and classroom practice. We focus on both continuity and change in analyzing traditional and current notions of the Chinese learner and pedagogical practices in the classroom.

*Where is the Chinese Learner?*

As was the case in the previous volumes, we consider the question of where Chinese learners are located. CHC classrooms vary across geographical locations, and local and overseas students learn differently because they are in different educational contexts. In considering the Chinese learner, we subscribe to the thesis put forward by Gieve and Clark (2005) that it is aspects of the social context, rather cultural heritage per se, that affects student learning. They note that a "Chinese culture of learning" should be seen not so much as the way they do things in China as the way learning takes place in contexts often found in China. Instead of focusing on the larger culture (in this case Confucian-heritage culture) we focus on specific situated responses to associated social and cultural factors. Hence, this volume does not adopt a notion of "Chinese-ness in learning" per se, but focuses more on learning in situ.

## Understanding Learning in Context

The unique responses of Chinese teachers and learners to learning demands are produced in response to their specific situational and contextual factors. Students from and in Confucian-heritage cultures share a common set of values and beliefs about learning that have been transmitted through the generations, and these beliefs and values as they relate to education influence students who have been exposed to them, regardless of where they live. As has been noted, such a situated approach is also congruent with current views of learning that focus on situated learning (Brown, et al., 1989; Lave & Wenger, 1991) and the recognition of the role of context in influencing learning in complex educational settings (see Sawyer, 2006). In short, pedagogy and learning are influenced by the sociocultural context, and in particular the value and belief systems in the societies in which they are embedded.

We believe that our approach, which acknowledges that elements of the system affect each other (Bronfenbrenner, 1979, 1989), is also appropriate for understanding the changing Chinese learner and Chinese teacher. Specifically, we regard the classroom as an ecosystem in which all of the components mutually affect each other (Biggs, 1993). As Biggs noted, it is not only the classroom that acts as a system, the classroom itself is also a system within the larger system of the school, which in turn is embedded in the system of the community. As each element of each system affects another, studying one factor in isolation will not provide a comprehensive understanding of behavior. Hence, the paradox of the Chinese learner and the Chinese teacher exists because learning and teaching do not exist in isolation but within the broader educational ecosystem. We cannot simply replicate Chinese pedagogical practices and expect them to have the same effects in another country, because teaching takes place in different systems and cultures. We need to consider teaching and learning, not just the Chineseness of students or teachers.

It is important to select the most suitable methodological approaches for studying "learning in context." The distinction between etic (from the term phonetics, which is concerned with universal language) and emic (from phonemics, which is concerned with language sounds and the meanings particular to a given language) is an important one in cross-cultural studies. With the etic approach, data collection and interpretation are guided by an a priori theory that is deemed to be universal, whereas with the emic approach data are gathered about beliefs and practices and subsequently interpreted in indigenous terms to reveal implicit assumptions. The first two volumes of the Chinese Learner emphasized the emic perspective, a tradition we continue and we also give a greater emphasis to observational and qualitative studies.

The goal of this volume is to examine the Chinese learner against the background of the changing educational context. In the following section, we examine the key conceptual themes that guide our inquiry and highlight the questions that need to be addressed.

## Student Learning and Understanding

The first theme is concerned with student learning in the changing Chinese classroom. The first two volumes in this series laid to rest the view that Chinese students are rote and passive learners. They also considered the relationship between memorization and understanding reported among Chinese learners, and provided important insights into how students learn discipline-based knowledge and skills. However, questions remain as to how Chinese learners "learn how to learn" and how they deal with novel educational practices. Some of the chapters in this volume address these issues.

We believe that both the old in the form of Confucian beliefs (Lee, 1996) and student cultural beliefs about learning (Li, 2002), and the new in terms of innovative pedagogy and educational reforms affect the conceptions and approaches to learning of the Chinese learner. The juxtaposition of traditional and novel views and practices often leads to conflict, and some chapters in the volume consider how Chinese students respond to the tensions engendered by this confluence.

Research on student beliefs about learning in Western contexts has shown that students vary in their conceptions of learning. Whereas some consider learning to mean the absorption of knowledge, others view it as involving knowledge construction and problem solving (Chan & Sachs, 2001; Lonka, Joram, & Bryson, 1996; Marton, Dall'Alba, & Beaty, 1993). Research has also shown that students who hold deeper conceptions and use active constructive learning approaches tend to achieve higher levels of learning outcomes than those who hold more shallow views of learning (Chan, 2001; Chan, Burtis, & Bereiter, 1997). Some of the chapters in this volume address the changes in teaching that have been engendered by reforms and other innovations, and show that there is clearly value in more in-depth, systematic investigations of student notions of learning and the processes that students undergo in making meaning.

Earlier volumes of the Chinese learner discussed research that used quantitative, qualitative, and mixed methods to study learning among Chinese students. Although surveys have revealed interesting distinctions between learners in Chinese and Western contexts, the findings from qualitative studies have been particularly illuminating. The authors of the chapters in this volume discuss studies that use technology-based innovations to probe more deeply into student conceptions of learning to gain a deeper understanding of the factors that mediate these conceptions.

## Pedagogical Practice

A second theme examines classroom practice in the changing Chinese classroom. Studies conducted in Western contexts have examined student inquiry (see Bransford et al., 2006) and the self-sustaining and generative changes made by teachers (Franke, Carpenter, Fennema, Ansell, & Behrend, 1998), but there is a dearth of such research in CHC classrooms. Against the background of educational reforms that may be at odds with teachers' cultural beliefs, there is a need to examine how pedagogy takes place in the changing socio-political-economic Chinese contexts.

Teacher and student characteristics, learning tasks, resource availability, the physical conditions of learning, and assessment tasks all affect the quantity and quality of classroom interactions. Given the strong performance of Chinese students in cross-cultural studies of achievement, considerable international attention has been directed toward understanding pedagogy in Chinese classrooms, and attempts have been made to adopt Asian educational practices in Western contexts. Hence, "lesson study" is becoming popular in the West, and in some Western countries there has been a "back to basics" movement. However, just as Western pedagogical approaches cannot simply be appropriated for Chinese contexts, "Chinese" pedagogy may not work in Western contexts. The mere transplantation of an approach without considering the context in which it is to be applied may doom it to failure (Biggs & Watkins, 2001), and highlights the importance of a systems perspective.

Watkins and Biggs (2001) discussed the importance of following a systems perspective in examining teaching and learning, noting that there are three levels at which one can understand teaching and learning. The first focuses on examining the characteristics of the students, the second focuses on identifying what teachers do, and the third level examines how teachers engage students in tasks that are appropriate to their cognitive levels in the broader cultural context. This reminds us that good teaching involves designing instruction and engaging students in learning in ways that are contextually appropriate.

*Teaching the Chinese Learner* examined how Chinese teachers could effectively use Western-based approaches such as constructivist learning (Chan, 2001), conceptual change (Ho, 2001), and problem-based learning (Pearson, Wong, Ho, & Wong, 2007; Stokes, 2001) to improve teaching and learning in Hong Kong. The chief questions addressed in this volume are how Chinese teachers align their beliefs and practices to meet the changing educational goals and demands of the 21st century and the kinds of pedagogical changes that they are making.

## Teacher Learning and Development

The third theme examines teacher learning and professional development in the context of education change. As has been mentioned, there are similarities and distinctions between Chinese and Western teachers' conceptions of their roles in student learning. Teachers in Hong Kong, like their Western counterparts, distinguish between transmission and constructivism in their conceptions of teaching (So & Watkins, 2005), whereas greater differences have been observed between the conceptions of Western and Chinese teachers. For example, research has shown that mainland Chinese teachers conceptualize teaching as preparation for examination and conduct guidance, views not found among teachers in Western contexts (Gao & Watkins, 2001).

With the introduction of new pedagogies as a sequel to educational reforms, teachers need to help students to develop problem-solving skills, to learn how to learn, and to work in teams. Teachers everywhere have to cope with the demands of continuing educational change. We consider how educational reforms (including the preparation of students for life-long and life-wide learning) influence conceptualizations of learning among students and teachers and actual classroom practice in Hong Kong and mainland China. The authors of the chapters in this volume present empirical research that illustrates the changes (and the lack of changes) in conceptions about learning and pedagogy based on interviews and fine-grained analyses of classroom proceedings. We reflect on the influence of these changes on conceptions of learning among Chinese teachers and students, and also consider teacher professional development and how teachers learn in the light of educational reform in the Chinese context.

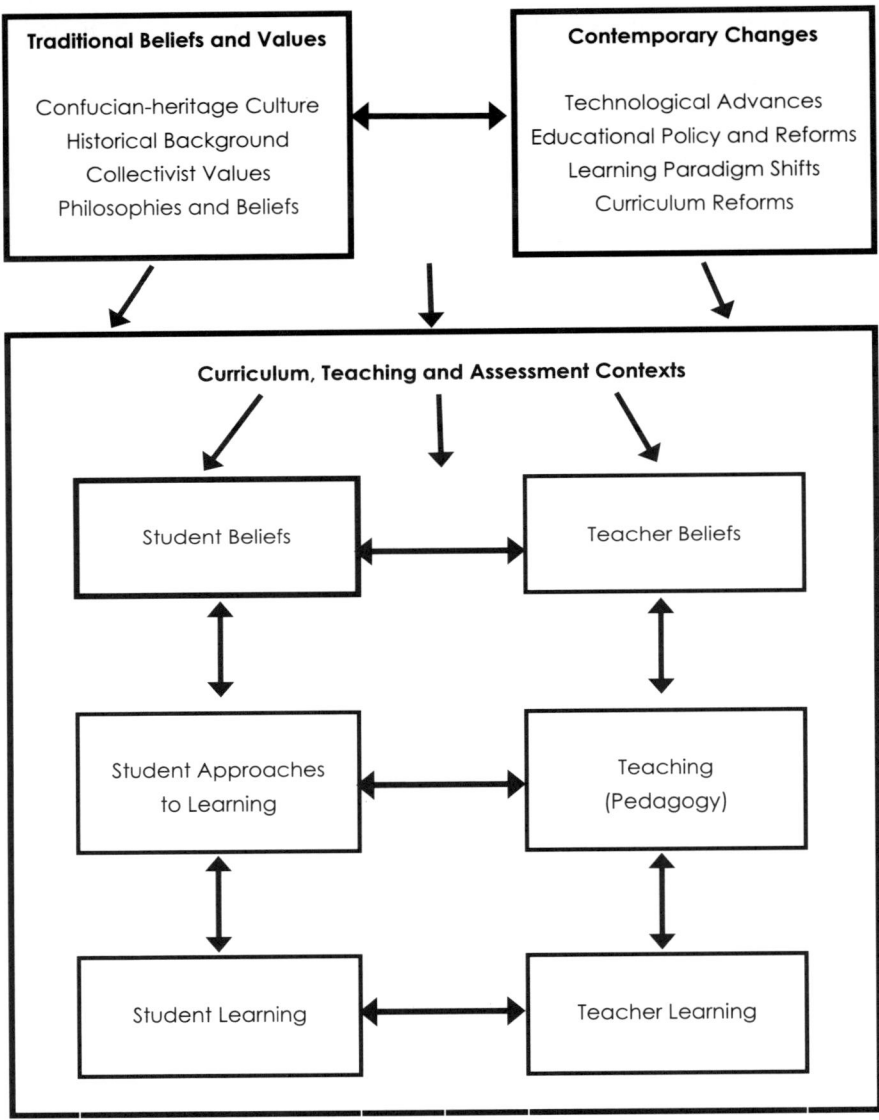

*Figure 1.1.* **Changing contexts, changing education**

# Overview of the Book

This chapter provides a framework for considering traditional conceptions of the Chinese learner and the contemporary changes that have affected the Chinese learner's beliefs about learning (see Figure 1.1, Row 1), and offers a rationale for *Revisiting the Chinese Learner*. Some of the chapters in this volume discuss the tensions between the old and new views of learning, and consider the influences of changes on students, teachers and the teaching/learning process brought about by recent research in instructional psychology, socio-political factors, economic development, and educational reforms (Figure 1.1, Rows 2 to 4). These changes are mediated by the curriculum, teaching, and assessment contexts. Other chapters consider the roles of teachers in changing educational practices and the impact of educational reforms on teacher development.

Chapters 2, 3, and 4 (Column 1, Rows 2 to 4) focus on student beliefs and approaches to learning. Li (Chapter 2) considers the value and meaning of learning for Chinese students, and Watkins discusses their views on competition in Chapter 3. In Chapter 4, Law and colleagues discuss student conceptions of learning in the light of educational reforms and contemporary approaches to learning.

The chapters that follow (Column 2, Rows 2 to 4) focus on teaching and teachers' professional development, beliefs, and practices. Marton and colleagues (Chapter 5) discuss how Chinese teachers prepare students for tomorrow's learning, and highlight that, like their counterparts in different parts of the world, Chinese teachers must respond to the changes brought about by educational reform. Accordingly, in Chapter 6, Chan focuses on the beliefs and practices of Chinese teachers as they appropriate Western-based pedagogy to promote computer-supported learning. The next chapters focus on pedagogical practices in the early and primary school years. In Chapter 7, Rao, Chi and Cheng consider how educational reforms have influenced teaching in urban and rural classrooms in mainland China. Globalization and internationalization have led to an increased emphasis on English proficiency in mainland China, and in Chapter 8, Siegel et al. discuss the efficacy of an English immersion model at the primary level in mainland China. In Chapter 9, Rao, Ng, and Pearson consider teaching at the preschool level and the fusion of traditional Chinese beliefs and Western notions of good educational practice. Teachers have to embrace the changes engendered by educational reforms (Row 3, Column 2). In Chapter 10, Tsui and Wong discuss models of professional teacher development used to support educational change in mainland China (Row 4, Column 2).

In the final chapter of the volume, Chan and Rao synthesize the findings from the preceding chapters and discuss issues relating to the conceptualization of the Chinese learner. In light of the findings of the preceding chapters, they examine how Chinese learners and teachers respond to changing cultural-contextual demands, and consider the contributions of research on the Chinese learner to knowledge about learning and teaching in different cultural contexts.

# REFERENCES

Alexander, R. (2000). *Culture and pedagogy: International comparisons in primary education*. Oxford, UK: Blackwell.

Andriessen, J. (2006). Arguing to learn. In K. Sawyer (Ed.), *Handbook of the learning sciences* (pp. 443-459). Cambridge: Cambridge University Press.

Bereiter, C. (2002). *Education and mind in the knowledge age*. Mahwah, NJ: Lawrence Erlbaum Associates.

Bereiter, C., & Scardamalia, M. (2006). Education for the knowledge age: Design-centered models of teaching and instruction. In P. A. Alexander & P. H. Winne (Eds.), *Handbook of educational psychology* (2nd ed., pp. 695-713). Mahwah, NJ: Lawrence Erlbaum Associates.

Bielaczyc, K., & Collins, A. (1999). Learning communities in classrooms: A reconceptualization of educational practice. In C. M. Reigeluth (Ed.), *Instructional design theories and models: A new paradigm of instructional theory* (pp. 269-292). Mahwah, NJ: Lawrence Erlbaum Associates.

Biggs, J. B. (1987). *Student approaches to learning and studying*. Melbourne: Australian Council for Educational Research.

Biggs, J. B. (1993). What do inventories of students' learning processes really measure? A theoretical review and clarification. *British Journal of Educational Psychology, 63*, 3-19.

Biggs, J. B. (1996). Western misperceptions of the Confucian-heritage learning culture. In D. A. Watkins & J. B. Biggs (Eds.), *The Chinese Learner: Cultural, psychological and contextual influences* (pp. 45-68). Hong Kong/Melbourne: Comparative Education Research Centre, The University of Hong Kong/ Australian Council for Educational Research.

Biggs, J. B., & Watkins, D. A. (1996). The Chinese Learner in retrospect. In D. A. Watkins & J. B. Biggs (Eds.), *The Chinese Learner: Cultural, psychological and contextual influences* (pp. 269-285). Hong Kong/Melbourne: Comparative Education Research Centre, The University of Hong Kong/Australian Council for Educational Research.

Biggs, J. B., & Watkins, D. A. (2001). Insights into teaching the Chinese Learner. In D. A. Watkins & J. B. Biggs (Eds.), *Teaching the Chinese Learner: Psychological and pedagogical perspectives* (pp. 277-300). Hong Kong/Melbourne: Comparative Education Research Centre, The University of Hong Kong/Australian Council for Educational Research.

Bond, M. H. (Ed.). (1986). *The psychology of the Chinese people*. Hong Kong: Oxford University Press.

Bond, M. H. (Ed.). (1996). *The handbook of Chinese psychology*. Hong Kong: Oxford University Press.

Bransford, J., Brown, A., & Cocking, R. (1999). *How people learn*. Washington, DC: National Academy Press.

Bransford, J., Vye, N., Stevens, R., Kuhl, P., Schwartz, D., Bell, P., et al. (2006). Learning theories and education: Toward a decade of synergy. In P. A. Alexander & P. H. Winne, *Handbook of educational psychology* (pp. 209-244). Mahwah, NJ: Lawrence Erlbaum Associates.

Bronfenbrenner, U. (1979). *The ecology of human development*. Cambridge, MA: Harvard University Press.

Bronfenbrenner, U. (1989). Ecological systems theory. In R. Vasta (Ed.), *Annals of child development: Vol. 6. Six theories of child development: Revised formulations and current issues* (pp. 187-249). Greenwich, CT: JAI Press.

Brown, J. S., Collins, A., & Duguid, P. (1989). Situated cognition and the culture of learning. *Educational Researcher, 18*(1), 32-42.

Chalmers, D., & Volet, S. (1997). Common misconceptions about students from South-East Asia studying in Australia. *Higher Education Research and Development, 16*, 87-99.

Chan, C. K. K. (2001). Promoting learning and understanding through constructivist approaches for Chinese Learners. In D. A. Watkins & J. B. Biggs (Eds.), *Teaching the Chinese Learner: Psychological and pedagogical perspectives* (pp. 181-204). Hong Kong/Melbourne: Comparative Education Research Centre, The University of Hong Kong/Australian Council for Educational Research.

Chan, C. K. K., Burtis, P. J., & Bereiter, C. (1997). Knowledge building as a mediator of conflict in conceptual change. *Cognition and Instruction, 15*, 1-40.

Chan, C. K. K., & Sachs, J. (2001). Beliefs about learning in children's understanding of science text. *Contemporary Educational Psychology, 26*, 192-210.

Chang, H. (1976). New Confucianism and the intellectual crises of contemporary

China. In C. Furth (Ed.), *The limits of change: Essays on conservative alterna-tives in Republican China* (pp. 276-302). Cambridge, MA: Harvard University Press.

Chang, W. C. (2000). In search of the Chinese in all the wrong places! *Journal of Psychology in Chinese Societies, 1*(1), 125-142.

Chen, C., & Stevenson, H. W. (1995). Motivation and mathematics achievement: A comparative study of Asian-American, Caucasian-American, and East Asian high school students. *Child Development, 66,* 1215-1234.

Cheng, K. M. (2007). Post-industrial workplace and challenges to education. In M. M. Suárez-Orozco (Ed.), *Learning in the global era: International perspectives on globalization and education* (pp. 175-191). CA: University of California Press.

Clarke, P. (2001). *Teaching and learning: The culture of pedagogy.* New Delhi: Sage.

Collins, A., Joseph, D., & Bielaczyc, K. (2004). Design research: Theoretical and methodological issues. *Journal of the Learning Sciences, 13,* 15-42.

Cortazzi, M., & Jin, L. (2001). Large classes in China: "Good" teachers and inter-action. In D. A. Watkins & J. B. Biggs (Eds.), *Teaching the Chinese Learner: Psychological and pedagogical perspectives* (pp. 115-134). Hong Kong/Melbourne: Comparative Education Research Centre, The University of Hong Kong/ Australian Council for Educational Research.

Dahlin, B., & Watkins, D. A. (2000). The role of repetition in the processes of memorizing and understanding: A comparison of the views of German and Chinese secondary school students in Hong Kong. *British Journal of Edu-cational Psychology, 70,* 65-84.

Entwistle, N. J. (1981). *Styles of learning and teaching.* New York: John Wiley & Sons.

Entwistle, N. J., (2007). Conceptions of learning and the experience of under-standing: Thresholds, contextual influences, and knowledge objects. In S. Vosniadou, S. Baltas & Vamvakoussi, X. (Eds.), *Re-framing the conceptual change approach in learning and instruction* (pp. 123-144). EARLI Advances in learning and instruction series. Oxford: Elsevier.

Evensen D. H., & Hmelo, C. E. (2000). *Problem-based learning: A research perspective on learning interactions.* Mahwah, NJ: Lawrence Erlbaum Associates.

Fan, L. H., Wong, N.Y., Cai, J. F., & Li, S. Q. (Eds.). (2004). *How Chinese learn mathematics: Perspectives from insiders.* Singapore: World Scientific.

Franke, M. L., Carpenter, T. P., Fennema, E., Ansell, E., & Behrend, J. (1998). Understanding teacher's self-sustaining, generative change in the context of professional development. *Teaching and Teacher Education, 14,* 67-80.

Gao L., & Watkins, D. A. (2001). Towards a model of teaching conceptions of Chinese secondary school teachers of physics. In D. A. Watkins & J. B. Biggs (Eds.), *Teaching the Chinese Learner: Psychological and pedagogical perspectives* (pp. 27-46). Hong Kong/Melbourne: Comparative Education Research Centre,

The University of Hong Kong/Australian Council for Educational Research.

Gieve, S., & Clark, R. (2005). "The Chinese approach to learning": Cultural trait or situated response? *System, 33*, 261-276.

Gow, L., Balla, J., Kember, D., & Hau, K. T. (1996). The learning approaches of Chinese people: A function of socialization process and the context of learning? In M. H. Bond (Ed.), *The handbook of Chinese psychology* (pp. 109-123). Hong Kong: Oxford University Press.

Hau, K. T., & Salili, F. (1996). Prediction of academic performance among Chinese students: Effort can compensate for lack of ability. *Organizational Behavior and Human Decision Processes, 65*, 83-94.

Hershock, P. D., Mason, M., & Hawkins, J. N. (Eds.). (2007). *Changing education: Leadership, innovation and development in a globalizing Asia Pacific.* CERC Studies in Comparative Education 20. Hong Kong/Dordrecht: Comparative Education Research Centre, The University of Hong Kong/Springer.

Hess, R. D., & Azuma, H. (1991). Cultural support for schooling: Contrasts between Japan and the United States. *Educational Researcher, 20*(9), 2-12.

Hess, R. D., Chang, C., & McDevitt, T. (1987). Cultural variations in family beliefs about children's performance in mathematics: Comparisons among People's Republic of China, Chinese-American, and Caucasian-American families. *Journal of Educational Psychology, 79*, 179-188.

Ho, A. S. P. (2001). A conceptual change approach to university staff development. In D. A. Watkins & J. B. Biggs (Eds.), *Teaching the Chinese Learner: Psychological and pedagogical perspectives* (pp. 239-254). Hong Kong/Melbourne: Comparative Education Research Centre, The University of Hong Kong/Australian Council for Educational Research.

Ho, D. Y. F. (1986). Chinese patterns of socialization: A critical review. In M. H. Bond (Ed.), *The psychology of the Chinese people* (pp. 1-37). Hong Kong: Oxford University Press.

Ho, D. Y. F. (1994). Cognitive socialization in Confucian-heritage cultures. In P. Greenfield & R. Cocking (Eds.), *Cross cultural roots of minority child development* (pp. 285-314). Hillsdale, NJ: Lawrence Erlbaum Associates.

Ho D. Y. F. (1996). Filial piety and its psychological consequences. In M. H. Bond (Ed.), *The handbook of Chinese psychology* (pp. 143-154). Hong Kong: Oxford University Press.

Hofstede, G. H. (1983). Dimensions of national cultures in fifty countries and three regions. In J. B. Deregowski, S. Dziurawiec & R. C. Annis (Eds.), *Explications in cross-cultural psychology* (pp. 335-355). Lisse: Swets and Zeitlinger.

Kember, D. (2000). Misconceptions about the learning approaches, motivation and study practices of Asian students. *Higher Education, 40*, 99-121.

Lave, J., & Wenger, E. (1991). *Situated learning: Legitimate peripheral participation.*

Cambridge, UK: Cambridge University Press.

Lee, W. O. (1996). The cultural context for Chinese Learners: Conceptions of learning in the Confucian tradition. In D. A. Watkins & J. B. Biggs (Eds.), *The Chinese Learner: Cultural, psychological and contextual influences* (pp. 25-41). Hong Kong/Melbourne: Comparative Education Research Centre, The University of Hong Kong/Australian Council for Educational Research.

Lee, W. O., & Mok, M. M. C. (Guest Editors). (2008). The construction and deconstruction of the Chinese Learner: Implications for learning theories [Special Issue]. *Evaluation and Research in Education, 21*(3).

Leung, F. K. S. (2005). Some characteristics of East Asian mathematics classrooms based on data from the TIMSS 1999 Video Study. *Educational Studies in Mathematics, 60,* 199-215.

Leung, F. K. S. (2006). Mathematics education in East Asia and the West: Does culture matter? In F. K. S Leung, K. D. Graf & F. J. Lopez-Real (Eds.), *Mathematics education in different cultural traditions: A comparative study of East Asia and the West: The 13th ICMI Study* (pp. 21-46). New York: Springer.

Li, J. (2001). Chinese conceptualization of learning. *Ethos, 29,* 111-137.

Li, J. (2002). A cultural model of learning: Chinese "heart and mind for wanting to learn". *Journal of Cross-Cultural Psychology, 33,* 248-269.

Li, J. (2003). The core of Confucian learning. *American Psychologist, 58,* 146-147.

Linn, M. C., Lee, H. S., Tinker, R., Husic, F., & Chiu, J. L. (2006). Inquiry learning, teaching and assessing knowledge integration in Science. *Science, 313,* 1049-1050.

Lonka, K., Joram, E., & Bryson, M. (1996). Conceptions of learning and knowledge: Does training make a difference. *Contemporary Educational Psychology, 21,* 240-260.

Ma, L. (1999). *Knowing and teaching elementary mathematics: Teachers' understanding of fundamental mathematics in China and the United States.* Mahwah, NJ: Lawrence Erlbaum Associates.

Marton, F., Dall'Alba, G. A., & Beaty, E. (1993). Conceptions of learning. *International Journal of Educational Research, 19,* 277-300.

Marton, F., Dall'Alba, G. A., & Tse, L. K. (1996). Memorizing and understanding: The keys to the paradox? In D. A. Watkins & J. B. Biggs (Eds)., *The Chinese Learner: Cultural, psychological and contextual influences* (pp. 69-84). Hong Kong/Melbourne: Comparative Education Research Centre, The University of Hong Kong/Australian Council for Educational Research.

Marton, F., & Säljö, R. (1976). On qualitative differences in learning – 1: Outcome and process. *British Journal of Educational Psychology, 46,* 4-11.

Marton, F., & Tsui, A. B. M. (2004). *Classroom discourse and the space of learning.* Mahwah, NJ: Lawrence Erlbaum Associates.

Marton, F., Watkins, D. A., & Tang, C. (1997). Discontinuities and continuities in the experience of learning: An interview study of high school students in Hong Kong. *Learning and Instruction, 7,* 21-48.

Marton, F., Wen, Q. F., & Wong, K. C. (2005). Read a hundred times and the meaning will appear: Changes in Chinese university students' views of the temporal structure of learning. *Higher Education, 49,* 291-318.

McClelland, D. C. (1961). *The achieving society.* Princeton, NJ: Van Norstrand.

Mok, I., Chik, P. M., Ko, P. Y., Kwan, T., Lo, M. L., Marton, F., et al. (2001). Solving the paradox of the Chinese teacher? In D. A. Watkins & J. B. Biggs (Eds.), *Teaching the Chinese Learner: Psychological and pedagogical perspectives* (pp. 161-180). Hong Kong/Melbourne: Comparative Education Research Centre, The University of Hong Kong/Australian Council for Educational Research.

Mullis, I. V. S., Martin, M. O., Gonzalez, E. J., & Chrostowski, S. J. (2004a). *TIMSS 2003 international mathematics report: Findings from IEA's trends in international mathematics and science study at the fourth and eighth grades.* Chestnut Hill, MA: Boston College.

Mullis, I. V. S., Martin, M. O., Gonzalez, E. J., & Chrostowski, S. J. (2004b). *TIMSS 2003 international science report: Findings from IEA's trends in international mathematics and science study at the fourth and eighth grades.* Chestnut Hill, MA: Boston College.

Mullis, I. V. S., Martin, M. O., Kennedy, A. M., & Foy, P. (2007). *PIRLS 2006 International report: IEA's Progress in International Reading Literacy Study in primary schools in 40 countries.* Chestnut Hill, MA: Boston College.

Nicholls, J. G. (1984). Achievement motivation: Conceptions of ability, subjective experience, task choice and performance. *Psychological Review, 91,* 328-346.

Organization for Economic Co-operation and Development. (2007). *PISA 2006 Science competencies for tomorrow's world.* Paris: Author.

Oyserman, D., Coon, H. M., & Kemmelmeier, M. (2002). Rethinking individualism and collectivism: Evaluation of theoretical assumptions and meta-analyses. *Psychological Bulletin, 128,* 3-72.

Paavola, S., Lipponen, L., & Hakkarainen, K. (2004). Models of innovative knowledge communities and three metaphors of learning. *Review of Educational Research, 74,* 557-576.

Paine, L. (1990). The teacher as virtuoso: A Chinese model for teaching. *Teachers College Record, 92,* 49-81.

Pearson, V., Wong, D. K. P., Ho, K. M., & Wong, Y. C. (2007). Problem based learning in an MSW programme: A study of learning outcomes. *Social Work Education, 26,* 616-631.

Pintrich, P. R., Smith, D. A., Garcia, T., & McKeachie, W. J. (1993). Reliability and predictive validity of the Motivated Strategies for Learning Questionnaire

(MSLQ). *Educational and Psychological Measurement, 53,* 801-813.

Ramsden, P. (1992). *Learning to teach in higher education.* London: Routledge.

Rao, N., Moely, B. E., & Sachs, J. (2000). Motivational beliefs, study strategies and mathematics attainment in high and low achieving Chinese secondary school students. *Contemporary Educational Psychology, 25,* 287-316.

Rao, N., & Sachs, J. (1999). Confirmatory factor analysis of the Chinese version of the Motivated Strategies for Learning Questionnaire (MSLQ). *Educational and Psychological Measurement, 59,* 1016-1029.

Rastall, P. (2006). Introduction: The Chinese Learner in higher education: Transition and quality issues [Special Issue]. *Language, Culture and Curriculum, 19,* (1).

Salili, F. (1996). Accepting personal responsibility for learning. In D. A. Watkins & J. B. Biggs (Eds.), *The Chinese Learner: Cultural, psychological and contextual influences* (pp. 85-106). Hong Kong/Melbourne: Comparative Education Research Centre, The University of Hong Kong/Australian Council for Educational Research.

Salomon, G. (1993). No distribution without individuals' cognition: A dynamic interactional view. In G. Salomon (Ed.), *Distributed cognitions* (pp. 111-138). New York: Cambridge University Press.

Sawyer, R. K. (2006). *The Cambridge handbook of learning sciences.* New York: Cambridge University Press.

Scardamalia, M., & Bereiter, C. (2003). Knowledge building. In J. W. Guthrie (Ed.), *Encyclopedia of Education* (2nd ed., pp. 1370-1373). New York: Macmillan Reference.

Serpell, R. (2002). The embeddedness of human development within sociocultural context: Pedagogical and political implications. *Social Development, 11,* 290-295.

Sfard, A. (1998). On two metaphors for learning and the dangers of choosing just one. *Educational Researcher, 27*(2), 4-13.

Shi, L. (2006). The successors to Confucianism or a new generation? A questionnaire study on Chinese students' culture of learning English. *Language, Culture and Curriculum, 19,* 122-147.

So, W. W. M., & Watkins, D. A. (2005). From beginning teacher education to professional teaching: A study of the thinking of Hong Kong primary science teachers. *Teaching and Teacher Education, 21,* 525-541.

Stevenson, H. W., Chen, C., & Lee. S. Y. (1993). Mathematics achievement of Chinese, Japanese and American children: Ten years later. *Science, 259,* 53-58.

Stevenson, H. W., & Lee. S. Y. (1990). Contexts of achievement: A study of Chinese, Japanese and American children. *Monographs of the Society for Research in Child Development, 55,* (1-2, Serial No. 221).

Stevenson, H. W., Lee. S. Y, & Stigler, J. W. (1986). Mathematics achievement of Chinese, Japanese and American children. *Science, 231*, 693-699.

Stigler, J. W., Gonzales, P., Kawanaka, T., Knoll, S., & Serrano, A. (1999). *The TIMSS-videotape classroom study: Methods and findings from an exploratory research project on eighth-grade mathematical instruction in Germany, Japan, and the United States*. Washington, DC: National Center for Educational Statistics.

Stigler, J. W., & Hiebert, J. (1999). *The Teaching gap*. New York: The Free Press.

Stokes, S. F. (2001). Problem-based learning in a Chinese context: Faculty perceptions. In D. A. Watkins & J. B. Biggs (Eds.), *Teaching the Chinese Learner: Psychological and pedagogical perspectives* (pp. 205-218). Hong Kong/Melbourne: Comparative Education Research Centre, The University of Hong Kong/ Australian Council for Educational Research.

Vygotsky, L. (1986). *Thought and language*. Cambridge, MA: The MIT Press.

Watkins, D. A. (1996). Learning theories and approaches to research: A cross-cultural perspective. In D. A. Watkins & J. B. Biggs (Eds.), *The Chinese Learner: Cultural, psychological and contextual influences* (pp. 3-24). Hong Kong/ Melbourne: Comparative Education Research Centre, The University of Hong Kong/Australian Council for Educational Research.

Watkins, D. A. (2000). Learning and teaching: A cross-cultural perspective. *School Leadership and Management, 20*, 161-173.

Watkins, D. A., & Biggs, J. B. (Eds.). (1996). *The Chinese Learner: Cultural, psychological and contextual influences*. Hong Kong/Melbourne: Comparative Education Research Centre, The University of Hong Kong/Australian Council for Educational Research.

Watkins, D. A., & Biggs, J. B. (Eds.). (2001). *Teaching the Chinese Learner: Psychological and pedagogical perspectives*. Hong Kong/Melbourne: Comparative Education Research Centre, The University of Hong Kong/Australian Council for Educational Research.

Wertsch, J. V. (1991). *Voices of the mind: A sociocultural approach to mediated action*. Cambridge, MA: Harvard University Press.

Wertsch, J. V. (1998). *Mind as action*. New York: Oxford University Press.

Whang, P. A., & Hancock, G. R. (1994). Motivation and mathematics achievement: Comparisons between Asian-American and non-Asian students. *Contemporary Educational Psychology, 19*, 302-322.

Yu, A. B. (1996). Ultimate life concerns, self, and Chinese achievement motivation. In M. H. Bond (Ed.), *The handbook of Chinese psychology* (pp. 227-256). Hong Kong: Oxford University Press.

Zhang L. F. (2008). Thinking styles and identity development among Chinese university students. *American Journal of Psychology, 121*, 255-271.

Zhang, L. F., & Sternberg, R. J. (2006). *The nature of intellectual styles.* Mahwah, NJ: Lawrence Erlbaum Associates.

## Endnotes

[1] Ho (1994) used the term Confucian-Heritage cultures to refer to East and South-East Asian cultures, both Chinese (China, Hong Kong, Singapore) and non-Chinese (Japan, Korea, Vietnam).

[2] Top performers in Grade 8:

TIMMS 1999 Mathematics: Singapore, Korea, Taipei, Hong Kong, Japan.

TIMMS 2003 Mathematics: Singapore, Korea, Hong Kong, Taipei, Japan.

TIMMS 2003 Science: Singapore, Taipei, Korea, Hong Kong, Estonia.

[3] Programme for International Student Assessment (PISA) (2006): Top performers at age 15

PISA 2006 Science: Finland, Hong Kong, Canada, Taipei.

PISA 2006 Reading: Korea, Finland, Hong Kong, Canada.

PISA 2006 Mathematics: Taipei, Finland, Hong Kong Korea.

# STUDENT BELIEFS AND APPROACHES TO LEARNING

# 2

# Learning to Self-Perfect: Chinese Beliefs about Learning

*Jin Li*

## Introduction

Learning is said to be the most remarkable human capacity (Segall, Dasen, Berry, & Poortinga, 1999). Humans have the capacity to learn necessary survival skills, achieve social and emotional understanding, obtain knowledge of the universe, and, perhaps most important of all, acquire culture. Humans are thus products of their own learning and are the carriers of the entire human cultural heritage. There is little wonder why human learning has been, since Greek antiquity, the focus of serious thinkers and scholarly endeavor in fields ranging from philosophy, modern psychology, and neuroscience to the ever-expanding realm of education.

The research topic of learning capacity is vast. Yet dwelling on capacity alone does not seem to lead us to a thorough understanding of how individual humans achieve learning. It is a truism that whereas some very bright children may end up not learning much, ordinary or mentally or physically impaired individuals can accomplish much learning (as illustrated by the heroic Helen Keller and dyslexic people as documented by Fink, 1998). Neither does a focus on learning capacity alone enable us to understand the vast variation found in human learning across cultures. Surprisingly, traditional research has largely neglected an essential area: the learner's outlook toward learning as an object of inquiry, which I term "beliefs about learning".

To be sure, beliefs about learning have been considered broadly by scholars such as Bruner (1986) and in research on conceptions of learning (e.g., Marton, Dall'Alba, & Beaty, 1993) and epistemological beliefs (Hofer & Pintrich, 2001). However, these studies still frame learning, to different extents, from the perspective of capacity and individual differences. The beliefs about learning under discussion in this chapter are those that constitute the self-relevant belief system that children develop parallel to their learning capacity, which is profoundly influenced by children's cultural values and orientation. To demonstrate this purported difference, consider the following learning scenarios.

In ancient Greece, Socrates tutored a slave boy in geometry (Plato, 1981). The boy started out with no mathematical understanding, but through Socrates' masterfully executed tutoring, he discovered geometrical principles himself. Socrates proved his philosophical claim about innate human knowledge and its home—the mind. The boy, one can imagine (even in the absence of historical records), sensed the power of his own mind and experienced a high degree of intrinsic enjoyment engendered by his self-discovery.

Centuries later in a much changed historical era in Europe, Rousseau (1979) in his provocative and spirited volume *Emile*, challenged the educational practices of his day with a radical learner who is naturally curious about the world, an independent thinker, innocent in outlook, and immune to human misery and corruption. Emile learns only according to his inner timetable, and his tutor does not lead the pupil but waits patiently to supply what Emile is ready to learn, to discover for himself.

Around the time of Greek antiquity, China also witnessed the flourishing of a learning tradition, and it, too, was blessed with an exemplary teacher—Mencius (a sage after Confucius). Unlike his Greek counterpart, Mencius (1970) did not tutor slaves but rather kings and dukes. It is said that Mencius led a king to awaken his own conscience. Mencius purportedly asked this king if it was true that he had felt compassion upon seeing a shivering ox about to be sacrificed. When the king confirmed this, Mencius claimed that the king possessed a noble moral sensibility, which the king did not believe he had (thereby permitting himself to be ruthless). Mencius urged the king to extend his compassion to his suffering people and to seek moral self-perfection with devotion and persistence. This is the Confucian way of ruling. It is recorded that the king was enlightened and transformed.

Flash forward to the present, to an ordinary evening on an American college campus, where a student from Taiwan was struggling with her physics homework. Her father had called from Taiwan, as he normally did. Upon learning that his daughter was about to quit, he quoted a well-known saying of Mencius:

> When heaven is about to confer a great responsibility on a man, it will first test his resolution, subject his sinews and bones to hard work, expose his body to hunger, put him to poverty, and place obstacles in the path of his deeds, so as to stimulate his mind [and heart], strengthen his nature, and improve wherever he is incompetent (Wu & Lai, 1992, p. 330).

The father was encouraging his daughter to persist. She did until she had solved all of the physics problems (Chang, personal communication, 2000). That experience, which can readily be understood among Chinese learners, awakens in the daughter personal strength and virtue—the true meaning of "responsibility" in Mencius' passage above.

The two Western scenarios depict two learners who are millennia apart. Much, of course, could be said of the differences between the two. Rousseau disagreed with and challenged Socratic and Platonic thought. Nevertheless, his Emile, viewed from a different culture and across the Western intellectual spectrum, rather than differing from, fundamentally resembles the slave boy. Both start out innocent, both exhibit a nascent curiosity and cherish self-discovery, and both end up triumphant. Together they embody the ideal learner and demonstrate a clear cultural lineage in present-day Western education, which is celebrated by progressive educators and exemplified by the new Reggio Emilia education.

The same can be said about the vast differences in time and space between the king and the college student from Taiwan. Yet, they hear the same message. Both the king and the father (on behalf of his daughter) turn to Mencius as a source of inspiration, not to discover objective knowledge and develop a great mind but to learn how to become a better person with moral virtues.

The two cultures' icons of learners are so different that the attributes of each is conceptualized and elaborated nearly to the exclusion of the other. Thus, we find that concepts such as the mind, reasoning, inquiry, and objective knowledge are rarely, if at all, part of Chinese learning parlance (despite the recent importation of these concepts into Chinese societies from the West). Similarly, the learning virtues of personal effort, endurance of hardship, perseverance, concentration, and humility are hardly discernible in iconic texts of the Western learning tradition despite their increased recognition in today's education (see, for example, Covington, 1992).

Children grow up in cultures that have different learning beliefs. These beliefs influence children's own beliefs in spite of their individual idiosyncrasies in thinking, affect, and behavior. Children's beliefs in turn guide their own learning and ultimately affect their achievement. Understanding learning capacity does not replace understanding learning beliefs. An able person may not be willing to learn; a willing person may not be able. What determines whether a person succeeds as a learner is his or her beliefs about learning. Thus, beliefs must be studied in their own right. Without understanding what the belief system of a learner is, how it emerges, and how it functions in learning, our knowledge of human learning will be deficient.

In this chapter, I present recent research that supports the view that children's learning beliefs are shaped by their cultural learning values. Using Confucian conceptions of learning, I examine the case of Chinese culture and children. I first critique traditional research on Chinese learning. I then discuss empirical research on both cultural- and individual-level beliefs and developmental research. Although I focus on Chinese beliefs, I place this discussion in a comparative context with Western learning beliefs to highlight the concepts that are specific to Chinese culture. I conclude the chapter with future research directions.

## Comparative Research on Western and Chinese Learners

The past few decades have witnessed increasing interest in cross-cultural research that compares Western and Asian school children's learning and achievement. Asian children have often been documented to have higher achievement than their Western peers, especially in math and science (Harmon et al., 1997; Kwok & Lytton, 1996; Stevenson & Stigler, 1992; Watkins & Biggs, 1996, 2001). Although Asian children do not always perform better on all mathematical tasks than do Western children (Cai & Cifarelli, 2004), most of the time, Asian children perform better than their Western counterparts regardless of how they are assessed. Stevenson and Stigler (1992) coined the term "learning gap" to capture these persistent achievement differences. Researchers have postulated a number of factors that could account for this learning gap, which include the following: Asian children attend school for a longer period and do more schoolwork

(Chen & Stevenson, 1989), Asian pedagogical practices are more effective (Hess & Azuma, 1991; Lewis, 1995; Matsushita, 1994; Stigler & Hiebert, 1999), Asian parents hold higher expectations and are more involved in their children's education (Au & Harackiewicz, 1986; Shon & Ja, 1982; Yao, 1985), Asian children's motivation for social mobility through education leads them to study harder (Salili, Chiu, & Lai, 2001; Sue & Okazaki, 1990), and, most importantly, Asians believe in effort whereas Westerners believe in ability (Hau & Salili, 1991; Holloway, 1988; Stevenson & Stigler, 1992).

This research has undoubtedly produced important knowledge about cultural variations in learning attitudes and achievement. However, research impediments remain, four of which are particularly obvious. First, research as a whole tends to rely on highly general, often dichotomous conceptual frameworks that divide people and the world's cultures based on opposites, for example, ability versus effort, success versus failure, intrinsic versus extrinsic motivation, inquiry-based versus rote learning, authoritative versus authoritarian parenting, and individualist versus collectivist/interdependent cultures and selves. These frameworks, although having some utility, function to reduce complex human psychological phenomena into single and simplistic thinking, affective, and behavioral types. Thus, while the high academic achievement of Chinese children is recognized worldwide, the portrayal of the process that leads to such achievement in learning has been caricatured at best and is contradictory at worst. On the one hand, the success of these students is claimed to lie in their belief in effort, not in their ability. On the other hand, they are said to be driven by extrinsic not intrinsic motivation, collective not individual goals, pushed to learn by rote not understanding, and harmed by authoritarian, but not fostered by authoritative parenting. A dichotomous framework does not permit the understanding of learners from any culture from perspectives beyond the framework. As a result, our knowledge remains incomplete, if not wholly distorted.

The second impediment is our comfort with a culture-free, individual-centered view of the learner. Much research on learning and achievement motivation in the West has been conducted from this perspective (Sternberg & Williams, 2002). This tendency is also observable within the Chinese research community. Take the well-known entity versus incremental theory of intelligence (Dweck, 1999) as an example. This theory was constructed based on empirical research on individual children presented with learning tasks of varying degrees of difficulties. The "entity view" pertains to those children who easily give up in the face of obstacles; they are found to subscribe to the view and their intelligence is born and fixed. On the other hand, the "incremental view" pertains to children who persist in the face of challenge or setbacks; they are found to subscribe to the view that intelligence can grow as the person learns more. The conclusion is that some individuals simply are entity learners whereas others are incremental learners. Although Dweck does not make an explicit universal claim about all learners, by implication such dichotomous models are often considered as universal models of learning.

However, most of the research by Dweck and colleagues has been done in the United States on individual children exclusively and without considering cultural influence, as if the United States were not a culture and therefore would not shape children's views of their intelligence (e.g., Dweck & Heckhausen, 1998; Dweck & Leggett, 1988). As it turns out, the so-called entity view (with an increasing number of children subscribing to this as they grow older) is deeply rooted in Western conceptions of intelligence, ability, and competence as significant parts of belief systems (Ruble & Flett, 1988; Stipek, 2002). However, this trend is not demonstrated in the beliefs of children from other cultures (Hau & Salili, 1991). For example, Chinese children do not start out focusing on the idea of intelligence or ability; hence, this theory of intelligence is not central, and could possibly be quite irrelevant to Chinese children's learning beliefs. Instead, they dwell much more on personal virtues (as will be discussed later), other personal and social purposes, and parental guidance among other thoughts and affects. These beliefs become more consistent as they grow older (Li & Wang, 2004). Clearly, individuals are far from free of cultural influences. Examining deep cultural beliefs and values can shed light on the nature and development of children's beliefs.

The third impediment comes from the widespread belief among researchers, Western or Chinese, that learning, particularly school learning, has one overwhelming purpose: to prepare individuals to make a living and all its associated goals for social mobility. Although researchers may not set out to study learning as it relates to social mobility, much of the actual research tends to focus on products of learning such as academic achievement and pragmatic gains that reflect the implicit notion of utilitarian purposes. Admittedly, economic goals may be valued by most learners. However, if making a living were the raison d'être of learning, then we would not care about children's natural questions about the world such as "Why do squirrels have bushy tails?" and "Why does the apple fall to the ground instead of flying away?" Neither would we admire adolescents who engage in philosophical debates about, for example, the meaning of justice. We would not continue to read about the slave boy under Socrates' tutelage or Mencius's advice on overcoming learning obstacles either. But we do, and we do so seriously.

In East Asia, school learning is predominantly dictated by the examination system, regardless of the social or political system of the country. This educational practice has been fiercely criticized from all sides. The historical development dates back to the Chinese civil service examination system established in the seventh century to select the most able and moral individuals to serve the royal court. An evaluation of this system is beyond the scope of this chapter. Suffice it to say that this system has been blamed for all of the ills associated with present-day examination-oriented education. To express the aversion toward this system, Ishisada (1974) used the phrase "examination hell." This loathing is now no secret to the world. Anyone with some degree of sanity must ask the obvious questions: why does this infamous system remain and why do Asians appear disinclined to stop it? To be sure, many attempts to find alternative systems have been made across East Asia. However, the system seems unlikely to disappear. Our innocent inquiry will inevitably lead to the discovery (but also great bewilderment) that most education policymakers in these societies are familiar with the "better" practices in the West, and that many of these leaders have themselves trained in Western education fields.

This absurd (as it seems) discovery demands some explanation. To my knowledge, no one has explained the legitimacy and vitality of this "examination hell" better than Samuel Peng (communication at a meeting of the Chinese American Educational Research and Development Association, July, 1998). According to Peng, Asian societies are "stuck" with the examination system because it is the only solution to a predicament that Asian cultures face. In the Chinese case, the dominant Confucian tradition regards respect for and honoring one's family as the moral foundation for oneself. At the same time, Chinese people and societies recognize another moral principle espoused by Confucius: equality of education for all regardless of personal background.

However, those holding power and access to education (e.g., college admissions officers) face a serious moral dilemma when their family members request favorable treatment (consider the case of a relative whose score is just a few points lower on a college exam, which, in all likelihood, indicates a trivial difference at most among students). If the request is denied, then the person with institutional power will violate the family moral code; if the request is granted, then the person will violate public ethical standards. Alternative means for evaluating students such as teacher recommendations and interviews all involve the same dilemma. There is no solution but to resort to the impartial test score. The only person responsible for advancement in education then is the student himself or herself. Viewed from this perspective, examination hell may not be as hellish as it first seems.

This predicament would not exist in the first place, though, if the whole populace did not desire and actually study to advance their learning. The question remains: why do Chinese feel that they must learn and advance in learning? The convenient reason "to make a living" may explain the purpose of people of lower socioeconomic status, but it does not explain the learning behavior of affluent people. On any university campus, either Asian or Western, it is common to see many Chinese students from affluent homes study just as hard as their peers from humble backgrounds. These students do not need to make a living by studying hard; their families can ensure them a comfortable life. However, they go through the ordeal willingly, as the story of the Taiwanese father and daughter illustrates. Thus, we are compelled to think that learning has to serve other purposes as well. Just because formal school learning in Chinese societies is examination directed does not mean that children's purposes, thoughts, affects, and behavior are all compromised by this examination system (Li, 2003b, 2006). Although a formal schooling structure may be related to cultural beliefs, the two are conceptually and functionally not identical. The retention of culturally based beliefs of immigrant Chinese learners across various school structures attests to the enduring power of culture (Li, Holloway, Bempechat, & Loh, 2008). As will be shown later, the beliefs that motivated the Taiwanese father and daughter are not idiosyncratic but pervasive among Chinese learners.

The fourth and greatest impediment is the continual reliance of researchers on Western concepts without considering indigenous or emic cultural meanings and their psychological manifestations in learning. Despite eloquent criticism by many culturally oriented scholars (Hwang, 2005; C. F. Yang, 2005; K. S. Yang, 2005), this problem still persists. Research on learning is no exception. The dichotomous frameworks mentioned earlier are routinely employed in the study of Chinese learners.

This kind of blind application of Western concepts to children from a very different culture can pose serious validity problems.

A case in point is made by H. S. Kim (2002), who investigated the widely noted phenomenon of the quietness of Asian students in the classroom. Kim examined the belief in and effect of speaking versus not speaking on thinking and task performance among European- and Asian-American college students. It has been a long-standing Western assumption that speaking promotes thinking and learning whereas not speaking impedes them. Asian learners are generally observed to be quiet in classrooms and are reluctant to speak in any public forum (Duncan & Paulhus, 1998; Kim & Markus, 2002; Tweed & Lehman, 2002; Winner, 1989). Kim found that whereas European-American students were more likely to believe in the causal effect of speaking on thinking and task performance, their Asian-American peers were much less likely to do so. Moreover, objective measures of how each group functioned vis-à-vis speaking showed that speaking did not interfere with the performance of European-American students but did with that of Asian-American students.

This study illustrates how some long-held Western assumptions about processes, efficacy, and effectiveness of learning cannot be readily applied to the study of learners from non-Western cultures. The reason is quite simple: these concepts and theories were developed by Western researchers to study Western people based on Western cultural norms and values. Given what we know about significant differences in many aspects of human psychology across cultures, it is perplexing why Western concepts are still dominant in much of the cross-cultural research on learning. Our understanding will be enriched if we look into learners' own thoughts, feelings, and behavior as they are developed in their respective cultural contexts.

## Chinese Learning Beliefs

Although research continues to face the aforementioned limitations, significant advancements in the understanding of Chinese learning beliefs have been made. Recent research yields important findings in three areas: culture-level beliefs about learning, their influence on individual-level learning beliefs, and children's developing beliefs.

# Culture-Level Beliefs

Research since the 1980s provides a general Chinese cultural model of learning. In their influential volume, *The Chinese Learner*, Watkins and Biggs (1996) presented basic beliefs and learning processes observed in Chinese learners that are distinctly Chinese. Lee (1996) offered a historical account of core Confucian values regarding learning and argued for their enduring impact on Chinese learners. According to Lee, most essential for the Confucian belief, in the pursuit of human self-perfection as the highest purpose of life, is through personal commitment to learning. This belief is linked to other beliefs such as social contributions, honoring family, and enhancing social mobility.

In support of Lee's argument, Cheng (1996) collected ethnographic data on Chinese people's beliefs about learning from both urban and rural populations. Cheng concluded that Chinese parents, whether well off or poor, send their children to school not to learn literacy and numeracy skills but rather to become knowledgeable about the world, able to function well in social relations, and most important of all, morally cultivated. In analyzing parent-teacher conflict, Ran (2001) found that whereas British teachers focused on recognizing and expressing satisfaction with the apparent high achievement of their Chinese students, Chinese parents in Britain were discontented, emphasizing the need for more demanding learning materials and their children's continual need to self-improve regardless of their achievement.

Jin and Cortazzi (1998) discovered that a good teacher was described by British students as one who is able to arouse the interest of students, explain concepts clearly, use effective instructions, and organize activities. However, a good teacher was described by their Chinese peers as one who has deep knowledge, is able to answer questions, and is a good moral model. Even Chinese science teachers, but not their Western counterparts, emphasize moral guidance in addition to cultivating students' adaptive attitudes toward learning (Gao & Watkins, 2001).

Research focusing on culture-level beliefs about the learning process has also yielded converging findings. For example, Marton, Dall' Alba, and Tse (1996) investigated rote learning and memorization, a commonly employed Chinese style of learning that has been heavily criticized in both Western and Chinese societies. They found that Chinese memorization was not an end in itself but was rather used as a strategy for achieving deeper understanding. In a related study comparing British and Chinese students, Dahlin and Watkins (2000) found that Chinese students used memorization and repetition more often than their British peers did, and that the two groups used these learning activities for different purposes. British students viewed understanding as a process of sudden insight and used repetition to check their memory. In contrast, Chinese students believed that understanding is a long process that requires extensive personal effort, and that memorization and repetition are two concrete ways of making such effort.

In exploring perceptions of teaching in Hong Kong, Pratt, Kelly, and Wong (1999) found that Western teachers often characterized Chinese students as quiet, receptive, and disinclined to challenge authority. However, Chinese students believed that learning is a gradual process that requires tremendous dedication and methodical steps. Typically, Chinese learners initially commit new material to memory to initiate learning (Wong, 2004), then they seek to understand it. Next, they try to apply the knowledge to real-life situations. Questioning and modifying the original material is the final step. Whereas the last step in their approach is verbally interactive by nature, the first three steps may call for more solitary learning and contemplation (which is an important aspect of the Chinese intellectual tradition; see de Bary, 1983).

Clearly, this learning orientation does not rely on or promote the immediate verbal exchange emphasized in Western learning beliefs, and can extend over a period of time (e.g., publishing a paper to challenge a teacher with whom one disagreed several years earlier). As noted previously, Asian students not only do not believe that speaking promotes thinking as do Western students, they believe the opposite: speaking interferes with thinking (H. S. Kim, 2002). This supports the observation by Pratt et al. (1999) that Chinese students often feel frustrated and bewildered when their Western teachers expect them to engage in questioning and analysis at the very beginning of the learning process.

These research efforts have greatly enhanced our understanding of Chinese learners. Notably, all of these studies were conducted with qualitative methods alone or in combination with quantitative methods, which were designed to uncover valid cultural meanings from emic views without imposing existing Western notions of learning, teaching, and achievement.

*Culture-Level Learning Beliefs as a Meaning System*

In spite of this enhanced understanding, knowledge of Chinese learning beliefs remains discrete. No systematic investigation of Chinese learning beliefs as an organized system of meanings had been done. I began researching this topic by adopting the emic perspective that learning beliefs constitute what anthropologists refer to as cultural models. Cultural models are established by historical and cultural processes and continue to be revised as a culture evolves. They are conceptual frames that shape the experiences of group members by supplying the group's shared ways of explaining, predicting, and interpreting people's minds, feelings, and behavior. These frames also guide people in forming their goals and motivate them to obtain their goals (D'Andrade, 1992, 1995; Harkness & Super, 1999; Quinn & Holland, 1987; Shweder, 1991). Chinese learning beliefs can be studied as such a conceptual system.

I conducted two studies comparing Chinese and American learning models. Prototype methods were used (D'Andrade, 1995; Rosch, 1975; Shaver, Schwartz, Kirson, & O'Connor, 1987). First, I asked 23 college students from each culture to free-associate the term learn/learning (*xuexi*) [學習] (Li, 2001, 2003b; Li & Fischer, 2004). These terms were determined to be closest in meaning based on word frequency and a cross-translation procedure (see Li, 2003b, for more detail). I initially collected nearly 500 terms from students from each culture. Using a rating procedure (60 participants from each culture) for relevance to learning, I obtained 225 Chinese (205 English) core terms. Then, 100 college students sorted these terms into groups based on similarity in meaning. Finally, using cluster analysis, the sorted groups were used to create a concept map of the Chinese learning process, as shown in Figure 2.1 (the American map is not shown but will be alluded to).

This map contains much detailed information but suffices to highlight the most relevant features. It displays the desirable versus the undesirable approaches to learning with a preference/value. The majority of terms fall on the desirable side, which contains two further distinctions: seeking knowledge and achievement categories and standards. Based on the assumption of prototype methods, a greater number of items indicates greater awareness/emphasis of the conceptions in that culture (Li, 2003b; Shaver et al., 1987).

Under seeking knowledge, the most significant groups are (1) heart

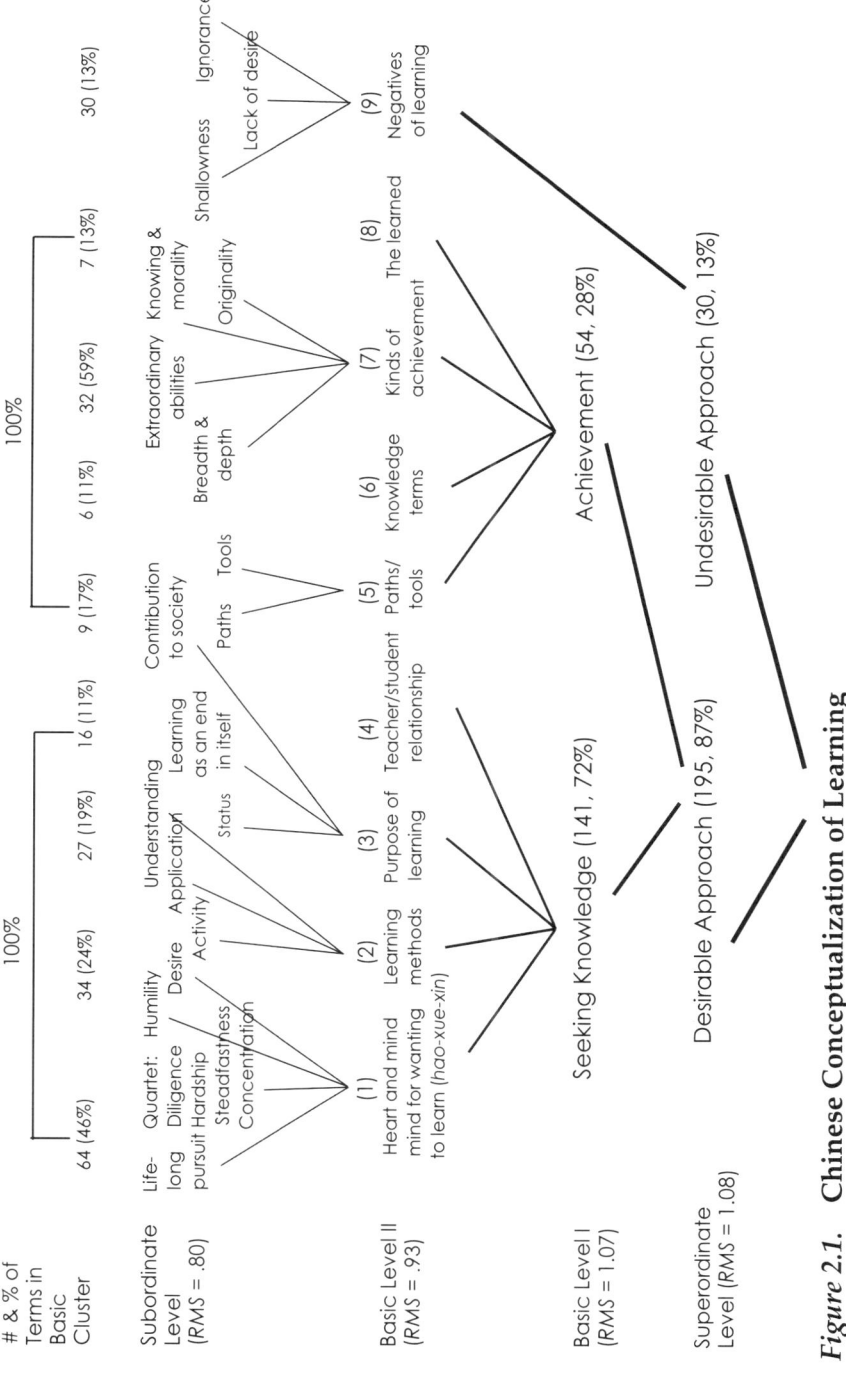

*Figure 2.1.*   **Chinese Conceptualization of Learning**

and mind for wanting to learn (*hao-xue-xin*) [好學心], which includes: (a) lifelong pursuit of learning, (b) a set of learning virtues (diligence, endurance of hardship, steadfast perseverance, and concentration), (c) humility, and (d) desire to learn; and (2) purpose of learning, which contains three essential notions: (a) learning as an end in itself, (b) status, and (c) contributions to society. Under achievement there is one significant dimension: kinds of achievement, including breadth and depth of knowledge, abilities, unity of knowing and morality, and originality.

In comparison, the American map did not display these dimensions, but featured two significant dimensions: (1) learning activities, which focused on (a) thinking, (b) inquiry, (c) active learning, and (d) communicating; and (2) learner's internal enabling characteristics which included (a) cognitive skills, (b) motivation, (c) open mindedness, and (d) intelligence.

In the second study, I asked 62 college students to describe the ideal learner in their respective cultures (124 students in the sample) (Li, 2002a; Li & Fischer, 2004). Ideal learner images instead of average learners were targeted because they provide what developmental researchers term the "optimum" in developmental outcomes. In addition, cultures have preferable "endpoints" (Bruner, 1986; Rogers, 1969) or "optimal ways of being" (Csikszentmihalyi & Rathunde, 1998) toward which younger members of culture are enculturated. Although no two children will achieve identical outcomes in the enculturation process due to diversity in individual characteristics and contextual influence, it is important to describe ideals because they exist in people's minds and guide people's behavior (D'Andrade, 1992). The image of the ideal learner, as opposed to words and phrases in the first study, would also compensate for the limitations inherent in the lexicon from which I derived the culture-level learning beliefs.

Thus, I probed four specific dimensions of the ideal learner: (1) thinking on the nature of knowledge, purposes and processes of learning, and views of intelligence and excellence; (2) understanding of the relationship between learning and one's moral development; (3) types of learning behavior in routine situations, including high achievement, high intelligence, failure, not understanding concepts, inability to learn despite effort, and boredom; and (4) emotional patterns associated with good or poor learning. The written descriptions of each of these dimensions were analyzed both qualitatively and quantitatively (Li, 2002a).

These procedures yielded four profiles corresponding to the four dimensions of the ideal learner for each culture.

The basic findings from the two studies converge to a comprehensive model of Chinese learning. Figure 2.2 shows a diagram of the proposed Chinese cultural learning model, which includes four broad dimensions: purpose, agency, achievement standards, and affect. Each dimension contains a number of subcomponents, which I will discuss next.

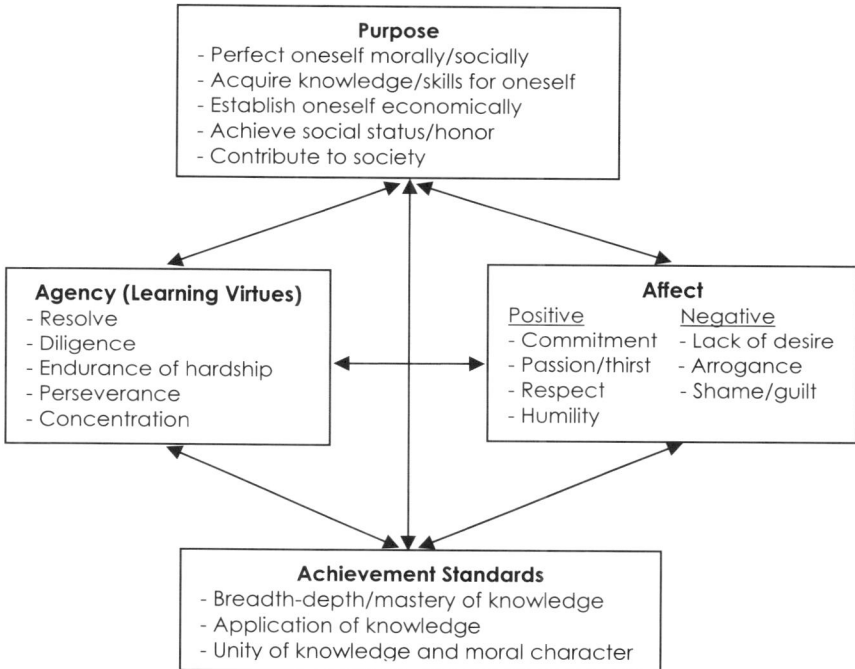

*Figure 2.2.* **The dynamic relationships among purpose, agency, affect, and achievement standards in the Chinese learning model**

*Purpose of learning.* Five main purposes were found: (1) perfect oneself morally/socially, (2) acquire knowledge/skills for oneself, (3) establish oneself economically, (4) achieve social status/honor, and (5) contribute to society. Students saw the foremost purpose of learning as the need to perfect oneself morally. This purpose is deeply influenced by the Confucian teaching of *ren* [仁], which is the lifelong striving to become the most genuine, sincere, and humane person that one can be (de Bary, 1983; Tu, 1979). Ren is regarded as the highest purpose of human life. However, a person is not born but rather learns to develop ren. Therefore, the most important purpose of learning is to engage in this process of one's own moral development. Such learning is called "great learning," as opposed to the narrowly defined "skill learning" (Lee, 1996; Li, 2003a). This great learning is the very model of life envisioned in Confucian thought and is deeply inspiring to Chinese. Indeed, such purpose of learning was Mencius' only concern in tutoring his king. It does seem to resonate among present-day Chinese learners (and teachers) as found by various researchers reviewed previously.

The second purpose was to acquire knowledge and skills for oneself, which is basically a cognitive goal, for one needs to understand how both the natural and social world operate. Knowledge is regarded as so powerful a personal asset that it is believed literally to lift people out of the darkness of ignorance. A person with knowledge is one who can see through deceptions and make wise judgments in life. The third purpose was to establish oneself economically. For Chinese ideal learners, knowledge and skill are also needed for their survival, self-sufficiency, and success in their careers.

The fourth purpose, achieving social status and honor, is related to the third purpose. It is rooted in the civil service examination system that lasted from the seventh century into the beginning of the twentieth century (Lee, 1996). This system, which aimed to make possible the Confucian ideal of equality of education for all, emphasized both moral self-cultivation and literary (literacy) achievement. Scholars from all walks of life, irrespective of their social stratum, partook in this exam. Those who were able to demonstrate both superior moral character and literary achievement succeeded. Once successful, they were appointed to various high governmental positions, thus accruing great political power in addition to their already superior moral and literary achievement. If one of these tripartite accomplishments alone was reason for respect and honor, then their combination only intensified the social status of the person and his/her kin. Although the old system was abolished, the present educational systems in Chinese regions continue to rely on examinations for selecting academically more able students to attend highly competitive higher education. High achievement is equivalent to better jobs and upward social mobility. Even if this pursuit results in examination hell, not having such aspirations and making such effort is tantamount to personal resignation from life.

The final purpose was to contribute to society, which has been a value in the Confucian learning tradition that has consistently inspired Chinese learners. It functions not only to validate the self-perfection of individuals and their pursuit of knowledge, but also binds these to a higher moral and social obligation. Learning is no longer delineated as an individual and personal matter; rather, it is linked to society and the commonwealth of which one is a part (Cheng, 1996; Li, 2002a; Wu & Lai, 1992).

These purposes are interrelated, and several are explicitly part of Confucian beliefs about learning and actively promoted among Asian families, communities, schools, and societies (Cheng, 1996; Gao & Watkins, 2001; Lee, 1996; Yu & Yang, 1994). However, Chinese people do not view the pursuit of socioeconomic success and status as contradictory to their pursuit of more "lofty" goals because a person needs all of these to lead a fuller life.

By comparison, the purpose of learning in the American model centered around developing the mind and understanding the world. When asked to define knowledge, for example, 79% of Chinese college students (but only 15% of European-American students) defined it as the "need to perfect oneself" and "spiritual wealth/power"; and 32% of Chinese students (as opposed to 96% of American students) defined it in terms of facts, information, skills, and understanding of the world. The mental references of American students included various kinds of thinking such as deductive and inductive reasoning, analysis, inquiry, and scientific discovery, which mirrors the goal of Socratic tutoring. Few Chinese respondents referred to thinking with such elaboration.

*Agency and learning virtues.* Agency refers to human acts done intentionally (Bandura, 2001). An agentic person in learning is one who plans for future action, anticipates consequences, selects a course of action, and self-regulates his or her learning to achieve his or her learning goals (Corno, 2004; Schunk & Zimmerman, 2003). As noted earlier, traditional research portrays Chinese learners as passive, deferent to authority, and lacking initiative and creativity (Keats, 1982; Pratt et al., 1999; Tweed & Lehman, 2002) because they learn to please parents and teachers, not for their own growth (U. Kim, 1997); they are extrinsically, not intrinsically, motivated. In other words, they lack a strong sense of personal agency in learning. However, as will be seen below, this image of the Chinese learner is not supported by the open-ended data that I collected. Rather, these data reveal a strong sense of personal agency, as demonstrated in the Chinese cultural learning model.

When the Chinese respondents were asked to describe how an ideal learner learns (i.e., what he or she does when encountering difficulties, failure, etc.), they surprisingly did not describe that which was considered a typical learning task or process (e.g., reading) by the American respondents. Instead, they wrote extensively about what I have termed "learning virtues" (Li, 2002a) (see "Quartet" in Figure 2.1). The term "learning virtues" was used because these virtues emphasize a morally good and desirable dispositional quality that underlies personal agency and action. Five such virtues emerged.

The *first* was the notion of resolve *(fen)* [奮] or *(fafen)* [發奮], which refers to the determination of a learner to come to a course of action and the degree to which he or she is prepared to follow through on his or her commitment. *Fen* is believed to be necessary to ensure one's goal clarification; the course of action one must take to realize one's goal; and a way to hold oneself accountable for one's temptation to stray from the course of action, or simply to give up in the face of obstacles. Frequently, upon making a resolution, people will share their *fen* with their family or close friends, who serve as witnesses. Such witnesses are invited to monitor, watch for, and even demand consistency between one's resolve and follow-up actions.

The *second* virtue was diligence *(qin)* [勤], which refers to frequent studying behavior and emphasizes much time spent on learning. If one is required to act in a manner that requires personal resolve, then diligence is the immediate measure and manifestation of that resolve. Therefore, resolve and diligence go hand in hand, and thus, the combined term in Chinese, *qinfen* [勤奮]. However, psychologically there are two steps although behaviorally only diligence is observable. Diligence is also believed to ensure familiarity, which in turn opens up opportunities for mastery (Li, 2001).

The *third* virtue was endurance of hardship *(keku)* [刻苦], which involves overcoming the difficulties and obstacles that one is bound to encounter in learning. Three kinds of difficulties were identified: (1) physical drudgery and poverty, (2) difficult knowledge and learning tasks, and (3) lack of natural ability. Physical drudgery and poverty are considered hardships and have been unavoidable throughout Chinese history. Despite recent improved living standards, excessive physical labor and poverty remain the harsh reality for many. Difficulty in understanding particular academic concepts is routine for any learner. Respondents clearly distinguished individual differences in natural capacity and acknowledged the impact of such differences on people's learning. However, there was also consensus that these obstacles are not reasons for not learning. Instead, one needs to develop the virtue of endurance of hardship (as the message the Taiwanese father conveyed to his daughter), which is believed to enable the learner to combat these hardships.

The *fourth* virtue was perseverance (*hengxin*) [恒心], which concerns one's general attitude toward learning and behavioral tendencies in the course of one's life. Perseverance is believed to be important because there are no shortcuts to learning. Knowledge comes only through a long process that is fraught with obstacles and distractions. Perseverance is believed to be crucial in helping a person stay on the course from the beginning to the very end, no matter how long it takes (Lee, 1996).

The *final* virtue identified, concentration (*zhuanxin*) [專心], is not defined exclusively in relation to specific tasks; rather, it is used to describe a general learning disposition. Concentration emphasizes studying with consistent focus and dedication. It also includes earnestness, patience, carefulness, and thoroughness of learning. Concentration is believed to allow the full engagement of one's mind and heart in study (Li, 2002a).

These five learning virtues form a coherent whole in the learning process. They all presume a desire to learn because without such a desire, these learning processes and type of behavior cannot be sustained. Without resolve and its associated value, commitment, diligence, endurance of hardship, and persistence may be limited by situational factors. Likewise, if concentration can be halted by hardship or if one lacks perseverance, then one's resolve may be aborted half-way.

Comparatively, the American notions of learning were more task oriented. They included active learning activities, specific thinking processes, scientific inquiry into the unknown world, task management skills, and communication (e.g., discussion, debate, self-expression). The beliefs of the two cultures differed markedly regarding agency and learning virtues.

*Achievement standards.* Three general achievement standards emerged as those at which Chinese model learners aim and against which they are measured. The *first* was depth and breadth and/or mastery of knowledge. Whereas breadth refers to extensive knowledge of different disciplines, depth concerns deep understanding of a subject or genuine scholarship. In addition, the integration of breadth and depth is also emphasized. The notion of mastery may not highlight breadth and depth but it does stress ownership of knowledge, and by implication, the broader and deeper is such ownership, the better. This achievement standard seems reasonable considering that the ultimate goal is self- perfection, which is open-ended and lifelong in nature.

The *second* standard was the application of knowledge. Stressed by the Chinese respondents was the *use* of what one has learned in real-life situations, not merely one's ability to solve problems per se, as was the case with the American respondents' image of ideal learner. The conceptual distinction lies in book knowledge versus knowledge in use. Whether such use of knowledge is personal or social in origin matters little. This standard thus includes the application of knowledge that may not be deemed as creative in any sense (e.g., using math to determine the best price), or for personal creative problem solving and insight and genuine advancement in one's field or historical impact on society as a whole. The *third* standard was unity of knowledge and moral character. Given the articulated purposes of learning as moral self-perfection and the acquisition of knowledge for oneself, achieving the unity of the cognitive/intellectual with the moral is only natural.

As noted previously, these achievement standards formed a coherent whole. Acquisition of depth and breadth of knowledge can enable one to better apply such knowledge, which in turn can further broaden and deepen one's knowledge. So long as one continues to self-perfect morally and socially, one will continue to seek breadth and depth of learning, which will increase one's ability to use one's knowledge in life.

The achievement standards of the American respondents centered around understanding the essentials of the subject and acquiring expertise. Personal insights, creativity, and achieving one's best were also emphasized. All of these standards highlighted individual brilliance and achievement.

*Affect involved in learning.* Chinese affect shows both positive and negative types. There were four types of positive affect: (1) commitment, (2) passion/thirst for learning, (3) respect, and (4) humility; and three types of negative affect: (1) lack of desire, (2) arrogance, and (3) shame and guilt.

The notion of commitment, *(lizhi)* [立志], to establish one's will, is part of one's learning purpose, but it is also a clear affect. It aims at helping the learner, often in middle childhood, to start pondering his or her life's purpose in order to come to a clear personal vision *(zhixiang)* [志向] or *(baofu)* [抱負]. This process is deliberately designed and practiced to lead the learner to imagine or envision something greater than his or her current (temporal sense) and own (individual sense) life. It is orienting one's learning toward one's future (parents and teachers frequently engage children in this discussion). In doing so, Chinese learners believe that they will not only find a more specific path to focus on (e.g., I want to be a physician) but also know to what path to attach their energy, dedication, emotion, and action (e.g., Therefore, I will study science hard). Thus, *lizhi* is a spiritually uplifting and emotionally positive process. It is important to point out that *lizhi* is not identical to career goal setting, although it may coincide with it; rather, it is searching for an inspirational purpose in the large framework in order to channel one's lifelong learning.

A passion and thirst characterized Chinese ideal learners, as intrinsic enjoyment did American ideal learners. However, a significant difference lies in the source of this affect between the two models. Whereas among American learners, intrinsic enjoyment, curiosity, and motivation were described as essential, this intrinsic source was not emphasized by Chinese respondents. In fact, many acknowledged that their ideal learners were initially not motivated to learn at a young age, but developed a passion for learning once they realized the importance of learning or their parents and/or teachers guided them through the process. Deliberate cultivation of love and passion on one's own and in one's social world corroborates recent research findings that personal autonomy and choice are less essential for the school learning of Asian American children than for that of European American children. The former enjoy and perform just as well when their learning activities are chosen by their trusted adults (e.g., mothers) and peers (Iyengar & Lepper, 1999).

Respect is another distinct affect that Chinese ideal learners express toward knowledge and teachers. Because learning in Confucian thought is not limited to academic learning but, more importantly, includes social and moral learning, respect for knowledge and teachers who ideally embody the self-perfecting process (Gao & Watkins, 2001; Li & Fischer,

2007; Jin & Cortazzi, 1998) is reasonable and expected. However, this general attitude of respect among Asian learners has been taken as a sign of obedience and lack of critical thinking (Keats, 1982; Pratt et al., 1999; Tweed & Lehman, 2002). This is a persistent misunderstanding (Inagaki, Hatano, & Morita, 1998; Li, 2003a). The deference that Asian learners show to teachers does not stem from their fear or blind acceptance of authority but from their deep sense of humility. Humility is regarded not as a personal weakness but as a personal strength because humble individuals are willing to self-examine, admit their inadequacies, and practice self-improvement. Humility also leads one to want to learn from anyone. Therefore, respect and humility go hand in hand. In these processes, one's ego or self-esteem is not seriously threatened by a lack of competence or a need for protection, as may be the case among some American learners (Brickman & Bulman, 1977; Ruble, Eisenberg, & Higgins, 1994). Chinese learners believe that one can always self-improve so long as one learns humbly and respectfully from others (Li & Wang, 2004).

The respect and humility of Chinese learners may be very different from the American learners' challenging attitude, especially in the form of immediate verbal exchanges in the midst of a discussion. Chinese respondents generally made few references to such challenging attitudes towards teachers, although their ideal learners did engage in discussions and debates with their peers. In general, one does not plunge into challenge until one thoroughly understands the issue in question or has mastered the field. This finding concurs with the findings of Pratt et al. (1999). The reluctance of Chinese learners to challenge their teachers face to face may also come from their sensitivity to the unavoidably painful social consequence: embarrassing teachers (Sun, personal communication, September, 2005). Not causing others to feel embarrassment or to lose face is a highly valued social skill in Chinese culture (Li, Wang, & Fischer, 2004). However, this does not mean that Chinese learners do not challenge others. In fact, many respondents wrote that challenging old knowledge or advancing new knowledge is an important goal.

When achieving well, Chinese learners normally do not display pride although they may be happy themselves (Li, 2002a). This tendency is quite different from their high-performing American peers who usually feel proud of themselves and like to share their joy with others (Mascolo, Fischer, & Li, 2003). Chinese ideal learners feel a need to remain humble. As discussed before, the need to be humble stems from the recognition that learning is a lifelong journey. Although others may acknowledge one's achievement publicly, focusing on celebration of *oneself* may be perceived as a negative tendency that diverts one from further self-perfection (Li & Wang, 2004).

Lack of desire, the opposite of a heart and mind for wanting to learn (Li, 2001), was described as the most severe negative affect. Many Chinese learning-related terms refer to this state, which lies at the heart of any motivational problem. Arrogance is an affect that refers to complacency and hubris, which is the opposite of humility. Learners who achieve highly are believed to be particularly vulnerable to an inflated sense of themselves. Given the importance of humility in Chinese learning beliefs, it is little wonder that pride/arrogance is a great concern among learners (Li & Wang, 2004).

Shame and guilt are the most frequently noted affective responses to poor learning, not only for learners themselves but also for their families. Shame is a powerful and prevalent emotion in Chinese culture (Li, 2002a; Li et al., 2004). Although shame in Chinese culture is an emotion of disgrace or humiliation, as in most cultures, it also refers to moral discretion and is a sensibility that people desire to develop (Fung, 1999; Fung & Chen, 2001). Thus, the meanings of shame and guilt overlap. Together they function to direct learners toward self-examination to recognize their inadequacies and motivate them to improve themselves The American respondents made fewer references to shame/guilt but more to low self-esteem.

## *Individual-Level Beliefs*

The foregoing research provides the description of a Chinese learning model at the *cultural* level, and should not to be taken as a model of individual learning. The previously described model is considered to be a cultural model of learning for two reasons. First, the model is derived from a learning-related lexicon that is a property of Chinese, the language that belongs to Chinese culture, not to specific individuals. Second, the ideal learner derived is not a specific, real person but rather a generalized ideal image, although a sample of participants, taken as representative of Chinese learners, described this image.

This cultural learning model is recognizable by the members of the culture. It also serves to influence and guide (but not determine) the members' thinking and action in learning. Individual learning beliefs are not termed as models because they are specific to individuals. Their own beliefs may differ from those in the cultural model because of social categories such as gender, socioeconomic status, and region of residence, context (e.g., political turmoil and decreased educational opportunities), and other changing factors such as age and role (e.g., parent versus student). Although models of culture-level beliefs do evolve over time, they tend to be stable relative to individual-level beliefs, which can change more rapidly (e.g., a less motivated learner becomes a parent, who then is much more motivated to guide her or his child in learning).

Given the Chinese cultural learning model, a central question about individual-level learning beliefs remains: Do ordinary Chinese learners themselves share these beliefs? Surprisingly, few researchers have directly assessed learners' own beliefs. To explore this essential question, I conducted two further studies.

In the first study (Li & Yue, 2004), we asked 1800 students in fifth through eleventh grade across six regions of China to respond to an open-ended questionnaire in writing, which inquired into how they themselves, not the "ideal learner," viewed the nature of knowledge, purpose(s) of learning, the origin of intelligence and excellence in learning, their moral aspirations and whether learning had anything to do with their own moral development, how they actually learned, and how they would respond emotionally to good versus poor learning. An analysis of a random set of the data from 187 adolescents revealed purposes and learning virtues mostly similar to those at the cultural level. Differences appeared to lie in the details of each purpose but not the basic categories. For example, regarding moral self-perfection, adolescents referred to finer distinctions in forging their moral character, finding meaning in life, and obtaining wisdom through learning. Regarding skill acquisition and mastery, they differentiated competence, development, expansion of horizons, and mastery of knowledge. Learning virtues almost converged with those at the cultural level.

As a follow-up effort, I used a revised version of the open-ended Twenty-Sentence Test (Kuhn & McPartland, 1954) to investigate the goals of learning and sense of agency among Chinese adolescents (Li, 2006). I asked 259 students in China aged 12-19 to answer ten times the same question "My goal of learning is ...." and "In learning I...." These adolescents named their learning goals and characterized themselves as learners. Examples of their responses to the first question are "My goal of learning is to get skills" and "My goal of learning is to become a leader."

Examples of their responses to the second question are "In learning I never give up no matter how badly things go" and "I impose strict self-discipline on myself." I used a multi-step procedure to code the data before conducting statistical analyses.

The results showed that Chinese adolescents harbored cognitive, lifelong striving, moral, and socioeconomic goals for themselves as individuals. They also held social goals such as contributing to society and honoring parents and teachers, seeking social acceptance, and developing good interpersonal relationships. However, they expressed significantly more individual than social goals. With regard to their sense of agency in learning, adolescents again overwhelmingly endorsed the learning virtues as their basic agentic orientation in learning. Although some of them accepted the demands and expectations of their parents and teachers and sought interaction with their peers, their learning activities were mostly structured around developing and exercising their learning virtues.

These data suggest that at the individual level, the learning beliefs of Chinese learners reflect those of their culture. It is important to stress again that the breadth and depth of the reflection of the cultural model may differ from individual to individual depending on his or her personal characteristics and socialization experiences (Spiro, 1987; Strauss, 1992).

## *Development of Learning Beliefs*

To trace the developmental origins of learning beliefs, I examined Chinese and American preschool children's beliefs (Li, 2002b, Li, 2004a, 2004b; Li & Wang, 2004). Preschool children aged 4-6 living in China and those of the same age living in the United States were told the beginnings of stories and asked to complete them. One set of stories depicted a child protagonist who liked to go to school and another who did not; another set showed a child who demonstrated the best performance in his or her class. Another set presented a hardworking bird who tried hard to learn how to fly and succeeded, as well as a bear who tried to learn how to catch fish but gave up in the end. The first set of stories elicited children's perceptions of the purposes of school learning; the second set elicited their perceptions of their achieving peers; and the third set focused on their construal of what the learning process involves. Whenever children responded with ideas that pertained to learning (e.g., knowledge, smart, understanding) or to feelings (e.g., "I like going to school", "Mom and Dad will be happy"), they were probed further with questions such as "What's good about ____ (e.g., knowledge)?" until they indicated that they were finished responding.

Data were coded qualitatively and then analyzed quantitatively. The results showed that, consistent with the Chinese cultural learning model, Chinese children as young as four talked more about the need to self-improve morally (e.g., "She learns, and she will be a good child"), mastery of knowledge (e.g., "The boy will know a lot in his head"), social contribution (e.g., "You can tell people things that they don't know"), and social respect/economic rewards (e.g., "People will like me" and "You will have a good job") as their purposes. Comparatively the American children told stories that stressed intelligence, literacy, friendship, and playing/fun as their purposes.

Regarding their perception of the achieving peers in the second of the three sets of stories, the Chinese children mentioned more often the social respect that the high achievers received and their ability to help others with their knowledge (compared to mental benefits, which were mentioned more often by the American children). Although the Chinese children voiced more often negative parental concerns about their lack of achievement compared with other students in the class, they often expressed respect for their high-achieving peers and the desire to emulate them. In addition, the high achievers were perceived to need to be humble (*bu jiaoao*) [不驕傲] in order to improve themselves further. The American children voiced more concerns about the negative conesquences of achieving well in school such as rejection and social isolation from peers, e.g., "Kids don't want to play with her any more because she is better than them".

In their construals of the learning process, the Chinese children were more likely to talk about the virtues of diligence, persistence, and concentration e.g., (*buneng sanxieryi*), [不能三心二意], whereas the American children were more likely to talk about ability and related mental processes, learning as a task to be tackled, and creative strategies. In addition, the observed trends in all three sets of narratives became more consistent as the children's age increased. These developmental data suggest that the Chinese cultural model of learning is likely to shape Chinese children's individual beliefs about learning.

# Summary

Based on the research reviewed thus far, Chinese beliefs center around a set of purposes that focus on perfecting oneself morally and socially, acquiring knowledge and skill for oneself, establishing oneself economically, achieving social status and honor, and contributing to society. To pursue these purposes of learning, one needs to develop the following quintet of learning virtues: resolve, diligence, endurance of hardship, perseverance, and concentration. These virtues are seen by Chinese learners as more essential than actual learning activities such as reading. They believe that once they have developed the learning virtues, they can apply them to all learning activities and processes.

These purposes and virtues are combined into four types of positive affect: (1) commitment; (2) passion/thirst for learning; (3) respect for teachers and knowledge as a whole, which does not mean blind obedience and acceptance of what is taught but rather personal receptivity and sincerity toward teachers; and (4) humility, which does not mean weakness but rather personal courage achieved through self-reflection and self-improvement. Such learning aims at breadth and depth of knowledge, its application to real-life situations, and unity of one's knowledge and moral character. When learners achieve learning, they remain humble; they also stay alert to complacency in order to continue the lifelong journey of self-perfection. When encountering failure and setbacks, they feel shame and guilt not only related to themselves but also in reference to those who nurtured them. These emotions, surprisingly, may not lead them to give up, but may motivate them to self-improve further. So long as they hold onto their ultimate purposes and believe in the potency of learning virtues, they may derive happiness and satisfaction from the never-ending nature of the process itself.

# Conclusion

In the introduction, I discussed four main impediments in research. It is worthwhile to revisit these issues in light of the research presented. First, both the existing research and my own work indicate that dichotomous thinking occurs rarely, if at all, among Chinese (and Western) learners. Individual concepts emerge in the data, but they are not expressed in dichotomous terms. For example, failure is not viewed as the opposite of success but rather as an integral part of learning. Therefore, the use of dichotomous frameworks may mislead research and raise serious concerns on examining any cultural group even though such frameworks can simplify topics and are convenient to researchers. Second, when comparative data are examined, it becomes clear that no learner is culture free: the beliefs that learners hold cannot be separated from the specific culture in which they grow up. It is thus imperative that cultural values be considered in any research that examines children's learning beliefs. Third, Chinese (and Western) learners have multiple (quite plausibly a taxonomy of) learning purposes and goals. Economic goals constitute just one of them. Neither does passing examinations emerge as an ultimate goal of learning. Learners express purposes and goals above and beyond success in examinations. Finally, as noted before, most of the research reviewed in this chapter did not rely on existing Western concepts to achieve understanding of Chinese learners. In fact, most of the studies used open-ended methods to collect culturally valid data. As a result, we understand much more about Chinese learning beliefs and processes.

This body of research charts an important new line of inquiry, but much remains to be studied. I venture here to consider directions for future research. First, considering that children begin to develop learning beliefs early in life, what is the developmental process in Chinese culture? What, specifically, do parents and teachers do to socialize children in the development of their learning beliefs? More systematic research in socialization will illuminate how children come to hold different beliefs.

Moreover, how should we think about learning beliefs and education from the perspective of increasing cultural exchange and international trends in education? Unfortunately, it is all too common that educational reforms fail rather than succeed. The American effort to eradicate achievement gaps between some minority groups and the mainstream group and the Chinese century-long attempt to foster children's creativity are two salient examples. One reason is that we do not fully understand how learning beliefs are formed and how they function in children's learning within and across cultures. How do people and education systems conceptualize learning beliefs in relation to their need to change? Learning beliefs, once constructed by an individual, are likely to be resistant to change: the developmental research reviewed here indicates that Chinese children's beliefs become stronger, not weaker, as they grow older. How, in that case, can educational practices, the purpose of which is to cause desirable change in children, respond to their learning beliefs? What happens when personal beliefs come into conflict with those held by the education system?

Today's world is witnessing frequent and extensive interactions among cultures. Ethnic diversity within a single society is becoming the norm rather than the exception. More and more children who are born and reared in one culture find themselves in another culture before they reach adulthood. Increasingly, many children grow up in multiple cultures. The general trend applies also to Chinese societies. How do acculturation and the development of learning beliefs proceed in these children? What are the consequences of such complex development? How do parents and schools respond to the mosaic of learning beliefs found in the same schoolyard?

Does the thinking of Socrates and Rousseau merge readily with that of Confucius and Mencius or, for that matter, other great thinkers on learning from different cultures and times? If so, then what enables the integration of such diverse perspectives? How are educators and parents from different cultures to achieve the goal of such integration? Answers to these and many more questions will undoubtedly shed needed light on the ubiquitous but still largely enigmatic existence of learning beliefs within and across cultures.

# REFERENCES

Au, T. K. F., & Harackiewicz, J. M. (1986). The effects of perceived parental expectations on Chinese children's mathematics performance. *Merrill-Palmer Quarterly, 32,* 383-392.

Bandura, A. (2001). Social cognitive theory: An agentic perspective. *Annual Review of Psychology, 52,* 1-26.

Brickman, P., & Bulman, R. J. (1977). Pleasure and pain in social comparison. In J. M. Suls & R. L. Miller (Eds.), *Social comparison processes: Theoretical and empirical perspectives* (pp. 149-186). Washington, DC: Hemisphere.

Bruner, J. S. (1986). Value presupposition of developmental theory. In L. Cirillo & S. Wapner (Eds.), *Value presuppositions in theories of human development* (pp. 19-28). Hillsdale, NJ: Lawrence Erlbaum Associates.

Cai, J. F., & Cifarelli, V. (2004). Thinking mathematically by Chinese Learners: A cross-national comparative perspective. In L. H. Fan, N. Y. Wong, J. F. Cai & S. Q. Li (Eds.), *How Chinese learn mathematics: Perspectives from insiders* (pp. 71-106). Singapore: World Scientific.

Chen, C., & Stevenson, H. W. (1989). Homework: A cross-cultural examination. *Child Development, 60,* 551-561.

Cheng, K. M. (1996). *The quality of primary education: A case study of Zhejiang Province, China.* Paris: International Institute for Educational Planning.

Corno, L. (2004). Work habits and work styles: Volition in education. *Teachers College Record, 106,* 1669-1694.

Covington, M. V. (1992). *Making the grade.* New York: Cambridge University Press.

Csikszentmihalyi, M., & Rathunde, K. (1998). The development of the person: An experiential perspective on the ontogenesis of psychological complexity. In R. M. Lerner (Ed.), *Handbook of child psychology. Vol. 1: Theoretical models of human development* (5th ed., pp. 635-684). New York: Wiley.

Dahlin, B., & Watkins, D. A. (2000). The role of repetition in the processes of memorizing and understanding: A comparison of the views of Western and Chinese secondary school students in Hong Kong. *British Journal of Educational Psychology, 70,* 65-84.

D'Andrade, R. G. (1992). Schemas and motivation. In R. G. D'Andrade & C. Strauss (Eds.), *Human motives and cultural models* (pp. 23-44). New York: Cambridge University Press.

D'Andrade, R. G. (1995). *The development of cognitive anthropology.* New York: Cambridge University Press.

de Bary, W. T. (1983). *The liberal tradition in China.* New York: Columbia University Press.

Duncan, J., & Paulhus, D. L. (1998, August). *Varieties of shyness in Asian-and European-Canadians.* Paper presented at the 106th Annual Convention of the American Psychological Association, San Francisco, CA.

Dweck, C. S. (1999). *Self-theories.* Philadelphia: Psychology Press.

Dweck, C. S., & Heckhausen, J. (Eds.). (1998). *Motivation and self-regulation across the life span.* New York: Cambridge University Press.

Dweck, C. S., & Leggett, E. (1988). A social-cognitive approach to motivation and personality. *Psychological Review, 95,* 256-273.

Fink, R. P. (1998). Literacy development in successful men and women with dyslexia. *Annals of Dyslexia, 48,* 311-346.

Fung, H. (1999). Becoming a moral child: The socialization of shame among young Chinese children. *Ethos, 27,* 180-209.

Fung, H., & Chen, E. C. H. (2001). Across time and beyond skin: Self and transgression in the everyday socialization of shame among Taiwanese preschool children. *Social Development, 10,* 420-437.

Gao, L., & Watkins, D. A. (2001). Identifying and assessing the conceptions of teaching of secondary school physics teachers in China. *British Journal of Educational Psychology, 71,* 443-469.

Harkness, S., & Super, C. M. (1999). From parents' cultural belief systems to behavior: Implications for the development of early intervention programs.

In L. Eldering & P. Leseman (Eds.), *Effective early education: Cross-cultural perspectives*. New York: Falmer.

Harmon, M., Smith, T. A., Martin, M. O., Kelly, D. L., Beaton, A. E., Mullis, I. V. S., et al. (1997). *Performance assessment in IEA's Third International Mathematics and Science Study (TIMSS)*. Chestnut Hill, MA: Boston College, Center for the Study of Testing, Evaluation, and Education Policy.

Hau, K. T., & Salili, F. (1991). Structure and semantic differential placement of specific causes: Academic causal attributions by Chinese students in Hong Kong. *International Journal of Psychology, 26,* 175-193.

Hess, R. D., & Azuma, M. (1991). Cultural support for schooling: Contrasts between Japan and the United States. *Educational Researcher, 20*(9), 2-8.

Hofer, B. K., & Pintrich, P. R. (2001). *Personal epistemology: The psychology of beliefs about knowledge and knowing*. Mahwah, NJ: Lawrence Erlbaum Associates.

Holloway, S. D. (1988). Concepts of ability and effort in Japan and the US. *Review of Educational Research, 58,* 327-345.

Hwang, K. K. (2005). The foundation of research methodology for indigenous psychology. In K. S. Yang, K. K. Hwang & C. F. Yang (Eds.), *Chinese indige-nous psychology* (Vol. 1, pp. 57-79). [in Chinese]. Taipei, Taiwan: Yuan Liu Press.

Inagaki, K., Hatano, G., & Morita, E. (1998). Construction of mathematical knowl-edge through whole-class discussion. *Learning and Instruction, 8,* 503-526.

Ishisada, M. (1974). The civil service examination: China's examination hell. *Chinese Education, 7*(1), 1-74.

Iyengar, S. S., & Lepper, M. R. (1999). Rethinking the value of choice: A cultural perspective on intrinsic motivation. *Journal of Personality and Social Psycho-logy, 76,* 349-366.

Jin, L., & Cortazzi, M. (1998). Dimensions of dialogue: Large classes in China. *International Journal of Educational Research, 29,* 739-761.

Keats, D. (1982). Cultural bases of concepts of intelligence: A Chinese versus Australian comparison. *Proceedings of Second Asian Workshop on Child and Adolescent Development* (pp. 67-75). Bangkok, Thailand: Behavioral Science Research Institute.

Kim, H. S. (2002). We talk, therefore we think? A Cultural analysis of the effect of talking on thinking. *Journal of Personality and Social Psychology, 83,* 828-842.

Kim, H. S., & Markus, H. R. (2002). Freedom of speech and freedom of silence: An analysis of talking as a cultural practice. In R. Shweder, M. Minow & H. R. Markus (Eds.), *Engaging cultural differences: The multicultural challenge in liberal democracies* (pp. 432-452). New York: Russell Sage Foundation.

Kim, U. (1997). Asian collectivism: An indigenous perspective. In H. Kao & D. Sinha (Eds.), *Asian perspectives on psychology* (Vol. 19, pp. 147-163). New Delhi, India: Sage.

Kuhn, M. H., & McPartland, T. S. (1954). An empirical investigation of self-attitudes. *American Sociological Review, 19,* 68-76.

Kwok, D. C., & Lytton, H. (1996). Perceptions of mathematics ability versus actual mathematics performance: Canadian and Hong Kong Chinese children. *British Journal of Educational Psychology, 66,* 209-222.

Lee, W. O. (1996). The cultural context for Chinese Learners: Conceptions of learning in the Confucian tradition. In D. A. Watkins & J. B. Biggs (Eds.), *The Chinese Learner: Cultural, psychological and contextual influences* (pp. 25-41). Hong Kong/Melbourne: Comparative Education Research Centre, The University of Hong Kong/Australian Council for Educational Research.

Lewis, C. C. (1995). *Educating hearts and minds: Reflections on Japanese preschool and elementary education.* New York: Cambridge University Press.

Li, J. (2001). Chinese conceptualization of learning. *Ethos, 29,* 111-137.

Li, J. (2002a). A cultural model of learning: Chinese "heart and mind for wanting to learn." *Journal of Cross-Cultural Psychology, 33,* 248-269.

Li, J. (2002b). Models of learning in different cultures. In J. Bempechat & J. Elliott (Eds.), *Achievement motivation in culture and context: Understanding children's learning experiences, new directions in child and adolescent development* (pp. 45-63). San Francisco: Jossey-Bass.

Li, J. (2003a). The core of Confucian learning. *American Psychologist, 58,* 146-147.

Li, J. (2003b). U.S. and Chinese cultural beliefs about learning. *Journal of Educational Psychology, 95,* 258-267.

Li, J. (2004a). "I learn and I grow big:" Chinese preschoolers' purposes for learning. *International Journal of Behavioral Development, 28,* 116-128.

Li, J. (2004b). Learning as a task and a virtue: U.S. and Chinese preschoolers explain learning. *Developmental Psychology, 40,* 595-605.

Li, J. (2006). Self in learning: Chinese adolescents' goals and sense of agency. *Child Development, 77,* 482-501.

Li, J., & Fischer, K. W. (2004). Thoughts and emotions in American and Chinese cultural beliefs about learning. In D. Y. Dai & R. Sternberg (Eds.), *Motivation, emotion, and cognition: Integrative perspectives on intellectual functioning and development* (pp.385-418). Mahwah, NJ: Lawrence Erlbaum Associates.

Li, J., & Fischer, K. W. (2007). Respect as a positive self-conscious emotion in European Americans and Chinese. In J. L. Tracy, R. W. Robins & J. P. Tangney (Eds.), *The self-conscious emotions: Theory and research* (pp. 224-242). New York: Guilford Press.

Li, J., Holloway, S. D., Bempechat, J., & Loh, E. (2008). Building and using a social network: Nurture for low-income Chinese American adolescents' learning. In R. W. Larson & L. A. Jensen (Series Eds.) and H. Yoshikawa & N. Way (Vol. Eds.), *New directions for child and adolescent development: Vol. 2008. Beyond the family: Contexts of Immigrant Children's Development* (pp. 9-25). San Francisco, CA: Jossey-Bass.

Li, J., Wang, L. Q, & Fischer, K. W. (2004). The organization of Chinese shame concepts. *Cognition and Emotion, 18,* 767-797.

Li, J., & Wang, Q. (2004). Perceptions of achievement and achieving peers in U.S. and Chinese kindergartners. *Social Development, 13,* 413-436.

Li, J, & Yue, X. D. (2004). Self in learning among Chinese adolescents. In M. F. Mascolo & J. Li. (Eds.), *Culture and developing selves: Beyond dichotomization* (New Directions in Child and Adolescent Development Series No. 104, pp. 27-43). San Francisco: Jossey-Bass.

Marton, F., Dall'Alba, G. A., & Beaty, E. (1993). Conceptions of learning. *International Journal of Educational Research, 19,* 277-300.

Marton, F., Dall'Alba, G. A., & Tse, L. K. (1996). Memorizing and understanding: The keys to the paradox? In D. A. Watkins & J. B. Biggs (Eds.), *The Chinese Learner: Cultural, psychological and contextual influences* (pp. 69-83). Hong Kong/ Melbourne: Comparative Education Research Centre, The University of Hong Kong/Australian Council for Educational Research.

Mascolo, M. F., Fischer, K. W., & Li, J. (2003). The dynamic construction of emotions in development: A component systems approach. In N. Davidson, K. Scherer & H. Goldsmith (Eds.), *Handbook of affective science* (pp. 375-408). New York: Oxford University Press.

Matsushita, K. (1994). Acquiring mathematical knowledge through semantic and pragmatic problem solving. *Human Development, 37,* 220-232.

Mencius. (1970). *Mencius.* (D. C. Lao, Trans.). Harmondsworth: Penguin Books.

Plato. (1981). *Five dialogues.* (G. M. A. Gruber, Trans.). Indianapolis, IN: Hackett.

Pratt, D. D., Kelly, M., & Wong, K. M. (1999). Chinese conceptions of "effective teaching" in Hong Kong: Towards culturally sensitive evaluation of teaching. *International Journal of Lifelong Learning, 18,* 241-258.

Quinn, N., & Holland, D. (1987). Introduction. In D. Holland & N. Quinn (Eds.), *Cultural models in language and thought* (pp. 3-40). New York: Cambridge University Press.

Ran, A. (2001). Traveling on parallel tracks: Chinese parents and English teachers. *Educational Research, 43,* 311-328.

Rogers, C. (1969). *Freedom to learn.* Columbus, OH: Merrill.

Rosch, E. (1975). Cognitive representations of semantic categories. *Journal of Experimental Psychology: General, 104,* 192-233.

Rousseau, J. J. (1979). *Emil, or on education* (A. Bloom, Trans.). New York: Basic Books.

Ruble, D. N., Eisenberg, R., & Higgins, E. T. (1994). Developmental changes in achievement evaluations: Motivational implications of self-other differences. *Child Development, 65,* 1095-1110.

Ruble, D. N., & Flett, G. L. (1988). Conflicting goals in self-evaluative goal seeking: Developmental and ability level analysis. *Child Development, 59,* 97-106.

Salili, F., Chiu, C. Y., & Lai, S. (2001). The influence of culture and context on students' achievement orientations. In F. Salili, C. Y. Chiu, & Y. Y. Hong (Eds.), *Student motivation: The culture and context of learning* (pp. 221-247). New York: Plenum.

Schunk, D. H., & Zimmerman, B. J. (2003). Self-regulation and learning. In I. B. Weiner (Series Ed.) and W. M. Reynolds & G. E. Miller (Vol. Eds.), *Handbook of psychology: Vol. 7. Educational psychology* (pp. 59-78). Hoboken, NJ: Wiley.

Segall, M. H., Dasen, P. R., Berry, J. W., & Poortinga, Y. H. (1999). *Human behavior in global perspective* (2nd ed.). Boston, MA: Allyn & Bacon.

Shaver, P., Schwartz, J., Kirson, D., & O'Connor, C. (1987). Emotion knowledge: Further exploration of a prototype approach. *Journal of Personality and Social Psychology, 52,* 1061-1086.

Shon, S. P., & Ja, D. Y. (1982). Asian families. In M. McGoldrick, J. K. Pearce, & J. Giordano (Eds.), *Ethnicity and family therapy* (pp. 134-163). New York: Guilford Press.

Shweder, R. A. (1991). *Thinking through cultures.* Cambridge, MA: Harvard University Press.

Spiro, M. E. (1987). Collective representations and mental representations in religious symbol systems. In B. Kilborne & L. L. Langness (Eds.), *Culture and human nature: Theoretical papers of Melford E. Spiro* (pp. 161-184). Chicago: University of Chicago Press.

Sternberg, R. J., & Williams, W. M. (2002). *Educational psychology.* Boston: Allyn & Bacon.

Stevenson, H. W., & Stigler, J. W. (1992). *The learning gap.* New York: Simon & Schuster.

Stigler, J. W., & Hiebert J. (1999). *The teaching gap: Best ideas from the world's teachers for improving education in the classroom.* New York: The Free Press.

Stipek, D. J. (2002). *Motivation to learn: Integrating theory and practice* (4th ed.). Boston: Allyn & Baker.

Strauss, C. (1992). Models of motives. In R. G. D'Andrade & C. Strauss (Eds.), *Human motives and cultural models* (pp. 1-20). New York: Cambridge University Press.

Sue, S., & Okazaki, S. (1990). Asian-American educational achievements: A phenomenon in search of an explanation. *American Psychologist, 45,* 913-920.

Tu, W. M. (1979). *Humanity and self-cultivation: Essays in Confucian thought*. Berkeley, CA: Asian Humanities Press.

Tweed, R. G., & Lehman, D. R. (2002). Learning considered within a cultural context: Confucian and Socratic approaches. *American Psychologist, 57,* 89-99.

Watkins, D. A., & Biggs, J. B. (Eds.). (1996). *The Chinese Learner: Cultural, psychological, and contextual influences*. Hong Kong/Melbourne: Comparative Education Research Centre, The University of Hong Kong/Australian Council for Educational Research.

Watkins, D. A., & Biggs, J. B. (Eds.). (2001). *Teaching the Chinese Learner: Psychological and pedagogical perspectives*. Hong Kong/Melbourne: Comparative Education Research Centre, The University of Hong Kong/Australian Council for Educational Research.

Winner, E. (1989). How can Chinese children draw so well? *Journal of Aesthetic Education, 23*(1), 65-84.

Wong, N. Y. (2004). The CHC learner's phenomenon: Its implications on mathematics education. In L. H. Fan, N. Y. Wong, J. F. Cai & S. Q. Li (Eds.), *How Chinese learn mathematics: Perspectives from insiders* (pp. 503-534). Singapore: World Scientific.

Wu, S. P., & Lai, C. Y. (1992). *Complete text of the four books and five classics in modern Chinese* [in Chinese]. Beijing, China: International Culture Press.

Yang, C. F. (2005). Research approaches to indigenous psychology. In K. S. Yang, K. K. Hwang & C. F. Yang (Eds.), *Chinese indigenous psychology* (Vol. 1, pp. 81-110). [in Chinese]. Taipei, Taiwan: Yuan Liu Press.

Yang, K. S. (2005). Significance and development of indigenous psychology. In K. S. Yang, K. K. Hwang & C. F. Yang (Eds.), *Chinese indigenous psychology* (Vol. 1, pp. 3-56). [in Chinese]. Taipei, Taiwan: Yuan Liu Press.

Yao, E. (1985). A comparison of family characteristics of Asian-American and Anglo-American high achievers. *International Journal of Comparative Sociology, 26,* 198-208.

Yu, A. B., & Yang K. S. (1994). The nature of achievement motivation in collectivist societies. In U. Kim, H. C. Triandis, C. Kagitcibasi, S. C., Choi & G. Yoon (Eds.), *Individualism and collectivism: Theory, method, and applications* (pp. 239-250). Thousand Oaks, CA: Sage.

# 3

# Motivation and Competition in Hong Kong Secondary Schools: The Students' Perspective

*David A. WATKINS*

## Introduction

Competition is the hallmark of Hong Kong and one of the key factors of success of East Asian economies .... In Hong Kong, the education system has brought frustration and a sense of failure to a lot of youngsters and does not provide sufficient channels for them to find their own career. Such a competitive mechanism can only produce a small number of distinguished talents and will not give Hong Kong a competitive edge. It has undercut social equity and has divided our society.

The reform package put forward by the EC aims to instill a new concept of competition and to introduce a new competition mechanism that takes account of selectiveness, fairness, social equity and the "no loser" principle. These principles are adopted in our proposals for school places allocation, examinations and admission (Education Commission, 2000, pp. 39-40).

It is clear from this quote that the Education Commission considers motivation and competition, in particular, to be serious problems in Hong Kong's education system, which needs to be reformed if Hong Kong is to be successful in the new millennium. In fact, statements along these lines have commonly been found in the mass media and in official reports for at least the past 15 years.

Intense competition has generally been seen as a necessity for the economic success of Hong Kong at the international level and for that of companies within Hong Kong at the local level. Fluctuating unemployment rates have also encouraged competition for good (or indeed any) jobs at the individual level. This role played by competition is consistent with traditional Chinese society in which many people competed against one another in civil service examinations to be selected to coveted government positions. These examinations were seen as a major motivation for learning, and this traditional emphasis on exams has become characteristic of the Hong Kong education system (Education Commission, 2000; Lee, 1996).

Accompanying this emphasis is the belief that success can be achieved through hard work, with innate ability being seen as much less important than it is in Western countries (Salili, 1996; Watkins & Biggs, 1996). Moreover, Hong Kong students have proved successful in a number of international comparisons of educational achievement (Rao & Chan, chap. 1, this volume). The examination system also served the purposes of the British colonial power to identify talented individuals who could join an administrative class capable of running Hong Kong. The emphasis on examinations led to an elitist education system in which there were relatively few winners and many losers.

Although a number of the reforms proposed by the Education Commission have been instituted, it appears that the underlying problems remain, as the following editorial from a leading local newspaper argues.

> At the very top end, Hong Kong's education system is consistently capable of producing outstanding students who can compete with the best from any school system anywhere . . .. The rest have largely been written off (*South China Morning Post*, 2004).

A disappointing feature of the debate over the role of competition in Hong Kong schools is the lack of a research base. How motivated are Hong Kong secondary school students, and how has this changed over the years? Just how much competition do these students actually experience? How do these schools foster competition? How do the students feel about it? Do the answers to these questions vary by ability or sex? This chapter provides empirical evidence to answer such questions.

# Motivation in Secondary Schools

Psychological problems among secondary school students have been reported in many countries. As Anderman and Maehr (1994, p. 287) put it, "Prominently associated with most definitions of the problem are issues of motivation: Adolescents either don't have it, have too much of it, or invest it in the wrong activities."

Motivation during the junior secondary school years has been reported to be declining in a number of studies in the U.S. (Anderman & Maehr, 1994; Gottfried, Fleming, & Gottfried, 2001; Ratelle, Guay, Larose, & Senecal, 2004). This is of particular concern to educators, as this is the period of life during which curriculum choices are usually made, thus influencing career opportunities, decision making and the necessary pre-paration for university, which requires intensive studying. Failure at this stage can seriously affect a student's economic and social future.

Despite the huge amounts of money poured into the U.S. educa-tional system, it seems that negative attitudes and a lack of confidence with regard to specific subjects become more common as students pro-gress. Anderman and Maehr (1994) refer to research that attributes this parlous situation not to pubertal changes, but rather to the learning environment in U.S. junior high schools (Eccles & Midgley, 1989; Simmons & Blyth, 1987):

> The typical middle grade school environment is characterized by few opportunities for students to make important decisions, exces-sive rules, and discipline, poor teacher-student relationships, homo-genous grouping by ability, and stricter grading practices than those in the elementary school years (Anderman & Maehr, 1994, p. 293).

Yet, adolescence is usually portrayed as a period of development during which autonomy, independence, and self-determination are sought. A typical U.S. middle school environment does not encourage such development. Anderman and Maehr (1994) propose that this mis-match between the demands of the school context and those of the growing adolescent are a major source of motivational issues.

## *Study 1 — Motivation*

Do Hong Kong students also experience such decreasing motivation as they progress through secondary school? To answer this question, I conducted a longitudinal investigation of cohorts of Form 1 (aged 12-13 years) and Form 3 (aged 14-15 years) students from three Hong Kong secondary schools as they progressed through one academic year. This allowed an investigation of their motivation in terms of stability over time and took into consideration age, sex, and ability group differences.

Western research on academic motivation has long been dominated by achievement goal theory (e.g., Ames, 1992; Dweck, 1986). Achievement goals are cognitive representations of the different purposes that students have, which may, in turn, differ according to the academic context. These goals are thought to be important, as they are likely to influence students' behavior, thoughts, and feelings as they become involved in academic tasks. Two main goals have been identified by theorists: *mastery* and *performance* goals. The belief that effort leads to success is central to a mastery (or learning or task) goal, and the intrinsic value of learning is salient. Individuals who adopt a mastery goal are likely to want to develop new skills, try to understand their work, improve their level of competence, and achieve a sense of mastery over a task. A performance (or ego or extrinsic) goal, in contrast, refers to a focus on one's sense of self-worth. Ability is demonstrated by outperforming others, by surpassing norms, or by achieving success with little effort. Performance goals are other-referenced, whereas mastery goals are self-referenced. Importantly for the quality of learning outcomes, mastery goals tend to be associated with deep-level learning strategies and performance goals with surface-level learning strategies (Covington, 2000). These findings are consistent with the motive/strategy model of approaches to learning (Biggs, 1987) in which external, intrinsic, and achievement motivation influence a student to adopt surface-, deep-, and achievement-oriented learning strategies, respectively. This model has been validated in a number of Western and non-Western countries and regions such as Hong Kong (Watkins & Biggs, 1996).

However, goal theory has major problems, particularly when applied to non-Western settings. First, it assumes a bipolar mastery versus performance goal continuum, although research suggests that these two types of goals are not incompatible and that students may hold both simultaneously (Maehr, 1984; Urdan & Maehr, 1995). Second, both types have a strong individualist flavor, as they give priority to the goals of the individual. Little attention is paid to more group-oriented goals, such as affiliation with other students or wanting to succeed for the sake of the family, which are likely to be salient in more collectivist cultures such as Hong Kong (Ho, 1986; Salili, 1996; Yang & Yu, 1988; Yu, 1996).

Based on Maehr's approach, McInerney, Young, and McInerney (2000, 2001) proposed a hierarchical, multidimensional model of goal orientation that is designed to reflect a wider range of goals relevant to both Western and non-Western students. At the base of this model are nine specific goals (task, effort, praise, feedback, competition, social status, extrinsic, social concern, and affiliation) that can be grouped into three more general goals (mastery, performance, and social), and at the apex is general motivation.

The Inventory of School Motivation (ISM) instrument was then developed to assess constructs salient to the model (McInerney, Roche, McInerney, & Marsh, 1997). The work of McInerney and his colleagues has involved not only psychometric research that demonstrates the reliability and factor structure of responses to the ISM from students from a number of minority groups, as well as Western students, but also qualitative research that has supported the relevance of the model's underlying constructs. The ISM has also been used in a series of studies that have looked at the motivational factors underlying academic achievement and school retention in different cultures (McInerney et al., 1997).

The participants of the study reported herein were Form 1 and Form 3 Hong Kong secondary school students. The schools were selected as typical of the region's schools. Of the total sample, 241 of the participants were from a high-ability band school, 230 from a medium band, and 226 from the lowest-ability band. Forty-nine percent were male, and the sex ratio was consistent across the band levels. The students were administered a Chinese version of the ISM (Watkins, McInerney, & Lee, 2002) during normal class periods at Time 1 and Time 2 early in the first terms some 12 months apart. The main analyses were repeated measures multivariate analysis of variance (MANOVA) with ability band, sex, and age as the between subject effects.

The ISM used in this study comprised 10 scales related to the following motivational goals (each item was answered on a five-point scale that ranged from 1 = strongly disagree to 5 = strongly agree).

- *Task-Effort (11 items)*: Interest in the task and willingness to expend effort to improve schoolwork. Examples of items that represent this dimension are "I like to see that I am improving in my schoolwork" and "I always try hard to understand something new in my school work."

- *Mastery goals (5 items)*: Motivation that comes from mastering learning. A typical item is "I am most motivated when I see my work improving."
- *Social concerns (5 items)*: Concern for other students and a willingness to help them with their school work. Examples of this dimension are "It is important for students to help each other at school" and "I like helping other students with their school work."
- *Affiliation (8 items)*: Belonging to a group or positive influence from friends when doing schoolwork. Examples of the dimension are "I can do my best work at school when I work with others" and "I like to work with other students at school rather than work alone."
- *Social goals (5 items)*: Motivation that comes from working with others. A typical item is "I am most motivated when I am in a group."
- *Competition (8 items)*: Competitiveness in learning. Examples of this dimension are "I like to compete with others at school" and "I am only happy when I am one of the best in the class."
- *Praise (9 items)*: Social recognition for schoolwork. Examples of this dimension are "I work best when I am praised at school" and "I like to be encouraged in my schoolwork."
- *Rewards (10 items)*: Tangible rewards for schoolwork. Examples of this dimension are "I work best in class when I get rewards" and "Getting good marks is everything for me."
- *Social status (7 items)*: Seeking social status through group leadership. Examples of this dimension are "I like being in charge of a group" and "I work hard at school to make the class notice me."
- *Performance goals (8 items)*: Motivation that comes from recognition for doing well and beating others. Typical items are: "I like my teacher to show my work to the rest of the class" and "I am most motivated when I am competing with others."

Table 3.1 presents the means, standard deviations, and internal consistency estimates of reliability for the responses to each of the scales at Times 1 and 2 in addition to the effect sizes that represent changes in the overall group means over this period.

**Table 3.1**

*Motivation Scale Means, Standard Deviations (SD), and Alphas at Times 1 and 2 and Effect Size*

| Scale | Time 1 | | Time 2 | | Effect | Alpha | |
| --- | --- | --- | --- | --- | --- | --- | --- |
| | Mean | SD | Mean | SD | Size | Time 1 | Time 2 |
| Mastery | | | | | | | |
| Task effort | 40.95 | 4.91 | 40.43 | 5.13 | -.10 | .74 | .78 |
| Mastery goals | 18.35 | 2.86 | 18.12 | 2.91 | -.08 | .74 | .76 |
| Social | | | | | | | |
| Social concerns | 18.01 | 2.62 | 18.01 | 2.60 | .00 | .68 | .69 |
| Affiliation | 16.95 | 3.18 | 16.56 | 3.09 | -.13 | .72 | .70 |
| Social goals | 16.19 | 2.90 | 16.09 | 2.99 | -.03 | .74 | .77 |
| Performance | | | | | | | |
| Competition | 26.07 | 5.31 | 25.71 | 5.46 | -.07 | .80 | .84 |
| Praise | 29.47 | 5.54 | 29.03 | 5.69 | -.08 | .84 | .86 |
| Rewards | 30.18 | 5.42 | 29.85 | 5.52 | -.06 | .75 | .78 |
| Social status | 19.97 | 4.36 | 20.04 | 4.31 | .02 | .80 | .81 |
| Performance goals | 26.11 | 5.01 | 25.65 | 5.23 | -.09 | .84 | .87 |

The alpha coefficients of the ISM scales obtained at Times 1 and 2 were generally satisfactory (with respective medians of .74 and .78). The effect sizes ranged from -.13 to .02, thus indicating the overall relative stability of the scale means over time (.20 is the generally accepted indicator of a moderate effect).

The results of the repeated measures MANOVA for the 10 motivation scales are shown in Table 3.2. Statistically significant effects were found for Band, Age, Sex, Time, Time x Band, Time x Sex, and Time x Band x Age. As the focus of this chapter is on changes over time, these are the effects discussed further here.

There was a statistically significant three-way interaction among time, band, and age. Social Concerns ($F$ (2, 621) = 5.34, $p < .005$), was the only motivation dimension that came close to contributing significantly to this interaction. An inspection of the means indicates that a slight lowering in those for Band 3 (the lowest-ability band) 13-year-olds is the reason.

## Table 3.2
### Summary of Repeated Measures MANOVA on Motivation Scales

| Effect | | Wilks' Lambda | F | df | Error df | Sig. |
|---|---|---|---|---|---|---|
| Between Subjects | band | 0.80 | 6.44 | 22 | 1222 | 0.00 |
| | age | 0.90 | 6.21 | 11 | 611 | 0.00 |
| | sex | 0.85 | 9.50 | 11 | 611 | 0.00 |
| Within Subjects | time | 0.58 | 40.45 | 11 | 611 | 0.00 |
| | time * band | 0.91 | 2.70 | 22 | 1222 | 0.00 |
| | time * age | 0.97 | 1.55 | 11 | 611 | 0.11 |
| | time * sex | 0.93 | 4.31 | 11 | 611 | 0.00 |
| | time * band * age | 0.94 | 1.67 | 22 | 1222 | 0.02 |
| | time * band * sex | 0.97 | 1.00 | 22 | 1222 | 0.47 |
| | time * age * sex | 0.99 | 0.61 | 11 | 611 | 0.82 |
| | time *band * age * sex | 0.97 | 0.88 | 22 | 1222 | 0.62 |

There were two statistically significant two-way interactions: Time X Sex and Time X Band. For the former, only Social Concerns, $F (1, 621) = 25.08$, $p < .001$, had a significant effect with the female scores rising over time. For the latter, four dimensions contributed to the overall differences: Social Concerns, $F (2, 621) = 17.55$, $p < .001$, Performance Goals $F (2, 621) = 4.25$, $p = .015$, Praise, $F (2, 621) = 4.25$, $p < .015$, and Mastery Goals, $F (2, 621) = 3.30$, $p = .037$. The Band 3 scores decreased over time for all of these scales.

There was also a main effect for time, with four of the motivation dimensions contributing to this overall effect: Affiliation, $F (2, 621) = 31.82$, $p < .001$, Social Goals, $F (2, 621) = 26.82$, $p < .001$, Social Status, $F (2, 621) = 3. 91$, $p < .048$, and Performance Goals $F (2, 621) = 3.85$, $p < .05$. In all cases, the means decreased over time.

### Summary

The foregoing results provide evidence of decreasing motivation over time among Hong Kong secondary school students, but it is the social scales and performance goals that exhibited these decreases. The trends also vary by ability band and sex. The scales related to mastery goals and intrinsic motivation showed no decrease, except for Band 3 students. These latter scales are those generally associated with deeper learning processes and higher-quality learning outcomes, both in Hong Kong and elsewhere (Watkins & Biggs, 1996). It should be noted though that as only one school was chosen from each ability band, the results that concern bands need to be treated with caution.

## The Nature of Competition in Hong Kong Schools

Much of the condemnation of the role played by competition in Hong Kong schools is based on criticisms in the Western literature. However, Fülöp (2005) argued that the concept of competition is interdisciplinary but has been treated superficially and quite inadequately in the psychological and education literature. In particular, a universal definition of competition seems to have been taken for granted, with it typically being viewed as the antithesis of, and less desirable than, cooperation (Fülöp, 2005). Major theorizing and research in social psychology (Deutsch, 1949, 1973) and education (Johnson & Johnson, 1989) have focused on cooperation and how it can be encouraged at the expense of competition. Fülöp's work, however, which is based on an ongoing research program (Fülöp 1999a, 1999b, 2001-2002, 2002, 2004; Fülöp & Berkics, 2002; Watkins, Fülöp, Berkics, & Regmi, 2003), shows clear cultural differences in perceptions of the nature and consequences of competition, and thus such social theorizing may be misguided. It seems that in collectivist societies such as Japan and Nepal, competition may have healthy consequences that go hand-in-hand with cooperation.

Fülöp's work has compared young people's perception of the role of competition using samples of school and/or university students from Canada, the U.S., the U.K., Japan, Nepal, and Hungary. The respondents from the first four economically advanced countries (and from the poorest, Nepal) tended to consider that they lived in relatively competetive societies. Most of the North American and U.K. students seemed to take this competition for granted and had relatively neutral views about its presence. Most of the Japanese and Nepalese respondents, however, had clearly thought about competition and were able to articulate sophisticated views of its positive effects on their societies and their own lives. Many of the respondents in these two countries saw competition as a process of mutual improvement that was beneficial both to them individually and to their society. In contrast, the respondents from Hungary, a country undergoing a transition from a controlled socialist society to a free enterprise economy, showed little understanding of the role of competition and typically expressed either neutral or negative sentiments towards it. The Hungarians, unlike the other respondents, frequently described the negative consequences of competition, such as cheating, bribery, corruption, jealousy, and aggression.

## *Study 2 – Competition*

How do students in Hong Kong, with their first-hand experience of a very competitive education system and a mix of Chinese and Western cultural values, feel about competition in their schools? This chapter reports two studies that have adapted the Fülöp approach of asking students to explain their perceptions of the characteristics of competition in their own words. The responses to the following three main questions are reported here.

(1)   Does your school encourage you to compete with other students? In Study 1, the focus was on competition through examinations, whereas in Study 2 it was widened to include any aspect of schooling.
(2)   In what ways does your school encourage you to compete?
(3)   How do you feel about competing with other students?

Each study also looked at specific issues, such as possible differences in views about competition, according to sex or achievement or ability level. In addition, each study involved students from different academic years to provide evidence of the effect of the level of schooling on views of competition.

Study 1 was originally a B.Ed. (Honors) dissertation by So (2003) that was supervised by the author. The participants were 86 Form 1 students randomly selected from a Band 1 (high-ability) secondary school. All of the students were ethnic Chinese, aged between 12 and 14 years of age, and 48 were female. They were also divided for analysis purposes into quartiles according to their performance in their first semester school examinations to allow for a test of differences in achievement.

Study 2 was an M.Ed. group research project supervised by the author. The participants were 257 Hong Kong Chinese students primarily between the ages of 16 and 18, of whom 169 and 88 were from Forms 4 and 5, respectively; 132, 42, and 83 were from Band 1 (high-ability), Band 2 (average-ability), and Band 3 (low-ability) schools, respectively; and 136 were female.

Each participant was asked to respond to a series of open-ended questions. This approach to data collection allows respondents to express their views in their own words, which means that the categories that emerge are based on the perspective of the respondents rather than that of the researchers. It does not allow probing to ensure that respondents have understood the questions or that their views are interpreted correctly, as would be possible with in-depth interviews. However, this approach is much less time consuming and allows much larger, more representative sampling and generally straightforward analysis. The questions were written in Chinese after a careful process of translation and back-translation, and the responses were later translated into English by the student researchers involved. With one exception, the latter were all experienced Chinese teachers.

Content analysis of Study 1 was initially carried out by only the B.Ed. student researcher. In Study 2, the M.Ed. students worked in groups of four and six, respectively. After a general discussion and analysis of the sample responses, they worked in pairs to carry out content analysis on a subset of the responses. Agreement between the pairs was checked and found to be over 90%. The responses to both studies were subsequently independently reanalyzed by the author.

*School encouragement of competition.* It was found that 67.4% of the respondents in Study 1 reported that their schools encouraged them to compete with other students during examinations. By way of comparison, the corresponding figure for 14- to 16-year-old Nepalese students was 93% (Watkins et al., 2003).

In Study 2, it was found that 81.3% of the respondents reported that their schools encouraged them to compete with one another. Although examinations were the most common arena for competition, other arenas mentioned included conduct awards, sports, and non-curricula activities.

*Feelings about school competition.* In both studies, the students' responses were classified according to whether they felt the competition encouraged during exams (Study 1) and by their schools more generally (Study 2) was "positive," "negative," "neutral," or "mixed" (both positive and negative). The frequencies of these responses are shown in Table 3.3.

**Table 3.3**

*Feelings about School Encouragement to Compete with Other Students*

|           | Positive | Negative | Neutral | Mixed |
|-----------|----------|----------|---------|-------|
| Study 1*  | 44.7%    | 35.0%    | 19.2%   | 1.0%  |
| Study 2   | 33.6%    | 30.1%    | 20.7%   | 15.6% |

*The responses focused on exams only.

It can be seen that the feelings about competition at school were slightly more positive than negative in both studies. About one-fifth of the responses were neutral: these students just accepted exams and other forms of competition as "facts of life," but had no emotional response. In the "mixed" views, positive or negative feelings often depended on whether the students had been successful. In Study 1, no differences between the sexes were found in terms of feelings, but lower achievers were much more likely to feel "nothing" about competition. In Study 2, the higher-ability Band 1 students tended to give more positive responses than did their Band 2 or 3 peers.

Positive comments typically focused on at least one of the following two factors.

*Competition is motivating/exciting* (35% and 22% of the responses in Study 1 and Study 2, respectively):

I hope to be the winner and get very excited.

[Competition] encourages me to improve myself. The feeling is quite good.

Competition motivates us to actively participate.

*Competition is a positive group experience* (5% and 16% of the responses in Study 1 and Study 2, respectively):

[Through competition] our school encourages us to learn from each other.

. . . our school always encourages us to compete with each other in a positive way . . . teachers hope students can be disciplined and further strengthen their abilities.

In exams we compete to make progress. This is a reminder from our school.

I feel very happy because in competition all of us improve.

However, another student warned:

The process of competition is joyful and cooperative, but in the end someone [the losers] will not be happy.

The negative comments typically referred to at least one of the following factors.

*The pressure of competition* (28% and 18% of the responses in Study 1 and Study 2, respectively):

Competition is hard work. I'm unable to breathe and want to give up.

Very hard, very great pressure. I do not want to compete with others.

I feel nervous and I am desperate to win.

*Competition affects relationships with other students* (10% and 12% of the responses in Study 1 and Study 2, respectively):

Classmates conceal their real ability from each other. They deceive each other . . . compete in a negative way.

Other classmates are enemies. It seems that there is no more friendship . . . others want to beat you badly.

[Competition] may badly affect relationships with others because the loser will be very unhappy.

Study 2 shed further light on relationships and competition. The respondents were specifically asked whether they respected their opponents in study and sports, and the great majority confirmed that they did (97.7% and 89.5%, respectively). The most frequent reasons given were that their opponents were all "friends or classmates" and that they should "respect everyone all of the time".

Also, a slight majority of respondents in Study 1 reported that they felt upset (51.2%) rather than any positive emotion (34.4%) when they were beaten by fellow students in exams. However, the most common response to such defeat was "to work harder" (16.3%), with another 7% reporting that they were "motivated to improve".

## Conclusions

The data reported in this chapter provide a counterpoint to the Education Commission of Hong Kong's assumption of widespread motivational problems in Hong Kong schools, at least at the junior secondary level. Future research is needed to determine whether this trend extends to the senior secondary level. Unlike the consistent U.S. findings reported by Anderman and Maehr (1994), the Hong Kong students investigated here generally showed stability rather than decline over a one-year period in intrinsic motivation and mastery goal orientation, both of which are very salient to higher quality learning outcomes.

There was, however, evidence of a drop in the mastery goal scores of the lower-ability Band 3 students. It was also found that students who attend lower-band schools have less positive attitudes towards competition. This suggests that many lower achieving students experience motivational problems. These problems are likely to both result from and, in turn, cause their poorer level of academic achievement. Thus, it appears that the Education Commission's change from a five-ability band to a three-ability band system and its changes in assessment procedures, which were intended to remove such problems, are not working. It should be kept in mind that several Hong Kong studies (Kong, Hau & Marsh, 2003; Wong & Watkins, 2001) have failed to support the often heard claim that lower-band students suffer from lower self-esteem.

The main evidence of motivational decline found here is in the areas of social concerns, affiliation, and general social goals. This may be due to the normal conflicts of young adolescents. However, there may be a need for students, particularly males, to become less self-centered and more concerned with the problems of others, and it may be that the new emphasis on Civic Education will help.

With regard to competition, the evidence presented here indicates that, once again, the Education Commission's assumptions may be over-stated. Although the majority of those sampled agreed that their schools encouraged competition, particularly with respect to exams, this percent-age was well below that reported for Nepal and comparable to Japan (Fülöp, 1999a, 1999b). However, the Hong Kong respondents had slightly more positive than negative views of such encouragement. Although the stress caused by competition was a common negative response, many pointed to its motivational value.

The latter view is consistent with the traditional Chinese view of the role of examinations (Lee, 1996). Moreover, in Study 2 it was found that the students respected their fellow competitors, which is contrary to Fülöp's (2001-2002) findings among Hungarian students, whose most common response was antagonism. Taken together with the view of competition "as a positive group experience" in which everyone can improve and cooperation is encouraged (similar to the Japanese views reported by Fülöp), this suggests an alternative to the Education Commission's policy. Instead of trying to minimize competition, Hong Kong schools could encourage its positive aspects by encouraging collaboration between students, group projects, and peer tutoring (Chan, chap. 6; Law et al., chap. 4, this volume). Such a policy would be consistent with the collectivist nature of Chinese society in which everyone is encouraged to work together for mutual benefits. Moreover, such an educational approach has been shown to work well in Hong Kong (see Watkins & Biggs, 1996, 2001, for examples).

# REFERENCES

Ames, C. (1992). Classrooms: Goals, structure, and classroom structure. *Journal of Educational Psychology, 84,* 261-271.

Anderman, E. M., & Maehr, M. L. (1994). Motivation and schooling in the middle grades. *Review of Educational Research, 64,* 287-309.

Biggs, J. B. (1987). *Student approaches to learning and studying: A research monograph.*

Melbourne: Australian Council for Educational Research.

Covington, M. V. (2000). Goal theory, motivation, and school achievement: An integrative review. *Annual Review of Psychology, 51*, 171-200.

Deutsch, M. (1949). A theory of cooperation and competition. *Human Relations, 2*, 129-151.

Deutsch, M. (1973). *The resolution of conflict: Constructive and destructive processes.* New Haven, CT: Yale University Press.

Dweck, C. S. (1986). Motivational processes affecting learning. *American Psychologist, 41*, 1040-1048.

Eccles, J. S., & Midgley, C. (1989). Stage/environment fit: Developmentally appropriate classrooms for early adolescents. In R. E. Ames & C. Ames (Eds.), *Research on motivation in education* (Vol. 3, pp. 139-186). New York: Academic.

Education Commission. (2000). *Learning for life learning through life: Reform proposals for the education system in Hong Kong.* Hong Kong: Author.

Fülöp, M. (1999a). Students' perception of the role of competition in their respective countries: Hungary, Japan and the USA. In A. Ross (Ed.), *Young citizens in Europe* (pp. 195-219). London: University of North London.

Fülöp, M. (1999b). Japanese students' perception of the role of competition in their country. *Asian and African Studies, 3*, 148-174.

Fülöp, M. (2001-2002). Competition in Hungary and Britain as perceived by adolescents. *Applied Psychology in Hungary, 3-4*, 33-53.

Fülöp, M. (2002). Intergenerational differences and social transition: Teachers' and students' perception of competition in Hungary. In E. Näsman & A. Ross (Eds.), *Children's understanding in the new Europe* (pp. 63-88). Stoke-on-Trent: Trentham Books.

Fülöp, M. (2004). Competition as a culturally constructed construct. In C. Baillie, E. Dunn & Y. Zheng (Eds.), *Travelling facts: The social construction, distribution, and accumulation of knowledge* (pp. 124-148). Frankfurt/New York: Campus Verlag.

Fülöp, M. (2005). The development of social, economical, political identity among adolescents in the post-socialist countries of Europe. In M. Fülöp & A. Ross (Eds.), *Growing up in Europe today* (pp. 11-39). Stroke-on-Trent, U.K./Sterling/USA: Trentham Books.

Fülöp, M., & Berkics, M. (2002). Economic education and attitudes towards enterprise, business and competition among adolescents in Hungary. In M. Hutchings, M. Fülöp, & A. Van Den Dries (Eds.), *Young people's understanding of economic issues in Europe* (pp. 129-152). Stoke-on-Trent: Trentham Books.

Gottfried, A. E., Fleming, J. S., & Gottfried, A. W. (2001). Continuity of academic intrinsic motivation from childhood through late adolescence: A longitudinal study. *Journal of Educational Psychology, 93*, 3-13.

Ho, D. Y. F. (1986). Chinese patterns of socialization: A critical review. In M. H. Bond (Ed.), *The psychology of the Chinese people* (pp. 1-37). Hong Kong: Oxford University Press.

Johnson, D. W., & Johnson, R. T. (1989). *Cooperation and competition: Theory and research*. Edina, MN: Interaction Book Co.

Kong, C.K., Hau, K. T., & Marsh, H. W. (2003). Cross-cultural validation of self-concept measures and theoretical models in the Chinese context. In F Salili & R. Hoosain (Eds.), *Teaching, learning, and motivation in a multicultural context* (pp. 117-145). Greenwich: Information Age Publishing.

Lee, W. O. (1996). The cultural context for Chinese Learners. In D. A. Watkins & J. B. Biggs (Eds.), *The Chinese Learner: Cultural, psychological, and contextual influences* (pp. 25-41). Hong Kong/Melbourne: Comparative Education Research Centre, The University of Hong Kong/Australian Council for Educational Research.

Maehr, M. L. (1984). Meaning and motivation: Towards a theory of personal investment. In R. E. Ames & C. Ames (Eds.), *Research on motivation in education* (Vol. 1, pp. 115-144). New York: Academic Press.

McInerney, D. M., Roche, L., McInerney, V., & Marsh, H. W. (1997). Cultural perspectives on school motivation: The relevance and application of goal theory. *American Educational Research Journal, 34*, 207-236.

McInerney, D. M., Young, A. S., & McInerney, V. (2000, April). *The meaning of school motivation: Multidimensional and hierarchical perspectives and impacts on schooling.* Paper presented at the annual meeting of the American Educational Research Association, New Orleans.

McInerney, D. M., Young, A. S., & McInerney, V. (2001). Cross-cultural validation of the Inventory of School Motivation (ISM). *Journal of Applied Psychological Measurement, 2*, 134-152.

Ratelle, C. F., Guay, F., Larose, S., & Senecal, C. (2004). Family correlates of trajectories of academic motivation during a school transition. *Journal of Educational Psychology, 96*, 743-754.

Salili, F. (1996). Accepting personal responsibility for learning. In D. A. Watkins & J. B. Biggs (Eds.), *The Chinese Learner: Cultural, psychological, and contextual influences*. Hong Kong/Melbourne: Comparative Education Research Centre, The University of Hong Kong/Australian Council for Educational Research.

Simmons, R. G., & Blyth, D. A. (1987). *Moving into adolescence*. Hawthorne, NY: De Gruyter.

So, W. M. (2003). *Perceptions of competition in Hong Kong schools*. Unpublished B.Ed. Honours dissertation, The University of Hong Kong, Hong Kong.

Urdan, T. C., & Maehr, M. L. (1995). Beyond a two-goal theory of motivation and achievement: A case study for social goals. *Review of Educational Research*, *65*, 213-243.

Watkins, D. A., & Biggs, J. B. (Eds.) (1996). *The Chinese Learner: Cultural, psychological, and contextual influences*. Hong Kong/Melbourne: Comparative Education Research Centre, The University of Hong Kong/Australian Council for Educational Research.

Watkins, D. A., & Biggs, J. B. (Eds.). (2001). *Teaching the Chinese Learner: Psychological and pedagogical perspectives*. Hong Kong/Melbourne: Comparative Education Research Centre, The University of Hong Kong/Australian Council for Educational Research.

Watkins, D. A., Fülöp, M., Berkics, M., & Regmi, M. (2003, July). *The nature of competition in Nepalese schools*. Paper presented at European Regional Conference of the International Association of Cross-Cultural Psychology, Budapest.

Watkins, D. A., McInerney, D., & Lee, C. (2002). Assessing the school motivation of Hong Kong students. *Psychologia*, *45*, 145-154.

Wong, M., & Watkins, D. A. (2001). Self-esteem and ability grouping: A Hong Kong investigation of the Big Fish Little Pond effect. *Educational Psychology*, *21*, 79-87.

Yang, K. S., & Yu, A. B. (1988, August). *Social- and individual-oriented achievement motives: Conceptualisation and measurement*. Paper presented at the symposium on Chinese Personality and Social Psychology, International Congress of Psychology, Sydney, Australia.

Yu, A. B. (1996). Ultimate life concerns, self, and Chinese achievement motivation. In M. H. Bond (Ed.), *The handbook of Chinese psychology* (pp. 227-246). Hong Kong: Oxford University Press.

## Acknowledgements

The author would like to thank Dennis McInerney, Clement Lee, and John Hattie for their contributions to the motivation study. That study was supported by a grant from the Hong Kong Research Grants Council. The author would also like to thank Ivan So and members of his M.Ed. classes for their contributions to the competition research, which was supported by a grant from the Committee on Research and Conference Grants of the University of Hong Kong.

# 4

# New Experiences, New Epistemology, and the Pressures of Change: The Chinese Learner in Transition

*Nancy W.Y. LAW, Allan H.K. YUEN, Carol K.K. CHAN,*
*Johnny K.L. YUEN, Nicol F.C. PAN, Ming LAI and Venus S.L. LEE*

## Introduction

A common underlying theme in education in the contemporary era is the need for change at all levels of education to prepare citizens for life in the knowledge society. The knowledge society is characterized by increasing globalization, progressively shorter half-lives of knowledge, the increasing importance of knowledge creation in sustaining development, and economic competitiveness, which requires increased collaboration in the workplace (Riel, 1998). The perceived need for major changes both in the goals and processes of education is felt not only in industrialized countries (European Round Table of Industrialists, 1997), but also in less developed countries (Gregorio & Byron, 2000).

In Asia, similar efforts to introduce large-scale reforms are evident in many countries. For example, in 1997 Singapore announced its vision of "Thinking Schools, Learning Nation" (TSLN) (Goh, 1997), which called for a fundamental review of the school curriculum and assessment system to better develop in students the creative thinking and learning skills required for the future and advocated a redefinition of the role of teachers and the adoption of new ideas and practices. In Hong Kong, the policy document *Learning to Learn – The Way Forward in Curriculum Development: Life-Long Learning and Whole-Person Development* (Curriculum Development Council, 2001) similarly highlighted the need for education to put a strong focus on helping students learn how to learn, "which involves developing their independent learning capabilities leading to whole-person development and life-long learning" (p. 10), and called for "the use of different methods of learning and teaching to achieve learning targets" to achieve these goals.

In fact, even before these formal reform documents were released, the rhetoric on the need for the reform of curriculum goals and pedagogy had already started in the community discourse on education in Hong Kong. Many new strategies, such as project work and collaborative inquiry that are more commonly found in Western societies had been introduced to schools and teachers. Moreover, much effort was put into providing professional development opportunities to encourage teachers to experiment with a wider diversity of pedagogical practices, and mechanisms were created to support the sharing of experiences in curriculum and pedagogical innovation across schools.

Although such reform initiatives are not unique to Hong Kong or other Confucian-heritage cultures, the curriculum and pedagogical ideals appear to move further away from the traditional teaching and learning practices in Chinese societies. The reforms call for developing the capacity of learners to handle new situations and new problems by helping them to build up their abilities to analyze problems, identify learning needs, and in the process generate new knowledge. On the other hand, expository teaching and high-stake examinations are common and Chinese learners adapt through using a memorization-understanding process (Marton, Dall'Alba, & Tse, 1996; Marton, Watkins, & Tang, 1997). The gap between the reforms and the traditional approach raises the questions of how Chinese learners and teachers in Hong Kong have responded to the educational reform initiatives that were set in motion at the beginning of the new millennium, what impacts the new practices have had on the epistemological beliefs and pedagogical practices of the Chinese learners and their teachers who have experienced these changes, and how the characterization of the Chinese learner has changed in light of these educational changes. It also calls for an examination of the dialectical relations among the socio-historical-political context, institutional educational practices, and the epistemological beliefs of learners in the changing world context.

This chapter presents a study that examined these questions through interviews with learners who engaged in more innovative forms of learning activities that were in line with the reform ideals and supported by their teachers. To provide historical and contextual perspectives on the study, the chapter begins with an examination of how Confucian teaching became part of the core state curriculum for the selection of officers in the feudal courts in China over a period of two millennia, and how its content, emphasis, and pedagogy changed over time under different social and political forces. This is followed by a brief review of studies that explore the paradox of the Chinese learner (see Rao & Chan, chap. 1, this volume, for a detailed discussion) and note that the predominant use of the memorization-understanding process by Chinese learners is possibly a result of an adaptive response to the pressures of high-stake public examinations that began in the early part of the first millennium. The study design and findings are then reported, and the chapter ends with a discussion of continuity and change in relation to Chinese learners and their teachers as they face the challenges of education in the 21st century.

## Learning and Teaching for the Chinese Learner

In examining the Chinese learner in transition, a fundamental issue is how the Chinese learner is characterized. This section provides perspectives related to understanding the Chinese learner from historical, psychological, and contextual perspectives. We start with a historical analysis of the conceptions of the learner and the teacher in Confucian philosophy to show how the Confucian notion of the ideal learner and teacher changed over time. This is followed by a review of contemporary psychological research conducted in both Western and Chinese contexts that illuminates the conceptions of teaching and learning among Chinese teachers and learners. We provide these perspectives as a context for understanding the challenges that the changing educational environment imposes on the Chinese learner.

### *The Chinese Learner: Historical Analysis and Changing Confucian Heritage*

Who is the Chinese learner? The traditional image of the Chinese learner is of one who learns studiously and respectfully from great master teachers. There is a general agreement that this notion of the Chinese learner is derived from the Confucian tradition (Ku, Pan, Tsai, Tao, & Cornell, 2004). Chinese scholars honor Confucius (551-479 B.C.) as a great teacher, and he has been given the title "the teacher for all ages" (Lin, 1972). Nonetheless, the aspiration of Confucius was not primarily to promote education, but to help the rulers of his time to realize his lofty political ideals. He only shifted his approach and began teaching his seventy-two disciples when his political aspirations failed to materialize (Ng, 2000). As a teacher, Confucius aimed to produce educated, moral persons who could contribute to the well-being of their society and state, eventually reaching sagehood. He believed that a society harmonized by poetry possesses a synchronized rhythm, and that the interaction among the people in such a society is like the natural flow of sympathetic responses to familiar musical tunes and dance forms. Thus, the full meaning of humanity is not an isolated individual act but a "communal act" (Tu, 1993, p. 12).

Confucius' writings reveal him to be a person who loved inquiry and believed in learning from others. In the opening remarks of the Analects, he wrote, "Is it not pleasant to learn with a constant perseverance and application?" (Analects 1:1). He related learning to "the mastery of significant empirical knowledge of the human past" (Schwartz, 1985, p. 98), and informed us that he was not "one who was born in the possession of knowledge; I am one who is fond of antiquity, and earnest in seeking it there" (Analects 7:19). He taught primarily by example and by questioning (Ng, 2000), and encouraged learning through asking, listening, and observing. He seemed to have a fervent faith in the integration of empirical learning and *su* [索] (analogous to thought). As he stated, "learning without thought is labor lost; thought without learning is perilous" (Analects 2:15). He also stressed practice and action in the learning process: "He acts before he speaks, and afterwards speaks according to his actions" (Analects 2:13).

Confucius used field trips as a pedagogical approach to provide authentic learning experiences of practice and action and to cater to the different talents of his students (Ng, 2000). His tenet of "teaching without distinction of persons" and "teaching according to each person's gifts" shows that he believed in equal access to education and practiced a student-centered, contextualized one-on-one teaching mode (Ng, 2000). To Confucius, a teacher should be an exemplary mentor who keeps abreast of new knowledge: "If a man keeps cherishing his old knowledge, so as continually to be acquiring new, he may be a teacher of others"

(Analects 2:11). He also believed in learning from peers: "when I walk along with two others, they may serve me as my teachers. I will select their good qualities and follow them, their bad qualities and avoid them" (Analects 7:21), which suggests a social perspective on learning and education. Ng compared Confucius' pedagogical approach with recent pedagogies, and concluded that Confucian pedagogy is not so different from some of our "modern" practices (pp. 313-314). This Confucian pedagogy is a complete contrast to the traditional image of the Chinese learner and Chinese pedagogy.

As mentioned, Confucius' teachings were underpinned by his political beliefs and aspirations. However, not only was Confucius relatively unsuccessful politically during his lifetime, his teachings were also ignored for several hundred years after his death. Things only took a different turn during the Han Dynasty (206 B.C.-24 A.D.), when the Confucian teachings were restored to favor, canonized, and taught by scholars in the national academies. Confucianism was systematized and institutionalized under *Tung Chung-shu* [董仲舒] (179-104 B.C.), who introduced a system of education built upon the teachings of Confucius. More important still was the introduction during the Han Dynasty of the institution of public examinations as a mechanism to select the most capable persons in the country to hold civil service positions, since which time classical literature and Confucian teachings have been a core component of the examination syllabus. These examinations caused learning to focus on "written words," which differed from the Confucian pedagogy and contributed to the establishment of a deep-rooted examination-oriented culture in Chinese education. Hence, the "Confucian tradition" took a significant twist during the Han dynasty when the examination became the predominant route for social advancement (Liu, 1998).

After the Han Dynasty, Confucianism underwent further changes. During the Sung-Ming period, the influence of Buddhism and Taoism gave rise to neo-Confucianism, which branched out into two schools, namely, the *li* [理] (principle) school and *hsin* [心] (mind) school. Chu Hsi [朱熹] (1130-1200), an eminent thinker of the *"li"* school during the Sung dynasty (960-1279) established a new philosophical foundation for Confucianism by organizing scholarly opinion into a cohesive philosophical system. He also contributed to the development of standard textbooks for schools and civil service examinations. Chu Hsi advocated knowing preceding practice, and considered reading, studying, and memorizing the Classics as effective ways to help one to grasp the *"li"* of things and events. Wang Yang-ming [王陽明] (1472-1529), the most influential Confucian scholar of the Ming dynasty (1368-1644), preached the unity and integration of knowledge and practice. His major proposition was that "apart from the mind, neither principle nor object" exists. Thus, one's major efforts should be put toward the development of the "pure knowing" of the mind: "the thousand sages are all passing shadows; it is pure knowing alone that is my teacher" (Nivison, 1996, p. 51). This focus on self-cultivation became a new perspective on learning and teaching that evolved over the Sung-Ming period, but it remained an intellectual endeavor only and was not further developed in pedagogical practice.

It is clear from the foregoing description that Confucianism, Confucian pedagogy, and the Chinese learner have evolved over time. In fact, scholars such as Liu (1998) have argued that the Confucian tradition started before Confucius, who "had inherited a rich tradition from the past" (p. 3). Confucian heritage has changed under cultural, social, and political forces. The integration of Confucian heritage into education has similarly undergone systemic changes and reforms mediated by sociopolitical and cultural influences, bringing tensions and changes to the "Chinese learner." The structural reform of education brought about by the institutionalization of Confucianism during the Han dynasty, and the theoretical reform through the philosophical integration of Buddhism and Taoism during the Sung-Ming dynasties are two prominent examples. At the beginning of the 20th century, Confucian heritage faced further challenges from the joint pressures of Westernization, modernization, and political instability. During the May Fourth cultural movement, which begun in 1919, Confucianism was blamed as a major factor contributing to the social ills and the tragic defeats by imperialist forces. "Down with the Confucian shop!" and "Throw the stitched volumes into the toilet!" were notable popular slogans of the time (Liu, 1998, p. 260). Now that we are at the beginning of the second millennium facing yet more challenges and new goals, we must ask ourselves whether Confucian thought and pedagogy will survive and what new insights they might bring to our study of the Chinese learner.

For about 2,000 years from the early Han period to the downfall of the Qing dynasty (1644-1911) at the beginning of the 20th century, Confucian teaching occupied the privileged position of being a core component in the state curriculum for scholars who aspired to hold a civil service position. The establishment of the civil service examinations further strengthened the importance of Confucian teaching in Chinese education through the ages. Interestingly, analyses of early Confucian teaching suggest that it bore a significant resemblance to modern theories of learning that emphasize questioning, interaction, and relevance. Nevertheless, perhaps because of the political and social importance of Confucianism through the ages, what was taught and emphasized as Confucianism changed with time. Further, as has been described, the conception of what constitutes the Confucian ideal of good teaching and learning also changed, and the tenets of Confucianism and related philosophies evolved under multifarious cultural, economic, and political influences over time. This brief historical analysis provides an important contextual backdrop for understanding the changing Chinese learner.

## The Chinese Learner: Psychological and Pedagogical Analyses

Since the last decade of the 20th century, there has been increased interest in examining what characterizes the Chinese learner and Chinese pedagogy. However, a distinction must be made between Chinese pedagogy and the aforementioned Confucian pedagogy. Building on research on student approaches to and conceptions of learning, researchers have reported an intriguing observation that is referred to as the paradox of the Chinese learner (Watkins & Biggs, 1996). As noted by Rao and Chan (chap. 1, this volume), decades of research in the West have shown that students vary both in their approaches to learning, with the primary distinction being between a surface and a deep approach (Biggs, 1987), and in their conceptions of learning, which vary from superficial memorization to understanding and transformation (Marton, Dall'Alba, & Beaty, 1993). However, when these studies have been replicated in the Chinese context, paradoxical observations have resulted. Chinese learners, who are often considered to rely heavily on rote memorization using a surface learning strategy, outperform their counterparts in international tests. Furthermore, studies have consistently shown that Chinese learners adopt a deeper approach to learning than their Western counterparts (Watkins & Biggs, 1996).

Watkins and Biggs (1996) and other researchers argue that it would be simplistic to consider Chinese learners as surface learners who rely on rote memorization, and Li (chap. 2, this volume) noted that it is inadequate to use constructs developed in the Western context to examine the Chinese learner. Two explanations have been put forward to account for the paradox. Studies by Marton and his colleagues report that whereas memorization and understanding are seen as distinct and different processes in Western studies of learning, these two processes are integrated for the Chinese learners (Marton et al., 1996). They further show that Chinese learners use memorization to help them understand the learning materials, and that understanding the materials helps students to memorize (Marton et al., 1996; Marton et al., 1997). Other similar studies report a developmental trajectory with increased differentiation and coordination of memorization and understanding (Marton, Wen & Wong, 2005).

A second explanation for the paradox is grounded in a systems model of the Chinese learner. Biggs (1996a) argues that different components of the system interact and they need to be examined from within the culture. He further noted that Chinese students adopt and adapt strategies that are effective in helping them to cope with the pressures of the education system in which they find themselves. As an example, collaborative learning was found to be practiced in an informal way among Chinese students in Hong Kong, although the Western model of collaborative learning was rarely observed in Hong Kong classrooms (Tang, 1996). Students were often found working together in study groups to help themselves prepare for examinations, indicating that they were able to adjust and adapt their approach in response to contextual demands.

These two explanations are complementary, rather than contradictory. We suggest that Chinese learners are not predisposed to engage in more memorization for understanding, although they may have more of such experiences due to cultural and contextual influences. Examinations continue to play a pivotal role in schooling in Hong Kong, and historical tradition and contextual demands may have led to the more predominant use of the memorization-understanding strategy by Chinese learners compared with learners from other cultures.

Research studies have shown that the Chinese learner can benefit from new and varied pedagogical approaches (Chan, chap. 6, this volume; Watkins & Biggs, 2001). For example, Chan and colleagues (Chan, 2001; van Aalst & Chan, 2007) examined the use of the constructivist approach with secondary students in Hong Kong and found that students benefitted from new ways of learning that required them to take active and constructive roles in their learning. Other studies with university students also show that Western approaches such as problem-based learning (Lam & Wong, 2007; Stokes, 2001) and the use of learning portfolios (Biggs, 1996b) have an effect on student learning and understanding. These studies support Biggs' argument that Hong Kong students are highly adaptive and when provided with contextual support; they are able to tune their learning in response to the new educational demands. However, although these studies examined the effects of constructivist and inquiry-based approaches, questions remain as to how Chinese students and teachers change their beliefs and epistemology when faced with new learning experiences.

Based on the literature reviewed, it is apparent that cultural and contextual influences have a profound impact on the beliefs and approaches of the Chinese learner. If the educational context continues to focus on content-based study and the regurgitation of information for examination, then memorization-understanding may continue to be the key feature characterizing the Chinese learner. However, there is currently a global trend, also evident in both Hong Kong and Mainland China, to call for fundamental reforms in curriculum and pedagogy in schools to foster the development of creative thinking, collaborative inquiry, and lifelong learning capacities, as described in the Introduction. How these reforms might influence the Chinese learner, how the Chinese learner will deal with the struggles and tensions produced by such reforms, and the kinds of experiences and impacts that Chinese learners and their teachers are undergoing during this period of change and reform are salient issues. In an attempt to address them, this study reported here examined the following questions.

1.   What are the changes, if any, in epistemology (i.e., beliefs about learning) that emerge in the Chinese learner exposed to new learning experiences?
2.   What are the changes, if any, in the beliefs about the roles of teachers in the Chinese learner exposed to new learning experiences or innovative pedagogies?
3.   How do students and teachers experience the tensions, constraints, and interactions brought about by educational changes and reforms?

## The Research Setting

The study aimed to explore the impact, if any, that new learning and teaching experiences may have on Chinese learners and their teachers. As it was an exploratory study, it was considered more appropriate to adopt an in-depth qualitative approach. Interviews were conducted with the participants, who were 48 students and seven teachers from four local secondary schools in Hong Kong. Education reform initiatives had formally started four years before the study was conducted, so it was not expected that pedagogical practices would yet have altered much in many schools, as the implementation of change is known to be a slow process. The study therefore selected schools that were known to have responded positively to the reform initiatives and teachers who were also known to have engaged in some pedagogical innovations in recent years. This was to ensure a high probability that the participants in the study had been exposed to new teaching and learning practices of the kind advocated in the educational reform.

The 48 students interviewed came from four secondary schools of average academic standard (not elite schools) in Hong Kong. They were nominated by their teachers for being able to express their ideas well. They were selected from different forms (Form 3 to Form 7) to allow us to solicit the views of students in the 14 to 19 age range. The focus in the student interviews was on the kinds of learning experiences that the students personally found to have made the deepest impact on them.

It was important for the purpose of the interviews that the students felt relaxed and free to express their views. It was also unnecessary to be able to trace which exact ideas were elicited from specific individual students. Focus group interviews were thus considered to be more suitable than individual interviews, as they make it easier to create an open, relaxed atmosphere for sharing. Focus groups were conducted between April and June of the year after the students had obtained some experience of a new learning approach. Thirteen focus groups were conducted, each with 4 to 5 students, and each focus group lasted for about one hour. The following interview questions were used.

1.  In the past year, which learning experience had the deepest impression on you? Why was it such a significant experience? What was the personal meaning of this experience for you?
2.  Are most of your learning experiences similar to this particular experience? How often does this kind of learning occur?
3.  Compare your typical learning experiences with this particular learning experience. Which one do you think will have a greater impact on your future?

The seven teachers invited to participate in the interviews taught different subjects, including the sciences, design and technology, the humanities, and Chinese language. Their teaching experience ranged from two to about twenty years. Five teachers' responses are quoted in the following sections. Four of the teachers were interviewed individually, and a group of three teachers from the same school was interviewed in a focus group. The teachers were asked to respond to the following questions.

1.  Describe one or two of the most satisfying experiences within the past two years that you feel made a significant impact on students' learning. Why were these experiences so satisfying? What distinguishes them from other experiences?
2.  What do you think the students learned from these experiences? Will these gains have a long-term impact on your students? Are these learning gains similar or different from those gained by your students through other "ordinary" learning experiences?
3.  What role did you play as a teacher in making the learning experiences happen? If yes, then please elaborate.
4.  Is there anything that you can do so that these learning experiences happen more often for your students? Would you anticipate any major obstacles in doing so?

It is important to note from the interview questions that we did not ask the students or the teachers what they thought about the reforms or their experiences with new learning and teaching activities arising from the education reform efforts. Instead, we asked them to describe what they found to be the *best* learning experiences from their own perspective and then to describe and explain why those experiences were so significant.

## Results and Analyses

All of the focus group interviews with students were transcribed and analyzed to identify the key characteristics of the most significant learning experiences as perceived by the students and the kinds of impacts that such learning experiences had made on them personally. The transcripts were repeatedly read and common themes were generated pertaining to different questions. These themes, supported by examples, were discussed among the research team to refine them and to generate categories. The process was reiterated until the team came up with co-herent themes that depicted the experiences of both students and teachers. The interview protocols revealed differences in the patterns of significant experiences among the students and their views about the desirability of new learning activities reflecting their changing concept-ions of learning and the roles of teachers. These patterns are reported in the following sections.

## The Changing Chinese Learner

In the interviews, the students were asked to describe their best or most significant learning experiences in the past year. It was clear from their descriptions that they not only enjoyed the experiences but also learnt a great deal from them. Although the specific experiences described were different, several common patterns could be identified. Several key themes emerge for why those experiences were so significant. First, most of the learning experiences were connected with authentic learning contexts. Second, the students enjoyed the intellectual challenge derived from interacting with diverse ideas. Third, they gained a socio-affective understanding of teamwork and leadership through the process, and fourth, some referred to the role of technology in their learning.

### Preference for Authentic Learning Contexts

The most significant learning experiences nominated by the students were predominantly associated with learning contexts that presented real-life problems or situations extending beyond the confines of the classroom. The nominated contexts included interschool competitions, adventure training camps, leadership training projects, and field trips. Although conventional classroom learning was considered to be impor-tant by virtue of its links to the prescribed curriculum, the students had difficulty perceiving the usefulness of such learning for real-life contexts. Quotes and discussions relevant to this point are presented in later sections. In contrast, the students felt that the learning gained from authentic contexts was highly valuable in preparing them for life and work in the real world. Although the specific learning tasks and settings involved were very different, they were all found to be truly engaging and enjoyable.

*Exposure to the world outside of school.* In authentic learning contexts, students have the chance to be exposed to the world outside of school. One of the authentic learning contexts described by the interviewed students was an interschool solar car competition organized by a nongovernmental conservation society. Many students were very impressed by the scale of the event and were proud to have represented their school in the competition. They did not mention winning or losing (even though they were the winning team), but valued it as an eye-opening experience that allowed them to see the work of peers from other schools.

> I think that the solar car competition was my best learning experience. We went to Victoria Park to participate in the big-scale event …. It was fun and eye opening.

> After having been students there for years, we could finally represent the school at Victoria Park and compete with other schools. We could see how other schools designed their solar cars and how they decorated their cars. We could see the creativity of others. We thought about why they [the other cars] were designed in those ways, and so it was like learning through a kind of interaction.

Various types of field trips were also mentioned by a number of students as their most significant learning experience. A Form 6 student told us about a trip she had made to Guilin [桂林] in Mainland China to learn about the local culture. She visited a local school and discovered that the learning atmosphere there was quite different from that in Hong Kong schools.

> We visited a primary school to see how they learned in class. The pupils were actively involved in the class and they quickly answered the teacher's questions. Although the facilities were not very good, for example [the teacher's] writing in chalk was unclear and difficult to read, the students concentrated hard. In Hong Kong, perhaps students are too lucky and do not cherish the opportunity to learn in class. They do not concentrate or pay attention in class. In Guilin [桂林], the students concentrated all the time.

*Authentic feedback and progressive problem solving.* Another feature of authentic learning contexts is the opportunity for repeated experimentation and authentic feedback during the problem-solving process, which the interviewed students found to be conducive to deep learning. One learning context that the students described was an interschool design competition organized by one of the universities in Hong Kong. The task was to design a small structure that could float on water. One student who participated reflected on how he benefited from learning through the cyclical design process of trial and error. He believed that he gained more through this process than when he was taught the same theories in class by the teacher. The feedback that he gained about his own learning in this situation was also far more helpful to his progress than ordinary school assessments by teachers.

> Although the teacher teaches us some physics theories, it is often too brief. When you come to solve practical problems, you might not use those formulae or theories at all. Sometimes, even though you are faced with lots of formulae, you cannot produce the final product. You have to go through the process of trial and error until you succeed.

In these experiences, trial and error was part of the process of progressive problem solving. When the construction of artifacts was part of the learning process, the performance or behavior of the artifact during different phases of the construction process became a rich and immediate source of feedback to the students. This learning process sometimes continued even after the formal end of the activity. One of the Form 6 students who considered the solar car competition to be his most significant learning experience reported that after the competition, the team evaluated their design and compared it with the designs of the other teams.

> After the competition, we thought about why one of the other cars turned upside down, why another car collapsed. We concluded that it was because of the angle and the speed of the car when it turned the corner. After the competition, we also evaluated our car and why it turned corners successfully. We compared [our car] with other groups' cars.

*Learning that matters, not simply as prescribed by the curriculum.* Learning in authentic contexts also implies that learning not only takes place in the classroom or as prescribed by the curriculum. The Form 6 student who took part in the floating structure competition reflected that in designing the product, they had to learn the theories of floating by themselves, as they had not yet been taught in class.

> When we went to the competition, what we saw and learned was new. For example, before we learned the theories about the force of floatation in the textbook, we had already tried to design a product that could float.

Another student in Form 4 described the depth of learning that resulted from having to face the challenges of dealing with things she had not learnt before when she took part in a physics design competition.

> I feel that the activity was very challenging. First of all, the things we learned from it were things we hadn't learned [from school]. So we had to develop an understanding of the things we hadn't learned. We learned with greater depth this way.

*Learning outcomes that are important in the real world.* An important characteristic that distinguishes authentic learning from traditional classroom learning is that the former is more conducive to the development of skills that are important in real life, such as those required in the workplace. A Form 3 student described how participation in an adventure training camp helped him to understand the meaning of teamwork and perseverance and why this was important.

> The hills we climbed were very high and very tough, we walked until we were out of breath, but you have to be tough and persist and tell yourself you can do it and you will be able to finish it …. I learned the spirit of teamwork and perseverance …. It's difficult to complete the task by yourself; the most important thing is collaboration.

Many students also pointed out that the learning gained from the authentic contexts they described would be difficult to bring about in the conventional classroom. Another Form 3 student described how her participation in leadership training helped her to learn about leadership and teamwork skills that would be useful for her future.

I learned a lot about the essential qualities of a leader, such as having a sense of responsibility, being able to make sacrifices, and having self-confidence …. I learned many skills, like improving myself to become a trustworthy leader …. Learning people skills and knowledge through group games … are different skills from classroom knowledge …. [These skills] will help my future work life, and to situate myself in society.

*Constructing personal understanding through direct field experiences.* Field trips appear to be somewhat different from other learning contexts in that students do not have to achieve specific goals or deliver concrete artifacts, but must instead develop their own understanding. A Form 4 student described how his visit to a historical site deepened his understanding of the historical events mentioned in the textbook, which he felt might also help to improve his examination performance.

My deepest learning experience was visiting the museums in Hu Men [虎門]. At that time we were studying the topic of the destruction of opium in Chinese history. We were able to visit the historical sites … [and] in visiting the museums my memory of the textbook knowledge was deepened. When we went to the site where the opium was destroyed, the tourist guide and the teacher told us more about the site. We remembered what the textbook had taught us about the "destruction of opium at Hu Men" [虎門銷煙]. It [the visit] deepened our impression of the textbook [knowledge], and will even have a positive effect on [our] examination results.

Field trips provide a chance for students to "look around and feel around." The two-dimensional knowledge presented in textbooks becomes three-dimensional when encountered in the real world. A Form 6 student also mentioned that geography field trips had deepened his understanding of the subject.

I think the best learning experience was going on field trips. In geography, it is much better when you make on-site investigations. For example, when you study rocks, you get to look at more examples, then it is easier to put them in your memory. It's like your head can process the images, and you learn very fast. And you gain understanding of things you didn't understand in class …. You can look around and feel around …. It creates a more lasting impression.

To summarize, authentic contexts provide learning experiences that break through the confines of the classroom walls, allowing students to connect with the real world and engage in progressive problem solving and to have opportunities for authentic feedback. Learning is no longer confined to the curriculum nor prescribed by the teacher, and students are given the space to decide on what to learn and to explore by themselves. Through hands-on experience, the academic knowledge normally conveyed through textbooks becomes more vivid through personal construction of understanding and experience. Further, the learning outcomes gained through the process matter in life beyond school.

## The Intellectual Challenge of Interacting with Diverse Ideas

Another prominent theme emerging from the students' descriptions of their best learning experiences was the value that they placed on the learning that they gained through discussions and debates with their peers. The focus was not on winning an argument per se, but on the opportunity to express one's own ideas, share and explore ideas, challenge or convince others, and sometimes arrive at a synthesis of views as a result of vigorous argument. Although answers provided by teachers may be clear and correct, the process of working through different ideas held by peers was found to be very valuable for developing understanding. It also helped the students to appreciate that no single person (not even the teacher) holds the ultimate answer to a problem.

*Learning through discussion with peers.* To students who rarely have the opportunity to express their own ideas in classes, a regular group discussion session opens up a whole new learning experience. Several Form 3 students who engaged in small group discussions in their Design and Technology (D&T) lessons explained why having an opportunity for everyone to express their ideas was so good.

When attending a class, it is very rare that a small group of people can sit around and discuss and express their own ideas. The D&T discussion sessions gave me the opportunity to practice how to express my own ideas and to listen to others' opinions.

The students were new to the use of online discussions for learning and had only used the Knowledge Forum® platform, a computer-supported learning environment, in their D&T subject for a few months before the interview took place. However, they already appreciated the space that opened up for them to conduct issue-based discussions, and wanted the discussion to go beyond the teacher-assigned topics.

> The Knowledge Forum® allows students to express their opinions on a certain issue and discuss it, and shows people that nobody is right or wrong. But I feel that the Knowledge Forum® is not enough, we are limited to talking about "slimming" [the topic assigned by the teacher], but we should be able to talk about more issues.

The experience of learning through discussing with peers prompted the students to want more of this kind of learning and more space for the expression and exchange of ideas. They were unhappy about the kind of hegemony that the teachers seemed to have.

> Give us more time to ask questions and express our opinions, because students don't understand everything that the teacher teaches .... The teacher usually does all the talking, and students seldom talk. We only listen .... If you talk about things that you don't understand, then you will have a better understanding of them. If you don't ask about things you don't understand, you'll never get it. It [asking questions] is very rare here. It should occur more often.

One of the Form 7 students who had participated in online discussions similarly argued that the most needed change to improve learning was not changing the curriculum per se, but rather the opening up of opportunities for learning through exploration with peers.

> In normal classes, even if the teacher tried every effort to make the curriculum more interesting, we would still feel like we were being "spoon fed." However, in discussions with classmates, it's a kind of self-learning. I think if you are actively involved in the discussions, it implies that you are ready to accept new views or new knowledge.

*Learning through exposure to diverse ideas.* One of the benefits of learning through authentic contexts and discussion with peers is the opportunity that it affords to come into contact with diverse ideas, thus heightening students' awareness of the complexities of the phenomena and concepts being studied. The Form 6 student who stated that field trip to Guilin [桂林] was her most significant learning experience described the learning experience that she gained through exposure to different ideas.

> I think it's quite different from attending classes. It's more one-way in classes, as the teacher gives the knowledge to you. In exploratory learning, you start by yourself and then search for different perspectives from different people. You can view the same thing from different angles, you can think in different angles. I think this kind of thinking is more complete.

One Form 7 student also explained the understanding he gained of the multifaceted nature of many of the phenomena around him.

> From the discussions, I understood that the same thing could be viewed from different angles, even angles that we might not expect. The effect on me was that now when I think about any matter, I seriously think about the different perspectives that could be adopted.

*Improved ideas about learning.* As a result of their experience of learning through interacting with different ideas, many of the students had changed their perceptions of the nature of knowledge. Knowledge came to be seen as limitless and no longer confined to a single authoritative source, which used to be the teacher in the classroom or the textbook. Knowledge was no longer seen as static truth, but as improvable through collective efforts to build on existing ideas. A Form 7 student who had more opportunities to learn through discussion with peers offered his insights on the nature of knowledge.

> Knowledge is infinite, so learning cannot be limited to teachers' teaching. Discussions among classmates can result in new knowledge, so I think I have widened my understanding of knowledge. My relationship with my classmates has also become more harmonious. Even when we cannot reach the same views in a discussion, we can reach a state of the peaceful co-existence of diverse views [和而不同的境界].

### Teamwork and Leadership as Key Socio-affective Goals and Conditions for Learning

The third major theme emerging out of the students' descriptions of their best learning experiences was learning through teamwork and learning how to work in a team. The various authentic learning experiences already mentioned, including competitions, field trips, and peer discussions, all involve different levels of teamwork. The socio-constructive aspect of learning figured prominently in the students' descriptions of their significant learning experiences, and was greatly valued by most both as a necessary condition for learning and as a learning outcome in itself. In an earlier study, Tang (1996) reported that Chinese learners are more positively inclined toward collaborative learning, and that it is more likely that students will adopt a deep rather than a surface approach to learning when they work in groups. The students we interviewed in this study certainly found working in teams to be conducive to deep learning. Furthermore, they were able to articulate deep reflections about how learning takes place and the role played by the socio-affective dimension of groups in determining the quality of learning outcomes, as is illustrated in the following sections.

*Student-student talk as constructive, rather than distracting.* Seeing peer discussion and collaboration as a desirable way to learn was not a view that the students had always held, but rather a view that resulted from their more recent learning experiences. For example, a Form 3 student described how she used to think that to learn well, she needed to listen intently in the classroom and not be distracted by talking to others.

> I felt that … usually in a class situation, everyone sat there and listened to the teacher's talk, and the learning was rather "dead" [rigid]. I personally thought that students should learn like that …. I felt that learning meant sitting there tightly and listening [to the lecture] seriously.

However, her views changed after being exposed to new learning experiences that involved the freedom to speak. She described what she now thinks to be an ideal classroom arrangement as follows.

[I imagine] people sitting around and if things come up [meaning if problems and questions come up], then we can talk or discuss …. [I like it because] there are more people and we are able to discuss and communicate.

*Socio-affective dimensions of competence in authentic learning context.* Many of the students also pointed out that the learning gained through the best experiences that they described went beyond cognitive outcomes. A Form 4 student who considered her participation in a solar cooker design competition to be her most significant learning experience described the richness of the learning outcomes she experienced through that process.

When I was very tired from the activities …, I'd think "what am I doing this for?" But after I completed it, I felt that I had not only gained in terms of knowledge, but also in terms of the people aspect, time management, and things like that. I really learned a lot.

Several of the Form 6 students who participated in the solar car competition drew on their experiences of learning outside of the traditional classroom to explain why the ability to communicate and work collaboratively with other people is so important.

The [solar] car could not be made by a single person; different people had different opinions, so we needed to arrive at a compromise. We needed to make clear our reasons [for holding certain positions], and in this process we learned about the importance of communication and collaboration.

For me, the meaningful thing was also communication. For example, you need to gain acceptance from people. If others oppose everything that you do, then you are not an outstanding leader.

I learned many skills – like improving myself to become a trustworthy leader …. I learned a lot about the essential qualities of a leader, such as having a sense of responsibility, being able to make sacrifices, and having self-confidence.

It is important to note that these aspects of learning are socio-affective outcomes that deeply influenced the students' understanding of the interdependence and socio-dynamics of working in teams, which is crucial to success in many real-life contexts. Some of the interviewed students were even able to articulate rather sophisticated insights on what constitutes real collaboration and teamwork. For example, one Form 3 student who went through the challenge of an adventure training camp elaborated on the nature of teamwork.

> Project work also needs team work and collaboration. But I feel that most of the time, a more capable person does most of the work and it is not collaborative ... and you don't experience the real spirit of collaboration and helping each other .... [Expeditions] require team work. For example, someone may have a stronger physique, and teamwork also means that we have to wait for those who are less strong. A team has to stick together. It's not like a person walks very far ahead, and another person lags so behind that you can't even see him .... The smarter kid will do all the work [in project work] ... because others don't know how to do it, and so will push the work on the smarter one .... Expeditions are different because you can't just let someone walk first, or walk later. You must collaborate; the whole team must reach [the destination] together.

### The Implicit Role of Technology in Supporting New Learning Experiences

Although the study did not specifically seek the views of students or teachers on the role of information technology in supporting learning and teaching, we found that the availability and use of specific forms of information technology were often taken for granted, and were integral to realizing the kinds of learning that the students described or wanted to experience. For example, a Form 6 student who greatly valued the inquiry-based lessons his geography teacher conducted described how this teacher used technology to provide extended learning opportunities, thereby making learning more effective and meaningful.

> He wouldn't just read from the books, he would give us some problems to think about. He would guide us in ways of thinking, and he let us use the Knowledge Forum® and made it possible to extend our class discussion after school. He used his own way to change someone like me, who initially didn't like geography that much ..., to develop an interest and understanding.

Apparently, the new generation of learners is able to conceptualize how even the best learning experience can be further enhanced by the appropriate use of technology. For example, one Form 3 student, who particularly appreciated the ten minutes of open discussion his Design and Technology teacher organized each lesson to follow up on the Knowledge Forum® discussions, proposed how such a mode of learning could become even better.

> For example, Sun Yat Sen did some things in Hong Kong, and we could do a field investigation to look at the old monuments and relics. I feel that would increase our [learning] enthusiasm … why not let us use the resources online for learning to change the view that we go online just to play video games …. To a certain degree, people tend to ignore it [the class online discussion in the Knowl-edge Forum®] because we are still confined to the school and home [experiences]. We just go online, find some material, and post it and say that we have found something. Wouldn't it be better to give us some time to explore, to go outdoors and discover something?

Another student from the same Design and Technology class de-scribed vividly how his desired learning scenario would require the use of a specific form of technology for its realization.

> [This form of learning] is not so rigid. Break the barriers of the classroom …, don't confine us to the classroom, let us find out more …. It's like [what I have heard is happening in] one of the primary schools: their learning occurs outdoors. The students take a Palm [handheld computer] with them, and when they see some-thing, they take a snapshot of it and send it to the computer. And if they don't know a word, they can check it online using the Palm …. Yeah, I like it.

Evidently, the most attractive aspect of this kind of learning for these students was that the learning was connected to the real world and that they could play a much more active role in directing the learning activities and contributing to the learning outcomes. To achieve this, access to technology that empowers the learner in the various facets of the learning process becomes essential.

## An Emerging Epistemology for the 21st Century

Our interviews revealed that the students were drawn toward new learning experiences that deviated from the traditional classroom and moved toward the ideals advocated by the current educational reform. In the process, they also developed new understandings of learning, valuing learning that addresses real-life issues and problems, and seeing it as a productive, knowledge-building process for solving authentic problems. Students who had engaged in new learning experiences appreciated the importance of idea diversity and engaging peer discussions to improve ideas, which in turn requires the establishment of social dynamics in collaborative inquiry. Furthermore, the use of appropriate technological tools to support collaborative knowledge building is already assumed by students who have grown up as the e-generation. This emerging epistemological understanding is a consequence of the students being exposed to new learning experiences devised by teachers who have experimented with new pedagogies that may be more appropriate for the 21st century.

# The Changing Chinese Teacher

In addition to describing their significant learning experiences, the students also talked about the desired roles and facilitation that they wanted their teachers to play in their learning. Aside from general guidance, the students generally wanted their teachers to create chances for them to learn how to learn, and to give them freedom of exploration beyond what was prescribed in the curriculum guidelines. The teachers, on the other hand, talked about the importance of constantly reflecting on different aspects of their teaching practice to meet the changing needs of their students. In this section, the expectations expressed by the students of the roles of teachers and the teachers' accounts of the changes that they have made to better support student learning are described.

## Changing Expectations of the Students

When the students talked about their significant learning experiences, a distinct change in the way that they perceived the relationship between teaching and knowledge could be observed. Some students articulated very clear visions of what learning was and how it should take place, and what the roles of teachers should be in those situations, as the following excerpt from the interview with the Form 6 student who went on a field trip demonstrates.

> I think the best learning is not when the teacher puts all the knowledge there for us to absorb, it is to let us have the opportunity to learn by ourselves. I think self-learning is very important .... If we can search for the information that we need and plan our own learning process, then it will be less confined than when the teacher decides what we should learn.

Similarly, when asked what teachers should do to allow students more opportunities to engage in the learning experiences that they now prefer, the Form 7 student who enjoyed the online discussion with classmates elaborated that teachers must play a less dominant role in the pedagogical process to give students opportunities to undertake self-directed learning.

> What should they do more? Rather, I think they should do less, they could let us have more space to do and learn, I think the outcome would be better .... Although the teachers teach you for the time being, it's only for a limited time, at most for ten more years. So I think the role of teachers should change from teaching us knowledge to guiding ..., because when you go to work in the future, there will no longer be a teacher beside you teaching you what to do; you need to learn by yourself.

This desire for teachers to be less dominant does not mean that the students no longer respected their teachers or the teaching profession; rather, they perceived a change in the roles played by some of their teachers in the new kinds of learning experiences that they now preferred. For example, a Form 6 student who enjoyed the learning experience in his geography class explained that a good teacher should possess knowledge and strong leadership, but should not dictate how learning must take place. He further elaborated the roles that his teacher played in supporting self-learning and why mastering the art of self-learning was so important.

> Our geography teacher did not simply teach us knowledge, but

helped us to [develop] attitudes toward learning as well. Although he was slightly strict, his way of teaching seemed to change our attitudes toward self-learning. For example, he would tell us about the things that we hadn't learned or the things that we needed to pay attention to. He wouldn't just read from the books, he would give us some problems to think about. He would guide us in ways of thinking, and he let us use the Knowledge Forum® and made it possible to extend our class discussion after school .... When you leave school, you no longer have a teacher to teach you things. When there's no teacher around, you need to learn by yourself. So obviously, before entering society, if you know how to self-learn, how to take the initiative to find [useful] materials, it should be a good thing .... I think it's at a different level, it is more important to have a good learning attitude. I think it is more important than the amount of knowledge [one obtains].

Although the students appreciated the opportunity to tackle new problems in authentic situations, they were not entirely confident of their own ability to cope with every situation by themselves. They wanted the teacher to be there watching over them like a "guardian angel," but remaining in the background and refraining from intervening unless absolutely necessary. Some of the Form 4 students we interviewed explained this as a gradual change process whereby the teacher's support gradually fades as students grow in competence.

The [desired] role of the teacher should be ... as a person who is standing beside you and quietly looking after you. He or she will suddenly appear to give a helping hand when you fall or when you are in need [of help], but when you are able to stand up again, he or she will slowly walk away and quietly watch you on the side again.

I think the role of the teacher should fade away as the students grow. In the higher forms [grade levels], the things we learn will be harder, so we need to put in more effort. It's impossible for the teachers to hold your hand and teach you everyday after school, like at kindergarten. When you enter university, the teachers will be even less close to the students. We will be simply listening to the lectures of the professors. It's impossible for the professors to hold your hand in your study.

Clearly, the students were no longer satisfied with learning from their teachers as the sole knowledge providers or the only authorities on the subject. They wanted teachers to play a supportive role as they become independent learners. However, in developing a system suitable to deliver education for the modern age, teachers must counter serious challenges and pressures, as the Form 3 student who enjoyed the discussion in the Design and Technology class observed.

> I feel it's like we are confined to the classroom. You are sitting in the back, and what can you do, it's very boring. First of all, it's boring, and besides, the teacher can't attend to your needs … and can't really help you to learn. We'd learn more by going outside [the classroom] …. [However, at school,] teachers teach us to prepare for examinations, such as by memorization. They lack the courage to try [new learning approaches] in major subjects. The curriculum is very tight … and teachers feel they need to cover all the chapters, and little time is left for these sorts of activities such as discussions.

## The Changing Roles and Aspirations of Teachers

In their interviews, the teachers were requested to describe the roles that they played in the pedagogical practices that they felt had had the most significant impact on their students. It was found that the teachers themselves were able to describe deep changes in their roles and practices, and that there was significant commonality in the descriptions that they provided. All of those interviewed were secondary school teachers. At the time of the interviews, Teacher A was a Physics teacher in the third year of his teaching career and Teacher B was a Geography teacher with more than 15 years of experience. Both Teachers C and D had more than 10 years of teaching experience: Teacher C was a Design and Technology teacher and Teacher D taught Chinese language. Teacher E had more than 16 years of experience in teaching Biology.

*Teachers as inquirers into their own teaching and self-development.* A common characteristic found among the interviewed teachers was that they had all experienced different degrees of dissatisfaction with their own teaching and had explored various ways of improving it. Teacher A recounted some of his pedagogical explorations.

> In my first year of teaching, I was very eager to know how to handle and cover the whole syllabus. However, in the second year, I felt that it was even more important to create authentic learning experiences for my students. For example, I was not very satisfied with the radiation experiment shown in the textbook because there were two shortcomings. Firstly, the human hand is not sensitive [as an instrument for measuring heat radiation differences] and secondly it is dangerous to use it. So I used tin foil and black paper to wrap two bars of chocolate and put both near a radiator to demonstrate the [effect of] heat radiation on different materials. When I opened the tin foil and the black paper after some time, I was very pleased to observe the different experimental outcomes and particularly the surprised look on the students' faces …. I knew my students had learned from the experiment when I saw the smiles on their faces.

Pedagogical innovations were shown by all teachers regardless of the subject that they taught. The following excerpt describes the process of pedagogical innovation carried out by Teacher B.

> It is never easy to plan educational innovations in a detailed way beforehand: they very often evolve through the change process itself. In the first term that KF [Knowledge Forum®] was launched, it was chaotic. The discussion guidelines for students were developed only after the discussions had started. It was also difficult to translate ideas related to knowledge-building into terms that were comprehensible to Form 3 students. It also depended on how much I understood those ideas. Sometimes I created different pedagogical designs that addressed specific issues found in the discussion process …. My attempts were rather ad hoc. Maybe it is my character that I always strive to do as well as I can to change something if I don't feel comfortable. Also, it is important for me to keep a clear overview of the situation while allowing time for myself to observe and make changes accordingly, whether it takes half year or one year. The idea is to make room for review and change.

Teacher C described the notion of lifelong learning when he talked about changing the mindset of his students toward learning.

Some students think that they finish learning once they graduate. In order to change this mindset, the first thing to do is to change the mindset of the teachers …. For example, I myself didn't have this idea of lifelong learning when I was a student. However, I now see that my role as a teacher involves being a lifelong learner as well. In this way, teachers also experience the difficulties in becoming lifelong learners, and in turn they can help the students to deal with this.

Apparently, teachers who provide authentic knowledge building activities for their students are themselves also knowledge builders and they engage in authentic pedagogical inquiry to address the identified problems.

*Teachers as fellow collaborators in pedagogical innovations.* Another insight that many of the teachers shared was the need for and the desirability of collaborating with their peers to design and facilitate new learning experiences that span subject and time schedule boundaries. Collaboration was often mentioned and deeply treasured by the teachers we interviewed, from both the professional development and student epistemological growth perspectives. For example, Teacher D argued for the benefit of collaboration to achieve a greater diversity of ideas.

So I think it's better to have interactions or sharing among colleagues, as the perspective of one single teacher is limited. It's better to have perspectives from others. It's not simply the interaction between teacher and students, but also among teachers, a kind of professional interaction …. It's also important to have input from other experts such as university professors.

Teacher C shared similar views, and stressed the importance of promoting teacher collaboration to break the artificial boundaries between subject disciplines.

Teachers should be able to break the barrier between subjects, to realize the coherence of knowledge beyond subject barriers …, to appreciate the overlapping of knowledge among subjects …. Subject knowledge should not be the focus of the classes, it should be the skills needed to learn [the ability to undertake self-directed learning].

*Teachers as collaborators with students.* One description that is often used to highlight the educational changes that are desired for the 21st century is that teachers should *"not be the sage on the stage but a guide on the side."* This change in the role of teachers was observed in many of the new learning experiences that the students reported, as has been described. In addition, we found that in some instances, the teachers actually played the role of collaborator with their students in the learning process. This more peer-like relationship was perceived by the teachers to be conducive to the development of better understanding and communication with the students, thereby placing them in a better position to influence and help the students when necessary. The following excerpt from Teacher A illustrates this view point:

> Although we won the solar car competition, my contribution was only a part of the whole. There were many things involved in [the construction of] the car that I did not know. Those were contributed by students and other teachers .... I believe teachers should spend time with students not only for the purpose of subject knowledge teaching, but also to be with students, to understand their needs. This is a good thing for teachers to achieve .... To be with students is very important in a good learning and teaching relationship. Good teachers are not only satisfied with what the students can do or perform when classes finish. If you look at students' personal growth along with their intellectual growth through being with them, you will be able to see what they have really gained in a few years' time.

Teacher D provided a more elaborated description, including the subtle details of her role.

> I want to talk about the role of a teacher using the metaphor of holding a rope. At first, when the students begin to learn, the teacher is holding the front of the rope, while the students are at the back. Then the rope becomes like a circle, everyone is holding the rope, including the teacher and the students, so their statuses are the same. At the end, the teacher will be outside the circle letting the students learn among themselves .... This process is not easy, as the teacher may find it difficult to judge the position in which she

should be situated: at the front pulling the rope, as a member of the circle, or outside the circle.

Our interviews with the teachers revealed evidence of a transformation taking place in teacher-student relationships. These teachers no longer perceived themselves to be the only source from which students can learn: they valued the many other sources and viewpoints that students could harness in their learning, such as peer interactions and the Internet. The role of teachers as collaborators with students on the journey of learning is thus given more prominence than the traditional roles of the teacher as coach or quality controller.

## Tensions Experienced: To Change or Not to Change

Although both the students and the teachers were positive about the outcomes of the significant learning experiences that they identified, they were still very hesitant about the status of such experiences within the formal school curriculum or how much of their learning time should be spent on them. The interviews revealed tensions between what they believed to be valuable learning in real-life contexts and what the system (educational and social) recognized as important learning.

### What Counts as Significant Learning?

A major concern expressed by both students and teachers was the impact of the significant learning experiences on assessment results as measured through formal examinations. Student performance in high-stake public examinations at the upper secondary level and in the basic competency assessment that the Education Bureau uses to monitor student achievement are still the most important benchmarks that the Hong Kong public uses to evaluate student learning outcomes, and hence school and teacher effectiveness. Both the students and the teachers knew very well that the valued learning outcomes derived from the significant learning experiences that they identified were not likely to help them to improve their performance in traditional examinations. The following excerpt from the interview with a Form 6 student who valued his participation in the interschool solar car competition as his most significant experience clearly illustrates the dilemma that he experienced.

From a utilitarian point of view, even when you win a competition outside [of the school], though you are happy and have really learned something, in Hong Kong it's still the academic results that matter. Academic results are important for your further studies or for finding a job.

Another Form 6 student who identified learning English by watching movies together in class as her most significant learning experience gave an even more explicit description of what really counts in learning.

I feel we are now living for examinations and we are studying for examinations .... Exams in Hong Kong are to test students' reciting and studying abilities, but are not able to detect a person's [real] capabilities.

In a similar vein, a Form 3 student whose most significant learning experience was a debate session in the Chinese language class mentioned that significant learning experiences rarely occurred and that the majority of what she learned may not be useful in the future.

They [significant learning experiences] are not very frequent. I feel that the things we learn [in the classroom] have no use for our future. They are not that practical. We probably won't be able to use them in our future work.

The Form 6 student who enjoyed learning English by watching movies in class exemplifies the frustrations and tensions many of the students experienced.

We should learn for learning's sake, not for examinations; [it should be] to learn out of interest. You learn because you really aspire to gain certain knowledge, not to gain good grades.

## Tensions in Setting Priorities

The realities of high-stake examinations have caused teachers to make pragmatic decisions in their teaching, as one of the Form 3 students observed.

I feel that this sort of dynamic learning style is confined to not so important subjects …, for example, Design and Technology and Home Economics. In the major subjects [those that are important in public examinations] such as Chinese, English, and Mathematics, teachers will not dare to try [new teaching approaches].

Only in some instances did the students perceive synergies between the significant learning experiences that they had gained and examination performance. One of the Form 4 students who mentioned the interschool competition as her most significant learning experience held this view.

Actually, they [the valuable learning experiences] are helpful experiences. What you learn leads to a deeper understanding, and if you have better understanding, then it is going to help with the exam.

A similar view was shared by the Form 6 student whose most significant learning experience was the cultural visit to Guilin [桂林]. She talked about the importance of achieving a balance between learning experiences outside the classroom and classroom learning, and that these should ideally be mutually complementary.

I think the most important thing is to get a balance. You cannot treat the visit as the whole or studying as the whole, both things should supplement one another. If you don't go on the visit, then you will not know how to think from different angles and to organize the information you have. If you only study, then the things you learn will be quite limited.

Even if significant learning experiences contribute to better examination results, yet another tension arises from the fact that these experiences generally require students to engage in learning tasks that take much more time than traditional classroom tasks. A Form 4 student framed this tension in a positive way by discussing her realization that she need to engage in careful time management in her learning.

The time spent on these projects is more than the daily classes. So you learn how to best use your time so that it won't interfere with your daily life and school.

This strong tension between the pressure to perform in summative, frequently high-stake examinations and the intrinsic appeal and value of authentic, inquiry-oriented learning needs to be resolved for these newer kinds of pedagogical practices to really take root in schools. On this point, Teacher E, a Biology teacher with more than 18 years of teaching experience, described the tension originating from the significant differences between the forms of learning treasured by students and the general public's expectations of learning and schooling. He hoped that more communication and collaboration among teachers would help to promote the kinds of pedagogical practices that he has come to value.

> I think knowing student's feelings is important. We should not impose what we think is good on the students …. One difficulty I face is that even if I think an idea is good, the students may not think so, and people around me [fellow teachers] may not support the idea. Sometimes I have the feeling that the idea may even be in conflict with society. Sometimes the expectations of the students and parents are not in line with our ideas; at those times we wonder whether we are wrong …. So I agree with the idea of sharing among teachers. We can share our opinions on those issues, reflecting on whether what we are doing is really useful.

## An Emerging Epistemology:
## The Chinese Learner in Transition

The study reported here aimed to explore the views and beliefs about learning among students who had experienced new pedagogical approaches in the context of the educational reforms brought in at the turn of the 21st century, to examine the impact that new learning and teaching experiences may have had on Chinese learners and their teachers, and to explore the dialectics among the tensions, constructs, and interactions of the various components of these experiences. The findings suggest that the students we interviewed were not only drawn toward new learning experiences that moved towards the goals advocated by the current educational reforms, but also developed a new understanding of learning in the process. An emerging epistemological understanding compatible with the demands of the 21st century was noticeable among the students, and there was evidence of a transformation taking place in terms of teacher-student relationships, with the role of the teacher as collaborator with the students on the journey of learning being very prominent, in contrast with the traditional roles of the teacher as coach or quality controller.

However, both the students and teachers were still very unsure about the status of such experiences within the formal school curriculum, and about how much of their learning time should be spent on them. The results reveal tensions between what they believed to be valuable learning in real-life contexts and what the system (educational and social) recognizes as important learning. One reading of this would be that the reform goals are achievable based on the findings from the students' and teachers' experiences but are not yet sustainable. We argue that the tensions need to be resolved through systemic change for the reforms to be sustainable.

## The Changing Chinese Learner and Teacher

This study contributes to our understanding of the Chinese learner in the light of changing socioeconomic, technological, and educational contexts, and extends current research on the Chinese learner. Our findings show that students have experienced new ways of thinking, learning, and understanding, and that there is evidence of the emergence of a new epistemology of learning. When the Chinese students in our study were exposed to new learning contexts and approaches, the learning that they gained through such experiences also scaffolded them to develop new ways of thinking about learning.

Previous studies have examined the Chinese learner primarily in traditional classroom setting. This study, on the other hand, examined their learning experiences and conceptions of learning in the changing educational contexts. An important theme is the emphasis on learning in authentic contexts. Interestingly, it could be argued that such emphasis somewhat resembles Confucian pedagogy with regard to the significance of learning in real-world contexts. Confucius himself used to take his students on "field trips" to seek a deeper understanding of people's lives and problems, and the students in our study felt it similarly important to experience authentic learning. Clearly, the stereotypical image of the Chinese learner as focusing on rote learning, which possibly results from the importance placed over public examinations for which memorization is required, needs to be reexamined. Given new opportunities, the Chinese learner now values new ways of learning and understanding.

This study further reveals interesting dimensions in the Chinese learner's conceptions of learning that have not been previously identified. For example, in earlier studies among English-speaking and Chinese-speaking students, both have been found to emphasize individual notions of learning. Specifically, researchers have identified the view of learning held by Western students as involving the accumulation of knowledge, memorization, application, understanding, and transformation (Marton et al., 1993), and research on the Chinese learner has shown student learning to be characterized by an intertwined process of memorization with understanding (Marton et al., 1996; Marton et al., 1997; Marton et al., 2005). However, these studies primarily focus on the notion of learning as an individual enterprise, and few have mentioned the role that collaboration plays in student conceptions of learning. In this study, the Chinese students' discussions of learning went beyond the roles of memorization and understanding, and they were engaged in new learning contexts outside of the traditional kinds of school learning. Their discussions indicate the emergence of a new epistemology that includes an understanding of how collaboration provides intellectual stimulation for idea diversity. The role of teamwork was also emphasized by the students, paralleling the changing educational emphasis in response to societal changes.

With the advent of new learning experiences in line with current educational reforms, research on student conceptions of learning needs to be broadened. The Chinese culture has often been characterized as a collective culture (Gu, 2006), although teaching and learning in classrooms does not usually exhibit collective aspects. However, there is evidence that students practice collaborative learning in informal settings in the Chinese context (Tang, 1996). Data from the present study may help to shed further light on how collective learning works among Chinese students as their epistemology evolves when they are learning in changing contexts. Nevertheless, how Chinese learners view the role of collaboration in their learning needs to be investigated further (Chan, chap. 6, this volume).

This study also extends what we know about Chinese teachers' conceptions of teaching and learning. Chinese teachers have been shown to focus on teaching as preparation for examination and moral guidance (Gao & Watkins, 2002). The findings from this study indicate that examinations still strongly influence Hong Kong Chinese teachers in their deliberations about teaching and learning, which often causes tensions for them. However, the picture is more complex than merely preparing students for examinations. Both the students and teachers interviewed pondered on how to reconcile the tensions between satisfying the demands of examinations and engaging in new ways of learning. For example, some of the students indicated that perhaps field trips could help improve understanding and even performance in examinations. These are emerging views that indicate changing conceptions of learning and teaching. The teachers taking part in this study did not perceive their teaching as either a cognitive or affective act, for example, preparation for examination can include elements of moral guidance. These Chinese teachers talked about collaborating with students as peers to inquire, thus possibly integrating both the affective and cognitive aspects of learning (Chan, chap. 6, this volume).

This study on the changing Chinese learner sheds light on the importance of considering the relations among the different conceptions of teaching, rather than considering them in isolation. Indeed, the interactions of different conceptions, such as the relationships between learning for examinations and learning for knowledge transformation, need to be considered together if we are to better understand the conceptions of teaching and learning among Chinese learners and their teachers in the changing socioeconomic, technological and educational contexts.

## Tensions and Reforms: Chinese Learners in the 21st Century

In this study, we have looked at change and continuity in the conceptions of learning and teaching among Chinese learners and teachers in Hong Kong as they engage in new modes of learning promoted by the recent educational reform efforts that began in 2000. We show that there is neither one orthodox interpretation of Confucianism nor a single ideal Chinese pedagogy. Our historical review demonstrates that Confucius' pedagogical views bore important commonalities with modern views on teaching and learning, but that there have been changes since the time of Confucius. The institution of the civil service examination system in China and the adoption of Confucianism as a core component of the examination syllabus brought the pressures of change to Confucianism itself and to Chinese pedagogy through the dynasties.

Similarly, recent research discussed by Rao and Chan (chap. 1, this volume) has challenged the stereotype of the Chinese learner as one who focuses on rote learning (Biggs & Watkins, 1996). Although public examinations still occupy centre stage in learners' and teachers' considerations of learning and teaching and will probably continue to be important, we show that new learning experiences that have arisen under the new contextual forces of the education reform in Hong Kong have brought about changing epistemologies and changing views of learning and teaching. Interestingly, the conceptions of learning that we have found among primary and secondary school students are very similar to those that learning scientists have been emphasizing in recent work on learning (Bereiter, 2002; Bransford, Brown, & Cocking, 1999; Scardamalia & Bereiter, 2003), that is, a move from an individual to a socio-constructivist view of learning.

The findings from this study support the argument of Biggs and Watkins (1996) about the importance of taking a systems perspective in studying the Chinese learner. The relations among the different components of the education system are complex, and the current reforms have made them even more so. There is evidence that Chinese learners are adapting to the changes in the educational system that have been taking place since the turn of the millennium, and are developing new strategies as they engage in new experiences in the course of the current reforms. Our study also reveals the many tensions and struggles faced by teachers and students in the course of change. The process of reform has started, but whether it can be sustained depends on continuing contextual influences and stakeholder perceptions of the new learning experiences. As Biggs (1996a) indicates, we need to go beyond looking at single components that focus on either learners or teachers, but must instead understand how these different components interact using a systems perspective.

This study is one of the few studies to examine the conceptions of learning and teaching among both Chinese students and teachers in the changing education context. Changes are taking place and new possibilities are opening up, but there are also tensions within the system. Continuing research is needed to understand the different forces that influence student learning in the Chinese context, and to examine how socioeconomic and educational changes in the 21st century affect Chinese learners and teachers.

# REFERENCES

Bereiter, C. (2002). *Education and mind in the knowledge age*. Mahwah, NJ: Lawrence Erlbaum Associates.

Biggs, J. B. (1987). *Student approaches to learning and studying*. Melbourne: Australian Council for Educational Research.

Biggs, J. B. (1996a). Western misperceptions of the Confucian-heritage learning culture. In D. A. Watkins & J. B. Biggs (Eds.), *The Chinese Learner: Cultural, psychological and contextual influences* (pp. 45-67). Hong Kong/Melbourne: Comparative Education Research Centre, The University of Hong Kong/ Australian Council for Educational Research.

Biggs, J. B. (1996b). Enhancing teaching through constructive alignment. *Higher Education, 32,* 347-364.

Biggs, J. B., & Watkins, D. A. (1996). The Chinese Learner in retrospect. In D. A. Watkins & J. B. Biggs (Eds.), *The Chinese Learner: Cultural, psychological and contextual influences* (pp. 269-285). Hong Kong/Melbourne: Comparative Education Research Centre, The University of Hong Kong/Australian Council for Educational Research.

Bransford, J. D., Brown, A. L., & Cocking, R. R. (Eds.). (1999). *How people learn: Brain, mind, experience, and school*. Washington, DC: National Academy Press.

Chan, C. K. K. (2001). Promoting learning and understanding through constructivist approaches for Chinese Learners. In D. A. Watkins & J. B. Biggs (Eds.), *Teaching the Chinese Learner: Psychological and pedagogical perspectives* (pp. 181-203). Hong Kong/Melbourne: Comparative Education Research Centre, The University of Hong Kong/Australian Council for Educational Research.

Curriculum Development Council. (2001). *Learning to learn – The way forward in curriculum development: Life-long learning and whole-person development*. Hong Kong: Author.

European Round Table of Industrialists. (1997). *Investing in knowledge: The integration of technology in European Education*. Brussels: ERT.

Gao, L., & Watkins, D. A. (2002). Conceptions of teaching held by school science teachers in P.R. China: Identification and cross-cultural comparisons. *International Journal of Science Education, 24,* 61-79.

Goh, C. T. (1997, June). *Shaping our future: Thinking schools, learning nation. Opening speech by the Prime Minister*. Paper presented at the International Conference on Thinking at the Suntec City Convention Centre Ballroom, Singapore.

Gregorio, L. C., & Byron, I. (Eds.). (2000). *Capacity-building for curriculum specialists in East and South-East Asia. Final report of the training seminar (Bangkok, Thailand, December 12-16, 2000)*. Paris: UNESCO Publishing.

Gu, M. (2006). An analysis of the impact of traditional Chinese culture on Chinese education. *Frontiers of Education in China, 1,* 169-190.

Ku, H., Pan, C., Tsai, M., Tao, Y. & Cornell, R. A. (2004). The Impact of instructional technology interventions on Asian pedagogy. *Educational Technology, Research and Development, 52*(1), 88-92.

Lam, D. O. B., & Wong, D. K. P. (2007). Problem-based learning in social work: A study of student learning outcomes. *Research on Social Work Practice, 17*, 55-65.

Lin, Y. (1972). *Chinese-English dictionary of modern usage.* Hong Kong: The Chinese University Press.

Liu, S. (1998). *Understanding Confucian philosophy.* London: Greenwood Press.

Marton, F., Dall'Alba, G. A., & Beaty, E. (1993). Conceptions of learning. *International Journal of Educational Research, 19*, 277-300.

Marton, F., Dall'Alba, G. A., & Tse, L. K. (1996). Memorizing and understanding: The keys to the paradox? In D. A. Watkins & J. B. Biggs (Eds.), *The Chinese Learner: Cultural, psychological and contextual influences.* (pp. 69-83). Hong Kong/Melbourne: Comparative Education Research Centre, The University of Hong Kong/Australian Council for Educational Research.

Marton, F., Watkins, D. A., & Tang, C. (1997). Discontinuities and continuities in the experience of learning: An interview study of high-school students in Hong Kong. *Learning and Instruction, 7*, 21-48.

Marton, F., Wen, Q. F., & Wong, K. C. (2005). "Read a hundred times and the meaning will appear . . ." Changes in Chinese university students' views of the temporal structure of learning. *Higher Education, 49*, 291-318.

Ng, G. (2000). From Confucian master teacher to Freirian mutual learner: Challenges in pedagogical practice and religious education. *Religious Education, 95*, 308-319.

Nivison, D. S. (1996). *The ways of Confucianism.* Chicago: Open Court.

Riel, M. (1998). Teaching and learning in the educational communities of the future. In C. Dede (Ed.), *Learning with technology: ASCD yearbook 1998.* Alexandria, VA: Association for Supervision and Curriculum Development.

Scardamalia, M., & Bereiter, C. (2003). Knowledge building. In J. W. Guthrie (Ed.), *Encyclopedia of education* (2nd ed., pp. 1370-1373). New York: Macmillan Reference.

Schwartz, B. I. (1985). *The world of thought in ancient China.* Cambridge, Mass.: Belknap Press of Harvard University Press.

Stokes, S. F. (2001). Problem-based learning in a Chinese context: Faculty perceptions. In D. A. Watkins & J. B. Biggs (Eds.), *Teaching the Chinese Learner: Psychological and pedagogical perspectives* (pp. 205-218). Hong Kong/Melbourne: Comparative Education Research Centre, The University of Hong Kong/Australian Council for Educational Research.

Tang, C. (1996). Collaborative learning: The latent dimension in Chinese students' learning. In D. A. Watkins & J. B. Biggs (Eds.), *The Chinese Learner: Cultural, psychological and contextual influences* (pp. 183-204). Hong Kong/Melbourne: Comparative Education Research Centre, The University of Hong Kong/Australian Council for Educational Research.

Tu, W. (1993). *Way, learning, and politics: Essays on the Confucian intellectual.* New York: State University of New York Press.

van Aalst, J., & Chan, C. K. K. (2007). Student-directed assessment of knowledge building using electronic portfolios. *Journal of the Learning Sciences, 16,* 175-220.

Watkins, D. A., & Biggs, J. B. (Eds.). (1996). *The Chinese Learner: Cultural, psychological and contextual influences.* Hong Kong/Melbourne: Comparative Education Research Centre, The University of Hong Kong/Australian Council for Educational Research.

Watkins, D. A., & Biggs, J. B. (Eds.). (2001). *Teaching the Chinese Learner: Psychological and pedagogical perspectives.* Hong Kong/Melbourne: Comparative Education Research Centre, The University of Hong Kong/Australian Council for Educational Research.

## Endnotes

*Original Text of the Analects in Traditional Chinese*

(Analects 1:1) 子 曰 , 學 而 時 習 之 , 不 亦 說 乎 , 有 朋 自 遠 方 來 , 不 亦 樂 乎 , 人 不 知 而 不 慍 , 不 亦 君 子 乎 .
(Analects 2:11) 子 曰 , 溫 故 而 知 新 , 可 以 為 師 矣 .
(Analects 2:13) 子 貢 問 君 子 . 子 曰 , 先 行 其 言 , 而 後 從 之 .
(Analects 2:15) 子 曰 , 學 而 不 思 則 罔 , 思 而 不 學 則 殆 .
(Analects 7:19) 子 曰 , 我 非 生 而 知 之 者 , 好 古 , 敏 以 求 之 者 也 .
(Analects 7:21) 子 曰 , 三 人 行 , 必 有 我 師 焉 , 擇 其 善 者 而 從 之 , 其 不 善 者 而 改 之 .
English translation: Legge, James. *The Chinese Classics,* vol. 1, 1861 (http://afpc. asso.fr/wengu/wg/wengu.php).

## Acknowledgements

This research was supported by competitive research grants awarded by the Hong Kong Research Grants Council, no. HKU 7158/01H, and the Hong Kong SAR Quality Education Fund, no. 2003/0410.

# TEACHER BELIEFS, CHANGING PEDAGOGY AND TEACHER LEARNING

# 5

# The Chinese Learner of Tomorrow

*Ference MARTON and the EDB Chinese Language Research Team*

## Introduction

Chinese learners are increasingly found to be good learners in classroom learning (Watkins & Biggs, 1996, 2001a). Marton, Wen, and Wong (2005) reported, however, on the capabilities of Chinese students to learn and study mainly on their own. The researchers followed a group of academically strong Chinese students through their first 20 months at university. The observations showed clearly how these students mastered their studies and at the same time developed a more complex understanding of what it takes to learn. Their ways of studying were characterized by reading the same texts in more than one way, using different sources to find out about the same topic, and sampling different views of the same problem from teachers and fellow students. They studied in a wide and widely varied way.

In recent educational reforms in China (in mainland China and Hong Kong), there has been a strong emphasis on developing the capability of learners to learn how to learn. Since 2001, the Ministry of Education of the People's Republic of China has published a series of reform documents that establish the framework for curricula from kindergarten to senior secondary level. A cooperative and interactive teaching approach is emphasized, which promotes independent learning and learning autonomy, and a major goal is the enhancement of student capabilities and attitudes in mastering and using knowledge (Ministry of Education of the People's Republic of China, 2001). A reform document published by the Curriculum Development Council of the Hong Kong Special Administrative Region (2001a), *Learning to Learn – The Way Forward in Curriculum Development: Life-Long Learning and Whole-Person Development*, also advances a learner-focused approach. The idea of focusing on "how students learn to learn" is that students of today, and more importantly, students of tomorrow, should be able not only to use the knowledge that they have been taught but also to learn new things in novel situations and make use of them in contexts that are not even possible to define at present. Being good at learning on your own means that you can rely on your own judgment, analyze and synthesize ideas and information, and draw your own conclusions. Such learning requires more critical thinking, flexibility, and creativity than does learning by being taught.

We report on a study that attempted to enhance students' capabilities to learn in a special, but also very common case. The study is about learning how to better understand argumentative texts and how to learn from them in more powerful ways. This is a dominant form of learning required in academic studies, but is also called for in both professional and private everyday life. Our attempt was based on certain ideas about learning outlined below in the proposed "variation framework." Before we present our study, however, we briefly describe a more common framework, which is an alternative to ours, to present our own approach by means of a contrast.

## Sociocultural Perspectives on Schema Theory

If we want to find powerful ways of improving the learners' capabilities to understand argumentative text, then a theory of understanding such texts is quite useful. Schema theory is an obvious candidate. Schemas, with a history that goes back at least to Kant, and possibly to Plato and Aristotle, refer to "organizing structures that mediate how we see and interpret the world" (McVee, Dunsmore, & Garelek, 2005, p. 535). The British psychologist Fredrick Bartlett is one of the best-known advocates of schema theory in modern time. Whereas Bartlett (1995) emphasized the social and cultural nature of schemas, throughout the 1970s and 1980s, when cognitive theories were popular, schemas were predominantly seen as structured mental representations of sets of situations or phenomena that are used for recognizing and remembering instances of those sets.

During the 1990s, the focus of research on learning shifted from what is going on in the heads of learners to what is going on in their world.

The term "schema" is used much less nowadays, although the concept is frequently referred to, especially in research on reading comprehension. In their review of schema theory, McVee et al. (2005) noted that the terms currently in use include "existing knowledge," "topic knowledge," "prior knowledge" and "previous knowledge" (p. 534). They argued for 1) the usefulness of schema theory, and 2) the sociocultural origin and nature of schemas. The cognitivist interpretation of schemas often implies fixed, rigid structures in spite of the "incredibly flexible and context-sensitive nature of comprehension" (Kintsch, 1998, p. 94).

There was previously little interest in the sociocultural origin of schemas. McVee et al. (2005) referred to Holland and Cole (1995), who suggested that schemas represent the conceptual aspect whereas discourse represents the material aspect of cognition. A schema, such as a historical narrative, for instance, can be seen as a cultural tool. When this tool is used, it is intertwined with "the particulars of the situation." Hence, it is not the schema but rather the situation or the event in which it is used that should be the unit of analysis. When a schema is used to make sense of a particular text in a situation, the two are mutually constitutive, rather than the former being more or less mechanically superimposed on the latter. In accordance with Vygotsky's notion of internalization, McVee et al. (2005) asserted, "schemas emerge from the social interactions between an individual and his environment" (p. 547), although the authors used a more complex model to emphasize that internalization is "not a reflection of the external, but rather a transformation of the external" (Robbins, 2003).

McVee et al. (2005) argued, with reference to Wertsch (1998), that students may fail to understand texts (such as historical narratives) because they have not mastered the necessary cultural tools (such as historical narratives). McVee et al. (2005) also suggested a number of ways to help students to master such tools: providing students with meaningful contexts in which they can engage with cultural activities and materials (p. 550), giving them opportunities for dialogical engagement instead of whole-class discussion (p. 554), and inviting them to be active participants in knowledge construction rather than passive recaptors of knowledge in teacher-directed activities in the classroom (pp. 554-555).

Not only are there texts with different genres and structures (e.g., narrative, argumentative), there are also different forms of narrative and argumentative texts. These different texts have certain distinguishing attributes, particularly in their structural nature. Schemas are complex, with distinctive features, and just like language, have sociocultural origins. Furthermore, it seems reasonable to see a reading event as situated in particular practices, whereas a schema is simply one aspect of the event, which appears to be closely intertwined with the material (such as discourse). Aspects of that event, instead of the schema being a mental construct, are more or less mechanically superimposed on the event or situation. We believe that when trying to make sense of texts in terms of particular structural features (or as characterized by certain schemas), learners are better off if they have appropriated those structural features. However, we disagree with the above mentioned line of reasoning about how this can be achieved.

As noted, McVee et al. (2005) suggested that learning can be enhanced by organizing learning in certain ways (dialogic rather than teacher-led whole-class discussion, giving more space to students, getting students to be more active in more meaningful contexts). These are reasonable ideas. Students might learn, and might appropriate that which they are supposed to learn and to appropriate, or they may not. It should be emphasized that the organization of learning is independent of what students are supposed to learn. Referring to how learning in the classroom is organized does not imply any distinctions between different things (different objects of learning) that the students are supposed to learn. If students are supposed to learn about a historical narrative, for instance, then how the narrative is presented and how the specific context of learning (as opposed to learning in general) is organized are not included in the definition of the approach to teaching the historical narrative.

## *The Variation Framework and Learning by Reading Argumentative Texts*

To further develop our argument, we must consider this question: What does it take to master (learn, appropriate) an object of learning (a schema, an object)? Mastering such an object of learning, in our view, amounts to making (or being able to make) a distinction between what this object of learning is and what it is not, and being able to distinguish among different instances of that object of learning. Distinctions can, in principle, be made in perception or in other actions (such as writing), but in this context we are primarily interested in the former. The reason for claiming that mastering something amounts to being able to distinguish it from other things (and being able to distinguish among its different instances) is related to our view that attributes have to do with how things differ from other things.

This view is related to de Saussure's theory of language (de Saussure, 1983) and, more generally, ideas inherent in the structuralist movement (Brügger & Vigsø, 2004), which stemmed from his work. De Saussure held that language is a system within which component parts derive their meaning from the position they occupy. One such component part, a word, for instance, can be understood, and in fact can only be understood, in terms of how it differs from other component parts, other words. For example, "young" is defined by not being "old" (and vice versa), and "male" is defined by not being "female." This principle applies to not only words, but also other parts of language. Phonemes, for instance, appear as pairs of opposites, an observation that has been elaborated by the Prague school of linguistics (Brügger & Vigsø, 2004, p. 31).

According to this line of reasoning, spoken or written language always has two contexts: one is the here and now, the syntagmatic context, the sentence in which the word appears, the situation in which the sentence is produced; the other is the paradigmatic context, the system in which we find the specific word, for instance, among other words that could have been said or written instead of the actual word, but were not.

These statements about language can be generalized to human experience in general. What we experience is how things differ from each other (see above), and what we perceive is difference (cf. Marton & Tsui, 2004). What is not present and what is ever present cannot be experienced. The illusion of induction is that if we show someone a number of cases that have one thing in common but differ in other respects, then the person should be able to discern what is common through induction.

Imagine, for instance, that we want to teach a child the concept of "green": we show her a green apple, book, ball, and shirt, and we point to each one and say "green." The child might grasp what we are trying to tell her but only if she has previously come across at least one other color, and if she is also simultaneously aware of her previous experience of other colors. The idea of "greenness" cannot be derived from different cases having green in common, but from the difference between green and at least one other color. So showing the child two balls, for instance, which are alike in all respects but color should work much better. Through such a contrast the child's attention is drawn to the colors compared and color is separated as a dimension of variation from other potential dimensions of variation (such as form, for instance) that do not

vary in the actual case. However, to distinguish green from its actual in-
stantiation (green ball), we need generalization, which implies pointing
to different instances that have green in common but vary in other
respects. This is actually the arrangement that does not work as induction,
but works for telling apart the concept from its instantiations. Hence, in
order to make a dimension of variation (e.g., color) and different "values"
in that dimension (e.g., different colors) visible, we need three patterns of
variation and invariance: contrast, separation, and generalization.

In many cases, a learner has to be able to discern and focus on two
or more dimensions of variation simultaneously. In Chinese, for instance,
every word integrates three aspects: form, pronunciation (initial and final), and meaning. Variation in sound and meaning is comparatively
easy for speakers of European languages to discern, but tone is difficult.
By exposing a learner to Chinese words that differ in tone but have the
sound in common, he or she can easily pick up the tone dimension
through separation. However, characters that differ in tone but not in
sound also differ in meaning. By drawing the learner's attention to variation in meaning at the same time that it is being drawn to variation in
tone, through fusion, the learner will experience variation in both respects simultaneously. It is the tonal feature of Chinese that constitutes
the greatest difficulty for Europeans when they are learning Chinese as a
second language (Ki & Marton, 2003).

The foregoing discussion is in accordance with our basic assumption that learning, to a considerable extent, amounts to learning to discern how something we encounter differs from other things. Enabling
learners to experience important differences through introducing things
that differ from each other in relevant respects, while they are the same
in other respects, means making it possible for learners to learn what
they are expected to learn.

If we apply the above line of reasoning, which we refer to as the
variation framework, to learning to understand argumentative texts and
hence learning more from them, then we might conclude the following.

1.    To enable learners to separate the act of learning (i.e., how they
      learn) from the content of learning (i.e., what they learn), the act of
      learning should vary while the content remains the same. This can
      be achieved by inviting learners to read a certain text first in one
      way (e.g., trying to memorize it) and then to read the same text

again, in a different way (e.g., trying to understand it). In this way, learners are likely to become aware of their own way of learning and of the potential variation in their own way of learning. Learners certainly have experiences of learning from different texts in different ways, but because in the past both the content of the text and the way of trying to learn from it has varied, it has not been easy to separate the way of learning (the act) from the content of learning.

2.  To enable learners to separate the meaning of a text from the words of the text, learners should be invited to inspect different accounts (e.g., originating from other learners) of the meaning of the same text. Then they can see how the same text can be understood in different ways; that is, the same words can have different meanings for different people. At the same time, they will find that different people can use different words to express the same meaning.

3.  To enable learners to become aware of the characteristics of different genres and separate those characteristics from the specific texts read, they should read texts that differ in genre (e.g., narrative, argumentative) but deal with the same theme, and read texts that belong to the same genre but deal with different themes.

4.  To enable learners to discern the structure of different texts, learners should read texts that deal with the same topic but have different structures (e.g., sequential, hierarchical), and read texts that have the same structure but deal with different topics.

In connection with each such exercise, the relevant distinctions should be thematized by the learners themselves when they together make comparisons aided by their teacher's guidance. The teacher should also summarize the conclusions after each exercise and point out the relations to other exercises.

These ideas about how to improve students' capabilities in learning how to learn through understanding argumentative texts were tested in a small-scale study carried out in two secondary schools in Hong Kong.

## The Study

### *Curricular Context of the Study*

In the new millennium, in accordance with the changes in educational policies mentioned earlier in this chapter, new curricula for primary and secondary schools were introduced in Hong Kong, which emphasized the development of students' capabilities to learn. The expression "learning to learn" was used as the slogan of the reform (Curriculum Development Council, 2001a). "Reading to learn" is one of the four key tasks that was put forward in the curriculum reform proposal, *Learning to Learn – The Way Forward in Curriculum Development: Life-Long Learning and Whole-Person Development*. Schools were strongly encouraged to promote a reading culture among children and provide "proper guidance, opportunity and motivation for them to enhance their learning capacity through reading" (Curriculum Development Council, 2001a). In response to the curriculum reform, a newly revised secondary Chinese Language curriculum was implemented in secondary one in September 2002. "Independent language learning" is one of the nine strands of this revised curriculum (Curriculum Development Council, 2001b) and reading is a major tool to attain that goal. Enhancing the ability of students to independently acquire and apply language-mediated new knowledge is the direction of the curriculum innovation.

In 2004, the Education and Manpower Bureau (now called the Education Bureau) published another consultation report, "Reforming the Academic Structure for Senior Secondary Education and Higher Education – Actions for Investing in the Future," which provided recommenddations for a new three-year senior secondary curriculum. The report stated that better progression and alignment to higher education were expected to "enable all students to be self-initiating and lifelong learners" to respond to the new challenges of the rapidly changing world (Education Manpower Bureau, 2004, pp. 1-2). The independent language learning promoted in the Chinese Language curriculum is in line with this goal.

In the study described in this chapter, we developed and tried out such a curricular unit using the variation framework to enhance learning how to learn through reading argumentative texts in accordance with the curricular goals. Our belief was that being able to extract meaning from argumentative texts is a key element of the ability "to independently acquire and apply language-mediated new knowledge." Argumentative texts are typically dealt with in secondary education in Hong Kong, but the comprehension of specific texts is emphasized rather than the enhancement of the capability of students to deal with new texts on their own.

In traditional teaching, teachers provide guidance for student learning. For each question asked, teachers already have a model answer in mind and give it directly if students do not produce it. Students need not put much effort into finding out the meanings of texts or choosing appropriate strategies for comprehension. Teachers explain the arguments, the bases of the arguments, and their proofs (these are considered the three crucial elements of argumentation) in texts. They discuss the characters, vocabulary, sentences, and paragraphs of a text, and often its related history and allusions. Teachers teach students how to divide a text into paragraphs, to conclude the central idea, and explain aspects of writing techniques including text and rhetorical structures and language attributes. Strategies for reading argumentative texts are also provided. The problem with this kind of teaching is that although the students might understand the content of the texts very well, they do not get better at dealing with novel texts in powerful ways on their own when they later encounter such texts in the future.

One of the intentions of the curriculum reform is a marked expansion of higher education. Such an expansion, with a radically higher proportion of new cohorts continuing beyond the secondary level, will put heavy demands on the secondary level regarding the preparation of students for tertiary studies. Developing students capabilities "to independently acquire and apply language-mediated new knowledge" should be seen as a key component in such preparation.

## Participants

Four teachers and 158 third-year secondary school students (about 15 years old) from two schools in Hong Kong participated in the study. An approximately equal number of girls and boys were enrolled in two classes in each of the two schools. There was one target and one comparison class in each school. In Hong Kong, secondary school students are streamed into three "bands" depending on their performance on ability tests. These students were of medium to high ability.

## Measures

### Measuring Text Understanding

*Design.* Six texts were used to assess the ability of students to understand argumentative prose: two were administered before students participated in the series of lessons, two immediately after the series of lessons had been completed, and two four months after the series of lessons had finished. Each class was randomly divided into two halves, and two pairs of text passages (AB and CD) were used for each of the four groups before and after the lessons (pre- and posttests) using a counterbalanced design to ensure that the text difficulty was similar for students across conditions. For the delayed posttest, the students read another pair of text passages (EF).

**Table 5.1**

*Design of the Reading of Text Passages for the Experimental and Comparison Classes*

|  | Pretest | Posttest | Delayed Posttest |
|---|---|---|---|
| Experimental |  |  |  |
| Half of Class 1 | A, B | C, D | E, F |
| Half of Class 2 | C, D | A, B | E, F |
| Comparison |  |  |  |
| Half of Class 1 | A, B | C, D | E, F |
| Half of Class 2 | C, D | A, B | E, F |

The design ensured that each class read the same texts before and after the series of lessons, but that each student did different tests before and after the lessons. In addition, the combined results were comparable before and after the series of lessons, but the results of the delayed posttest were not directly comparable with the results of the pre- and posttests (as the texts were different).

Each text had an identifiable "gist" (at least from the point of view of the researchers), which was illustrated by means of one or more examples (see Appendix A). The length of the text was, on average, 700 words. The students were asked to read each text "for understanding" within ten minutes and then to write what they thought the author of the text was trying to say. One single-lined A-4 page with the question was provided for each text. The responses of students (when translated into English) were, on average, 100 words.

*Scoring of text understanding.* The answers of the students were analyzed qualitatively in accordance with the phenomenographic research tradition (see Marton & Booth, 1997, pp. 110-136). This approach involves two steps. First, the similarities and differences in the ways that the students captured the gist of a particular text were evaluated against the researchers' understanding of the text. In accordance with the principles of phenomenography it was assumed that this variation could be captured in terms of a limited set of categories that were hierarchically related to each other. After a preliminary grouping of the differing understandings of the gist, we focused on how one group could be distinguished from another; that is, we identified critical differences. The relationships among the categories of different understandings were also examined. After determining a set of categories (the number of categories varied from three to five for the different texts) and the relationships between them were finalized, the second step started. All of the student answers were categorized based on the system established by two independent judges. The degree of agreement varied from 80 to 90% for the different texts; in the event of disagreement, the two judges reached agreement after negotiation. Finally, to simplify the comparisons, only two categories were retained, "the best" understanding of each text versus "the other" understandings, scored as 1 or 0. It is reemphasized that the categories were not defined in advance, but rather were derived from the analysis of the answers of the students.

*Views of the Participants*

Each lesson was observed and followed by a (taped) discussion (lasting for approximately 15-40 minutes) between the observer and the observed teacher. After the sequence of lessons was completed, nine students from each target class were interviewed about their experience. The student interviews lasted approximately 10-15 minutes.

# Teaching Plan

Based on the variation framework, a teaching plan was developed jointly by the two teachers of the "target classes" and the research team. The plan was designed to enhance the ability of students to make sense of novel argumentative texts. This was done by making aspects of argumentative texts and the acts of reading visible to the students through their participation in activities designed to keep certain aspects invariant (i) while other aspects vary (v). Table 5.2 shows the different sub-goals (objectives), patterns of variation, and activities.

# Table 5.2
## Teaching Plan for Learning from Argumentative Texts Using the Variation Approach

| Objective | Pattern of variation[a] | | | | Activities |
|---|---|---|---|---|---|
| | text | act | meaning | learner | |
| **1. Memorization vs. understanding**<br>Making students aware of their own reading acts by contrasting memorization and understanding | i | v | | i | Students read text 1 with the aim of remembering (act 1) as much of it as possible<br><br>Students write all that they remember (text removed)<br><br>Comparing how much the students remember<br><br>Students read text 1 again, but now with the aim of understanding (act 2) it as well as possible<br><br>Students write what they think the author was trying to say<br><br>Students reflect on whether they have read the text differently on the two occasions |
| | text | | meaning | learner | |
| **2. Meaning vs. text/ words**<br>Making students aware that the same word can have different meanings and that the same meaning can be expressed with different words | i<br>v | | v<br>i | v<br>v | Comparing the students' accounts of what the author was trying to say<br>• Different meanings?<br>• Same meaning? expressed in different ways? |
| | text | act | | learner | |
| **3. Understanding vs. understanding**<br>Making students aware of their reading acts through generalizing the act of understanding across different texts | v | i | | i | Students read text 2 with the aim of understanding it as well as possible<br><br>Students write what they think the author was trying to say<br><br>Students reflect on their ways of reading through comparison of the first with the second way of reading text 1 (aiming for understanding)<br><br>students discuss the issue in groups and report to the class |

| Objective | Pattern of variation | | | Activities |
|---|---|---|---|---|
| | text | meaning | genre | |
| 4. *Argumentative text vs. narrative text* | | | | Students read text 3 (same content, different genre) |
| Making students aware of genre-related differences by comparing argumentative and narrative texts | > | i | > | Students try to find differences and similarities between texts 2 and 3 |
| | | | | Students discuss the issue in groups and report to the class |
| 5. *Different genres* | text | meaning | genre | Students read texts 4 (narrative), 5 (descriptive), 6 (lyric), 7 (expository), and 8 (argumentative) at home and complete relevant worksheets aimed at comparing the texts |
| Developing students' understanding of the characteristics of different genres | > | > | > | Group work in class |
| | | | | 1. Each group receives paper strips with fragmentary information about the text concerning |
| | | | | - the authors' points |
| | | | | - style of writing |
| | | | | - content |
| | | | | 2. Students categorize and reorganize the paper strips and stick them onto blanks on work-sheets |
| | | | | 3. Groups present their findings and the teacher summarizes the characteristics of the different genres |
| | text | genre | character-istics | |
| 6. *Narrative text vs. narrative text* | | | | Students read text 9 (narrative) and compare it with text 3 (narrative) |
| Making students aware of differences between texts within the same genre | > | i | > | Students read texts 10 and 11 (both argumentative) and look for differences and similarities between them |
| 7. *Argumentative text vs. argumentative text* | text | genre | character-istics | |
| Developing students' understanding of the characteristics of argumentative texts | > | i | i/v | With reference to these two texts and others read before, the teacher summarizes the characteristics of argumentative texts |

| Objective | Pattern of variation | | | Activities |
|---|---|---|---|---|
| | scenario/ perspective | account | learner | |
| 8. *Scenario and perspectives* | | | | Students watch a certain scenario (on video) and describe what they see |
| Making students aware that the same scenario can be described in different ways (different accounts given) depending on differences in perspective | i/i | v | v | In groups, students share what they have seen |
| | i/v | v | i/v | Students describe the same scenario from two given perspectives; e.g., patient at a home for the elderly vs. an advertisement producer |
| | | | | Different accounts compared in class |

| Objective | Pattern of variation | | Activities |
|---|---|---|---|
| | argument | basis of argument (example) | |
| 9. *Argument vs. rationale for argument* | | | Students read two extracts (different bases of argument) and figure out the argument (same) |
| Making students aware of the distinction between an argument and the basis of an argument | i | | |
| | v | | Students read texts 12 and 13 (same basis of argument, different arguments) and compare them |
| | | v | Teacher summarizes the relationship between an argument and the basis of the argument |
| | | i | Students read text 14 and separate the argument from the basis of the argument |

| Objective | Activities |
|---|---|
| 10. *Conclusion* | Teacher summarizes the series of lessons with a specific focus on the following |
| Encouraging students to engage in independent learning and reflect on their ways of learning | • Learning by reading<br>• What to learn? How to learn?<br>• Reflecting on one's way of learning |

ᵃ Patterns of variation are described in terms of what varies (v) and what is invariant (i).

*Implementing the Lessons*

The plan was carried out by both teachers with slight differences: 12 lessons (each 80 min. long) were taught in school A and 13 lessons (each 55 min. long) were taught in school B. Teacher A used one more lesson to cover pattern 3 than did teacher B, one less for each of patterns 4, 5, and 8, and allocated one-half lesson after pattern 8 for students to practice giving accounts based on various sources (about the same topic). This means that teacher A put relatively more emphasis on the pattern of variation/invariance, which we call generalization (the same idea and style applied to different instances, meaning is derived from sameness), and less on contrast (meaning is derived from differences) compared to teacher B. Generalization is the most common teaching approach, so although the main contribution of the variation framework is its emphasis on meaning that is derived from differences, we would say that teacher B was somewhat uncompromising, which is illustrated in the following example of how the teaching took place in the two classes.

For pattern 5 (see above), when students came to class, they had already read five texts that represented five different genres. They had also used worksheets that helped them to capture the meaning of the texts and their genre-related characteristics (without having the actual genres given). During the lesson, students worked in groups, each of which received 15 paper strips with one of three descriptors (meaning, style, content) for one of the texts, without stating the nature of these descriptors. The students had to organize these descriptors by finding the three dimensions of variation (discern them from each other) and finding the right combination of "values" in these dimensions for each text.

Teacher A thought that the task was too complicated for the students and therefore told them what the three dimensions were (meaning, style, content). Students had only to find the matching combination of "values" for each text. In contrast, teacher B followed the original plan. Although the task was indeed difficult, in the end the students in both of the classes managed to complete it successfully.

*Teaching in the Comparison Class*

At the same time that the set of lessons was being carried out in the two target classes, the object of teaching, argumentative text, was also being taught in the comparison classes. The topic was dealt with in 12 lessons (each 40 min. long) in the comparison class in school A and 8 lessons (each 55 min. long) in the comparison class in school B, in what we call the "traditional way of teaching argumentative texts," which is characterized as follows.

Teachers in Hong Kong usually teach passages in a standard way, starting from the smallest unit, that is, a character, and then discussing vocabulary, sentences, paragraphs, the whole passage, the author's information, and other relevant knowledge of the passage (such as that related to the author or the historical context of the passage), respectively. Instructed by teachers, students divide the passage into paragraphs, determine the idea of each paragraph and the central idea of the passage, and discuss the content of the passage.

After discussing the contextual clues of the passage (pointing out the general meaning of characters, vocabulary, sentences, and paragraphs), teachers analyze the passage in terms of genre characteristics and writing method. For instance, three crucial elements of argumentation, the argument, the basis of the argument and its proof, and distinctive ways of establishing proof, such as proof and disproof (establish an argument by refutation) are highlighted.

To integrate the teaching of reading and writing, teachers usually employ reading materials as exemplars when teaching writing. Teachers neither design reading lessons from the perspective of enhancing the reading comprehension capability of students nor give students the opportunity to discover ways to independently comprehend the text or think critically. For example, teachers usually guide students in the appraisal of writing techniques, but do not teach them to verify the author's viewpoint, rationale for his or her argument, or type of proof. Students need not share their own views or feelings, as teachers typically provide the model answers at the end of a lesson. The ability of students to master argumentative writing is assessed in two ways: whether they are able to write an argumentative text (e.g., establishing an appropriate argument, the basis of the argument, and the proof), and whether they are able to answer questions relating to the content (e.g., idea of a sentence or paragraph) and writing technique (e.g., genre characteristics).

Sometimes teachers introduce students to certain reading strategies, such as looking for keywords and key sentences, but this is done in an isolated manner. As lecturing is the dominant teaching mode, teachers usually give hints on the selection of strategies and they may even give them model answers. Students become accustomed to taking a passive role, and are not trained to develop their own style of reading such as selecting and applying appropriate reading strategies to solve reading difficulties, or to construct their own knowledge.

*Lessons between the Posttest and Delayed Posttest*

Teacher A taught her own class during the experiment and continued doing so afterwards. Teacher B taught the target class in her school only during the study. Afterwards, she changed classes with the teacher of one of the comparison classes and continued teaching that class. Independent learning and argumentative texts were not objects of teaching in either of the classes during the period between the posttest and delayed posttest.

## *Results*

*Test on Text Reading*

From Table 5.3, we can see that the proportion of students "getting the point" was the average for the four texts read on each occasion. As discussed in the Method section, students in each class were divided into two groups, and each student read two text passages counterbalanced across the conditions at the pre- and posttests. Altogether, four texts were read by students in each class on each occasion. We took the average scores of the two text passages. We can see that whereas the target group from school B did somewhat better than the corresponding comparison group (in the sense of improvement), the target group from school A did less well than the corresponding control group. In general, we did not find much difference between the target and comparison groups regarding differences between the two tests.

**Table 5.3**
*Relative Frequency (%) of "Getting the Point" (Texts Combined)*

|  | Target Group | | Comparison Group | |
| --- | --- | --- | --- | --- |
|  | Pretest | Posttest | Pretest | Posttest |
| School A | 31 | 22 | 30 | 35 |
| School B | 20 | 27 | 36 | 33 |
| All | 25 | 25 | 33 | 34 |

However, based on the results shown in Table 5.4, there was a significant difference ($p < .01$) found between target and comparison groups in their performance on the delayed posttest, for which two novel texts were used, four months after the curriculum unit on reading argumentative texts. The results suggest that the effects of the programme were stronger after some time rather than immediately after the unit was taught.

**Table 5.4**
*Relative Frequency (%) of "Getting the Point" (Texts Combined)*
*on the Delayed Posttest*

|  | Target Group | Comparison Group |
| --- | --- | --- |
| School A | 61 | 45 |
| School B | 69 | 47 |
| All | 65 | 46 |

Note: $t = 2.45$, $p < .01$.

*Views of the Participants*

As previously mentioned, each lesson was observed and followed by a (taped) discussion between the teacher and the observer. Eighteen students (nine from each of the two target schools) were interviewed after the sequence of lessons was completed. Various features of the experiment appeared to be new experiences for the study participants. We found that the participants, each of whom had had different experiences of the Hong Kong educational system in general and of teaching/learning how to deal with argumentative texts in particular (prior to the study), noticed certain aspects in which the lessons differed from what they were used to, which include the following:

1.  Aim of the sequence of lessons
2.  Design and implementation of the lessons (how the lessons worked)
3.  Teacher and student perceptions of the lessons (how they felt about the lessons)
4.  What the students actually learned

*Aim of the sequence of lessons.* In Hong Kong, school teachers commonly emphasize text features (such as genre characteristics) and reading strategies (such as reading the first and last paragraph). However, if text features and reading strategies are simply memorized and applied mechanically, then no improvement will result. In accordance with the programmatic statement, "The kind of capabilities we focus on are those that empower learners to deal with situations in powerful ways, that is, to simultaneously focus on features critical for achieving a certain aim" (Marton & Tsui, 2004, p. 20), the sequence of lessons was aimed at alerting students to critical aspects of reading such as the reading act, meaning, account, perspective, genre, and genre characteristics.

> In fact, we never understand much of reading, such as the psychology of reading. Many things are related to reading . . . like thinking. That's true! This is a big problem because thinking is something fundamental. You have to develop your thinking before building up those strategies. (Teacher B)

> In our usual practice, we give our students a certain direction, . . . which has somehow restricted their reading. (Teacher B)

*Design and implementation: How the lessons work.* The basic idea behind the design of the sequence of lessons was that by holding certain aspects of the reading of argumentative texts constant while varying other aspects, the students would have the opportunity to discern the various aspects, and subsequently be able to combine them. According to the theory, someone who is good at making sense of argumentative texts is someone who can discern different aspects of the text and by doing so, grasp both its form and content. Both teachers seemed to find this a powerful idea and made it their own.

> The principle is that if you don't compare two things, then their features can't be discerned. That's a crucial point. I can't deny the brilliance of variation. But surely there is a difference between giving [students] the variation directly and letting them discover it themselves. The latter is far more impressive [to students] and leads to great reflection on pedagogy [by teachers]. (Teacher B)

> If students are able to explain how they got the answer, then the teacher can ascertain what students can and cannot understand. Students with similar answers can then compare the similarities

and differences [between their answers] and [those] of other students. Therefore, this design is capable of catering for individual differences. (Teacher B)

In addition to the systematic use of variation, perhaps the most striking feature of the lessons was their interactive, dynamic nature. The teachers really tried to learn from their students to be able to help them to learn, and to build on what they expressed. This meant two important things: first, the teachers had a genuine interest in what the students thought and felt, and did not expect them to try to guess the "right answers". Second, as the teachers could not predict what the students would say, they had to take into account the students' responses on the spot, and had to act on them immediately.

I had never realized that learning is much more important than teaching. . . . I realize that this process is very important. Only when students speak up can I discover their concerns. "Why is this wrong?" I'm then given the opportunity to tell them. Maybe I need to provide (them) with further such opportunities (to get to know problems), and these opportunities are created through the process. (Teacher B)

In the latter part of the lesson, I think that the use of the blackboard together with recess aided my teaching. After the students had written down their findings and left [the classroom], I could quickly think over their answers or reading methods. I tried to combine and organize them. I find that teachers have to do much reflection during the lesson. This is a problem of professionalism. However, if [professionalism] is developed, then the spontaneous learning of students can be enhanced. Just now, they've provided me with an opportunity to analyze their understanding. (Teacher A)

I think these lessons are very novel – I've never had them before. We students are closer now and have more topics to discuss with each other. In the past we had to be attentive during teaching and raise our hands before asking or answering questions. Now it's more interactive. The teacher says something and we have to respond. There are more exchanges of ideas among students. In the past, those who were less attentive would chat and fool around. Only those who were attentive, usually two persons in your classroom, would discuss what was being taught. I find it a rare chance to listen to the opinions of the entire class. If we have group presentations, then I can listen more. (Student B1)

This student's observation about the change in the pattern of interaction is paralleled by the reflection of the teacher who taught that class.

In the past, I would often ask my students, "How did you find [the answer]?" I would first divide them into groups and let them discuss the matter among themselves. . . . Finally, they'd come up with a model answer (because the capabilities of my students are not low). Then I'd give feedback such as "Right! That's the answer!" But this design allows students to review or articulate the ways in which they find their answers. Because there were six types of answers, we could cater for students with different capabilities. This is different from the traditional "cooperative learning" approach. In the past, I thought that I could cater for students [of different abilities]. But that's not true! Looking back, low achievers wouldn't speak much [during group discussion]. Therefore, a method to discern different types of answers helps to reveal how low-ability students think and why they think in that way. This is a great reflection! I used to think that I'd planned group discussion in my lesson such that students of different ability were guaranteed the opportunity to express their opinions. But in fact, that was not the case! (Teacher B)

*Teacher and student perceptions of the lessons.* The dynamic, interactive nature of the sequence of lessons put a great strain on the teachers, who had to act or respond immediately, without being able to predict the flow of events in advance. The arrangement was challenging for the students too, in part because of its demanding nature and the repetitive elements of the patterns of variation and invariance that were used.

When teaching students about thinking, I find it very exhausting as my brain has to function quickly. This is because I have to pick out students with different answers and point out their differences. (Teacher A)

The teacher is under great pressure when she has to respond instantly to students' answers. That's very stressful. (Teacher B)

Some of us felt exhausted while reading ... because we were reading the same article .... Probably we'd been reading it in too complicated a way ... too much in depth. (Student A1)

It was boring . . . because we read the same articles again and again the first day and re-read them the following day. (Student A2)

*What the students actually learned.* Despite occasionally feeling frustrated, most of the students who were interviewed gave positive accounts of what they felt they had learned.

We needed to ponder over more questions .... I got to know the problems of my classmates so that I could learn from them. Student answers were quoted and we could read and learn from all of these answers. (Student B2)

I think that the great difference is that she [the teacher] asked us to be more active. She stimulated our thinking by asking us dozens of questions. She always urged us to answer her questions. The atmosphere was better. (Student B1)

You had to keep thinking while reading the examples. No one would tell you the meaning of the examples and the writing methods adopted. You had to think about this on your own. (Student A3)

I think different people think differently. I usually think on my own and read from my own perspective. I seldom read from other angles .... I discovered that people perceive the same thing differently from one another. (Student A4)

Previously, if the time was set, then I would be afraid of running out of time and would read very quickly. In fact, I did not read [the text] in detail, but just aimed at roughly grasping the main idea. Later I realized that I might have missed some crucial sentences, which may have given clues to the theme. But I'd neglected them.

And when formulating my answers about what the author wanted to say, I would actually answer in my own words, and not so objectively sometimes …. I would add my own thinking to the answer. In fact, I should try to answer as though I were the author. (Student B1)

For example, when we read for comprehension, sometimes we just used our own point of view in reading. Now, after attending so many lessons and reading others' answers, I realize something: we shouldn't use our own point of view to read, but the point of view of the author instead …. That is we have used so many … so many …. For example, we find it hard to understand if you just simply say it. But this time, we read a great number of our class-mates' answers. Why were the answers so different? We'd then go wondering, and understand later. (Student A5)

## Discussion

The results of the study are discussed below in terms of three themes: first, the curricular context; second, the short- and long-term effects of student participation in the sequence of lessons, designed and carried out in accordance with the variation framework; and third, the "Chinese-ness" of the Chinese learner.

### *Curricular Context*

As mentioned in the introduction, the present study considered an approach to work towards an objective introduced by the new curriculum reform in Hong Kong, namely, the enhancement of "independent language learning," that is, the development of students' capabilities to learn on their own, mainly through reading. This objective is close to the central ideas of the curriculum, implied by its introduction with the expressions "learning to learn" and "reading to learn." The curriculum reform aims at promoting learner autonomy and assisting learners to become creative and critical thinkers who are good at dealing with novel situations in an unknown and unpredictable future. Accordingly, the new curricula advocates arrangements for learning believed to be conducive to such aims, including learner-centered modes of instruction, group work, interactivity, and active forms of participation. These recommendations are consistent with what McVee et al. (2005) suggested as the means for improving students' capabilities to learn.

Through the reactions of the participants (see the Results section), we could see that the learning of the target groups was organized in accordance with the principles advocated by the new curriculum. We emphasize, however, that the organization of learning was not the point of departure in the target groups. That is, the planning did not start with the assumption that the teacher's role should be reduced, that the lessons should be interactive, or that students should work in groups. The point of departure was the object of learning, theoretically conceptualized as the capability to discern various aspects and parts of novel texts, and the point of departure was the theoretical ideas about what it takes to develop it. It turned out, however, that we could not create the conditions necessary to develop this particular capability without giving more space to the students or without making interaction more dynamic. The way in which learning was organized was not an end in itself but a means towards specific and specified learning objectives.

## Immediate and Long-Term Effects

The most striking results originating from this study was the combination of no immediate effects and strong long-term effects of the mode of instruction. These results are in agreement with the research of Schwartz and Bransford (1998; see also Bransford & Schwartz, 1999; Schwartz & Martin, 2004) on preparation for future learning. These researchers have shown that certain designs of learning conditions do not immediately yield superior results regarding learning outcomes; rather, learners excel when they subsequently encounter novel learning resources: even if they have not learned what they were learning better, they have become better at learning from other sources. The difference is that in Bransford, Schwartz and their colleagues' studies, the researchers experimentally introduce particular learning resources, while in our case occasional reading experiences during the four months (between the posttest and the delayed posttest) were "the novel learning resources". We believe that we have shown a case of generative learning (Holmqvist, Gustavsson, & Wernberg, 2008; Marton, 2006), that is, learning that generates new learning. This was, of course, what was meant to happen and what was expected to happen (in accordance with the earlier results just mentioned) as an effect of students' having participated in the experiment. The way it is assumed to have happened is as follows.

During the sequence of lessons, the students encountered patterns of variation and invariance aimed at bringing out contrasts, differences, and distinctions through the juxtaposition of cases according to some systematicity. Now, every time the learner encounters a new case, that is, each new text to be read, is a new learning occasion for these learners. Ideally, they are simultaneously aware of the new text and previous text(s) they have read. The patterns of variation and invariance, which were brought out by means of specific combinations of cases during the experiment, have made the different features of the texts visible. But as the learner is simultaneously aware of "the old" texts and the new texts, the former makes features of the new text visible too (an effect we would not find in the comparison group). However, the addition of the new text may retrospectively enrich the perception of the "old" texts, because the set of texts of which the learner is simultaneously aware of is enlarged and more varied. The effect of generative learning is thus cumulative: the longer is the time that passes, the stronger the effect gets.

One could raise the question: why would students get better at extracting meaning from texts they read by having become better at discerning characteristics of genres, structures of texts, and styles of writing? According to the theoretical point of departure of the study described in this chapter, what we (humans) notice is difference. When we read a text, we notice how it differs from other texts, for example, how its structure differs, how its style differs, and how its main point (i.e., its meaning) differs. Noticing differences amounts to discerning the aspects in which texts differ from each other and vice versa. If we fail to discern a particular aspect, then we cannot notice the corresponding dimension of variation. The two things are two sides of the same coin. We might fail to notice a difference (given that it exists), to discern the dimension of variation, because other things differ, or vary, at the same time. Simply stated, if everything varies, then nothing can be discerned. This is the case before you learn to discern any aspects of texts. Once you have discerned a particular dimension of variation, or noticed a way in which texts differ from each other, you can attend to that particular aspect and "bracket it," that is, neglect it momentarily. The greater is the number of differences between texts that you have learned to notice, the easier it is for you to notice any of them, because you can "think away" all of the differences but one and focus completely on that one (e.g., the point, or meaning).

Without the ability to distinguish the different ways in which texts differ from one other, you will not be able to find out how texts differ from each other given that they differ in many ways.

Of course, texts do not always differ in many ways. Children who have listened to many tales of the same kind (narrative texts) can accurately answer the question "What can we learn from this tale?" exactly for the reason that the texts that they have come across so far have only differed in one respect – content/meaning. However, when they come across a text of another kind, an argumentative text, for instance, they might encounter great difficulty when trying to answer the above question (What can we learn from this text?), because the new text differs in too many respects from the texts they have come across earlier (e.g., in structure, style, and meaning).

There are, naturally, alternative explanations that cannot be ruled out by means of the design adopted. Although it was not our primary aim to introduce more active, interactive, and dialogical forms of learning to help the students to appropriate the object of learning, the teachers made use of such forms of learning to a greater extent than did the teachers in the comparison groups. So, in principle, this difference could have explained the differences in outcomes. In similar studies, however, we find dramatic differences in learning outcomes, in spite of the absence of differences in the level of activity and interactivity in the classroom (e.g., Marton & Pang, 2006; Pang & Marton, 2003, 2005). What differed in these cases, however, was the patterns of variation and invariance, which in our interpretation, made the critical difference in the conditions of learning. We can also refer to von Wright's (2007) recent inquiry into whether activity in learning is necessarily observable. Discernment has always to be brought about by learners. It is the central act of learning, in our view, and discernment is necessarily active and necessarily non-observable. Activity in learning is thus a necessary, but not sufficient condition of learning. "Activity" may or may not imply discernment, while "discernment" always implies activity.

Still, one may question how such a highly structured approach to teaching can be conducive to the development of the ability of students to learn independently. The answer is that the structure had to do with the choice of tasks to be addressed and texts to be read. What the teachers did actually enlarged the space of variation (Runesson & Marton, 2002), that is, the range of alternatives the students encountered, the range of aspects they could discern and pay attention to, the range of things they could do, and the range of ideas they could explore.

## The "Chineseness" of the Chinese Learner

The theoretical idea underlying this paper is that being good at dealing with something amounts to seeing that particular thing in a certain way, or in certain ways. Being good at learning amounts thus to seeing learning in certain ways, and being good at learning through a certain kind of medium (such as argumentative texts) amounts to seeing learning in certain ways and seeing that medium in certain ways (noticing its different features, i.e., how it differs from other forms of presentations and how its different instances differ from each other). In addition, being good at learning a certain kind of content through a certain kind of medium amounts to seeing learning in certain ways, seeing that medium in certain ways, and seeing the kind of content in certain ways (i.e., noticing how it differs from other kinds of content and how its different instances vary from each other). This means that someone who is good at learning may be good at learning certain things, but not necessarily good at learning other things. People are not good at learning in general. Learning is always the learning of something, and learning to learn is always the learning of learning something. In this study, this "something" has been "dealing with argumentative texts with a certain kind of general content (basically, deliberations about human nature)." We have shown that secondary school students can learn to learn this "something." However, there is no art of learning that makes someone good at learning everything. Realizing this is as far as one can get in mastering the art of learning.

Now, is there anything especially Chinese in our way of characterizing the capability aimed at or in our way of trying to nurture that capability?

First, our approach to the advancement of independent learning takes its point of departure from what the students are supposed to become better at learning from. We have not been dealing with independent learning in general, but rather with independent learning through reading argumentative texts. When doing so, we have tried to help students to focus on the content, or more precisely, "the gist" of the texts. Teachers in Confucian-heritage cultures are seen as more content oriented than their Western counterparts. Gao and Watkins (2001) demonstrated nicely that content has a critical position in most of the different conceptions of teaching identified among Chinese teachers. Also, the contradiction between views of teaching as teacher centered/content oriented and student centered/learning oriented, so common among Western educators, does not seem to exist among Chinese teachers (Biggs & Watkins, 2001; Watkins & Biggs, 2001b). Our own study was, for instance, teaching centered (not teacher-centered) and learning oriented at the same time.

So what about the means by which we have tried to achieve our objectives? Chinese views of learning are characterized by strong beliefs in human perfectibility, and by the willingness of learners to learn (Li, chap. 2, this volume), and willingness of parents to support their children's learning. None of this has explicitly been a part of our project for two reasons. First, we wanted to explore one specific aspect of learning. Second, we believed that the series of lessons would have an indirect motivational effect. We have tried to help students become better at understanding the texts they read: becoming better at understanding texts by reading should make readers more interested in reading for understanding.

Tse and Marton (2005) reported on a parallel study, which also aimed at developing students' capabilities to learn by encouraging them to read on their own (i.e., independent learning), conducted in Hong Kong during the same school year as the present study. Twelve Chinese language teachers and 453 Form 1 students participated in Tse and Marton's study, which was carried out over the course of one year. The students were divided into target (experimental) and comparison (control) groups. The approach adopted was much wider than that of the study described in this chapter. A great deal of effort was made to facilitate the reading habits of students, such as having them read more literature outside school and engaging the parents (to talk with their children about literature and to create better conditions for studying at home). In addition, lesson plans and teaching materials were developed collaboratively by teachers and researchers according to the same theoretical framework used in the present study. The Progress in International Reading Literacy Study (PIRLS) reading test was used to measure the ability of students to understand the texts that they were reading (see, for instance, Rosén, Myrberg, & Gustafsson, 2005). Whereas the comparison group's test result increased from $M = 62$ (SD = 15) to $M = 71$ (SD =

14), the target group's test result increased from M = 59 (SD = 13) to M = 75 (SD = 11) from the beginning to the end of the school year. The change was about .62 standard deviation units in the comparison group and 1.3 standard deviation units in the target group; that is, the change in the latter was more than twice as much that in the former. Although these results should be interpreted with caution as the PIRLS test is developed for younger students, the additional gain in reading comprehension generated by the experimental program is of such a size that a corresponding increase for all Hong Kong students would catapult them to become the "best in the world," based on the PIRLS test.

According to the PIRLS 2006, students from Hong Kong primary 4 classes comprised one of two groups who did the best in the world in reading comprehension and also one of two groups that had improved most since 2001. To what extent new approaches to the teaching of reading, writing, and reading comprehension adopted in many Hong Kong schools recently, within the space created in the wake of the ongoing curriculum reforms, have contributed to these results has still to be investigated. One of these approaches, is based more or less on the framework used in the present study (Tse & Marton, 2005; Tse, Marton, Ki, & Loh, 2007).

In the study described in this chapter and in that of Tse and Marton (2005), the lessons were designed based on the variation framework. This means that the conditions for learning were carefully orchestrated. This is typical, we would suggest, of Chinese teaching, or at least, of good Chinese teaching (cf. Ko & Marton, 2004). In addition, the systematic use of variation and invariance is very common in the teaching of mathematics in China. It is called *bien shi* [變式] (variation), and similar principles are used in other subjects (cf. Gu, Huang, & Marton, 2004). We would like to suggest that even if the way we tried to advance independent learning is far from being uniquely Chinese, it is a special case of a general approach to teaching that is more common in China and other Confucian-heritage cultures than in the Western world.

Earlier studies (Marton, Dall'Alba, & Tse, 1996; Marton, Watkins, & Tang, 1997; Marton, Wen, & Wong, 2005) have pointed out a unique feature of Chinese views of learning: memorization and understanding are not seen as opposites as they are in many other cultures. A developmental trajectory has also been shown: to begin with, memorization and understanding are undifferentiated in children's perception. Subsequently, they are completely differentiated and form a stark contrast, but eventually merge again in the learner's experience: they are seen as two sides of the same coin. A possible explanation of the close relationship between memorization and understanding is the central role of variation and repetition in Chinese pedagogy (see Marton & Tsui, 2004) and in approaches to studying adopted by Chinese students.

In the introductory section of this chapter, we referred to the study of Marton, Wen, and Wong (2005). They argued that at least some Chinese students are, or are becoming, very good at learning on their own: they are, or are becoming, good at developing their own capabilities to learn independently. Interestingly, these students are making use, either consciously or unconsciously, of the same principles as those used by the teachers in the target groups (in both studies discussed here). Our point is that although the systematic use of variation and invariance is not unique to Chinese culture (see above and Marton, 2006), the former is deeply ingrained in the latter. We suggest that you take a look at *The Book of Changes* (《易經》).

# REFERENCES

Bartlett, F. C. (1995). *Remembering*. New York: Cambridge University Press.

Biggs, J. B., & Watkins, D. A. (2001). Insight into teaching the Chinese Learner. In D. A. Watkins & J. B. Biggs (Eds.), *The Chinese Learner: Cultural, psychological and contextual influences* (pp. 277-300). Hong Kong/Melbourne: Comparative Education Research Centre, The University of Hong Kong/Australian Council for Educational Research.

Bransford, J. D., & Schwartz, D. C. (1999). Rethinking transfer: A simple proposal with interesting applications. *Review of Research in Education, 24*, 61-100.

Brügger, N., & Vigsø, O. (2004). *Strukturalism*. Lund: Studentlitteratur.

Curriculum Development Council. (2001a). *Learning to learn – The way forward in curriculum development: Life-long learning and whole-person development*. Hong Kong: Author.

Curriculum Development Council. (2001b). *Secondary Chinese language curriculum guide (Secondary 1-5)*. Hong Kong: Author.

de Saussure, F. (1983). *Course in general linguistics*. London: Duckworth.

Education and Manpower Bureau. (2004). *Reforming the academic structure for senior secondary education and higher education – Actions for investing in the future*. Hong Kong: Author.

Gao, L., & Watkins, D. A. (2001). Towards a model of teaching conceptions of Chinese secondary school teachers of physics. In D. A. Watkins & J. B. Biggs (Eds.), *Teaching the Chinese Learner: Psychological and pedagogical perspectives* (pp. 27-45). Hong Kong/Melbourne: Comparative Education Research Centre, The University of Hong Kong/Australian Council for Educational Research.

Gu, L., Huang, R., & Marton, F. (2004). Teaching with variation: A Chinese way of promoting effective mathematics learning. In L. H. Fan, N. Y. Wong, J. F. Cai & S. Q. Li (Eds.), *How Chinese learn mathematics: Perspectives from insiders* (pp. 309-347). Singapore: World Scientific.

Holland, D., & Cole, M. (1995). Between discourse and schema: Reformulating a cultural-historical approach to culture and mind. *Anthropology and Education Quarterly, 26*, 475-490.

Holmqvist, M., Gustavsson, L., & Wernberg, A. (2008). Variation Theory – An organizing principle to guide design research in education. In A. E. Kelly, R. Lesh, & J. Baek (Eds.), *Handbook of design research methods in education* (pp. 111-130). New York: Routledge.

Ki, W. W., & Marton, F. (2003, August 26-30). *Learning Cantonese tones*. Paper presented at the 11th biennial conference of the European Association for Research on Learning and Instruction, Padova, Italy.

Kintsch, W. (1998). *Comprehension: A paradigm for cognition*. New York: Cambridge University Press.

Ko, P. Y., & Marton, F. (2004). Variation and the secret of the virtuoso. In F. Marton & A. M. B. Tsui et al., *Classroom discourse and the space of learning* (pp. 43-62). Mahwah, NJ: Lawrence Erlbaum Associates.

Marton, F. (2006). Sameness and difference in transfer. *Journal of the Learning Sciences, 15*, 501-537.

Marton, F., & Booth, S. (1997). *Learning and awareness*. Mahwah, NJ: Lawrence Erlbaum Associates.

Marton, F., Dall'Alba, G. A., & Tse, L. K. (1996). Memorizing and understanding: The keys to the paradox? In D. A. Watkins & J. B. Biggs (Eds.), *The Chinese Learner: Cultural, psychological and contextual influences* (pp. 69-83). Hong Kong/Melbourne: Comparative Education Research Centre, The University of Hong Kong/Australian Council for Educational Research.

Marton, F., & Pang, M. F. (2006). On some necessary conditions of learning. *Journal of the Learning Sciences, 15*, 193-220.

Marton, F., & Tsui, A. B. M. (2004). *Classroom discourse and the space of learning*. Mahwah, NJ: Lawrence Erlbaum Associates.

Marton, F., Watkins, D. A., & Tang, C. (1997). Discontinuities and continuities in the experience of learning: An interview study of high-school students in Hong Kong. *Learning and Instruction, 7*, 21-48.

Marton, F., Wen, Q. F., & Wong, K. C. (2005). "Read a hundred times and the meaning will appear...": Changes in Chinese university students' views of the temporal structure of learning during the first two years of their studies. *Higher Education, 49*, 291-318.

McVee, M. B., Dunsmore, K., & Garelek, J. R. (2005). Schema theory revisited. *Review of Educational Research, 75*, 531-566.

Ministry of Education of the People's Republic of China. (2001). *Jichu jiaoyu kecheng gaige gangyao (shixing)* 《基礎教育課程改革綱要（試行）》 [Outline for Basic Education Curriculum Reform (trial version)]. Available from Ministry of Education of the People's Republic of China web site, http://www.moe.edu.cn/

Pang, M. F., & Marton, F. (2003). Beyond "lesson study" — comparing two ways of facilitating the grasp of economic concepts. *Instructional Science, 31*, 175-194.

Pang, M. F., & Marton, F. (2005). Learning theory as teaching resource. *Instructional Science, 33*, 159-191.

Robbins, D. (2003) *Vygotsky's and A.A. Leontiev's semiotics and psycholinguistics: Applications for education, second language acquisition and theories of language.* Westport, CT: Praeger.

Rosén, M., Myrberg, E., & Gustafsson, J. E. (2005). *Läskompetens I skolår 3 och 4. Nationell rapport från PIRLS 2001 I Sverige.* Göteborg: Acta Universitatis Gothoburgensis.

Runesson, U., & Marton, F. (2002). The object of learning and the space of variation. In F. Marton & P. Morris (Eds.), *What matters? Discovering critical conditions of classroom learning.* Göteborg: Acta Universitatis Gothoburgensis.

Schwartz, D. L., & Bransford, J. D. (1998). A time for telling. *Cognition and Instruction, 16*, 475-522.

Schwartz, D. L., & Martin, T. (2004). Inventing to prepare for future learning: The hidden efficiency of encouraging original student production in statistics instruction. *Cognition and Instruction, 22*, 129-184.

Tse, S. K., & Marton, F. (2005). *Developing students' independent learning capabilities in secondary Chinese language curriculum project* (Final report). The University of Hong Kong.

Tse, S. K., Marton, F., Ki, W. W., & Loh, E. K. Y. (2007). An integrative, perceptual approach for teaching Chinese characters. *Instructional Science, 35*, 375-406.

von Wright, M. (2007). Where am I when I am at ease? Relocating the notion of activity in education. *Nordisk Pedagogik/Nordic Educational Research, 27*, 222-235.

Watkins, D. A., & Biggs, J. B. (Eds.). (1996). *The Chinese Learner: Cultural, psychological and contextual influences*. Hong Kong/Melbourne: Comparative Education Research Centre, The University of Hong Kong/Australian Council for Educational Research.

Watkins, D. A., & Biggs, J. B. (Eds.). (2001a). *Teaching the Chinese Learner: Psychological and pedagogical perspectives*. Hong Kong/Melbourne: Comparative Education Research Centre, The University of Hong Kong/Australian Council for Educational Research.

Watkins, D. A., & Biggs, J. B. (2001b). The paradox of the Chinese Learner and beyond. In D. A. Watkins & J. B. Biggs (Eds.), *Teaching the Chinese Learner: Psychological and pedagogical perspectives* (pp. 3-23). Hong Kong/Melbourne: Comparative Education Research Centre, The University of Hong Kong/Australian Council for Educational Research.

Wertsch, J. V. (1998). *Mind as action*. New York: Oxford University Press.

## *Appendix*

The six texts used in the study, "the gist" being defined in terms of "the best student understanding" according to the researchers, were as follows.

Text A
Title:        Learning: not for scoring
Topic:      By translating the English slogan "Learning: It's more than scoring" into Chinese as "Learning: not for scoring," the translators upset many people who thought that the slogan would make children lazy (by encouraging them not to care about tests). The actual intention of the translator was to attract people's attention and make them reflect, by creating a contradiction.

Critical features:
The means: replacing "not only for scoring" with "not for scoring".
The goal: to capture attention and bring about reflection.

Text B
Title:        Children
Topic:      Children may not become successful adults because they are spoiled

Critical features:
Cause: Children are spoiled today.
(Possible) effect: they may not become successful adults.

Text C
Title:        Discussion of McDonald's' sales strategy
Topic:      The old Chinese saying "To know one's own strength and the enemy's is the sure way to victory" is illustrated by how McDonald's created Snoopy fever in Hong Kong. Customers were offered a limited number of plastic figures, a different one each day for 28 consecutive days, when they purchased a McDonald's Happy Meal. By capitalizing on Hong Kong people's weakness of not wanting to miss out on potential benefits, long queues were created outside McDonald's restaurants.

Critical features:
The importance of knowing others' strengths and weaknesses.

Text D

Title:      Protecting oneself against ridicule

Topic:      Different examples of how people endure difficulties by showing what may be called "breadth of mind": being tolerant, generous, forgiving, and relaxed.

Critical feature:

"Breadth of mind".

Text E

Title:      The second one

Topic:      The first one, the innovator, or the leader of the troop in the battle is always hailed, and honored. But without the second one, who develops the innovation further, following and backing the leader in battle, the efforts of the first one would be in vain.

Critical feature:

The achievement of "the first one" is dependent on the achievement of "the second one".

Text F

Title:      Deposit bit by bit for whole withdrawal

Topic:      We might save a little bit of money every month during a long period of time and then withdraw a big lump sum later. We can find the same principle in many other contexts. You cannot learn to write well, for instance, if you do not accumulate a great number of small improvements.

Critical feature:

"Deposit bit by bit for whole withdrawal" is relevant for things other than money.

## Acknowledgements

We would like to thank the teachers and students who participated in the study described in this chapter. They are the real heroes and heroines of our story. We are also grateful for the insightful comments that we have received from the editors of this book and three anonymous reviewers.

# 6

# Classroom Innovation for the Chinese Learner: Transcending Dichotomies and Transforming Pedagogy

*Carol K.K. CHAN*

## Introduction

Since the pioneering work on the paradox of the Chinese learner (Watkins & Biggs, 1996; 2001), there has been growing enthusiasm for examining teaching and learning for Chinese learners (Fan, Wong, Cai, & Li, 2004; Lee & Mok, 2008; Rastall, 2006). Biggs (1996) examined Western misperceptions and discussed the importance of sociocultural, contextual and systems perspectives for interpreting learning in the Chinese context. Marton and his colleagues identified the use of the memorization-understanding process in explaining the paradox of the Chinese learner (Marton, Dall'Alba, & Tse, 1996). These research efforts have primarily debunked the myth that Chinese students are passive and rote learners. Major advances have now been made examining the influences of cultural and contextual influences on Chinese learners.

As noted in the Introduction (Rao & Chan, this volume), although there is continuing growing interest in the Chinese learner, relatively less attention, thus far, has been given to examining the contemporary Chinese learner in the light of changing global and educational contexts. Educational reforms throughout Asia and in different countries of the world now place emphasis on developing citizens' capabilities in learning how to learn, innovation, and knowledge creation needed for 21st century education. These changing educational demands have presented major challenges for teachers and students (Darling-Hammond, Bransford, LePage, Hammerness, & Duffy, 2005; Hargreaves, 2003). To address global changes, the Hong Kong government has initiated a series of major educational reforms. The first major effort, described in a document entitled *Learning to Learn – the Way Forward in Curriculum Development: Life-Long Learning and Whole-Person Development* (Curriculum Development Council, 2001), illustrated a set of new educational goals and aims. Over the years, continuing reform efforts have expanded and are now taking place at all levels of schooling, such as the structural change in senior secondary school levels and the introduction of a compulsory subject called Liberal Studies (Law et al., chap. 4; Marton et al., chap. 5, this volume).

With changing technological, socioeconomic and educational contexts, how do Chinese teachers adapt and adopt classroom innovations as they help students to achieve new educational goals? Previous research has focused on academic achievement and school performance (Watkins & Biggs, 1996, 2001), and comparatively less attention has been given to examining the Chinese learner in the light of new educational goals and task demands such as learning how to learn. This chapter investigates such questions in the context of examining how an innovative pedagogical approach, computer-supported knowledge building, was implemented in Chinese classrooms. Specifically, the chapter reports on case studies of how two expert Chinese teachers transformed their pedagogical practices; how these changing practices led to emerging epistemologies among students and teachers; and how these changes illuminated the notion of teaching the Chinese learner for the 21st century.

## The Paradox of the Chinese Learner

To understand Chinese students' learning in the contemporary era, we start with the question of the paradox of the Chinese learner. This intriguing phenomenon has been discussed in the Introduction (Rao & Chan, chap. 1, this volume) and various chapters (Li, chap. 2; Law et al., chap. 4, this volume). Because of the centrality of this notion in understanding the changing Chinese learner, this chapter provides further explanation as background to the reported studies. Traditionally, many assumptions have been held noting that Chinese learners are passive learners adopting surface approaches and studying in crowded classrooms. However, since the 1990s, researchers have found that Chinese students consistently outperform Western students in international tests of academic achievements, as well as on measures of deep approaches to learning (Mullis, Martin, Beaton, Gonzalez, Kelly, & Smith, 1997; Mullis, Martin, Kennedy, & Foy, 2007; Watkins, 1996). This puzzling phenomenon of how Chinese learners can be both rote learners and high achievers has been coined the "paradox of the Chinese learner" (Biggs, 1996; Watkins & Biggs, 1996).

There are different interpretations of the paradox of the Chinese learner, alluding to the Confucian-heritage culture, in which high priority is given to learning (Lee, 1996; Wong, 2004). Biggs and Watkins (1996) noted that teaching and learning is embedded culturally and there exist various misinterpretations when learning and teaching are examined from a Western perspective. They argue that Western theories cannot explain Chinese students' performance adequately; student learning needs to be interpreted in relation to contextual and cultural perspectives. Chinese students are attuned to contextual influences, and they develop various approaches to meet their learning needs. For example, although it is uncommon to have collaborative learning in Hong Kong classrooms, cooperative learning is widely practiced informally among Chinese students in preparation for public examinations (Tang, 1996).

Another explanation examines the memorization-understanding approach observed among Chinese learners. Marton and his colleagues argue that whereas memorization and understanding are seen as distinct in the West, they are intertwined processes for Chinese learners (Marton et al., 1996). Various studies have shown that Chinese learners use memorization to help them understand the materials; and at the same time understanding the materials helps students to memorize (Marton et al., 1996; Marton, Watkins & Tang, 1997). More recently, Marton, Wen and Wong (2005) identified a developmental trajectory with increased differentiation and coordination of memorization and understanding among Chinese learners.

These various interpretations relating to cultural and contextual influences generally refute the myth of the rote-learning Chinese student. Chinese learners may not be inherently predisposed to use memorization-understanding, but they use this approach more because of cultural beliefs about efforts and perceived task demands. In traditional Chinese culture, there is a deep-rooted tradition of public examinations for the selection of candidates for social and economic advancement, and this tradition continues to play a pivotal role in schooling in China and Hong

Kong. The historical tradition and contextual demands of examination, together with attribution beliefs in effort, may influence students to develop and to experience the memorization-understanding process more than do learners from Western cultures.

Biggs (1996) discussed the "cue consciousness" of Chinese learners and how they can adapt to new task demands, and he used examples of how overseas Chinese students changed their strategies when faced with new tasks within the first year of university schooling. The explanation emphasizing contextual influences is consistent with the recent emphasis on the "discursive construction" of the Chinese learner (Clark & Gieve, 2006) that suggests how sociocultural and contextual factors mediate the characterization of the Chinese learner. Given the changes in educational reforms and new goals for learning, there will now be new learning tasks and different perceived task demands. This chapter explores how contemporary Chinese learners respond to these new contextual demands in the context of experiencing the new pedagogy of knowledge building.

## *The Paradox of the Chinese Teacher*

The question has also been posed as to how it is possible for Chinese teachers teaching in unfavorable conditions (e.g. crowded classrooms) to help students to attain high achievement (Watkins & Biggs, 2001). One explanation is that, in this respect, it should be noted that teaching is a cultural activity (Stigler & Hiebert, 1999) and it is important to examine teaching activity in relation to interactions between different components of the system (Biggs & Watkins, 2001). For example, large classes may not be considered conducive to learning, but in mainland China, teachers have highly effective ways of orchestrating learning with large class sizes supported by an elaborate teacher professional development system (Cortazzi & Jin, 2001; Tsui & Wong, chap. 10, this volume). Students may not seem as if they are able to express themselves well, but they can develop high levels of cognitive engagement with different manifestations (Biggs & Watkins, 2001). Chinese teachers hold both cognitive and affective conceptions of learning that emphasize cultivating roles in which teaching is considered as "preparation for examination" and "providing moral guidance" (Gao & Watkins, 2002).

Biggs and Watkins (2001) discussed the importance of examining teaching and not just teachers, and noted that there are various levels for understanding teaching and learning. The first level focuses on examining the characteristics of students, the second focuses on identifying what teachers do, and the third level examines how teachers engage students in tasks that are appropriate to their cognitive levels in the broader context of cultural and contextual influences. Good teaching is not merely transplanting the Western approach or adding on another approach; rather it involves designing instruction and engaging students in learning in ways that are aligned with the cultural and contextual forces for *transforming* student learning.

With changes in educational goals and demands, we need further investigation into how to develop pedagogical practices that help Chinese learners *learn how to learn* in the knowledge-based era. We also need to explore how teachers think about and transform classroom practices to align them with the new approaches. Research has shown that teachers nowadays need to be communities of learners and inquirers themselves (Chan & Pang, 2006; Cochrane-Smith & Lytle, 1999; Putnam & Borko, 2000) in order to achieve sustainable and generative change (Franke, Carpenter, Fennema, Ansell, & Behrend, 1998; Richardson & Placier, 2002). Whereas educational reforms are making major strides in Asia and Confucian-heritage culture classrooms, limited research has been conducted to examine how new pedagogy can be implemented for the Chinese learner for education reform.

Previous research on teaching Chinese learners has shown that various Western-based approaches such as constructivist learning (Chan, 2001), problem-based learning (Taplin & Chan, 2001; Stokes, 2001), and conceptual change (Ho, Watkins, & Kelly, 2001) can help foster student learning in the Chinese classroom. Less attention, however, has been given to detailed analyses of how these approaches can be implemented in the Chinese classroom, negotiating the tensions between cultural beliefs, contextual demands and Western ideas. With the changing education context, Chinese teachers and students will encounter further experiences of new pedagogy. The research reported in this chapter extends earlier studies and focuses on how a new pedagogy called "knowledge building" was adapted and adopted in the Chinese classroom.

## Knowledge Building Innovation and 21st Century Education

The term "knowledge building" is used rather loosely in the literature; we use it here to refer to the model focusing on "the production and continual improvement of ideas of value to a community" postulated by

Bereiter and Scardamalia (2006). Knowledge building is based on decades of cognitive research on intentional learning (Bereiter & Scardamalia, 1989; Chan, Burtis, & Bereiter, 1997), expertise (Bereiter & Scardamalia, 1993), and restructuring schools as knowledge-building communities (Scardamalia & Bereiter, 1994). Similar to scientific inquiry, ideas can be examined, critiqued, refined and improved through the *collective efforts* of members of the community. In knowledge-building communities, members make progress not only in improving their personal knowledge, but also in developing collective knowledge through progressive discourse (Bereiter, 2002; Scardamalia & Bereiter, 2003, 2006).

With the advent of the knowledge-based era, Scardamalia and Bereiter (2006) argue that the goals of schooling need to go beyond the acquisition of knowledge. Schools in the 21st century need to focus on helping students to improve their ideas, develop new ways of thinking, and advance collective learning. Knowledge building goes beyond focusing on tasks with a mere shift from teacher-centered to student-centered learning. It reflects an underlying philosophical shift about what schooling is about – students and teachers need to become members of a community *creating* and improving knowledge for the community.

To support the knowledge-building approach, Scardamalia and Bereiter and colleagues have developed a computer-supported forum called Knowledge Forum® (Scardamalia & Bereiter, 1994). Using networked computers, a number of users (i.e., students or teachers) can simultaneously create notes (text or graphics) to add to the database; search for and read existing notes; comment on other students' notes; or organize notes into more complex structures. By seeing different ideas and models, students can reflect on their own thinking and improve their metaconceptual awareness. At the same time, the database provides a space for tracking the growth of collective understanding. In knowledge-building classrooms, students typically begin by posing their questions and ideas; they then build on each others' inquiry and continue to search for a deeper understanding, integrating classroom and online discourse.

The knowledge-building approach was developed in Canada, beginning in the mid-1980s, but is now used in many countries. Decades of research have shown its role in promoting student understanding, inquiry and collaboration (e.g., Scardamalia, Bereiter, & Lamon, 1994; Zhang, Scardamalia, Lamon, Messina, & Reeve, 2007). In Asia, researchers and educators in Japan, Taiwan, Singapore, and Hong Kong have implemented Knowledge Forum in the classroom. Studies in Hong Kong have examined knowledge building in teacher education (Chan & van Aalst, 2006), international collaboration (Lai & Law, 2006) and assessment for scaffolding knowledge building (Lee, Chan, & van Aalst, 2006; van Aalst & Chan, 2007).

The studies reported in this chapter examined the implementation of the knowledge building approach in the Chinese classroom for teaching the Chinese learner of the 21st century. The key notions of the knowledge-building approach seem particularly relevant for the Chinese context. For example, one of the key constructs of knowledge building is "collective cognitive responsibility," and the idea of working collectively in a community seems to align well with the emphasis on collective aspects in the Chinese context. Another notion of "improvable ideas" accords well with the emphasis on effort among Chinese students as ideas can be improved through continued and sustained work.

## Research Goals and Questions

This chapter examines the characterization of the Chinese learner and the nature of the pedagogy appropriate for Chinese learners for 21st century learning in the context of examining the implementation of the knowledge building approach. To this end, the chapter reports on two case studies of teachers who implemented knowledge building in Hong Kong classrooms. These studies show how the two teachers transformed their classroom pedagogy, taking into account both traditional practices and contemporary influences, and how teachers and students changed their beliefs and understanding. The major research goals were: to examine the roles and effects of the knowledge-building pedagogy with Chinese learners; to characterize the beliefs and approaches to learning of the Chinese learners; and to explore teacher beliefs and pedagogy for learning and innovation in the Chinese classroom. Specifically, the following questions were examined.

(1) How did the teachers implement the new pedagogy of the knowledge building approach? In particular, how did they transform the pedagogy and how was innovation implemented in the Chinese context?

(2) What were the roles of the transformed pedagogy of knowledge building on student learning? Specifically, in what ways did students improve in their learning outcomes, approaches and beliefs?

(3)   What characterized changes in teacher beliefs and practice when they implemented the new pedagogy of knowledge building in the Chinese context?

The first teacher, Teacher A adopted the new pedagogy early on. The second teacher, Teacher B, was initially a skeptic, but both had experienced major growth and change. Both teachers joined the author's research project on implementing the knowledge building approach. The research method adopted was design-based research (Brown, 1992; Collins, Joseph, & Bielaczyc, 2004), where researchers and teachers worked collaboratively and iteratively to improve design and practice. Whereas action research focuses on teacher reflection and practice, design research emphasizes refinement of theory and design principles in complex classroom settings. There were regular visits and meetings with the teachers to discuss the design of the knowledge building pedagogy. The Knowledge Forum databases were monitored and examined by the researchers and teachers to track student responses. Teacher and student interviews, classroom observations, analyses of student discourse, and conceptual understanding tests were employed as data sources.

These two case studies were selected because they illustrate different facets of the same theme – both teachers developed a deep understanding of the new pedagogy; they adopted seemingly contradictory approaches, but they transcended the dichotomy as they appropriated the innovation. Through these cases, we sought to examine how Chinese teachers and students approached new learning and innovations in the classroom and how we can conceptualize the nature of teaching and learning in the Chinese context in the contemporary era.

## Study One: Knowledge Building and Conceptual Inquiry

### Participants

Teacher A had ten years of teaching experience when he first started to use the knowledge building approach in his teaching. Having done a Master's degree, he was keen to explore new ways of facilitating student learning. Teacher A started his classroom use of knowledge building with a group of Form Six students (aged 16-17 years) in his geography class, consisting of fourteen students. Students came from a regular subsidized school with students of high-average ability. As they were Form Six students, they were working on the curriculum in preparation for the university-entrance examination. The medium of instruction was English and students wrote in English in Knowledge Forum.

## *Transformed Pedagogy and Classroom Implementation*

This section considers how the teacher appropriated and adapted the Western-based knowledge-building pedagogy. Teacher A, working with the university researchers, developed an instructional sequence that combined sociocognitive principles with the sociocultural constraints in Hong Kong classrooms integrating both structured and emergent pedagogy synergizing dialectic tensions (Figure 6.1). We have described the instructional design elsewhere (Lee et al., 2006; van Aalst & Chan, 2007); this chapter highlights aspects of the pedagogical transformation of knowledge building in the Chinese context.

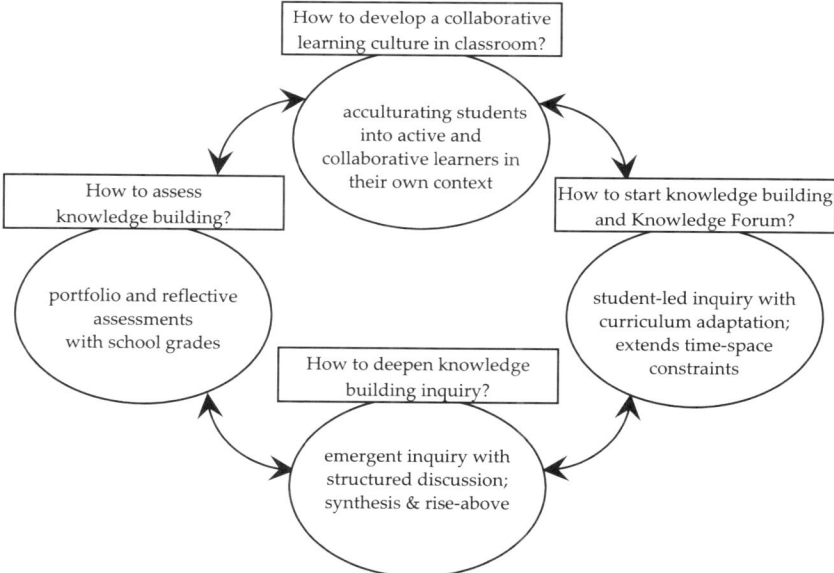

*Figure 6.1.* **Design of knowledge building and transformed pedagogy**

*Phase 1 – Developing a collaborative classroom culture.* The teacher was concerned with how he could appropriate the knowledge building pedagogy in his classroom. Instead of simply viewing Chinese students as passive learners, we considered how students could be acculturated into active and collaborative learners in their own context. Rather than starting on Knowledge Forum, we worked on developing a collaborative culture aligned with regular classroom routines. For example, Teacher A provided opportunities for students to express themselves and build on others' ideas; he asked them to summarize and to present both textbook and other information, thus making their ideas go public; he used concept mapping, student-generated questions and other metacognitive strategies to support collaborative inquiry. Teacher A gradually moved from teacher talk to student talk; he tried out new approaches in the context of adapting regular curriculum materials such as textbook and teacher notes. We emphasized acculturating Chinese students to the new practices, taking into account student and curriculum needs.

*Phase 2 – Addressing inquiry and curriculum adaptation.* After the initial phase of collaborative learning, the students were introduced to Knowledge Forum. Instead of the usual approach of teacher asking questions, students were scaffolded to generate their questions. Given the packed curriculum and perceived time constraints, they were asked to continue to pursue questions on Knowledge Forum after school; a practice quite different from how knowledge building pedagogy has been used in other countries, but well aligned with the context of the Chinese classroom. The discussion in the database was adapted to be part of the homework routine for the students. Instead of spending time doing worksheets or practicing essays, which is a common homework practice in Hong Kong, the students were encouraged to pose and inquire into questions and to develop explanations to extend class discussion.

Figure 6.2 shows a discussion view of the computer database where students were engaged in collaborative inquiry, building on others' questions and ideas. Whereas most teachers in Hong Kong have complained that they could not apply new pedagogy in their classrooms due to the lack of time, the teacher used Knowledge Forum in ways that created more time and space for the students as they fulfilled their homework requirements.

*Phase 3 – Deepening learning through structured discussion and emer-*

*gent inquiry.* The teacher was concerned with how to increase his students' level of collaborative knowledge-building inquiry. We designed a variety of strategies using "rise-above notes," asking students to pool questions and explanations for deeper inquiry. The teacher employed both Western ideas of open and emergent inquiry and the Chinese pattern of *structure* to help students deepen their discussion. Selected students were asked to be "view managers" to encourage others to contribute and to maintain the discussion views. "Group leaders" are commonly used in Hong Kong classrooms (van Aalst, Fung, Li, & Wong, 2007), and Teacher A capitalized on that to help the students further their inquiry; student ownership and agency was given a different and richer meaning with the combined use of structured and emergent strategies.

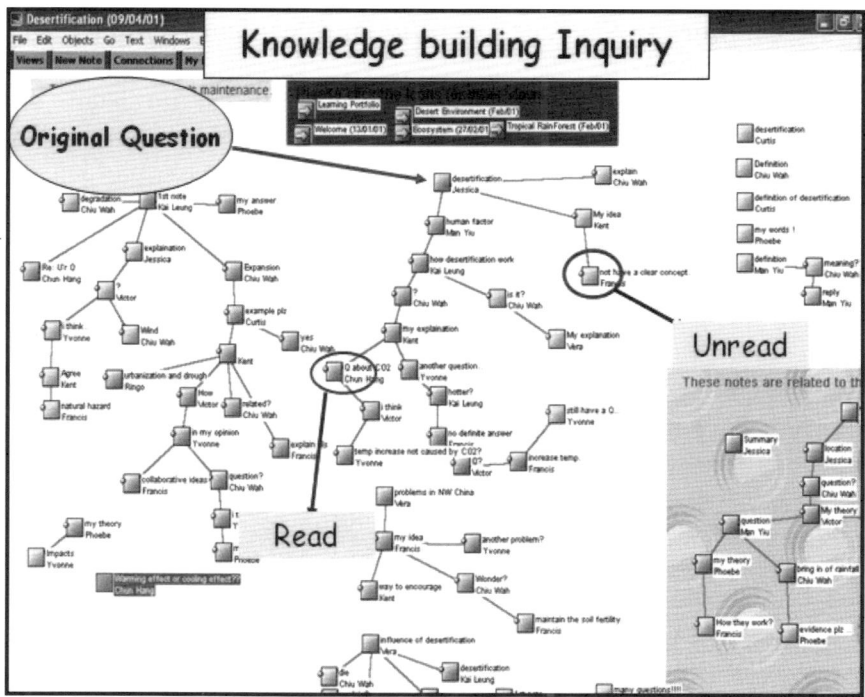

**Figure 6.2.** An example of students' knowledge-building inquiry on Knowledge Forum

*Phase 4 – Portfolio assessment and school grades.* We capitalized on the perceived importance of assessment for Chinese students. Working with the research team, the teacher adapted an innovative artifact called "knowledge-building portfolios" first used in a graduate course that required the students to identify the best clusters of notes in the discussion forum and to write explanatory notes to explain why and how these notes showed knowledge building guided by a set of principles (Chan & van Aalst, 2004; van Aalst & Chan, 2007). He asked the students to submit this knowledge-building portfolio, a sophisticated sociocognitive design for assessing knowledge building, and these portfolios were considered to be required, assessable assignments. While the notion of scaffolding students' deep collaboration with the required portfolios seems to contradict the focus on self-agency in knowledge building, it is an arrangement the teacher deemed necessary in the Chinese educational context.

## Changes in Student Learning and Student Beliefs

Evaluation of student learning outcomes was conducted (for details, see van Aalst & Chan, 2007). The following section highlights several key results of the effects of the pedagogical transformed approach of knowledge building on student learning processes, outcomes and beliefs.

### Student Learning Process and Domain Understanding

*Participation and collaboration in Forum discussion.* This study assessed students' growth in learning and collaboration through examining their participation in the computer forum. Several knowledge-building indices derived from the Analytic Toolkit (Burtis, 1998), a software developed by Knowledge Building Research Team, were employed. These indices included notes written, revision of notes, and scaffolds (metacognitive prompts), and others that included notes read, keywords and links used. The indices reflected the students' participation and efforts to collaborate with others and, as measures of knowledge building activity, have been employed and validated in research on knowledge building (Lai & Law, 2006; van Aalst & Chan, 2007; Zhang et al., 2007).

Table 6.1 shows the mean scores of student participation and collaboration in Forum discussion in early and late phases of the instruction. Statistical analyses using paired t-tests indicated that there were significant increases from Periods 1 to 2 in the numbers of notes created, $t(13) = 4.2$, $p < .01$; number of scaffolds used, $t(13) = 6.8$, $p < .001$, and percentages of linked notes, $t(13) = 3.6$, $p < .04$. The findings suggest more sophisticated patterns and growth in student participation and collaboration in the use of Knowledge Forum over time.

**Table 6.1**

*Student Participation and Collaboration on Knowledge Forum for Early and Later Phases, Indicating Improvement over Time*

|  | Period 1 Mean (SD) | Period 2 Mean (SD) |
|---|---|---|
| Number of notes created | 26.3 (11.4) | 34.9 (10.9) |
| Number of revisions | 23.4 (10.7) | 27.4 (18.2) |
| Number of scaffolds | 19.0 (12.5) | 42.4 (20.2) |
| Percentage of notes linked | 76.9 (9.8) | 88.6 (3.9) |
| Percentage of notes with keywords | 49.1 (21.7) | 52.2 (11.8) |

*Deepening inquiry over time.* Question asking is commonly used as an index of deep thinking important for developing expertise and learning how to learn (Bereiter & Scardamalia, 1993). The quality of student questions was examined using a 4-point scale (Table 6.2). A random set of responses constituting about 40% of all questions was coded and inter-rater reliability was 0.87. Analyses were conducted to examine whether students made progress in asking deeper questions over time as they worked on Knowledge Forum. Levels 1 and 2 were combined to form "low-level" questions, and Levels 3 and 4 questions were combined to form "high-level" questions.

**Table 6.2**

*Mean Frequency of Different Levels of Questions for Early and Later Phases, Indicating Improvement over Time*

|  | Period 1 Mean(SD) | Period 2 Mean (SD) |
|---|---|---|
| Level 1 | 1.0 (1.0) | 0.3 (0.8) |
| Level 2 | 4.4 (3.2) | 1.7 (1.8) |
| Level 3 | 2.4 (2.1) | 4.9 (3.5) |
| Level 4 | 0.3 (0.6) | 1.5 (1.7) |
| Total | 8.0 (5.1) | 8.4 (5.3) |

Paired t-tests on the total number of questions showed no differences between Periods 1 and 2. However, significant differences were obtained for both low-level questions, $t$ (13) = 4.2, $p < .01$; and high-level questions, $t$ (13) = 3.8, $p < .03$. These findings suggested that students improved in asking deeper questions over time (Table 6.2).

*Domain understanding.* To examine the effects of the pedagogy on conceptual understanding, students in the Knowledge Forum group (n=14) and comparison group (n=9) were given writing tests to assess their domain understanding. The comparison group was taught similar curriculum topics by another teacher with comparable qualifications and years of experience. We controlled for differences among students using similar school banding and prior academic achievements based on their public examination results (i.e., Hong Kong Certificate of Education Examination, HKCEE). The students were asked to complete two tasks that included both public-examination essay-questions and new-learning questions. Table 6.3 shows the mean scores of the two groups. Statistical analyses indicated that significant differences were obtained favoring the Knowledge Building students: Global Essay Scores, $F$ (1, 22) = 9.8, $p < .005$; Detailed Essay Scores, $F$ (1, 22) = 14.5, $p < .001$; and Detailed Learning Scores, $F$ (1, 22) = 10.3, $p < .004$.

**Table 6.3**

*Mean Scores of Domain Understanding for Knowledge-Building and Comparison Classes*

|  | Knowledge Building Mean (SD) | Comparison Mean (SD) |
|---|---|---|
| Essay (Global) Scores (Max = 6) | 4.4   (1.2) | 2.7   (1.3) |
| Essay (Detailed) Scores (Max = 24) | 18.4   (4.4) | 10.6   (4.9) |
| Learning (Global) Scores (Max = 6) | 5.0   (1.0) | 3.44  (1.5) |
| Learning (Detailed) Scores (Max = 24) | 19.28 (4.1) | 12.56 (5.6) |

Correlation analyses also indicated that students' knowledge building activities were related to each other and also correlated significantly with domain understanding. Specifically, students' inquiry (question-asking) scores were correlated significantly with participation in the forum measured by Analytic Toolkit ($r$ = .56, $p < .05$) and with domain understanding measured by writing tests ($r$ = .53, $p < .07$). Students' portfolio scores, indicating knowledge building advances, were correlated with their domain learning ($r = .67$, $p < .05$).

*Public examination results.* A key concern among Chinese teachers working on new pedagogy such as knowledge building is that it may have adverse effects on students' public examination outcomes. Although this group of Form Six students continued working on Knowledge Forum in the first semester of Form 7, it was to a lesser degree. They were primarily engaged in more regular instruction in Form 7 and sat for the Geography Advanced-Level public examination several months later. Hence the public examination was a kind of a delayed posttest to see how they could use their understanding. The pass rate for this group of students was 94%, comparatively higher than earlier cohorts studying geography from that school, and the pass rate was higher than all other humanities subjects for the same cohort of students.

The very positive results of the public examination gave a strong boost of confidence to the teacher for continued implementation. Generally the effect of inquiry-based pedagogy on public examinations is very difficult to ascertain because there can be inconsistencies in matches between instructional goals and assessment formats in examinations. Through teacher and student interviews (see following sections), we obtained some preliminary evidence suggesting how pedagogical transformation might have influenced student and teacher beliefs that mediated student learning for both new educational goals and examination results in the changing educational context.

## Student Beliefs about Learning

Students were asked to participate in focus-group interviews at the end of the year to examine their experience with knowledge building pedagogy and to understand how they approached classroom innovation.

*Learning how to learn.* Interview excerpts suggest that these students had positive views about the new learning experience. When asked why they would use Knowledge Forum one student said:

> The lesson time is very short and often I still have many ques-
> tions .... We can go home and sit in front of the computer and talk
> and discuss with my classmates .... I think it helps our problem-

solving skills ... um ... because we have to ask and answer others' questions ... and we have to read and think. (Student #7)

Many teachers in Hong Kong are concerned that there is not enough time to complete the syllabus, but these students, although noting the time constraints, suggested that Knowledge Forum could provide a learning environment where they could continue to learn on their own.

The students also seemed to develop learning how to learn strategies as they indicated how they could transfer inquiry strategies to other subject areas. When asked what they had learned, one student said:

I learned ... useful ways to study such as linking topics together, useful discussion [skills] by asking more questions, and further learning using concept mapping. *Our teacher, [Teacher A], forced us to think a lot in class.* I also used these skills in other subjects ... When I am reading a newspaper, especially international news [now], I always ask myself why this or that happens ... (Author Note; Italics for emphasis) (Student #12)

*Collective learning.* Students showed their understanding of the role of knowledge building in supporting reflection and community learning. For example, one student said:

When our teacher gave us some material to read, sometimes we found it to be quite difficult to understand because it is new to us. Some classmates ... posted notes on Knowledge Forum asking questions and others responded to these questions. I read these notes and I can understand more and see what others think ... It made me want to write there because the forum is ours and ... um ... actually I can learn from it. (Student #8)

Similarly, other students seemed to be developing their views of learning as collective learning, reflecting the emphasis on teamwork and community. Another student said:

*In the past we thought that some were just stupid questions. Now we know you can't go on without these stupid questions? because ... you can use the stupid questions and further elaborate to other productive questions. For example, you may think "what is a desert?" an easy question ...*

Actually, everyone can just say that a desert is mainly sandy land, but actually you can think ... What are the different kinds of desert? Why did the desert appear? How does it affect people? Because of this simple or "stupid" question, you can elaborate to include many questions. We cannot build on [together] and have more questions ... without that first question. You can't miss the importance of stupid questions ... and we improve together. (Student #011)

These interview excerpts suggest how these students may have developed their views, seeing themselves as active agents emphasizing inquiry, question asking, and community knowledge, and thus to some extent reflecting *21ˢᵗ century learning orientation.*

### Intertwined Beliefs about Inquiry and Revision

Another major theme sheds light on the notion of the transformed learning for the Chinese learner. The students showed how they approached the integration of the Western-based notion of collaborative inquiry with an emphasis on preparing for examinations. Interestingly, some students juxtaposed collaborative inquiry on Knowledge Forum with the pragmatic purpose of preparing for examination. For example, one student said:

When working on Knowledge Forum I really study and revise geography ... Because for other subjects, I will have questions but I don't know how to ask them or whom to ask. But for geography, we have a group of classmates and there is a place for me to ask questions and to think and to have some records there. (Student #13)

Another explained how collaborative inquiry in Knowledge Forum and preparation for examination can complement each other:

When we have to respond to other classmates' questions, first we have to read a lot of notes and read our books ... and other sources to answer the questions. But later on, we do not need to read that much, and *I think this helps to shorten the time when we study for the exam* because we are already developing this kind of thinking in normal time when we are working on Knowledge Forum. *I think I am already spending time to understand and to study when I am working on Knowledge Forum ... um ... it seems like what we are discussing is already there in our minds.* (Student #07)

Another student made the connection between revision and inquiry more explicit. She said:

Knowledge Forum is time consuming, but it is a valuable use of time ... because *it can help with our revision.* During the process we can learn much more ... For example, if we just have individual learning by ourselves, we can only read the teacher notes ... but all the classmates adding together (laughing) ... *Then now there are 14 people and 14 brains must be better than one brain.* (Student #12)

Students also had a sense of the tensions between collaborative inquiry on Knowledge Forum and preparing for examination but they seemed able to find ways to transcend them. One student said:

There are lots of times ... the questions on Knowledge Forum posted by our own classmates may be out of the syllabus. If you just concentrate on working on such questions, there may be a contradiction with the examination. But still when we are discussing, um ... and in the process, we read and understand more. When doing the portfolio, we have to ... follow the notes and read other materials, the quality of our writing is higher. Um ... maybe there is something not related to what we *must* study, it is still helpful for us ... (Student #11)

In summary, the Chinese learners developed some interesting ways of interpreting how learning takes place. Working on Knowledge Forum was seen to be useful in helping to familiarize them with the materials, and so it became easier when they needed to revise such materials. Interestingly, students interpreted their learning experiences in relation to cognitive and contextual demands.

## Changes in Teacher Beliefs and Teacher Learning

### Changing Beliefs about Student Learning

As Teacher A was an early user of Knowledge Forum, he already had a rather sophisticated view at the start, which continued to develop over time. He developed his views about learning, shifting from an individual to a collective perspective, and continued to surpass his own good practice. Rather than seeing Western and Chinese ways of learning and teaching as conflicting, he drew from both worlds to improve his understanding of pedagogy. Teacher A commented:

> In the past, I thought the more you teach, the more students learn. Now I understand it is not like that.

Later, Teacher A was more explicit about his role. He said:

> Now I emphasize shifting the responsibility of learning back to students. That is the main change. I do not say too many things in Knowledge Forum or in my classes and by doing this, things are shifted back to them. *They control their learning. They start the question. They start the response to the question and they get the answer and sometimes these ideas go back to the lesson for further discussion.* So that is the main difference in my teaching.

When asked why he adopted the approach, Teacher A explained how his approach could address the problem of student learning and contextual constraints. In a way, what Teacher A said aligned very well with what the students said. For example:

> An advantage of Knowledge Forum is that students can continue their learning after school. This attracts me a lot because I find that when we ask them, "do you have any questions?" they usually look so puzzled … But after school it is very natural because … they may go over the notes and then they can see if there are [questions] etc.. There are also students who may be scared to share in class, but they are free to share on the Forum …. I can usually find out more about students, whom I never thought could think in such deep ways.

## Intertwined Beliefs about Constructivist and Didactic Pedagogy

Another interesting theme is how Teacher A aligned and put together new and old approaches, bridging the differences between process and products; he viewed them as related, not distinct or opposing, approaches. In the same quote, he referred to student learning relating to explanation, theories and linkages as well as digesting things; he linked both content and learning to learn, process and product.

> *I look at Knowledge Forum as a source of improving the learning process, but I also believe that it will also help to improve the product finally.* By product I mean the Advanced-Level examination or final school examination. I can use Knowledge Forum to check my students' progress; I can check [the] type of questions, their explanations, their theories and the linkages. I can find out if … they are following the lessons …

When asked how he viewed the conflict in implementing innovation in the presence of public examinations, interestingly, Teacher A explained how he used both inquiry and drilling as he considered cognitive and contextual factors. He said:

> It is not adequate just to use the knowledge-building approach. I also use drilling and practicing examination papers to help students learn … *But the deep understanding they derived when they were engaged in knowledge building would be important for them in recalling the information for the examination.*

Teacher A explained more explicitly how he planned his teaching in the two years of Advanced-Level Study so that different approaches could work together. He noted:

> It is a good time to use Knowledge Forum in Form Six to help students develop a deep understanding of the subject matter and to develop motivation and deep learning. *This actually facilitates their understanding and helps them with their memorization* as they need that in preparing for their exam in Form 7.

## Long-Term Impacts and Sustained Practice

Study One shows that students benefited from working on Knowledge Forum for learning how to learn goals as well as for traditional examination. Although it is common to dichotomize, Teacher A's practice and beliefs were more nuanced. As a Chinese constructivist teacher, paradoxically, he structured the learning environments to help students to become independent learners, and to enable them to control their own learning process. He was both didactic and constructivist; as one of his students wrote: "Mr. A forced us to think."

After the initial success, Teacher A had a set-back in the second year of his work working with junior form students. However, instead of blaming the approach or the students, he reflected on his practice and sought improvement. Mr. A engaged in further practice of pedagogical transformation over the following years (for details, see Chan, 2008). He discovered that the textbook topics were highly fragmented and that this impeded deep inquiry. In the subsequent years, he developed further alignments between knowledge-building pedagogy with contextual constraints – he pooled the topics and put them under some major questions. He also extended the use of portfolio assessments for his Form Three students and later for examining how the approach could cater for both high- and low-achievers.

Often new pedagogy that is transplanted from Western cultures may not last because the pedagogy may not align well with the Chinese cultural context. This section has described the transformed pedagogy and changes in learning beliefs in order to highlight the impact on students and teachers. Mr. A continued with his new classroom practices after the research was completed and has emerged as a teacher leader, helping other teachers to develop knowledge-building pedagogy in their own teaching contexts. The ingenuity of designing knowledge-building that integrates both Chinese and Western wisdom may have led to continuing positive results.

## Study Two: Knowledge Building and Reading to Learn

### *Participants*

Teacher B was an experienced secondary school teacher of Chinese, who had been teaching for 12 years when the study was conducted. She had rich experience with a number of approaches including thematic instructtional units for teaching language and reading. She worked with other teachers in her school and the research team in implementing the pedagogical innovation of knowledge building.

The students were attending a secondary school in the New Territories in Hong Kong. They were from a school for medium to high ability students and were mainly from families of working-class background. There were four classes of Form Three students (aged 13-14 years); two using the Knowledge Forum approach taught by two teachers (n=78), and two other classes not using Knowledge Forum. (n=75). There was no streaming in the school, and these students from different classes were of similar academic levels. In the comparison classes, the teachers used the regular approach of teacher explanation and questioning. After school, as Knowledge Forum students worked online, students in the comparison classes worked on other kinds of homework including exercises on reading comprehension. Students wrote in Chinese in Knowledge Forum.

## *Transformed Pedagogy and Classroom Implementation*

In Hong Kong, there is increasing emphasis in the Chinese curriculum on teaching reading to learn in current Curriculum Reforms (Marton et al., chap. 5, this volume). Teacher B emphasized the importance of reading, adapting the knowledge-building approach relevant to the curriculum. Working with the university researchers, she also employed several phases of instruction, integrating new pedagogy with her current practice (Figure 6.1).

*Phase 1 - Developing a collaborative classroom culture.* As a language teacher, Teacher B started by helping students to develop strategies for reading to learn in collaborative context. We adapted the use of reciprocal teaching (Palincsar & Brown, 1984), a highly successful cognitive-strategy program that translates theory into practice (Constas & Sternberg, 2006), in consideration of the classroom context in Hong Kong. As she had to deal with a larger class typical in a Chinese classroom (35-40 students), instead of reading together with a group of students, Teacher B arranged students into groups of four, each including high- and low-achievers, making sure that all students would need to contribute. Students took turns as group leaders or teachers helping other group members to understand the text. Typically the high achievers would start first thus providing modeling for the others. Using a more structured approach, Teacher B asked the students to write down their questions and ideas so that they were all actively engaged and she could also have a record of their thinking. They also followed specific prompts that ensured they experienced all the four reading-to-learn strategies: summarizing, clarifying, questioning and predicting. Teacher B's approach, compared to reciprocal teaching employed in Western classrooms, took on a much more *structured* format in scaffolding her students to engage in higher-order reading.

*Phase 2 – Addressing inquiry and curriculum adaptation.* Teacher B also asked students to do homework using Knowledge Forum after school to address the problems of time and lack of computer access. For curriculum design, she chose an interesting problem, asking the students to start with discussing school rules. The design was not just for discussing something related to students' daily experience; it was based on pedagogical principles of developing "core ideas" (Brown & Campione, 1994) and "deepening inquiry" (Scardamalia & Bereiter, 2006). The discussion of school rules led to students inquiring into the notions of "rules of propriety and rituals", *li* [禮], a central philosophical concept in Chinese culture. Students engaged in collaborative inquiry in Knowledge Forum to deepen their understanding, examining beliefs and values related to Chinese philosophies and culture. They were asked to interpret Chinese classical texts from Confucius and modern writing. Teacher B used seemingly contradictory approaches; while designing for open inquiry, she also used a highly structured approach. She set up requirements that students had to write and respond to their classmates' ideas, and she closely monitored student contributions to the forum.

*Phase 3 – Deepening learning through structured discussion and emergent inquiry.* After the early phases of having students write on the Forum, Teacher B continued with her efforts to deepen student understanding and improve their work using various strategies. She used "knowledge-building talk", developing a discourse community, encouraging students to talk about their ideas on Knowledge Forum in class and developing supportive social dynamics. She worked to help students move beyond superficial discussion with higher-level themes, but she also used highly structured approaches; she assigned students to summarize threads of notes both in class and in forum discussion, so that they needed to identify and synthesize different viewpoints. They were asked to produce concept maps as rise-above notes to share their collective understanding. Teacher B combined deep collaborative inquiry with a high degree of structure; she specified rise-above summary notes and synthesis as homework that students needed to complete.

*Phase 4 – Portfolio assessment with school grades.* Assessment was also made an integral part of the knowledge building pedagogy, and both formative and summative assessments were used. Similar to the strategy employed in Study one, the students' note writing in the forum was incorporated formally into their assignments for grading, and the students worked continually on self- and peer-assessments to extend their community understanding. In this way, they could develop both cognitive skills and the social skills of working with others. In addition, Teacher B would identify quality forum notes from the students, which she would then ask the students to build on or ask each others questions. For synthesis of understanding the students worked on a portfolio identifying good clusters of notes guided by rubrics and principles. In all, there was an interesting mix of pedagogical design involving highly structured activities together with an emphasis on developing emergent inquiry through reading to learn, and developing good relationships.

## Changes in Student Beliefs and Student Learning

Here we report the evaluation of student learning to demonstrate the roles of the transformed knowledge building pedagogy in student learning.

### Student Inquiry and Reading to Learn

A major educational goal for the 21st century and curriculum reform is developing students' capacity in reading to learn (Marton et al., chap. 5, this volume). This study assessed students' text processing with a reading test which examined the students' ability to extract information from text. This test included several reading passages, and students had to respond to written questions that required them to summarize their understanding of the text passages and to explain what they had learned.

The means and (standard deviations) on the assessment measures are given below. The scores for the two knowledge-building classes were 94.18 (17.13) and 98.41 (11.91), and the scores of the comparison classes with regular teaching were 89.32 (15.11) and 85.82 (14.16) (Max score = 200). Analyses were conducted controlling for academic achievement (Hong Kong Attainment Test scores) obtained from school records. Statistically significant differences were obtained favoring Knowledge Building over Comparison classes, $F(3, 147)=3.95$, $p < .05$. These results provided some evidence suggesting that the Knowledge Building classes performed better on text comprehension than the comparison classes.

## Student Beliefs about Learning

Focus group interviews were conducted to examine the students' views on knowledge building. Their comments suggested that they were developing towards more sophisticated views about learning.

*Self-learning.* The students seemed to have developed good insights into their own learning and how learning can take place. For example, one student said:

> Even when teachers try very hard, it is often quite spoon-feeding, but through discussion with classmates in the forum, *it is about self-learning.* When you are willing to put effort into discussion and let others know your idea, it means … it means you are motivated to learn … you want to learn because things learned through discussion are much more memorable … (Student #27)

Another student noted how the approach helped her to compare her own ideas with others' thinking:

> When we are working on the forum, we can see what other students have written and *with that we can compare what they think with what we thought, and so we can do some analyses* … I think the forum helps because *it provides a record of our thinking.* Sometimes in class discussion there are too many ideas and you will forget … or you will not have time to respond to them. But with the computer forum, I can go home and read and think over them and respond more carefully. (Student #18)

Another student discussed how her writing had improved:

> There are scaffolds [thinking prompts] on Knowledge Forum to help us write … sometimes when we write, it can be a bit confusing … but when there are the prompts, *it helps us to organize our thoughts. I am sometimes quite amazed how I can write such a long piece* … (Student #28)

*Collective learning.* When students commented about their own thinking as they shared their experience of engaging in knowledge building, they also referred to the collective aspect of learning:

> In using Knowledge Forum, I can understand how my classmates think and their standpoints and how they think. *You see there are more than 30 students, and they may be quite different. Now I can make reference to their different views, and then I can improve my thinking ... At the same time, I can also work with other classmates with my ideas and ways of thinking.* (Student #19)

Other students discussed the notion of knowledge that reflected some developing views of epistemology; they noted that knowledge can be extended with collective learning. One student said:

> Through discussing with others ... It helps me to think and to develop knowledge. I could see that many things have multiple views ... and many interesting ideas may exist ... so in future, when I have to think, I will think more of different possibilities ... *I think knowledge is unlimited* ... so learning is not just from teachers ... it can occur among us, and discussion can bring out new ideas ... knowledge is broadened. (Student #26)

## *Intertwined Views – Cognitive Inquiry and Social-Affective Aspects*

Although Knowledge Forum focuses on cognitive inquiry, some students interpreted it as something useful for developing relationships among classmates, and some referred to socio-affective aspects. For example, one student said:

> *One time we are discussing school rules and people have different views. I feel it improves the relationships with students ... even if we have different views, we can still agree.* Some students may accept our views ... and we can *refine our views* ... and sometimes we come to *new ideas* ... we can come to similar viewpoints even when we disagree ... (Student #21)

Another student noted:

> *It is a place for learning and for pleasure and for sharing ... I do not feel*

*much pressure* ... Although chat room is similar there is no system to express our ideas and views ... there is no *issue* ... but usually in Knowledge Forum, with the use of scaffolds, we are able to express our views and show our ideas. (Student #19)

One student noted how she related her new learning with aspects of friendship in everyday life. She said:

What I learn most is to look beyond the surface ... Now when people talk, I will not just accept, but now I will think more ... if that is appropriate, and if there are other ways to think about them ... Um ... it is good and bad for me because sometimes my friends may think why I question them and may not like it ... but I think it is ... good because I really think more. (Student #8)

## *Changes in Teacher Beliefs and Teacher Learning*

### *Changing Beliefs about Student Learning*

It was interesting to observe the growth of Teacher B. Earlier she was skeptical about the role of knowledge building in the subject of Chinese language; as she said in an early interview at the start of the project:

Chinese language is different from other subjects; Knowledge Forum can work for English-speaking students in the West and maybe with Hong Kong students for science, but the Chinese language is different.

However, there was some gradual change over time as she engaged in the work and witnessed student growth. She said:

In the past we as teachers had to ask students good questions. I didn't know they could ask good questions on their own ... I did not know they could go so high ... I did not know they could reflect ... the happiest thing is that in their notes I can see what they have understood. When using group discussion, it is good, but not so clear as to what they have learned, but when reading their computer notes, I can see much more clearly ...

Teacher B described how she was changing her pedagogy and belief according to her gradual understanding of the approach:

> Over time from last year, I think I understand the approach more now ... at first, *I really did not know if I could really just let students go on their own; would it become a mess,* and would we have to teach things all over? I see we have to trust in the students. We have to let them go ...

> Now I think ... um I understand the approach better ... I can feel it much more strongly now ... As I see what students can do ... *my ideas and views have changed ... I have found that students can share their knowledge and build their knowledge together* ... so I now see more about *individual* and *collective* worlds.

### Intertwined View – Cognitive Inquiry and Values Formation

Teacher B also integrated different conceptions of learning in considering how the innovations could be adapted in the context of the Chinese classroom. Interestingly, she referred to affective aspects of knowledge building:

> Knowledge building can change students' attitudes ... In Knowledge Forum, at the beginning, students may be contradicting and arguing against each other. Later, I saw that they were learning how to accept others and use other words ... and use different views ... *People can own knowledge together,* collectively and harmoniously.

> I think there is an *affective* aspect ... about student communication ... one student will start a note; another builds on one note ... and others will follow; some will be passionate ... others will build on a note ... sometimes they are working late at night and still going ... you can see emotions flowing among students as they share ideas.

Reflecting on her own understanding, Teacher B, as a Chinese language teacher, referred to Chinese philosophy and culture as lenses to help her understand the Western innovation integrating cognitive and affective aspects. She said:

In the past, I thought if students can use the reading strategies to learn, that is already very good. Now when I look at Knowledge Forum, I think we can go further. *When you think of Chinese philosophy or maybe ... about the Kung Fu masters, you do not just perfect yourselves ... you need to disseminate your ideas, your kung-fu styles and ideals.* Just as we are doing knowledge building now, it is more than internalizing some understanding for yourself, it is about making things go further ... so ideas can go far. Just as our great masters and teachers in the past, we want to um ... want more people to benefit ... So knowledge building is like that too. We ... we can share knowledge and make it better ... even if some have more and others less initially ... We each contribute something and after that these ideas cross ... with other ideas [cross-fertilize]. We can build more understanding ... it is really like a community.

## Struggles and Tensions and Striking a Balance

Teacher B noted what motivated her to change, but she also discussed her struggle in using this new approach; a struggle which pertained to deeper issues of teaching for new educational goals:

In the past I underestimated their ability, but now I see their ability much better. I have never thought my students are so capable. I really "see" their thinking process and I like it more as I can see how they have improved. The *struggle* is that sometimes I would like to intervene as a teacher, but then I know it is better to be *a member of the group*.

Undoubtedly, the innovation is not easy for teachers, and they face struggles because the teaching context has such a strong emphasis on public examination. She had to tackle the problem of aligning the new pedagogy with sociocultural context. Teacher B noted:

I felt we have this extreme approach; on one side is the traditional teaching and on the other side is this modern approach such as knowledge building. I still struggle with ... this pendulum. Could we have something in the middle ... maybe we still need some traditional work in relation to the examination ... maybe some worksheets and exercises are still needed, but we may continue to work to find a balance?

Teacher B's comments somewhat reflect a Chinese way of thinking of seeking a middle ground reflecting the Doctrine of the Mean [中庸之道] as she tried to strike a balance.

*Long-Term Impacts and Sustained Practice*

Teacher B started as a late adopter of Knowledge Forum, and when she was first introduced to it she was somewhat skeptical. For her, there were various barriers; knowledge building is a Western approach, and examples are often given in the literature on science subjects. Typically, Hong Kong teachers want professional development that is highly contextualized, with examples shown in their own subject area.

Teacher B took quite a long time before adopting the knowledge building pedagogy in her classroom, but after her initial success, she continued with the knowledge-building pedagogy; she had sustained the practice and made it her regular approach. Currently she is acting as a mentor for teachers who have begun to use Knowledge Forum in her school, and even in other schools. Over the years, Teacher B has sustained the trajectory of improving her practice. Her questioning attitude and her continued effort suggest how contemporary Chinese teachers may take the best of both worlds – she is persistent and diligent but she also questions and inquires deeply. Possibly, such a combination is what is needed for expert teachers to develop and to learn in the current knowledge era. Certainly some researchers have identified 'persistence' as a characteristic of the Chinese learner (Li, chap. 2, this volume).

# Discussion

This chapter has examined the nature and characterization as well as the pedagogy appropriate for the Chinese learner of the 21st century in the context of examining the implementation of a knowledge-building approach. Case studies of two expert teachers have indicated what is possible and how teachers adopt *pedagogical transformation* for developing innovation. The impact of the transformed pedagogies on student and teacher beliefs and pedagogy have also been examined. This section examines the roles of the knowledge-building approach in fostering learning in the 21st century among Chinese students and considers the characterization of the Chinese learner and Chinese teacher in the light of adopting new pedagogy and classroom innovation.

## *Knowledge Building for Teaching the Chinese Learner of the 21st Century*

The two case studies have provided some evidence suggesting the roles of the knowledge-building approach in fostering 21st century learning. The findings showed that the students participated actively and improved in their collaboration using Knowledge Forum; they asked deeper and more high-order questions over time (Study 1), and they improved in tests of text processing (Study 2). Moreover, these improvements were not made at the expense of content learning. There were positive relationships between knowledge-building activity and conceptual understanding, and there were gains in public examination results (Study 1).

Regarding student beliefs and approaches, the students' responses revealed their developing capacity for learning how to learn. Students discussed how they could apply their strategy use to different subjects; some noted how they could reflect on and examine their own work in relation to others' models. Students developed more sophisticated views of ideas as improvable through collective effort, and they showed epistemological views noting that knowledge is unlimited. They also developed views of learning as involving social and affective aspects and considered how such changes brought about by their new experience might influence their everyday lives.

Through working with their classmates, the students had opportunities to develop more sophisticated notions about learning how to learn, problem solving and collaboration. As shown in the interviews, when working on the forum, students needed to pose questions – thus developing inquiry and agency. They worked collaboratively, contributing to community knowledge – thus developing teamwork; and they developed metacognition as they examined different models and compared them to their own. It is useful to point out that knowledge building is much more than online discussion – the students identified problems that needed inquiry, co-constructed explanations, synthesized various points of view and developed coherent explanatory accounts. Their experience of engaging in developing ideas appears to have helped students to change their views about learning.

The positive results obtained from this study are consistent with research showing the positive impact of knowledge building on student inquiry and understanding (Scardamalia et al., 1994; Zhang et al., 2007). It is apparent, however, that these results need to be interpreted with caution because of the small sample sizes, and it needs to be recognized that comparison studies are complex because of numerous factors involved typical of technology studies in the classroom. The results have emphasized the design aspects of knowledge building pedagogy and provided preliminary evidence of the positive effects. We have replicated the findings in a series of other studies suggesting the possible roles and effects of knowledge building in enhancing inquiry and learning for Chinese students (Chan & van Aalst, 2006; Lee et al., 2006; van Aalst & Chan, 2007). It has been argued, although from different perspectives, that helping students to be aware of variation is a powerful means of improving student learning (Marton & Tsui, 2004; Marton et al., chap. 5, this volume). The knowledge-building environment may provide such settings to help students become aware and reflect on these varied models of understanding.

The author also conjectured that knowledge building is an approach that may work well in the Chinese context. The notions of learning in the Chinese context, in which effort is emphasized, may align well with the emphasis of knowledge building on "improvable ideas" and "community knowledge". The students in this study responded well to the need to help each other to learn. The Chinese language teacher's comments suggest that she was making sense of knowledge building in relation to Chinese cultural traditions. Thus, the idea of working collectively and contributing to community knowledge may be congruent with Chinese ways of thinking. Further investigations are needed to examine aspects of relevance as perceived by students and teachers and how these may influence how they approach 21st century learning.

## The Paradox of the Chinese Learner and Transcending Dichotomies

These case studies examining learning among Chinese learners in the knowledge-based era have provided further support for the idea that

Chinese learners are not inherently passive rote-learners; they respond in ways appropriate to the contextual background and different pedagogical approaches and task demands. When provided with learning opportunities and new task demands, they are able to develop sophisticated notions of learning and collaboration needed for 21st century learning (Law et al., chap. 4, this volume). While earlier research on the Chinese learner has been concerned mainly with memorization-understanding focusing on individual learning (Marton et al., 1996; Marton et al., 2005), this study has focused on roles of inquiry for collaborative learning. With current changes in education and reform, collaboration has become a more salient feature in students' views of learning, and investigation into students' views of collaboration is needed as we move to new approaches and new visions of teaching the Chinese learner.

Just as Chinese learners are able to combine both memorization and understanding (Marton et al., 2005), the participants integrated collaborative inquiry with preparation for examinations. As the students engaged in new ways of learning, they used an integrated and dialectical approach, putting seemingly contradictory ideas together. For example, they saw collaboration as important because information from different classmates can be helpful for them to understand and to prepare for examinations. Some noted that this approach helped them both to see things from more perspectives and to gather more points for the examination. Some also analyzed the approach, noting that by reading and writing ideas collaboratively on the forum, they were actually continually doing revision; the students viewed collaborative inquiry and preparation for examination as mutually consistent.

Research on the Chinese learner has highlighted the key theme that learning and teaching need to be considered in relation to cultural, psychological and contextual influences (Watkins & Biggs, 1996). With the current education system in Hong Kong, Chinese students' conceptions of learning are greatly influenced by examinations. Yet deep learners do not necessarily only use deep approaches recognized in Western countries; they create approaches that help them make meaning relevant to the sociocultural context. The Chinese learners in the study saw how collaborative inquiry in Knowledge Forum could help them develop thinking as well as help them prepare for examinations, and some thought that discussion could help them develop better relationships with their peers.

These findings support earlier research on going beyond dichotomies (Biggs, 1996; Li, chap. 2, this volume) when viewing learning from a different cultural context. Moreover, they have shown that Chinese learners may indeed integrate and intertwine seemingly opposing approaches. They may develop ways of interpreting information and approaching learning in ways that are meaningful to them. We may consider the Chinese learners in the study good learners because they understood the need to understand, to collaborate and to engage in new ways of thinking. At the same time, they could do so in a contextually appropriate manner and accommodate examination demands.

## *The Paradox of the Chinese Teacher and Transforming Pedagogy*

Influenced by sociocultural and contextual demands and factors, Chinese learners may develop intertwined and synthesized views and approaches that transcend a polarized distinction of learning processes. Similarly, the Chinese teachers involved in the two studies reported here employed a transformed pedagogy – they integrated the innovation of knowledge building with their usual classroom practice. The different instructional phases indicated that they implemented new pedagogy in ways that took into account students' cognitive levels, classroom structure and schooling demands. All phases encompassed key cognitive principles – develop a collaborative culture, align with the curriculum, encourage student agency and use assessment to foster learning – but the two teachers also adapted an innovative design to suit the cultural and contextual background.

The two Chinese teachers we examined are both *didactic* and *constructivist*. On the one hand, they used scaffolding to foster students' abilities to articulate and express their views, to ask and to pursue questions while students worked on their ideas in knowledge building inquiry. On the other hand, they conducted teaching in a structured manner, a common approach in Chinese classrooms (Paine, 1990), which led the students to develop what they believed to be important to foster. Unlike many Western teachers who tend to be more open to following student interests, Teacher A insisted on students engaging in deep thinking and collaboration through portfolio assessment, while Teacher B engaged students in deep discourse and progressive inquiry, with structured activities to guide their collective inquiry.

It is paradoxical that open inquiry and structure coexist in the Chinese classroom, but such transformed pedagogy is not merely an add-on strategy; the learning experiences reported in these two studies were designed by thoughtful teachers who understood students' cognitive levels and were in line with contextual and system requirements; and they led to success in deep learning, thus helping these teachers to sustain the practice. Certainly, how teachers adopting new pedagogical innovation will understand the deep principles involved and not just follow the routines, and whether they will remain at a certain phase or continue to advance their practice are important questions for future investigation.

Teacher beliefs from interviews illustrate further the notion of an integrated and transformed approach. Research on conceptions of teaching among Chinese teachers has shown them to encompass preparation for examination and conduct guidance (Gao & Watkins, 2002). Teacher A noted that knowledge-building inquiry can go alongside examinations – he indicated that he would require his students to practice examination papers if that was what was needed to help students pass the examination. Teacher A believed that working on Knowledge Forum could help students develop their ideas, thus helping them to understand and also prepare themselves better for the examination. In this way, the distinction between student-centered and teacher-centered approaches becomes blurred. This is apparently also recognized in Western classrooms, but the Chinese classrooms in the study bring it into sharper focus.

Another interesting dimension of teacher beliefs pertains to the intertwined nature of cognitive and affective dimensions. Teacher B noted, with reference to affective aspects of working on the forum, how students could learn to relate well to other students and how they could change their attitudes. When interpreting the knowledge-building approach, she highlighted the parallels between knowledge building and traditional Chinese culture, which emphasizes the importance of working not only for oneself but for the benefit of the community. Teacher B interpreted the new approach as striking a familiar chord in relation to affective aspects and values emphasized in schooling in the Chinese context.

Through our case studies, we found that the Chinese students adapted their learning in response to perceived new goals and new task demands. The teachers also used a transformed pedagogy; they combined classroom structure with an innovative and emergent knowledge building approach in meaningful ways. These Chinese teachers of the knowledge-based era found ways to make innovation work for developing 21ˢᵗ century goals within the constraints of examination rather than seeing them as contradictory. They saw collaborative knowledge building as incorporating affective and moral dimensions – collective learning is interpreted in relation to Chinese traditional values of collective responsibility.

Biggs and Watkins (2001) examined cross-cultural differences in teaching and argued that good teaching and learning are common across cultures at a deep level although they could have different manifestations influenced by social and cultural factors. Good teaching in the knowledge-based era is about developing students' capacity to advance their own knowledge and aligning innovation with classroom conditions and socio-cultural contexts. The intertwined conceptions and pedagogical transformed approach may have different manifestations. We provided such illustrations in the Chinese context in order to examine how innovations can take place in classrooms.

This analysis of knowledge building in the Chinese context is consistent with the idea of social infrastructure when implementing classroom innovation (Bielaczyc, 2006). For any innovation to work, there needs to be consideration of cultural and contextual influences. The form of knowledge building in Western and Asian countries could be different, but the underlying notion of focusing on students' understanding, reflection on beliefs, and consideration of cultural and sociocontextual factors may be applicable across cultures when considering classroom innovation.

## Conclusion

The knowledge-building accounts among Chinese teachers and learners suggest how the knowledge-building model may be a useful framework for teacher and student learning in the 21ˢᵗ century. The case studies of two expert teachers implementing knowledge building in Hong Kong classrooms also help to illuminate the characterization of Chinese learners and teachers – the Chinese learners used seemingly contradictory approaches to make meanings that transcended polarized distinctions of learning approaches, given task demands and contextual dynamics. Similarly, the Chinese teachers developed a transformed pedagogy that took into account student cognition and social infrastructure, integrating Chinese and Western approaches in scaffolding student inquiry, collaboration and understanding. These case studies, while showing how knowledge building is implemented in Chinese classrooms, also illuminate the importance of investigating how innovations take place in cross-cultural contexts.

# REFERENCES

Bereiter, C. (2002). *Education and mind in the knowledge age*. Mahwah, NJ: Lawrence Erlbaum Associates.

Bereiter, C., & Scardamalia, M. (1989). Intentional learning as a goal of instruction. In L. B. Resnick (Ed.), *Knowing, learning, and instruction: Essays in honor of Robert Glaser* (pp. 361-392). Hillsdale, NJ: Lawrence Erlbaum Associates.

Bereiter, C., & Scardamalia, M. (1993). *Surpassing ourselves: An inquiry into the nature and implications of expertise*. Chicago and La Salle, IL: Open Court.

Bereiter, C., & Scardamalia, M. (2006). Education for the knowledge age: Design-centered models of teaching and instruction. In P. A. Alexander & P. H. Winne (Eds.), *Handbook of educational psychology* (2nd ed., pp. 695-713). Mahwah, NJ: Lawrence Erlbaum Associates.

Bielaczyc, K. (2006). Designing social infrastructure: Critical issues in creating learning environments with technology. *Journal of the Learning Sciences, 15*, 301-329.

Biggs, J. B. (1996). Western misperceptions of the Confucian-heritage learning culture. In D. A. Watkins & J. B. Biggs (Eds.), *The Chinese Learner: Cultural, psychological and contextual influences* (pp. 45-67). Hong Kong/Melbourne: Comparative Education Research Centre, The University of Hong Kong/ Australian Council for Educational Research.

Biggs, J. B., & Watkins, D. A. (1996). The Chinese Learner in retrospect. In D. A. Watkins & J. B. Biggs (Eds.), *The Chinese Learner: Cultural, psychological and contextual influences* (pp. 269-285). Hong Kong/Melbourne: Comparative Education Research Centre, The University of Hong Kong/Australian Council for Educational Research.

Biggs, J. B., & Watkins, D. A. (2001). Insights into teaching the Chinese Learner. In D. A. Watkins & J. B. Biggs (Eds.), *Teaching the Chinese Learner: Psychological and pedagogical perspectives* (pp. 277-300). Hong Kong/Melbourne: Comparative Education Research Centre, The University of Hong Kong/Australian Council for Educational Research.

Brown, A. L. (1992). Design experiments: Theoretical and methodological challenges in creating complex interventions. *Journal of the Learning Sciences, 2*, 141-178.

Brown, A. L., & Campione, J. C. (1994). Guided discovery in a community of learners. In K. McGilly (Ed.), *Classroom lessons: Integrating cognitive theory and classroom practice* (pp. 229-270). Cambridge, MA: MIT Press.

Burtis, J. (1998). *The analytic toolkit for Knowledge Forum.* Knowledge Building Research Team. Toronto: The Ontario Institute for Studies in Education, University of Toronto.

Chan, C. K. K. (2001). Promoting learning and understanding through constructivist approaches for Chinese Learners. In D. A. Watkins & J. B. Biggs (Eds.), *Teaching the Chinese Learner: Psychological and pedagogical perspectives* (pp. 181-203). Hong Kong/Melbourne: Comparative Education Research Centre, The University of Hong Kong/Australian Council for Educational Research.

Chan, C. K. K. (2008). Pedagogical transformation and knowledge building for Chinese Learners. *Evaluation and Research in Education, 21*, 235-251.

Chan, C. K. K., Burtis, P. J., & Bereiter, C. (1997). Knowledge building as a mediator of conflict in conceptual change. *Cognition and Instruction, 15*, 1-40.

Chan, C. K. K., & Pang, M. F. (Eds.). (2006). Teacher collaboration in learning communities [Special Issue]. *Teaching Education, 17*(1).

Chan, C. K. K. & van Aalst, J. (2004). Learning, assessment, and collaboration in computer-supported collaborative learning. In J. W. Strijbos, P. Kirschner, & R. Martens (Eds.), *What we know about CSCL and implementing it in higher education* (pp. 87-112). Kluwer Academic Publishers.

Chan, C. K. K., & van Aalst, J. (2006). Computer-supported knowledge building in teacher education: Experience from Hong Kong and Canadian teachers. *Teaching Education, 17*, 7-26.

Clark, R., & Gieve, S. N. (2006). On the discursive construction of 'the Chinese Learner'. *Language, Culture and Curriculum, 19*, 54-73.

Cochrane-Smith, M., & Lytle, S. L. (1999). Relationships of knowledge and practice: Teacher learning in communities. In A. Iran-Nejad & P. D. Pearson (Eds.), *Review of Research in Education* (pp. 249-305). Washington, DC: American Educational Research Association.

Collins, A., Joseph, D., & Bielaczyc, K. (2004). Design research: Theoretical and methodological issues. *Journal of the Learning Sciences, 13*, 15-42.

Constas, M. A. & Sternberg, R. J. (Eds.). (2006). *Translating theory and research into educational practice: Developments in content domains, large scale reform, and intellectual capacity.* Mahwah, NJ: Lawrence Erlbaum Associates.

Cortazzi, M., & Jin, L. (2001). Large classes in China: "Good" teachers and interaction. In D. A. Watkins & J. B. Biggs (Eds.), *Teaching the Chinese Leaner: Psychological and pedagogical perspectives* (pp. 115-134). Hong Kong/Melbourne: Comparative Education Research Centre, The University of Hong Kong/Australian Council for Educational Research.

Curriculum Development Council. (2001). *Learning to learn – The way forward in curriculum development: Life-long learning and whole-person development.* Hong Kong: Author.

Darling-Hammond, L., Bransford, J., LePage, P., Hammerness, K., & Duffy, H. (Eds.). (2005). *Preparing teachers for a changing world: What teachers should learn and be able to do.* San Francisco, California: Jossey-Bass.

Fan, L. H., Wong, N. Y., Cai, J. F., & Li, S. Q. (2004). *How Chinese learn mathematics: Perspectives from insiders.* Singapore: World Scientific.

Franke, M. L., Carpenter, T., Fennema, E., Ansell, E., & Behrend, J. (1998). Understanding teachers' self-sustaining, generative change in the context of professsional development. *Teaching and Teacher Education, 14*, 67-80.

Gao, L., & Watkins, D. A. (2002). Conceptions of teaching held by school science teachers in P. R. China: Identification and cross-cultural comparisons. *International Journal of Science Education, 24*, 61-79.

Hargreaves, A. (2003). *Teaching in the knowledge society: Education in the age of insecurity.* New York: Teachers College Press.

Ho, A. S. P., Watkins, D. A., & Kelly M. (2001). The conceptual change approach to improving teaching and learning: An evaluation of a Hong Kong staff development programme. *Higher Education, 42*, 143-169.

Lai, M., & Law, N. (2006). Peer scaffolding of knowledge building through collaborative groups with differential learning experiences. *Journal of Educational Computing Research, 35*, 123-144.

Lee, E. Y. C., Chan, C. K. K., & van Aalst, J. (2006). Students assessing their own collaborative knowledge building. *International Journal of Computer-Supported Collaborative Learning, 1*, 277-307.

Lee, W. O. (1996). The cultural context for Chinese Learners: Conceptions of learning in the Confucian tradition. In D. A. Watkins & J. B. Biggs (Eds.), *The Chinese Learner: Cultural, psychological, and cultural influences* (pp. 25-41). Hong Kong/Melbourne: Comparative Education Research Centre, The University of Hong Kong/Australian Council for Educational Research.

Lee, W. O., & Mok, M. M. C. (Eds.). (2008). The Construction and deconstruction of the Chinese Learner: Implications for learning theories [Special issue]. *Evaluation and Research in Education, 21*(3).

Marton, F., Dall'Alba, G. A., & Tse, L. K. (1996). Memorizing and understanding: The keys to the paradox? In D. A. Watkins & J. B. Biggs (Eds.), *The Chinese Learner: Cultural, psychological and contextual influences* (pp. 69-83). Hong Kong/Melbourne: Comparative Education Research Centre, The University of Hong Kong/Australian Council for Educational Research.

Marton, F., & Tsui, A. B. M. (2004). *Classroom discourse and the space of learning.* Mahwah, NJ: Lawrence Erlbaum Associates.

Marton, F., Watkins, D. A., & Tang, C. (1997). Discontinuities and continuities in the experience of learning: An interview study of high-school students in Hong Kong. *Learning and Instruction, 7*, 21-48.

Marton, F., Wen, Q. F., & Wong, K. C. (2005). "Read a hundred times and the meaning will appear..." Changes in Chinese university students' views of the temporal structure of learning. *Higher Education, 49*, 291-318.

Mullis, I. V. S., Martin, M. O., Beaton, A. E., Gonzalez, E. J., Kelly, D. L., & Smith, T. A. (1997). *Mathematics achievement in the primary school years: IEA's Third International Mathematics and Science Study*. Chestnut Hill, MA: TIMSS International Study Centre, Boston College.

Mullis, I. V. S., Martin, M. O., Kennedy, A. M., & Foy, P. (2007). *IEA's progress in international reading literacy study in primary schools in 40 Countries*. Chestnut Hill, MA: Boston College.

Paine, L. (1990). The teacher as virtuoso: A Chinese model for teaching. *Teachers College Record, 92*, 49-81.

Palincsar, A. S., & Brown, A. L. (1984). Reciprocal teaching of comprehension-fostering and comprehension-monitoring activities. *Cognition and Instruction, 1*, 117-175.

Putnam, R. T., & Borko, H. (2000). What do new views of knowledge and thinking have to say about research on teacher learning? *Educational Researcher, 29*(1), 4-15.

Rastall, P. (Ed.) (2006). The Chinese Learner in higher education – Transition and quality issues [Special Issue]. *Language, Culture and Curriculum, 19*(1).

Richardson, V., & Placier, P. (2002). Teacher change. In V. Richardson (Ed.), *Handbook of research on teaching* (4th ed., pp. 905-939). Washington, DC: American Educational Research Association.

Scardamalia, M., & Bereiter, C. (1994). Computer support for knowledge building communities. *Journal of the Learning Sciences, 3*, 265-283.

Scardamalia, M., & Bereiter, C. (2003). Knowledge Building. In J. W. Guthrie (Ed.), *Encyclopedia of education* (2nd ed., pp. 1370-1373). New York: Macmillan Reference.

Scardamalia, M., & Bereiter, C., (2006). Knowledge building: Theory, pedagogy and technology. In R. K. Sawyer (Ed.), *The Cambridge handbook of the learning sciences* (pp. 97-115). New York: Cambridge University Press.

Scardamalia, M., Bereiter, C., & Lamon, M. (1994). The CSILE project: Trying to bring the classroom into World 3. In K. McGilly (Ed.), *Classroom lessons: Integrating cognitive theory and classroom practice* (pp. 201-228). Cambridge, MA: MIT Press.

Stigler, J. W., & Hiebert, J. (1999). *The teaching gap: Best ideas from the world's teachers for improving education in the classroom*. New York: Free Press.

Stokes, S. F. (2001). Problem-based learning in a Chinese context: Faculty perceptions. In D. A. Watkins & J. B. Biggs (Eds.), *Teaching the Chinese Learner: Psychological and pedagogical perspectives* (pp. 205-218). Hong Kong/Melbourne: Comparative Education Research Centre, The University of Hong Kong/Australian Council for Educational Research.

Tang, C. (1996). Collaborative learning: The latent dimension in Chinese students' learning. In D. A. Watkins & J. B. Biggs (Eds.), *The Chinese Learner: Cultural, psychological and contextual influences* (pp. 183-204). Hong Kong/Melbourne: Comparative Education Research Centre, The University of Hong Kong/ Australian Council for Educational Research.

Taplin, M., & Chan, C. K. K. (2001). Developing problem solving practitioner. *Journal of Mathematics Teacher Education, 4*, 285-304.

van Aalst, J., & Chan, C. K. K. (2007). Student-directed assessment of knowledge building using electronic portfolios. *Journal of the Learning Sciences, 16*, 175-220.

van Aalst, J., Fung, A. W. H., Li, M. S. M., & Wong, A. P. W. (2007). Exploring information literacy in secondary schools in Hong Kong: A case study. *Library and Information Science Research, 29*, 533-552.

Watkins, D. A. (1996). Learning theories and approaches to research: A cross-cultural perspective. In D. A. Watkins & J. B. Biggs (Eds.), *The Chinese Learner: Cultural, psychological and contextual influences* (pp. 3-24). Hong Kong/Melbourne: Comparative Education Research Centre, The University of Hong Kong/Australian Council for Educational Research.

Watkins, D. A., & Biggs, J. B. (Eds.). (1996). *The Chinese Learner: Cultural, psychological and contextual influences*. Hong Kong/Melbourne: Comparative Education Research Centre, The University of Hong Kong/Australian Council for Educational Research.

Watkins, D. A., & Biggs, J. B. (Eds.). (2001). *Teaching the Chinese Learner: Psychological and pedagogical perspectives*. Hong Kong/Melbourne: Comparative Education Research Centre, The University of Hong Kong/Australian Council for Educational Research.

Wong, N. Y. (2004). The CHC learner's phenomenon: Its implications on mathematics education. In L. H. Fan, N. Y. Wong, J. F. Cai & S. Q. Li (Eds.), *How Chinese learn mathematics: Perspectives from insiders*, (pp. 503-533). Singapore: World Scientific.

Zhang, J., Scardamalia, M., Lamon, M., Messina, R., & Reeve, R. (2007). Socio-cognitive dynamics of knowledge building in the work of 9- and 10-year olds. *Educational Technology Research and Development, 55*, 117-145.

## *Acknowledgements*

This research was supported by a grant from the Committee on Research and Conference Grants (No. 07176180) and The Strategic Research Theme on *Sciences of Learning* of the University of Hong Kong. The author would like to thank the teachers and their students for their participation and valuable contributions to the project. My thanks also go to Doris Y. K. Law for developing and conducting the reading tests for the Chinese language classes.

# 7

# Teaching Mathematics: Observations from Urban and Rural Schools in Mainland China

*Nirmala RAO, Jin CHI and Kai-ming CHENG*

## Introduction

The outstanding performance of Chinese students in cross-national studies of mathematics achievement has attracted international attention. Explanations put forward to account for this have included inter-dependent factors such as parental beliefs and behaviors, motivation and self-regulation of learning, the Chinese educational system and teacher beliefs and practices (Hess, Chang, & McDevitt, 1987; Leung, 2005; Rao, Moely, & Sachs, 2000; Stevenson & Lee, 1990; Stevenson & Stigler, 1992). Investigators who have sought to understand why Chinese students have done so well despite large class sizes and what is considered less student-centered pedagogy have focused on understanding classroom practice in the Chinese context (Huang & Leung, 2004; Leung, 2005; Stevenson & Stigler, 1992; Watkins & Biggs, 2001; Zhang & Zhou, 2003).

    Mathematics teaching is influenced not only by teacher and student characteristics, but also by cultural and social factors. The latter are re-flected in the design of educational goals and the curriculum and notions about instruction. This chapter is based on a larger study of teaching and learning in the world's largest school system, and considers how socio-contextual factors, including educational reform (Ministry of Education of the People's Republic of China, 2001), have influenced instructional practices in the teaching of mathematics in primary school Grades 3 and 5. Research on classroom processes in China has typically been conducted in urban areas, even though officially about 67% of China's population lives in rural areas. In the study described in this chapter, we also included mathematics teaching in rural schools. The specific objectives of the study were: (i) to examine commonalities and distinctions in the teaching of mathematics by comparing urban and rural primary school classrooms, and (ii) to compare the mathematics achievement of children from urban and rural schools.

We begin by considering the influence of sociocontextual factors on mathematics learning. Next, we review the literature on mathematics teaching in elementary schools in Mainland China, paying particular attention to the guidelines on teaching from the Educational Reform documents. We then turn to our empirical study and describe the sample, methods and findings. Finally, we argue that changes heralded by the educational reforms have led to new pedagogies, which necessitate *revisiting* previous notions about teaching the young Chinese learner.

## Sociocontextual Influences on Mathematics Learning

Zhang and Zhou (2003) review sociocontextual influences on Chinese children's mathematical learning and discuss the facilitative influences of parental beliefs and behaviors, the Chinese number-naming system, and the use of numerals in daily life on children's early mathematical learning.

### Parental Beliefs and Behaviors

In Chinese culture, an emphasis is placed on the early learning of mathematical concepts, and parents in major Chinese cities teach children basic arithmetical operations in the home context prior to school entry (Zhang & Zhou, 2003). It is widely acknowledged that Chinese parents ascribe a high value to education and this is reflected in their socialization practices (Ho, 1994; Rao, McHale, & Pearson 2003). Chinese parents emphasize effort over ability in explaining their children's academic performance (Stevenson & Lee, 1990), and ethnic Chinese parents hold higher standards for their children's mathematics achievement than do Euro-American ones (Chen & Stevenson, 1995). These expectations may indeed lead to Chinese children spending more time and exerting more effort in mathematics learning (Stevenson & Stigler, 1992).

## Number-naming System

It has been argued that characteristics of the Chinese number naming system and the use of numerals to denote days of the week, months of the year and family relationships in Chinese languages, afford advantages to young children in learning basic arithmetical concepts and operations. The Chinese numeration system is a decimal (base 10) system and a unique feature is that the written form indicates the number in each base, together with the base. Hence, Chinese children have significantly less difficulty learning to count and to understand place values than English children because of the nature of the number system.

## Characteristics of the Chinese Language

Certain other characteristics of the Chinese language enable children to acquire and practice numerical concepts in daily life without specialized instruction (Miller, Smith, Zhu, & Zhang, 1995; Zhang & Zhou, 2003). In Chinese, relatives are known by their order in the family; for example, the eldest brother is referred to as Brother Number 1. The names of the days of the week and months of the year are referred to by numbers (Weekday No. 1, Weekday No. 2, etc., and Month Number 1, Month Number 2, etc.). The way in which the months of the year are named in Chinese is assumed to account for the fact that second and fourth grade Chinese children had faster reaction times and better accuracy than English-speaking children in solving problems which involve calendar operations (Kelly, Miller, Fang, & Feng, 1999).

In summary, sociocontextual factors, the Chinese number naming system, and the prominence of numbers in the Chinese language provide Chinese children with advantages in mathematical understanding in the early years. We now turn to the teaching of mathematics in primary schools.

## Teaching of Mathematics in Primary Schools in Mainland China

In their review of mathematics teaching in primary schools in Mainland China, Zhang and Zhou (2003) discuss classroom teaching methods which have contributed to Chinese students' relatively high performance in comparative international studies of mathematics achievement. They believe that the emphasis on basic number facts, the particular way teachers use concrete objects to teach abstract constructs, the strong emphasis on practice, and the nature of the elementary mathematics curriculum in China, all facilitate mathematical understanding. Each of these will be considered briefly.

## Promoting Mathematical Understanding

Zhang and Zhou state that Chinese children memorize 45 easy to learn phrases to help them learn multiplication facts, and that once they master these, they can solve arithmetic problems rapidly. They also maintain that the way teachers use concrete objects and the extent of their use help children learn abstract concepts. However, it can be argued that all good teachers, regardless of where they live, use such techniques to promote mathematical understanding. Zhang and Zhou also highlight the spiral nature of the mathematics curriculum in China. Again, mathematics curricula in all parts of the world build on skills presented in lower grades.

Zhang and Zhou (2003) give examples of how teachers in China use a variety of well-presented and carefully sequenced examples to help students acquire concepts and provide immediate feedback to students. This, along with the interactive nature of their large-class teaching (Huang & Leung, 2004; Stevenson & Stigler, 1992), their posing of high level questions (Perry, VanderStoep, & Yu, 1993), their insistence that students practise newly taught concepts by completing worksheets and problems in the textbook (Ma, Zhao, & Tuo, 2004) and the way they effectively use practice to hone children's arithmetical competencies may be what sets Chinese teachers apart from their counterparts in other parts of the world. Further, Chinese teachers prepare detailed lesson plans which are constantly modified and discussed with their peers, reflecting their belief that it is possible to create and deliver a perfect lesson (Stevenson & Stigler, 1992).

## Whole-Class Instruction

Chinese mathematics teachers promote mathematical understanding using expository methods, and primary school mathematics teachers in China spend most of their instructional time engaged in whole class instruction. However, children are actively engaged in the discussion of difficult problems during this time (Stevenson & Stigler, 1992). Other studies on mathematics teaching in secondary schools have illustrated that large class instruction in Chinese contexts does not preclude active student engagement (Huang & Leung, 2004; Mok et al., 2001). Indeed, Schleppenbach, Perry, Miller, Sims, and Fang (2007) found that extended discourse (questioning and discussion led by the teacher after students had provided a correct response) was more frequent, lasted a longer time and included more discussion of mathematical procedures, and rules and reasoning in primary school mathematics classes in China than in classrooms in the United States.

## Differences between Urban and Rural Schools

Ma, Zhao and Tuo (2004), compared mathematics teaching in primary schools in urban and rural areas in China and found differences in lesson preparation and classroom teaching between urban and rural schools. Teaching was observed in different grades in different schools, and as both children's developmental characteristics and the syllabus affect the mode of teaching, it is not clear whether identified variations between teaching in urban and rural schools were mainly due to differences in location. However, Ma et al. provide systematic documentation of the differences in instruction between rural and urban primary schools.

Urban and rural classes differed very little in the ways in which lessons were structured. Lessons lasted for 40 minutes, and about 15 minutes were spent by the teacher in front of the class questioning students, while students completed exercises from the textbook for another 13 minutes. The question/answer format for checking understanding was commonly used in both urban and rural schools. Teachers posed the majority of the questions and students seldom raised them. The questions were typically close-ended, requiring short answers and provided little opportunity for critical thinking (Ma et al., 2004). Both urban and rural teachers tended to use textbooks and an exercise oriented approach. Teachers focused on explaining examples from the textbook, and then had students complete the exercises in the textbook. Teachers' cultural beliefs, reflected in proverbs such as "Practice makes perfect," "Integrating teaching and exercise," and "Teaching the essential and ensuring plenty of exercises," were manifest in classroom practice (Ma et al., 2004). Teachers spent a considerable time during and after class checking students' exercises as they believed that practice with more mathematical problems would enhance mathematics achievement.

There were a few differences between urban and rural teachers' instructional methods, with urban teachers asking more challenging questions and providing students with a wider range of activities than their rural counterparts. The authors attributed these differences to larger school size and higher levels of teachers' professional training in urban schools. As there was only one class per grade in rural areas, this provided less opportunity for rural teachers to discuss lesson preparation with colleagues teaching the same grade level. The researchers also found that urban teachers had higher levels of professional training and pedagogical content knowledge than rural teachers. Ma et al. (2004) also noted that urban teachers had more opportunities for professional development and a larger number of instructional resources available to them than their rural counterparts.

## *The Educational Reform*

In 2001, Mainland China embarked on a major reform of basic education with the publication of the *Guidelines on Curriculum Reform of Basic Education*. This is the eighth reform undertaken since the establishment of the People's Republic of China (PRC), and is unprecedented in terms of its scope, intensity and speed (Zhang, 2005). According to Zhu Muju, the former Deputy Director-General for Basic Education in the Ministry of Education of the People's Republic of China, the goals of the reform are to "bring forth a new generation of high-caliber citizens, people who are competent enough to serve China's modernization drive. To achieve the purpose, competence oriented education is being stressed and the kind of education irrelevant to the practical needs of society and which focuses on preparing students for examinations is being phased out" (Wang, 2005). Zhu (2007) maintains that the curriculum reform (i) has adapted curriculum structure and content to meet contemporary needs, (ii) has established a model of teaching and learning that is student-centered and focuses on promoting students' learning to learn, and (iii) uses assessment to provide feedback on students' learning needs to improve teaching and to promote student development.

In 2001, new curricula were issued for 21 subjects, including mathematics. We now turn to a discussion of the guidelines for mathematics education at the primary school level. To fully appreciate the degree of the changes prescribed for mathematics teaching, it is important to gain an understanding of the historical and current context of mathematics teaching in primary schools.

Zhang (2005) described the stages of the primary mathematics curriculum in China. After the Chinese Communist Party gained power in 1949, the Soviet model of education was espoused, and teachers, the curriculum and teaching methodology were the foci. In 1963, new guidelines were issued which stressed basic knowledge and skills, and emphases were placed on computational skills, logic and analysis. Careful teaching and giving students opportunities for extensive practice were highlighted. The Cultural Revolution (1966 to 1976) adversely affected all levels of education, but in the 1980s, western ideas about the focus of mathematics instruction were evident in China. For example, an emphasis on "problem-solving" in mathematics was evident (Zhang, 2005), and new teaching methods such as discovery learning and cooperative learning were advocated. Until the 1990s, China followed a common national curriculum and the same textbooks were used for elementary school mathematics all over the country. That has since changed and there has been an emphasis on developing and reforming the educational system.

The Mathematics Curriculum Standards for Full-Time Compulsory Education were developed in 1999, and were formally adopted in 2001 (Ministry of Education of the People's Republic of China, 2001). These Mathematics Curriculum Standards included the following sections: preface, curriculum goals, standards for mathematical content and suggestions on how to use the standards. Several changes were noted in the educational goals and curriculum of primary mathematics education. These included (i) broadening the educational goals beyond the emphasis on numbers and computational ability to include spatial concepts and logical thinking ability; (ii) changing the guidelines on syllabi and textbooks from "one syllabus, one textbook" to "one syllabus, many textbooks," then to "many syllabi, many textbooks" in order to suit the different educational needs in different contexts in China; and (iii) training students from being skilful in calculating, to mastering the "two basics" (basic concepts and basic skills), and then to problem solving ability (Ma et al., 2004; Zhang & Zhou, 2003).

Of particular relevance to this chapter, the Mathematics Curriculum Standards advocated a shift from knowledge transmission to developing learning ability and preparing students for lifelong learning. They also focused on enhancing students' learning experiences. This was to be achieved by choosing learning activities which were close to students' daily experiences; providing classroom experiences which were interesting and lively; and by guiding students to observe, experiment, problem-solve and communicate. The use of calculators for complex problems was to be encouraged so that students could spend more time in exploratory and creative mathematical activities (Zhang, 2005). In short, these reform guidelines imply that students will be more active in the learning process and the teachers' role will change to help students become more self-directive, collaborative, creative, and enhance their communication skills. Technology will also be integrated into pedagogy.

How successful has the reform in primary school mathematics been to date? It was thought that by 2004, much progress had been made as teachers had undergone professional development to update their educational ideas. Teaching and learning methods had become more student-centered, a more democratic relationship between teachers and students had been established, and parents were involved in curriculum reform (Zhou, 2004). However, the long history of central government control of curriculum and textbooks continues to have a marked influence on teaching. It takes time to move teachers from valuing students' conformity to appreciating students' individuality and creativity in learning. Therefore, it may take time for education reform ideas to be evident in classroom instruction. Furthermore, changes are easier to effect in urban schools than in rural schools as teachers have more opportunities for professional development in the former (Ma et al., 2004).

Against this background, this paper, which is based on a larger study of teaching and learning, considers the teaching of mathematics in Grade 3 and 5 classrooms. Earlier research has documented teaching practices in primary school mathematics, but we are unaware of any published studies that have systematically compared mathematics teaching and student achievement in urban and rural areas. We also believe that increased professional knowledge, globalization and educational reform have precipitated changes in teacher practices and hence, necessitate revisiting our notions of the Chinese learner.

The specific objectives of this study were (i) to examine commonalities and distinctions in the teaching of mathematics by comparing urban and rural primary school classrooms, and (ii) to compare the mathematics achievement of children from urban and rural schools. Based on previous research, we expected to find "better" teaching and higher student achievement in urban schools than in rural ones. However, we did not know the exact nature and extent of the differences we could expect. This is because many features of the Chinese education system, such as national curriculum, common textbooks, common school design, common teacher education program syllabi, may have worked together to promote convergence in educational practice. At the same time, differences in family background variables between urban and rural families (including family size, parental educational level and socioeconomic backgrounds) and differences in resource availability and teacher qualification between urban and rural schools, may influence student attainment.

## Observations from Urban and Rural Primary Schools in Mainland China

### Research Site and Schools

The aim of this section is to highlight the physical and structural factors which characterize the schools involved in this project, and to consider their impact on school learning. Examination of structural aspects of children's learning allows greater understanding not only of classroom interactions, but also of the range of educational needs and priorities that exist. For example, the level of facilities ranges from new buildings and a suite of audiovisual facilities in some schools, to no toilet for children in others.

*Location and geographical features of the research sites.* We conducted our study in a province on China's southeast coast, Zhejiang. China's coastal provinces are generally more developed than inland rural areas, and this province has a relatively well developed economy. However, it differs from its coastal neighbors in that it is mountainous and has areas that are relatively hard to access. This has led to considerable disparity in economic and educational development within the province. Towns and villages located in the south-western, mountainous regions of Zhejiang are much less developed than those located on the coast.

The six schools used in the study were located in three areas: rural areas, semi-rural areas, and the provincial capital. The most isolated rural school in our study was located in a remote, mountainous village with a population of approximately 2000. The nearest major town was a 45 minute drive away and the nearest large city a 3-hour drive. The roads surrounding this village are un-tarmacked, and public transportation is limited. As Chi and Rao (2003) report, due to its remoteness, the village tends to adopt government policy well after it has been officially implemented. For example, the one-child policy was not enforced in the village until 10 years after its enactment in urban areas.

Hangzhou, the capital city of Zhejiang and home to two of the schools involved in this study, is highly developed in relation to many other cities in China. It is known for its handicraft industries and has attracted foreign investment. The other two schools were located in semi-rural areas of the province.

*Physical features and learning facilities.* The schools involved catered for between 950 and 1700 students. Of the two schools located in rural areas, one was significantly more remote and located in a mountainous region, while the other was located in a rural area near one of the province's main cities. The latter school, catering for almost 1200 children, enjoyed relatively good facilities, with new buildings, a playground, a computer for teachers' use, and designated toilet amenities. Although the more remote school had received funding from a local non-governmental organization to build a new school building, classroom facilities were basic and varied. Children had to walk to the local village to use the toilet as there were no facilities at the school. During break times, children went to the local village to buy food and drinks.

The two semi-rural schools enjoyed somewhat better facilities than the schools located in rural areas. The larger school, located in one of the provincial towns, was housed in new buildings and covered an area of 9,000 square meters. Its classrooms were fitted with AV facilities including a projector. The second semi-rural school offered boarding facilities and also enjoyed relatively modern facilities, with a television and projection equipment, specialized science and language laboratories, a health centre and a large canteen. This school had also received funding donations from local people. Facilities in the urban schools were impressive, with specialized music, dance and computer rooms, and one of the schools planned to install its own campus network in the near future.

*Class size.* Class size varied across the schools, with some classes consisting of 31 children (a rural school) and others comprising over 60 students (an urban and one semi-rural school). Class sizes are indicated in Tables 7.2 and 7.3.

*Instructional time.* Although timetables were more uniform across the semi-rural and urban schools, daily activities were more varied in the urban schools and allowed for development of a wider range of skills, such as music, computing and the English language. Children attended between six and seven 40-min classes each day, and students in the semi-rural and urban schools were required to complete homework tasks.

## Method

*Participants.* Participants were mathematics teachers (n=12) and students in Grade 3 (n=285) and in Grade 5 (n=230). As mentioned above, our sample of 12 classes came from 6 schools located in three areas: rural areas, semi-rural areas, and the provincial capital. Two schools were selected from each of the three areas and one Grade 3 and one Grade 5 class were selected from each school.

*Procedure.* One mathematics lesson from each of the twelve schools was videotaped and a checklist with items related to the physical settings for learning was completed. All students in the observed classes were given a curriculum-based mathematics attainment test at the end of the academic year. Different tests were used for students in Grades 3 and 5. The tests included items which assessed students' memorization and understanding of concepts (fill in the blanks, true/false), calculation ability (addition, subtraction, multiplication and division), application (word problems), and logical reasoning (deducing the value of symbols). The test for the Grade 5 children also included problems involving fractions and decimals. Teachers were also interviewed after their lessons to obtain standard background information.

## Results

### Data Management

*Coding of observations.* Two observers coded the first 35 minutes of each video-taped lesson in 30-second segments, using a protocol developed for the study. They noted what the teacher was doing (administration, reviewing, introducing new material, giving instructions); the method of instruction (whole class versus small-group); the teaching aids used (textbook, blackboard, worksheets); the teaching strategies (textbook based, repetition, explanation, questioning); and the methods of encouraging student participation (checking understanding, requesting responses, acknowledging correct responses, praising/criticizing). Interobserver agreement was 96%.

*Lesson transcripts.* All lessons were transcribed and translated by Chinese-English bilingual students. The accuracy of the translation was favorably evaluated by an independent bilingual rater. The first author and another independent rater repeatedly reviewed the transcripts and, using a broad-brush approach, characterized the primary method of teaching and teacher feedback.

## Classroom Observations

*Physical settings for learning.* There were marked discrepancies among the urban, semi-rural and rural classrooms in the physical conditions under which school learning occurred. For example, unlike the rural classrooms, the urban ones had computers and PowerPoint projection facilities. Also, the village school had poorer lighting and smaller classrooms than the other schools and had no heating in the winter.

*Classroom management.* In all classes, urban and rural, children were very well-disciplined and very engaged in the learning process. Despite the large class sizes, teachers did not have to spend time managing disruptive behavior. The classroom atmosphere was very pleasant, with teachers praising children for their responses and encouraging other classmates to praise their peers for solving problems correctly. Children were seldom criticized.

*Lesson structure.* Results indicated that teachers instructed Primary 3 and 5 students in a similar fashion. Further, there was consistency in the overall structure of the lesson across schools and grades: the teacher typically introduced a new topic, questioned students, assigned class work and finally summarized the lesson.

As mentioned earlier, the first 35 minutes of each lesson were coded. Table 7.1 shows the amount of time teachers spent engaged in different activities. Teachers spent 23.2 minutes introducing new material and 3.8 minutes reviewing previously taught material.

**Table 7.1**

*Time (in Minutes) Spent by Teachers on Different Activities*

|  | Mean | SD |
|---|---|---|
| **What was the Teacher Doing?** | | |
| Introducing New Material | 23.2 | 10.5 |
| Reviewing Material | 3.8 | 8.4 |
| Giving Instructions | 0.4 | 1.2 |
| Administration | 0.4 | 1.2 |
| **Method of Instruction** | | |
| Talking to the whole Class | 14.5 | 7.5 |
| Demonstrating to the whole Class | 8.4 | 7.1 |
| Supervising Individual Seat Work | 3.1 | 4.2 |
| Teaching Large groups | 0.8 | 1.9 |
| Teaching Small groups | 0.4 | 0.9 |
| Interactive supervision | 1.0 | 1.3 |
| **Teaching Aids** | | |
| Textbook | 1.4 | 2.9 |
| Blackboard | 12.3 | 8.7 |
| Worksheets | 4.4 | 6.4 |
| Others | 9.3 | 8.2 |
| **Teaching Strategies** | | |
| Textbook based | 0.9 | 2.0 |
| Repetition/chanting | 1.2 | 2.1 |
| Explanation | 4.1 | 2.9 |
| Questioning | 18.1 | 7.9 |
| No Supervision | 0.8 | 1.6 |
| **Encouraging Student Participation** | | |
| Checks understanding | 5.9 | 8.8 |
| Requests response from a student | 12.3 | 9.7 |
| Acknowledges correct response | 4.3 | 5.3 |
| Elaborates task related comment | 4.0 | 3.6 |
| Praise | 0.5 | 1.0 |
| Criticism | 0.0 | 0.0 |

*Method of instruction.* Teachers spent an average of about 23 minutes engaged in teaching the whole class. They either talked (explained concepts) ($M = 14.5$) or demonstrated procedures to the whole class ($M = 8.4$ minutes). They also asked individual students and/or small groups to answer questions, explain a concept, or demonstrate procedures (usually at the blackboard) to the whole class.

*Teaching aids.* Teachers relied on the blackboard for an average of about 12 minutes, while students completed worksheets for about 4 minutes of the class time.

*Teaching strategies.* Nine of the 12 teachers observed did not use text-books to teach. Instead they used the question-answer method for the majority of the class time ($M$ = 18.1 minutes). They also relied on explanation ($M$ = 4.3 minutes) to elucidate concepts and procedures.

*Methods of encouraging student participation.* Teachers spent a considerable amount of time engaging students in learning. They requested responses from individual students ($M$ = 12.3 minutes), checked students' understanding through questioning ($M$ = 5.9 minutes), acknowledged correct responses ($M$ = 4.3 minutes), or elaborated students' task related comments ($M$ = 4 minutes).

A quantitative analysis of the data provides a picture of active teachers working hard to get students engaged in the learning material. Whole-class teaching predominated, but even with these large classes, teachers did spend a considerable amount of time calling on individual students to give responses. The question and answer method was the most common method.

## Lesson Transcripts

*Questions and answers.* Teachers posed all the questions in classes. Questions were directed either at the whole class or to individual students, and the majority of teachers called individual students by their names. In general, questions were short and required closed-ended replies by the students. Many students were asked the same question, for example, "Which month is your birthday?" Most of the questions started with "What" as teachers were asking students for the answers to problems. A few teachers posed "How" questions, but this was not common. These teachers asked students to explain the way they had come up with the answer, or to demonstrate the procedure to solve the problem. Only one teacher asked "Why" questions. That stated, the students were often taught procedures – how to determine the radius and diameter of a circle, the procedure to solve numerical problems, how to apply fractions; and so perhaps the phrasing of "why" questions was not appropriate for students of this age. The teacher who did pose "Why" questions frequently elaborated on students' task-related responses. We did not observe students asking any questions, but they paid attention to teachers and willingly answered all the teachers' questions.

*Examples used*. Teachers were also sensitive to children's back-grounds. For example, we observed "Year, Month and Date" presented in an urban, a semi-rural and a rural school. In all three schools, children were taught about leap years and how to find out if a year was a leap year. The semi-rural school catered for children of Communist Party members and in this school, children were asked to state why certain years were significant for China and then say whether they were leap years. These years included the establishment of the PRC (1949), the transfer of Hong Kong's sovereignty to China (1997), the transfer of Macau's sovereignty to China (1999), the year China successfully bid to hold the Olympics (2000), and the year of the Olympics in Beijing (2008).

Teachers did not typically use examples from children's daily life to explain to or question children. However, the Grade 3 teachers tended to relate the material to children's lives more than the Grade 5 teachers, who tended to present decontextualized written problems. For example, the Grade 3 teachers asked children to look for objects or shapes in the classroom, asked children to solve problems that would be similar to the ones they encountered when shopping (unit cost, discounts), asked them the month they were born, and asked them how they spent their days when explaining the difference between telling the time with a 24 hour format versus a 12 hour format.

In two classes, teachers asked students to memorize and chant in unison mathematical formula and procedures (e.g. the radius of the circle, distributive law of multiplication, exchange law of addition). However, in general, teachers focused on promoting children's understanding of procedures through their questions.

## Similarities and Differences between Urban and Rural Classes

*Classroom teaching*. Urban and rural classes did not differ in terms of the structure and format of lessons, and there were striking similarities between how different teachers in 3 different schools tackled the same topic. The topic of "Year, Month, and Date" was videotaped in Primary 3 classes in an urban, a semi-rural and a rural school. The structure of the lesson was similar across the classes and all teachers used the same example about mid-way through the class. All three teachers demon-strated the same strategy to work out the number of days in a month: they instructed students to put their hands in front of them and move a finger across the knuckles. The teachers then explained that the knuckles represented months with 31 days while the depressions represented months with 30 or less days. All the teachers also discussed leap years and taught students how to determine which years were leap years. In addition, all three teachers asked some students in the class to state the months in which they were born.

Urban and rural teachers did, however, differ in some ways. Compared to rural teachers, those in urban classes tended to use activities to introduce a topic and examples to make abstract concepts meaningful to students. Urban teachers also used more extended discourse than did rural ones. On the other hand, rural teachers emphasized the use of correct procedural knowledge to solve mathematics problems more than did urban teachers.

*Mathematics achievement.* There was a significant difference across schools in the mathematics achievement of Primary 3 students, $F (5,279) = 22.4$, $p<.001$. Follow-up tests indicated that children in the rural village (School 5) showed significantly lower achievement than children in all the other 5 schools. Further, children in the other rural school did significantly less well than children in the highest performing semi-rural school.

There were also significant school differences in the mathematics performance of Primary 5 students, $F (4,225) = 20.5$, $p<.001$. Children in the two rural schools showed significantly lower attainment than children in the two urban schools and children in the one semi-rural school where test results were obtained. In addition, the performance of children in the semi-rural school was significantly lower than students in one of the urban schools. Means, standard deviations and class sizes are shown in Tables 7.2 and 7.3.

## Table 7.2
### *Mathematics Achievement of Children in Primary 3*

| School | Mean | SD | Number of Students in each class |
|---|---|---|---|
| Urban 1 | 14.1 | 2.4 | 41 |
| Urban 2 | 13.6 | 1.7 | 36 |
| Semi-rural 1 | 14.5 | 1.8 | 61 |
| Semi-rural 2 | 15.2 | 1.3 | 55 |
| Rural 1 | 12.9 | 3.5 | 31 |
| Rural 2 | 11.2 | 2.7 | 61 |
| Mean | 13.6 | 2.6 | 48 |

**Table 7.3**

*Mathematics Achievement of Children in Primary 5*

| School | Mean | SD | Number of Students in each class |
|--------|------|-----|----------------------------------|
| Urban 1 | 10.6 | 2.3 | 52 |
| Urban 2 | 12.0 | 1.7 | 49 |
| Semi-rural 1 | 9.6 | 2.7 | 60 |
| Rural 1 | 8.8 | 2.6 | 35 |
| Rural 2 | 7.7 | 2.5 | 34 |
| Mean | 9.9 | 2.7 | 46 |

## Discussion

The objectives of this study were to examine commonalities and distinctions in mathematics teaching and achievement between urban and rural schools. There were marked similarities in the teaching approaches adopted in the 6 schools studied, and these common pedagogical approaches are a consequence of the school system, including the centrally-determined syllabus, common textbooks, and a uniform teacher training curriculum.

Lesson structure was very similar across all schools and grades. All teachers used large-class teaching for the majority of the lesson, but employed strategies to ensure that children were actively involved in learning. Our findings are consistent with those of Ma et al. (2004), who found that teachers spent about 15 minutes in front of the class questioning students, and other researchers who have reported on the interactive nature of large-class teaching in Mainland China (Cortazzi & Jin, 2001; Huang & Leung, 2004; Schleppenbach et al., 2007).

Teachers in all the schools relied on a question-and-answer format to engage children in learning. Children paid close attention to the teacher and volunteered to respond to teachers' questions, but they never asked any. Teachers did elaborate on students' responses, but they mainly posed questions that required simple responses.

There were marked differences between urban and rural settings. Urban classrooms were much better equipped than rural ones and urban teachers were able to use computer simulations to show how to solve a problem. However, despite differences in resource availability and teacher qualifications between urban and rural settings, variations in actual pedagogy did not appear to be so significant. Students generally were actively involved in tackling mathematics contents and solving problems under teachers' guidance.

Despite common teaching approaches and lesson structure, there were significant differences in mathematics achievement between children in urban and rural schools. It could be that family-related factors may have more influence on children's mathematics achievement than actual classroom teaching. For example, urban parents tend to be more educated than rural ones and to have only one child, unlike their counterparts in rural areas. Further, unlike rural children, those in urban schools may have benefited from after-school tutoring.

## Educational Reform and Classroom Practice

In the past, China emphasized "examination-oriented book-education" and rote learning. The teacher was typically considered a fountain of knowledge who "force-feeds Peking ducks"; that is, a transmitter of knowledge rather than a facilitator of learning. Further, the primary mathematics syllabi emphasized basic knowledge, computational skills, logic and analysis, and it was believed that these competencies could only be developed through rigorous practice. Instruction was teacher centered and practicing mathematical procedures was emphasized.

However, it was felt that the previous educational goals and practices did not promote student development, critical thinking or independent problem solving, and the new educational reform advocated new educational goals, promoted new approaches to instruction, and recommended the integration of technology into pedagogy. The classes that we observed were implementing these recommendations. For example, consistent with educational guidelines, teachers made efforts to actively engage students in the learning process through class discussions and questioning. All teachers tended to follow a principle of "returning time to students". They paid more attention to students' responses and building connections between knowledge and the real world. Hence, our observations suggest that traditional Chinese beliefs about learning have begun to take a back seat to what is considered good educational practice. It is indeed possible that traditional approaches may be reinforced in the home setting.

China has always stressed the precise implementation of State edu cational guidelines and it appears from this study that the new educational reform may have prompted teachers to change their practices. There were marked similarities in the way in which teachers in different schools addressed the same topic. Lesson structure and the explanations of difficult points were almost the same, which showed that teachers were following the curriculum faithfully. This was in line with the findings of most studies on mathematics teaching and reform in China (e.g., Ma et al., 2004; Zhang & Zhou, 2003). A common curriculum, the public examination system, mandated professional development activities, and teachers collaborating to draft the most effective lesson plan for a particular topic, may all work together to forge similarities.

In summary, education reforms have recently been implemented in Mainland China as they have in other parts of the world. These reforms, which represent a marked change from previous ideas about teaching and learning in primary schools, have facilitated the development of a more student-centered pedagogy and perhaps necessitate revisiting our notions about the Chinese learner.

# REFERENCES

Chen, C. S., & Stevenson, H. W. (1995). Motivation and mathematics achievement: A comparative study of Asian-American, Caucasian-American, and East Asian high school students. *Child Development, 66*, 1215-1234.

Chi, J., & Rao, N. (2003). Parental beliefs about school learning and children's educational attainment. *Ethos, 31*, 330-356.

Cortazzi, M., & Jin, L. (2001). Large classes in China: "Good" teachers and interaction. In D. A. Watkins & J. B. Biggs (Eds.), *Teaching the Chinese Learner: Psychological and pedagogical perspectives* (pp. 115-134). Hong Kong/ Melbourne: Comparative Education Research Centre, The University of Hong Kong/Australian Council for Educational Research.

Hess, R. D., Chang, C. M., & McDevitt, T. M. (1987). Cultural variations in family beliefs about children's performance in mathematics: Comparisons among People's Republic of China, Chinese-American, and Caucasian-American families, *Journal of Educational Psychology, 79*, 179-188.

Ho, D. Y. F. (1994). Cognitive socialization in Confucian-heritage cultures. In P. Greenfield & R. Cocking (Eds.), *Cross-cultural roots of minority child development* (pp. 285-314). Hillsdale, NJ: Lawrence Erlbaum Associates.

Huang, R., & Leung, F. K. S. (2004). Cracking the paradox of Chinese Learners: Looking into the mathematics classrooms in Hong Kong and Shanghai. In L.

H. Fan, N. Y. Wong, J. F. Cai, & S. Q. Li. (Eds.), *How Chinese learn mathematics: Perspectives from insiders* (pp. 348-380). Singapore: World Scientific.

Kelly, M. K., Miller, K. F., Fang, G., & Feng G. (1999). When days are numbered: Calendar structure and the development of calendar processing in English and Chinese. *Journal of Experimental Child Psychology, 73*, 289-314.

Leung, F. K. S. (2005). Some characteristics of East Asian mathematics classrooms based on data from the TIMSS 1999 Video Study. *Educational Studies in Mathematics, 60*, 199-215.

Ma, Y., Zhao, D., & Tuo, Z. (2004). Differences within communalities: How is mathematics taught in rural and urban regions in Mainland China? In L. H. Fan, N. Y. Wong, J. F. Cai, & S. Q. Li (Eds.), *How Chinese learn mathematics: Perspectives from insiders* (pp. 413-441). Singapore: World Scientific.

Miller, K. F., Smith, C. M., Zhu, J., & Zhang, H. (1995). Preschool origins of cross-national differences in mathematical competence: The role of number-naming systems. *Psychological Science, 6*, 56-60.

Ministry of Education of the People's Republic of China. (2001). *Mathematics curriculum standards for full-time compulsory education*. Beijing, China: Beijing Normal University Press.

Mok, I., Chik, P. M., Ko, P. Y., Kwan, T., Lo, M. L., Marton, F., et al. (2001). Solving the paradox of the Chinese teacher? In D. A. Watkins & J. B. Biggs (Eds.), *Teaching the Chinese Learner: Psychological and pedagogical perspectives* (pp. 161-179). Hong Kong/Melbourne: Comparative Education Research Centre, The University of Hong Kong/Australian Council for Educational Research.

Perry, M., VanderStoep, S. W., & Yu, S. L. (1993). Asking questions in first-grade mathematics classes: Precursors to mathematical thought. *Journal of Educational Psychology, 85*, 31-40.

Rao, N., McHale, J. P., & Pearson, E. C. (2003). Links between socialization goals and child-rearing practices in Chinese and Indian mothers. *Infant and Child Development, 12*, 475-492.

Rao, N., Moely, B. E., & Sachs, J. (2000). Motivational beliefs, study strategies and mathematics attainment in high and low achieving Chinese secondary school students. *Contemporary Educational Psychology, 25*, 287-316.

Schleppenbach, M., Perry, M., Miller, K. F., Sims, L., & Fang, G. (2007). The answer is only the beginning: Extended discourse in Chinese and US mathematics classrooms. *Journal of Educational Psychology, 99*, 380-396.

Stevenson, H. W., & Lee, S. Y. (1990). Contexts of achievement: A study of American, Chinese, and Japanese children. *Monographs of the Society for Research in Child Development, 55* (1-2, Serial No. 221).

Stevenson, H. W., & Stigler, J. W. (1992). *The learning gap: Why our schools are failing and what we can learn from Japanese and Chinese education.* New York: Summit Books.

Wang, J. (2005, September 29). *Curriculum reform of elementary education in China.* Retrieved January 28, 2008, from http://www.chinese-embassy.org.uk/eng/zt/Features/t214562.htm

Watkins, D. A., & Biggs, J. B. (Eds.). (2001). *Teaching the Chinese Learner: Psychological and pedagogical perspectives.* Hong Kong/Melbourne: Comparative Education Research Centre, The University of Hong Kong/Australian Council for Educational Research.

Zhang, H., & Zhou, Y. (2003). The teaching of mathematics in Chinese elementary schools. *International Journal of Psychology, 38,* 286-298.

Zhang, L. (2005, October 25). A review of China's elementary mathematics education. *International Journal for Mathematics Teaching and Learning, October 25 2005.* Retrieved January 28, 2008, from http://www.cimt.plymouth.ac.uk/journal/zhang.pdf

Zhou, M. S. (2004). *Ensuring students' skills to participate in the 21st century economy through curriculum reform: Views and policies of China.* Paper presented at the APEC Summit on Educational Reform, Beijing, P. R. China.

Zhu, M. (2007). Recent Chinese experiences in curriculum reform. *Prospects, 37,* 223-235.

# 8

# Teaching English to Chinese-Speaking Children

*Linda SIEGEL, Ellen KNELL, Miao PEI,*
*Haiyan QIANG, Wei ZHAO and Lin ZHAO*

## Introduction

The aim of this chapter is to develop an understanding of English language learning among Chinese children and to present evidence on the effectiveness of a program designed to help develop English language skills. The particular technique in question is called English immersion. This chapter describes that method, which is widely used to teach English to children in China. In English immersion classrooms, a teacher who is a non-native English speaker and whose first language is Chinese conducts lessons entirely in English for approximately half the school day. We describe the details of the program, as well as the benefits this method has for children's performance of English and Chinese reading and language tasks.

## The History of Immersion Language Teaching

First, we briefly describe the history of the concept of English immersion. More than thirty-five years ago, a group of Canadian parents living in French-speaking Quebec realized that existing French instructional programs did not prepare their English-speaking children to communicate adequately in French. As a result, these parents convinced a local school board to hold a trial run in a single kindergarten class based on a language immersion model. Due to the success of this initial immersion class, many other immersion programs were initiated in Canada. Since then, Canadian immersion programs have expanded dramatically, and 324,495 students had participated in them as of the 2000-2001 school year (Canadian Official Languages Annual Report, 2000-2001). Virtually every territory and province in Canada offers a variety of immersion programs, including alternative forms such as late and partial immersion, which are described below.

A foreign language immersion system provides majority-language students with an opportunity to master a second language in much the same way as they master a first language (i.e., by being immersed in a language environment that promotes natural, meaningful communication). An immersion program is meant to establish a solid base in oral skills prior to introducing reading and writing. The process of second language acquisition is an incidental result of learning academic content through a second language medium (Genesee, 1995). Rather than exclusively focusing instruction on the direct mastery of second language rules and grammar, immersion programs adopt a content-based language approach that provides the means to increase the amount of comprehensible second language input by delivering subject content in the target language (Genesee, 1991, 1995).

Immersion programs vary according to the amount of instructional time spent in the second language, as well as with the age at which immersion begins. Early immersion programs begin when the child enters school in kindergarten and usually continue until middle school, although in some circumstances they may continue through the secondary level. Delayed immersion programs may begin in fourth grade, and late immersion programs typically begin in secondary school (Cummins, 1996; Genesee, 1995). Partial immersion programs, as distinguished from total immersion programs that provide instruction entirely in the target language in the first few years, have also been implemented. This form of instruction is subject–driven, with part (usually half) of the instruction in partial immersion programs being delivered in the native language and the remaining part being delivered in the target language from the first year of program initiation.

Based on the Canadian model of French immersion, English immersion programs were implemented in elementary schools in several major Chinese cities in 1997 in an attempt to expose students to more authentic English input at an earlier age. The longest running program is in Xian. These programs emerged in response to dissatisfaction with the common public school practice of teaching English through rote memory and grammar drills, methods that seemed inadequate for developing functional listening and speaking skills. In an attempt to improve the quality of instruction, a content-based language program that immerses children in English and promotes communicative language was introduced.

## Studies on Immersion Education

Immersion programs have been studied since they were first introduced more than 35 years ago (Genesee, 1995). In Genesee's study, a synthesis of the extant research in this field consistently and clearly demonstrated that Canadian French immersion children did not experience any long-term deficits in native language skills and scored equal to or better than their monolingual peers in academic achievement tests. The French language skills of immersion students were superior to those of students that received traditional French language instruction for a set period each day. Although their skills were not near-native, French immersion students had high levels of proficiency in reading and writing, as well as in speaking and listening comprehension (Genesee, 1995).

# English Immersion in Chinese Settings

## Hong Kong

Marsh, Hau, and Kong (2000) examined the effectiveness of late English immersion programs by evaluating both English and Chinese performance, including the assessment of subject content areas, among 12,784 middle school students in Hong Kong. They compared subject scores from students in English medium schools, which would qualify as late immersion programs, to the scores of students enrolled in Chinese medium schools. They found that late immersion students scored higher in English and Chinese, but significantly lagged behind their peers in Chinese medium schools in history, geography and science. Although Chinese and English language skills were better among students enrolled in late immersion programs, Marsh et al. (2000) concluded that English immersion had not enabled students to successfully access language and content in academic subject areas. They recommended that their study be extended to the high school years to determine whether the positive effects of immersion are subsequently realized over a longer time period. It was also recommended that future evaluation include assessment of English oral fluency, as this was not measured in their study, and may have improved significantly.

## Singapore

In spite of the fact that the majority of the population in Singapore speaks a form of Chinese at home, English has been used as the primary language of instruction in Singaporean schools since 1987 (Pakir, 1993). The teaching method adopted in primary schools in Singapore can be considered a total early immersion system because all children are instructed in English from kindergarten onwards. English is recognized as an official language in Singapore and, in addition to being designated as a common language for all ethnic groups, is the primary language of business and technology. International mathematics and science evaluations (administered in English) for Grades 4 and 8 place Singaporean students at or near the top worldwide (Mullis, Martin, Gonzales, & Chrostowski, 2004a, 2004b). Singaporean students scored first in the world in 8th grade science and math, leaving students from other English-speaking countries in their wake. The results of pilot studies in which adaptations of UK-normed English tests have been administered at the beginning of primary school show that while children from Singapore are behind UK school children in the early grades, they catch up in the later primary years. In addition, Singaporean students have scored well above UK children in mathematics tests at every level (Gupta, 1994). Although many variables (sociocultural, educational, political) undoubtedly have an impact on these results, it is possible that beginning English immersion in the early primary grades is an important factor that contributes to academic success among Singaporean students in subjects taught in English.

Although the immersion programs noted above take place in communities where the majority of people speak a form of Chinese, the educational, social and political environments of Hong Kong and Singapore are very different from that of China. No study to date has investigated early English immersion programs in China. English immersion programs in public primary schools, which represent the realization of a new concept in language instruction in China, provide a unique opportunity to examine the generalizability of Canadian immersion models in a very different educational setting.

## Mainland China

For the most part, English instruction in China is designed to help students pass English exams. These exams are required for students wishing to gain admittance to and graduate from universities and colleges (Anderson, 1993; Chen & Zhang, 1998), and they measure other important language benchmarks from primary school through to high school (Penner, 1995). Oral communication has not been a priority in traditional English instruction, and until the mid- to late-1980s, it was not uncommon to find college students who had studied English for many years but were unable to speak more than a few selected words (Chen & Zhang, 1998). Although a communicative language approach is gaining popularity in China (Anderson, 1993), it is still the case that functional oral English skills are seldom taught in the public school environment. The majority of students are instructed through rote drills and grammar-translation techniques, methods that do not lend themselves well to the development of an overall fluency in speaking and understanding oral English (Zou, 1998). School administrators and teachers may be resistant to the use of communicative, interactive language techniques because they worry that students will not pass national written exams designed to test grammar, reading, vocabulary and writing (Anderson, 1993).

Because the early immersion program in Xian emphasizes oral language and communicative, task-based language teaching, it may enable students to develop confidence and fluency in spoken English. Early immersion, in particular, has been shown to positively affect the development of speaking skills (Turnbull, Lapkin, Hart, & Swain, 1998). Turnbull et al. (1998) examined a large database of evaluative studies conducted in Canada involving over 1,160 12th grade students enrolled in a variety of French immersion programs. An analysis of studies comparing early immersion with late or delayed immersion programs revealed that although students in delayed or later immersion programs scored as well as early immersion children in some measures, especially L2 (the second language, English) literacy, early immersion children were better able to speak in the target language. Early English immersion programs implemented in public school settings in China may provide a means for young children to build their English listening and speaking skills before grammar and language rules are intensively taught and memorized for the purpose of passing written exams that begin in middle school.

*The Xian program structure.* The early English immersion program in Xian operates at the Shaanxi Normal (Teachers) University's Affiliated Primary School and begins in kindergarten. Enrollment in the immersion program is on a voluntary basis, and is determined by the children's parents. Approximately 300 children are enrolled in the immersion program (K-3), with one experimental class at each grade level. While the remaining children at the school do not participate in the immersion program, they still study English for two periods each week.

Primary school education in China follows a national curriculum and is departmentalized in that children change classrooms and teachers for each subject. The vast majority of teachers (95%) in this primary school have university degrees. English immersion teachers must pass an oral and written English exam and participate in training seminars given by professionals from Canada, in which communicative language techniques are taught. Non-immersion English teachers also participate in these seminars. Although these requirements are considered rigorous for primary school teachers in China, the English teachers at the school do *not* have near-native English language proficiency, and difficulties with pronunciation and English grammar are common.

The immersion program at the Shaanxi Normal University's Affiliated Primary School is a partial immersion program in that 50% of the curriculum is taught in English and 50% is taught in Putonghua (the national language). Subjects taught in English include: English language arts, moral education, art, physical education, music and science. Chinese and math are taught in Chinese. Children have six hours of mathematics lessons and ten hours of Chinese reading and calligraphy lessons each week. The required subjects and time allotments are the same for both immersion and non-immersion students, the only difference being that non-immersion students are not taught half of the curriculum in English.

Although immersion students have half of their subjects taught in English, both immersion and non-immersion children have the same amount of time devoted to formal English study: only two 45-minute periods each week. Immersion teachers are encouraged to use communicative teaching methods in the classroom during this time and to use teacher manuals specially written for the purpose. Non-immersion teachers use a traditional text and tend to teach English in a more traditional way.

# Language Learning

Immersion programs are based on certain principles of language learning. When considering the teaching of English to children for whom it is a second language, it is important to understand how children learn their first language. A child's first language is learned by listening and speaking. Reading and writing come much later after a good foundation in oral language skills has been established.

Children first speak in single words, followed by increasingly longer sentences. Children first learn nouns, adjectives and verbs. Articles, prepositions and function words appear much later. Good language teaching stresses listening and speaking skills to help develop comprehension and reading skills. Conversation and oral language skills are especially important in the early stages of learning a language. Reading and writing skills must be based on a sound oral language foundation. Listening skills reflect the ability to extract meaning from a string of words. These are aural skills. Reading is about extracting meaning from a series of words and involves visual skills.

## *Vocabulary, Syntax and Phonological Awareness*

A child cannot extract meaning from spoken language without understanding the meaning of words. The teaching of English in an immersion setting involves the teaching of vocabulary and syntax. To teach reading skills in English, which is an alphabetic language, it is important to develop phonological awareness skills. Phonological awareness skills refer to the ability to segment spoken language into small segments, such as words, syllables, and individual sounds called phonemes.

In teaching English, it is important to develop vocabulary skills and an understanding of the basic syntax of the language, as well as to develop oral language skills before the introduction of reading. In many English language teaching programs operated in China, English has traditionally been taught through the medium of writing. Nevertheless, it is important that writing not be taught too early. Good English language teaching involves conversation and fostering an understanding of oral language. Fluent and accurate reading skills cannot be developed without sound oral language skills.

*Vocabulary.* Understanding the meaning of words is obviously a fundamental aspect of learning any language. Vocabulary teaching usually starts with the labeling of pictures and objects. It is important to begin with nouns, adjectives and simple verbs in the present tense.

*Syntax.* To speak any language, a child must develop an understanding of the basic grammar of the language. Chinese and English are very different in terms of their grammatical structure. Chinese has no verb tenses, plurals, articles or prepositions. These aspects of English grammar can be very difficult for Chinese-speaking children to learn. It is important for the teacher to provide models of these structures in English.

## The Study – The Xian Immersion Program

The immersion program in Xian incorporates a number of important activities that are designed to build literacy skills. For example, children participate in centers such as a pretend bank, restaurant or grocery store, and are required to act out scenarios in English appropriate to those places. For example, the teacher may read a story to the children using *Big Books* so the children can see the pictures. The children then act out the stories and draw pictures based on them. The children learn simple songs and rhymes in English, and sing and recite them with actions.

As far as possible, only English is used in the classroom. The goal of the immersion program is to build the vocabulary of the children and develop their ability to follow instructions in English. Games and storytelling are used to provide a rich English language environment.

All children begin Chinese literacy instruction in the first grade. Prior to learning any Chinese characters, they initially learn Pinyin (a Romanized spelling of Chinese characters that acts as a mediating system designed to aid in learning pronunciation and character recognition). It is common in many early immersion programs in Canada to introduce literacy in the second language. For Chinese-speaking students, certain considerations may need to be taken into account to accommodate the complex literacy systems that they are required to master in their native language (Cummins, 2000). For this reason, literacy is initially introduced through the L1 (the first language, Chinese) for immersion students at Shaanxi Normal University's Affiliated Primary School.

Although the major emphasis for students in the early grades is on receptive and expressive language skills, all students are exposed to some written English words in the second grade; however, no formal literacy instruction or alphabet instruction is given until the third grade. By the end of the third grade, just prior to testing, both non-immersion and immersion students have been exposed to most of the English alphabet and a limited number of English words (mostly high-frequency nouns). English literacy instruction begins in Primary 1 and phonological awareness training in kindergarten.

The structure of the classes in Xian is such that there is a high student-to-teacher ratio (most of the classes have approximately 50 students). The immersion program operates as part of a public school, and funds are scarce, which directly affects the availability of resources. There are limited English materials available at the present time, as materials from English-speaking countries that are appropriate for L1 English students at this level contain vocabulary and syntax that is too difficult for L2 Chinese children. The immersion teachers are non-native English-speakers and do not have near-native English proficiency. In addition, there is little opportunity for children to hear English spoken outside the school environment; moreover, few parents speak any English.

The present study examined the performance of immersion and non-immersion students at Shaanxi Normal University's Affiliated Primary School by measuring English oral proficiency, as well as literacy and vocabulary in Chinese and English, all of which are factors that are crucial to school and language success. In addition, phonological awareness measures were administered in English and Chinese. Phonological awareness is the ability to perceive and manipulate sublexical phonological units such as syllables, rhymes and phonemes, and has been shown to have a strong correlation with proficient literacy acquisition in both English (Adams, 1990; Goswami & Bryant, 1990; Siegel, 1993; Wagner et al., 1997) and Chinese (Ho & Bryant, 1997a, 1997b; Hu & Catts, 1998).

## *Method*

### *Participants*

One hundred and eighty-three students took part in this study. Approximately half of the participants from each of the immersion and regular classes (Grades 1 to 3) were randomly assigned for testing. The participants (96 boys and 87 girls) included 51 first graders, 61 second graders, and 71 third graders. Ninety-two of the children were from the immersion group, and 91 were from the control classes. All of the classes were from the same school.

## English Measures

*Oral language interview.* A 24-item oral interview, based in part on primary school English interview forms from Clifford International School in Guangzhou, was administered in English. This measure was designed to test listening comprehension and the ability to express oneself in English. There were three sections to the interview: directions, basic conversational questions, and sentence comprehension. The directions section included eight basic directions such as "put the book on the table" and "give me the pencil." Students received one point for correctly completing each direction. The conversational questions section included ten questions designed to elicit personal information, such as "what do you like to do after school?" and "when is your birthday?" The sentence comprehension task included two items from small vignettes of between two and five sentences. The sentences were read to the children, after which between two and four comprehension questions we asked. The testing administrator was allowed to repeat each question twice if necessary. The student's response was scored on a scale from zero to two. The student was given one point for a partial response or for a response that indicated that the student understood the question but could not produce an adequate answer. The student received two points for a correct, understandable response and no points for a wrong answer or no response. There was a maximum possible score of 40 points.

*English vocabulary.* English vocabulary was measured using the Peabody Picture Vocabulary Test – Revised (PPVT-R) Form M (Dunn & Dunn, 1981). This test requires the student to point to one of four pictures to identify the vocabulary word presented orally by the test administrator.

*Word identification (WRAT-3).* English word identification was assessed using two measures. The first was an abridged version of the word-reading subtest of the Wide Range Achievement Test 3 (WRAT-3) (Wilkinson, 1995). The Blue Form of this test, which has 15 uppercase letters and 20 words arranged in ascending order of difficulty, was used. The student was told to read each of the letters and words on the page. Examples from the word list include *book, finger, stretch* and *abuse.*

*English word list.* The second word identification task was a graded word list. Twenty words were selected from the Fry word list (Fry, Polk, & Fountoukidis, 1984) and the primer and first grade word lists compiled by the Center for Applied Research in Education (1993). Four teachers from the control and immersion classes selected words from the lists that they knew the children had been exposed to in English class. It is important to note that formal reading instruction had only begun in the third grade with the introduction of the letters of the alphabet; however, most of the students had been exposed to some whole words, although they had not been explicitly taught how to read them. The 20 words were arranged in a column on two sheets of paper. The test administrator would point to the word and ask the child to read it aloud. Word samples from the graded word list include *ball, three, yellow* and *jump.* The Cronbach alpha reliability coefficient for this test was .93.

*Letter recognition.* The 26 lowercase letters of the English alphabet were randomly arranged on a page, and each student was asked to say the name of the letter as the examiner pointed to it. Only the third grade students had been taught the names of the letters directly and at the time of testing had been instructed in over half of the alphabet letters; however, the teachers reported that it was not uncommon for students to have been exposed to the letters, and most students were familiar with the English alphabet song. If, during testing, the student gave a Pinyin sound for the letter, he was asked to give the name of the letter in English. Only English letter names were scored as correct. The Cronbach Alpha reliability coefficient for this task was .95.

## English Phonological Awareness

*Onset-rime detection.* The first part of the onset-rime measure assessed initial sound (onset) detection. There were 10 test items with three demonstration items. Each student was first given a stimulus word and then given three more words. The child was asked which of the three words had the same first sound as the first word. During the three training items, the child was given corrective feedback. The items could be repeated if the child requested it. Pictures were provided during this task in an attempt to reduce memory load and provide a purer measure of phonological awareness (see Schatschneider, Francis, Foorman, Fletcher, & Mehta, 1999). The picture cues may have been especially important for this task as some of the children might not have been familiar with the English words used.

The second part of the onset-rime measure was a rhyme detection subtest that included 10 items. As in the onset detection task, the child was given a stimulus word and asked to choose the word that rhymed with it or had the same final sound from a list of three words. Once again, pictures were used for all the words to reduce memory load. There were three demonstration items and the examiner gave corrective feedback if the child responded incorrectly. The phonological awareness score for this measure was a composite score which included both the onset and rime tasks. The Cronbach's alpha for the onset-rime detection task was .67.

### Chinese Measures (Phonological Awareness)

*Chinese onset-rime detection.* The first part of the onset-rime task assessed the child's ability to detect initial sounds, with the second part assessing the child's ability to detect final sounds. The first part of the test, which was designed to assess initial sound detection, included 10 items and two practice items. The child was told "I am going to say four characters and I want you to find the two characters that start with the same sound." The child was given corrective feedback during the two practice items.

The second part of the Chinese onset-rime task was adapted from So and Siegel (1997) and included 15 experimental trials and two practice items. This rhyming task, which was originally designed to be used with Cantonese-speaking children in Hong Kong, was adapted into Putonghua for this study. As in the initial sound detection task, each trial was composed of four characters, two of which rhymed. The examiner explained the task by saying "I am going to read aloud four characters and you must listen carefully. Say these four characters after me, and tell me which two characters rhyme with each other." If the child had difficulty during the two practice trials, the examiner explained that two characters rhyme if they have the same final sounds. The phonological awareness score for this measure was also a composite score that reflected both the onset and rime tasks. The Cronbach's alpha for the onset-rime task was .89.

*Chinese phoneme deletion.* The Chinese phoneme deletion task was composed of 16 items and four practice items. The initial phoneme was deleted in the first eight experimental trials and the final phoneme was deleted in the last eight trials. The child was told "if I say the word *che* [車] (car) without the 'ch,' what sound is left?" Occasionally during the practice trials, the child would say the deleted sound instead of the remaining sound, in which case the examiner would ask for the remaining sound. The Cronbach's alpha was .72 for this measure.

*Character identification.* Chinese character identification was assessed using an instrument developed to test emerging literacy in Chinese preschool and primary school children. The Preschool and Primary Chinese Literacy Scale (PPCLS) developed by Li (2000) includes a character recognition subtest. Characters were randomly selected from those commonly listed in the course syllabi of Chinese primary schools. The character recognition subtest includes 75 characters arranged in ascending order of difficulty, with four single characters presented on each page. The examiner asked the child to read each character aloud. The child was told to guess if he or she was unsure of the character. The test was discontinued after eight consecutive wrong answers. The coefficient alpha reported for the character recognition subtest of the PPCLS was .74.

*Chinese vocabulary.* The revised Peabody Picture Vocabulary Test (PPVT-R), Form L, was translated into Chinese to assess Chinese receptive vocabulary. Form L was used to prevent any test learning from the Chinese version to the English version in which Form M was utilized. Test items were translated and adapted by a group of native Chinese speakers (two teachers and a professor) from Shaanxi Normal University. As in the English version, students were told "I'm going to say a word and I want you to point to the picture of the word." The student was required to choose from four pictures arranged on a page. The student was given three trial items in which corrective feedback was given. Testing was discontinued after eight consecutive errors.

## Procedure

The measures were individually administered by a team of eight Chinese-English bilingual college seniors (psychology and education majors) recruited from Shaanxi Normal University and two bilingual university teachers. These college students and teachers were trained to administer the English and Chinese measures. All testing took place in a large conference room in the elementary school. The English testing session lasted approximately half an hour and the Chinese testing session required approximately 45 minutes to complete. The testing sessions were administered consecutively, with half of the children being tested first in Chinese and the other half being tested first in English. During the English testing session, the examiners gave the directions for the English measures in both Chinese and English to ensure each student understood the directions.

## Results

The immersion group performed at a significantly higher level than the control group in the English oral language interview at each of the three grade levels. However, there was no significant difference between the immersion and control groups in the English phonological awareness task at any of the grade levels (Figure 8.1).

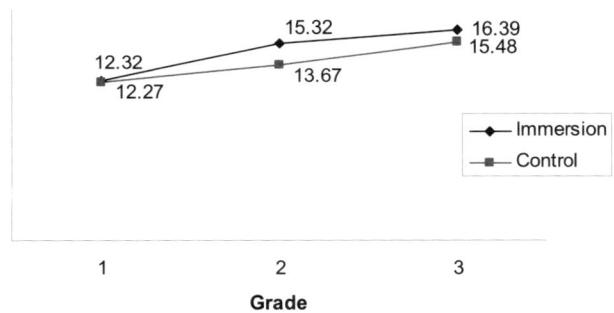

*Figure 8.1.* **English phonological awareness skills**

In terms of English vocabulary skills, English reading and English WRAT, the immersion group performed at a statistically significant higher level than the control group at each grade level. In Grades 2 and 3, the immersion group knew three times as many words as the control group as measured by the English reading and English WRAT (word recognition) tests (Figures 8.2, 8.3 and 8.4).

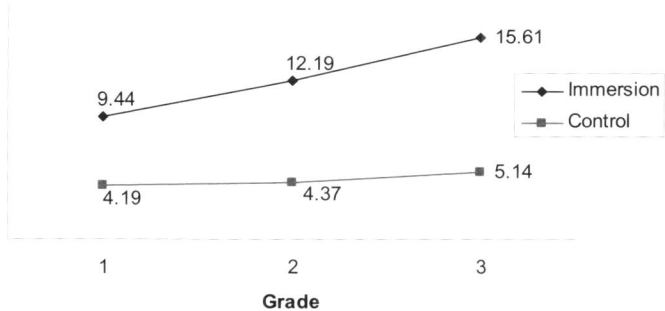

*Figure 8.2.* **English vocabulary skills**

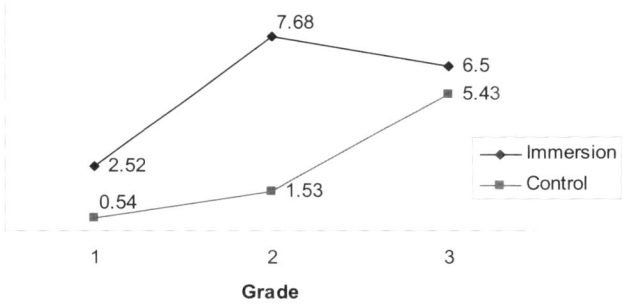

*Figure 8.3.* **English word list**

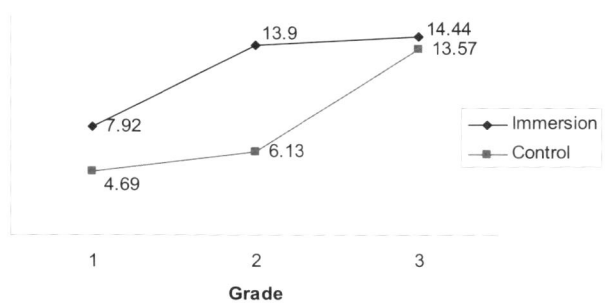

*Figure 8.4.* **English WRAT skills**

While letter recognition skills were significantly more advanced for the immersion group in Grades 1 and 2, the control group had caught up to the immersion group by Grade 3 (Figure 8.5).

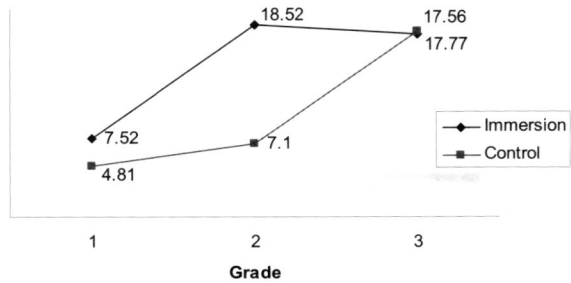

*Figure 8.5.* **English letter knowledge skills**

There were no statistically significant differences between the immersion and control groups in the Chinese character recognition (Figure 8.6), Chinese phonological awareness (Figure 8.7) or Chinese phoneme deletion tasks (Figure 8.8). Nor was there any significant difference between the immersion and control groups in the Chinese vocabulary test.

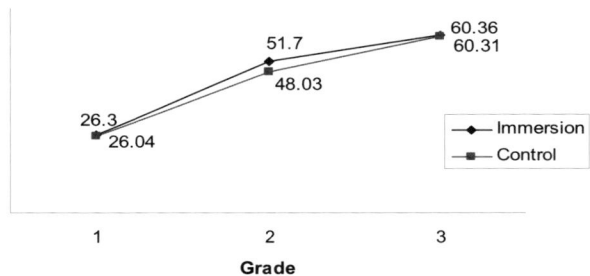

*Figure 8.6.* **Chinese character identification skills**

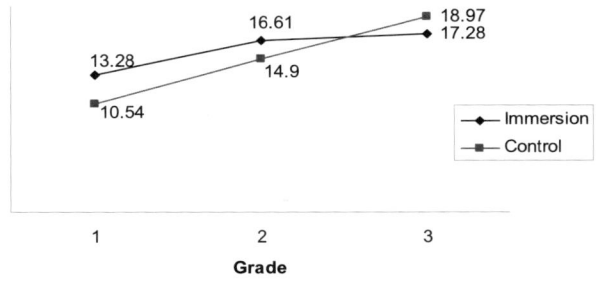

*Figure 8.7.* **Chinese phonological awareness skills**

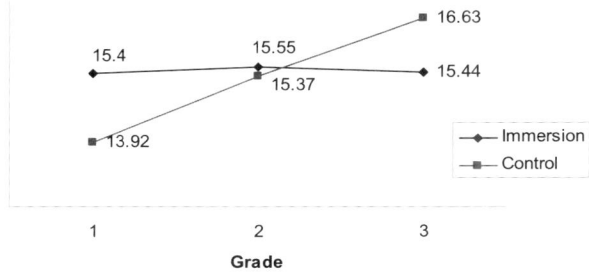

*Figure 8.8. Chinese phoneme deletion skills*

## *Discussion*

Two major findings emerged from this study. First, the immersion students scored significantly higher than the control students in the English literacy, vocabulary and oral language measures. These differences existed at each grade level, the only exception being that by the third grade there were no longer any significant differences between the two groups in reading skills. In the third grade, both groups had begun receiving reading instruction, which included teaching on the alphabet and repeated exposure to certain function words; this may have eliminated any difference that existed between the groups in spite of any immersion effect.

There was a particularly large difference between the groups in the oral interview measure, indicating that the immersion students were much more able to comprehend and express concepts in English. Previous studies (Turnbull et al., 1998) have found that children enrolled in early immersion programs are better able to speak in the second language than students enrolled in delayed or late immersion programs. As many students in China are especially lacking in functional verbal communication skills, it may be that early immersion provides a good educational alternative because it significantly improves students' ability to speak in the target language. This could be an advantage in China, where many students are required to focus on grammar drills and the rote learning of rules to pass technical English exams in middle and high school. As a result of this emphasis, students often concentrate their efforts on written English comprehension rather than oral proficiency. Exposure to English instruction at an early age using an interactive, communicative approach may enable students to acquire functional English skills in a meaningful context that promotes the development of oral fluency before the need for grammatical accuracy becomes more pressing in middle school. The difference favoring the immersion group occurred in spite of the fact that their language instructors did not have near-native English ability and taught in the context of a public school where resources are limited.

The second major finding of this study was that no difference was observed between the two groups of children in terms of their ability to recognize Chinese characters. Although the English immersion children had studied Chinese characters for the same amount of time as the control students, they had not been exposed to the same amount of Mandarin as their non-immersion peers. One of the principal curriculum objectives for primary school children in China is the mastery of approximately 4,000 characters (Hanley, Tzeng, & Huang, 1999). It is evident from the results of this study that the acquisition of Chinese characters by immersion children had not suffered any ill effects. In fact, their mean score for this task was slightly higher than that of the control group. This suggests that the learning of English in the immersion program is an additive process and does not detract from the acquisition of Chinese character reading skills. Parents may hesitate to enroll their children in immersion programs due to fears that native language development will be impaired. The results of this study support previous studies (Genesee, 1995) which have shown that language immersion students do not experience any long-term deficit in native language skills.

The Xian English immersion program is a partial early immersion program. Swain (1996) summarized research conducted on immersion programs in Canada and reported that children in partial immersion programs did not perform as well in French as children in total immersion programs. The decision to introduce a partial English immersion program in Xian was made to ensure that children receive adequate instruction in Chinese characters during their primary school years. Administrators, parents and teachers collectively felt that the partial immersion model provided the most effective way of improving students' communicative English skills, while maintaining adequate instructional support for Chinese.

Traditionally, English has been taught in China through a whole word type of instruction, with very little attention being given to the direct mastery of sound-symbol correspondences. Furthermore, because Chinese is typically parsed at the level of the onset-rime and because Pinyin is taught as onset-rime units (Cheung, Chen, Lai, Wong, & Hills,

2001), it may be especially appropriate to use this knowledge when teaching English by beginning English literacy instruction with the introduction of rhyming word families (*cat, bat, rat*). In the present study, the English onset-rime identification task was strongly related to English word identification among immersion students, indicating that a sensitivity to onset-rime units predicted reading success in English.

Our observations indicated that the children in the Xian immersion program really enjoyed learning English and were quite eager to speak it with foreigners. Unlike many children, they were not shy and even asked the female members of the observer team what their age was. One mature woman said "25," and the children laughed.

Pronunciation was quite a problem for the children, as they did not have native speaker models. Although one solution to this problem is to use videos, tapes and DVDs, this was not feasible as the material available in English is too advanced for children at this level. They do not yet have the vocabulary required to understand these media. Another solution is the use of tapes made locally by native speakers. This solution, while excellent, does require funding.

The teachers really made an effort to speak only English in the classroom. One seven year old boy even asked his Chinese teacher (in Chinese), "if you do not speak Chinese, how come you can understand my Chinese?"

## Conclusion

This was the first study to investigate aspects of early English immersion in a Chinese public primary school. The study found that Chinese children enrolled in an early immersion program in Xian performed significantly better in measures of English oral proficiency, vocabulary and literacy than their non-immersion peers; furthermore, their participation in the immersion program did not have a detrimental effect on their acquisition of Chinese character identification skills. The differences between the immersion and non-immersion groups were especially pronounced in oral proficiency, with the immersion children much more able to understand and speak English. This may be an important advantage for Chinese children, because oral competency is not typically emphasized in Chinese public schools, and many students lack this skill. Children who have participated in immersion programs will most likely begin middle school with better spoken English and comprehension skills. Whether these differences continue to be as pronounced once the students attend middle school should be the focus of further study.

The learning of Pinyin in first grade by Chinese students and the possible increase in Chinese phonological awareness such learning brings may provide a foundation on which to build English literacy. Teaching methodologies which emphasize sound-symbol correspondences and phonological awareness may be very beneficial for students of this age, and should be the focus of future research.

Children who were exposed to a classroom environment in which only English was spoken and in which there were many opportunities for interaction and conversation showed significant improvement in English compared to children taught in traditional classrooms. We conclude that it is possible to foster English language fluency in children whose first language is Chinese if one uses a program which emphasizes listening skills, phonological awareness, and oral language comprehension.

# REFERENCES

Adams, J. (1990). *Beginning to read: Thinking and learning about print*. Cambridge, MA: MIT Press.

Anderson, J. (1993). Is a communicative approach practical for teaching English in China? Pros and cons. *System, 21*, 471-480.

*Canadian Official Languages Annual Report*. (2000-2001). Available from the Canadian Heritage web site, http://www.pch.gc.ca/index-eng.cfm

Chen, C., & Zhang, Y. (1998). A perspective on the college English teaching syllabus in China. *TESL Canada Journal/Revue TESL du Canada, 15*(2), 69-75.

Cheung, H., Chen, H.-C., Lai, C. Y., Wong, O. C., & Hills, M. (2001). The development of phonological awareness: Effects of spoken language experience and orthography. *Cognition, 81*, 227-241.

Cummins, J. (1996). *Negotiating identities: Education for empowerment in a diverse society*. Los Angeles: California Association for Bilingual Education.

Cummins, J. (2000). *Language, power and pedagogy*. Clevedon: Multilingual Matters Ltd.

Dunn, L. M., & Dunn, L. M. (1981). *British Picture Vocabulary Scale: Revised manual for forms L and M*. Circle Pines, MN: American Guidance Service.

Fry, E. B., Polk, J. K., & Fountoukidis, D. (1984). *The reading teacher's book of lists*. London: Prentice-Hall Inc.

Genesee, F. (1991). Second language learning in school settings: Lessons from immersion. In A. Reynolds (Ed.), *Bilingualism, multiculturalism, and second language learning* (pp. 182-201). Hillsdale, NJ: Lawrence Erlbaum Associates.

Genesee, F. (1995). The Canadian second language immersion program. In O. Garcia & C. Baker (Eds.), *Policy and practice in bilingual education: Extending the foundations* (pp. 118-133). Clevedon: Multilingual Matters Ltd.

Goswami, U., & Bryant, P. E. (1990). *Phonological skills and learning to read*. Hillsdale, NJ: Lawrence Erlbaum Associates.

Gupta, A. F. (1994). *The step-tongue: Children's English in Singapore*. Clevedon: Multilingual Matters Ltd.

Hanley, J. R., Tzeng, O., & Huang, H. S. (1999). Learning to read Chinese. In M. Harris & G. Hatano (Eds.), *Learning to read and write: A cross-linguistic perspective* (pp. 173-191). Cambridge: Cambridge University Press.

Ho, C. S. H., & Bryant, P. (1997a). Learning to read Chinese beyond the logographic phase. *Reading Research Quarterly, 32,* 276-89.

Ho, C. S. H., & Bryant, P. (1997b). Phonological skills are important in learning to read Chinese. *Developmental Psychology, 33,* 946-951.

Hu, C. F., & Catts, H. W. (1998). The role of phonological processing in early reading ability: What we can learn from Chinese. *Scientific Studies of Reading, 2,* 55-79.

Li, H. (2000). *Contributors to Chinese literacy development: A longitudinal study of preschoolers in Beijing, Hong Kong and Singapore*. Unpublished doctoral dissertation, The University of Hong Kong, Hong Kong.

Marsh, H., Hau, K. T., & Kong, C. K. (2000). Late immersion and language of instruction in Hong Kong high schools: Achievement growth in language and nonlanguage subjects. *Harvard Educational Review, 70,* 302-350.

Mullis, I. V. S., Martin, M. O., Gonzales, E. J., & Chrostowski, S. J. (2004a). *TIMSS 2003 international mathematics report: Findings from IEA's trends in international mathematics and science study at the fourth and eighth grades*. Chestnut Hill, MA: Boston College.

Mullis, I. V. S., Martin, M. O., Gonzales, E. J., & Chrostowski, S. J. (2004b). *TIMSS 2003 international science report: Findings from IEA's trends in international mathematics and science study at the fourth and eighth grades*. Chestnut Hill, MA: Boston College.

Pakir, A. (1993). Two tongue tied: Bilingualism in Singapore. *Journal of Multilingual and Multicultural Development, 14,* 73-90.

Penner, J. (1995). Change and conflict: Introduction of the communicative approach in China. *TESL Canada Journal/Revue TESL du Canada, 12*(2), 1-17.

Schatschneider, C., Francis, D. J., Foorman, B. F., Fletcher, J. M., & Mehta, P. (1999). The dimensionality of phonological awareness: An application of item response theory. *Journal of Educational Psychology, 91,* 1-11.

Siegel, L. S. (1993). The development of reading. In H. Reese (Ed.), *Advances in child development and behavior* (Vol. 24, pp. 63-97). San Diego, Ca: Academic Press.

So, D., & Siegel, L. S. (1997). Learning to read Chinese: Semantic, syntactic, phonological and working memory skills in normally achieving and poor Chinese readers. *Reading and Writing: An Interdisciplinary Journal, 9*, 1-21.

Swain, M. (1996). Discovering successful second language teaching strategies and practices: From programme evaluation to classroom experimentation. *Journal of Multilingual and Multicultural development, 17*, 89-104.

Turnbull, M., Lapkin, S., Hart, D., & Swain, M. (1998). Time on task and immersion graduates' French proficiency. In S. Lapkin (Ed.), *French second language education in Canada: Empirical studies* (pp. 31-55). Toronto and Buffalo: University of Toronto Press.

Wagner, R. K., Torgesen, J. K., Rashotte, C. A., Hecht, S. A., Barker, T. A., Burgess, S. R., et al. (1997). Changing relations between phonological processing abilities and word-level reading as children develop from beginning to skilled readers: A 5-year longitudinal study. *Developmental Psychology, 33*, 468-479.

Wilkinson, G. S. (1995). *The Wide Range Achievement Test – 3*. Wilmington, DE: Jasak Associates.

Zou, Y. Y. (1998). English training for professionals in China: Introducing a successful EFL training programme. *System, 26*, 235-248.

# 9

# Preschool Pedagogy:
# A Fusion of Traditional Chinese Beliefs and Contemporary Notions of Appropriate Practice

*Nirmala RAO, Sharon S.N. NG and Emma PEARSON*

This chapter considers pedagogical practices in Hong Kong kindergartens. First, it addresses some macro-level changes which have influenced classroom practice. Second, it considers how professional knowledge about early instruction, educational policy and traditional cultural beliefs about learning have affected teacher-child interactions. Next, through the use of examples, the chapter illustrates current and emerging pedagogical practices in kindergartens and discusses the role of various cultural-contextual factors in shaping the form of early childhood pedagogy. Finally, it argues that a distinct Hong Kong-Chinese early childhood pedagogy is discernible from systematic observations of classroom practice.

## Worldwide Change and Early Childhood Pedagogy

There are many factors which affect what goes on in the preschool classroom. These include child characteristics, teacher attributes and behaviors, the availability of educational resources, school philosophy, parental beliefs and behaviors and educational policy. However, in recent years, educational policy and reforms relevant to the early years have had the foremost influence on classroom practice in Asian countries where early childhood services are expanding and changing. This is because the governments in these countries have been active in setting

255

benchmarks for teacher qualifications, limiting class size, issuing curriculum guidelines and determining whether or not early childhood education should be part of the compulsory education provision. Policy relevant to early education is itself influenced by a number of factors: research, national goals and development, the ratification of international conventions, the desire to respect diversity, governments' beliefs about their role in early childhood education, technological advances, and the desire to prepare children for a globalized world (Rao, 2006). In-depth discussion of all these factors is beyond the scope of this chapter. However, some of them are considered in the following section, particularly research on the importance of the early years for human development, and new conceptions of effective teaching and learning in the preschool years. Both have affected pedagogical practices in Hong Kong preschools.

*Research*. Research indicates that the brain develops most rapidly in the first years of life and that environmental stimulation positively affects the developing brain (Shonkoff & Phillips, 2000). Further, research has also drawn attention to the larger economic returns of government investment in early childhood education compared to later education (Heckman, 2004; Lynch, 2004). These findings have presumably influenced the Hong Kong government in its increased focus on the provision and quality of early childhood services.

We know more about early child development and learning now than ever before, and it is clear that views about child development and learning influence classroom practice. The dominant philosophical/theoretical perspectives in early childhood education have been the constructivist, social constructivist and behaviorist approaches that are representative of the views of Piaget, Vygotsky and Locke/Skinner, respectively. Each of these views is associated with different roles for the adult-teacher and the child. For example, under the cognitive-development perspective associated with Piaget and constructivism, the adult provides guidance to the child by observing, assessing and supporting development. The child is described as a "little scientist," who actively explores and constructs meaning about the world. The social constructivist perspective, which is based on Vygotsky's Sociocultural Theory, assumes that adults play an important role in cultural transmission. The adult provides engagement by scaffolding and transforming learning. During the development process, the child co-constructs knowledge based on interactions with adults. In contrast to these two perspectives, the Behaviorists view the child as a passive recipient of environmental stimuli, while the adult's role is to provide direction for the child and respond appropriately to the child's behavior. This perspective also assumes that children's minds are tabulae rasae, empty containers to be filled with knowledge (Trawick-Smith, 2006). Following a major paradigm shift in educational psychology some decades ago, the focus of teaching in Western contexts moved from knowledge transmission (behaviorist) to knowledge construction. Teachers were encouraged to move from being transmitters of knowledge to facilitators of learning and creativity. This shift is now occurring in many Asian contexts including Hong Kong, where contemporary concepts such as acknowledgment of play as a valuable medium for learning have increasing importance in the early childhood curriculum.

*National development and globalization.* Wide-ranging social, economic, and technological changes have markedly affected educational policy and practice. Globalization has affected early childhood practice in both positive and less desirable ways. Improved communications and knowledge of what is happening in other countries have led to preschool education reform in different parts of the world. However, globalization has also led to the devaluing of traditional values. In many regions of the world, there is tension between a culture promoted by globalization and that of traditional culture. For example, there is a dissonance between progressive views of how early learning should come about (such as learning through play) and more teacher directed approaches, still prevalent in some kindergartens in Hong Kong. This conflict is reflected in the findings reported here, which highlight the pervasive role of cultural beliefs in teachers' classroom practices.

*Technological advances.* Curriculum and instruction in preschools have also been influenced by technological advances in society. For example, most preschools in Hong Kong have computers for children. Chinese software programs have been developed, and in some classrooms computers are used to enhance children's learning, and to promote peer collaboration. However, these are typically still used for games and reinforcing academic concepts and not to promote more complex cognitive skills.

## Factors Influencing Pedagogical Practices in Hong Kong

Hong Kong's sociopolitical, educational, geographical, and cultural contexts have had, and continue to have, a significant influence on Hong Kong's early childhood policies and practice. Informative accounts of early childhood education in Hong Kong are available (see Chan & Chan, 2002, 2003; Opper, 1992, 1996; Pearson & Rao, 2006; Rao, 2002; Rao & Koong, 2000; Rao, Koong, Kwong, & Wong, 2003; Wong & Rao, 2004). In the following section, we limit our discussion to the influences of professional knowledge about instruction, educational policy and cultural beliefs on teaching in Hong Kong kindergartens. Figure 9.1 illustrates the relationship between the various factors which influence classroom practice and will be explained in more detail later in the chapter.

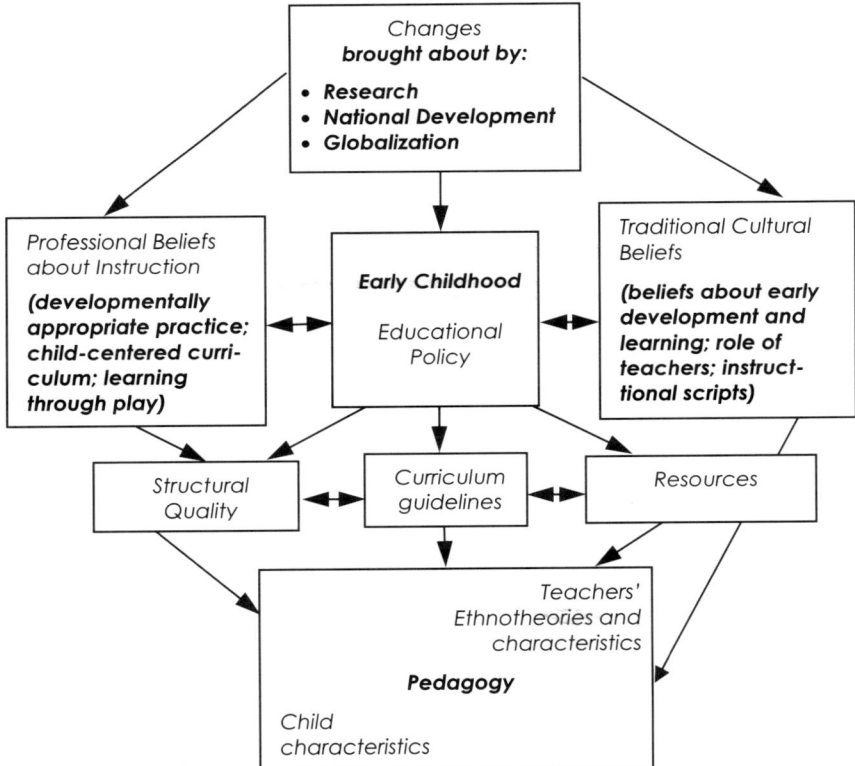

*Figure 9.1.* **Factors influencing kindergarten pedagogy**
*Source: Rao (2005)*

*Professional knowledge about early instruction*. The beliefs of early childhood professionals, such as notions about developmentally appropriate practice, child-centered curricula, and play-based learning have affected the classroom behaviors of kindergarten teachers all over the world. Indeed, teacher-training programs in Hong Kong reflect Western emphases upon child individuality, child-centeredness and learning through play. Kindergarten teachers in Hong Kong have expressed their concerns over the conflict between primary school entry requirements and the desire to become more child-centered in their teaching, but their actual behaviors often reflect Chinese traditional values and norms (Ng, 2005; Pearson & Rao, 2004).

*Educational policy*. Western political, economic and educational ideas and systems were introduced to Hong Kong during the British colonial rule, and Westernized pre-primary education first emerged in the mid-1800s. The demand for preschool education substantially increased after the influx of refugees from Mainland China in the 1940s. Between the 1950s and 1970s, the number of kindergarten places in Hong Kong rose from 13,000 in 1953 to 198,351 in 1979 (Rao & Koong, 2000). Although preschool provision increased, the number of qualified teachers markedly decreased and class sizes increased. Hence preschool quality was adversely affected. Many kindergartens introduced entrance examinations as a consequence of the high demand for preschool education. Parental concern over entry into primary schools advanced an orientation towards academic curricula into early childhood education. Large class sizes in kindergartens also led to a strong emphasis on discipline.

Despite its unofficial status in educational policy, preschool education in Hong Kong has been and continues to be closely aligned with primary schooling by both parents and teachers. Historically, Hong Kong's education system has been regarded as relatively didactic and geared primarily towards examination success (Biggs & Watkins, 1996). Pedagogical objectives at pre-primary level have therefore tended to focus on preparing children for the highly performance-oriented, structured learning environment that children experience at primary level. This is done by ensuring that children achieve formal literacy and numeracy skills through direct instruction. Indeed, preschool professionals have in the past expressed concern over the push-down effect of the primary school curriculum on both teaching and assessment methods in preschools (Chan & Chan, 2003) and the tendency for practitioners in kindergartens and nurseries to adopt formal teaching methods with children as young as 3 years of age (Opper, 1992; Sweeting & Ching, 1988).

Notwithstanding these concerns, preschool education forms a significant part of early childhood experience in Hong Kong, where almost all children are enrolled in some form of preschool provision. In 2006, as many as 140,783 children aged between three and six years were enrolled in 1015 kindergartens and kindergartens-cum-child care centers (Educational Bureau, 2008), and about 95 per cent of children between the ages of three and six years attend either kindergartens or child care centers (Rao et al, 2003). The extent of coverage reflects both government policy and the value that Chinese parents traditionally attach to early childhood education. The government does not provide free early education[1] and the responsibility for the provision of such services rests with private organizations. However, the government's fee remission scheme for needy parents ensures that no child is deprived of preschool education because of financial reasons.

*Preschool quality.* The authority to determine, monitor, and enforce standards in preschools rests with the government. The current standards reflect minimum criteria for the initial and continued registration of kindergartens: there are no independent accreditation bodies. However, while Hong Kong has very lax regulatory standards for the operation of preschools, policies and incentives are improving the quality of preschool education. Rao et al. (2003), found considerable variability in preschool quality, with higher quality evident in preschools which exceeded government requirements.

Adult-child ratios are a major indicator of preschool quality and the mandated teacher-child ratio has progressively become more favorable since the 1980s. The ratio is currently about 1:9.3 in kindergartens (Education Bureau, 2008). Group size and adult-child ratio have a significant influence on the type of activities which can take place in the amount of time teachers have to give individual attention to a child.

*Curriculum guidelines.* National governments have typically been reluctant to require kindergartens to rigidly follow a prescribed curriculum, and the same is true of the Hong Kong government. There are several reasons for this: a realization that a curriculum for preschools should be broad and holistic, individual differences in rates of early development, the emphasis on learning-through-play, and a belief that the young child should be an active participant in the learning process rather than a passive recipient of teacher-delivered knowledge. However, by necessity, many governments have issued broad curriculum guidelines for pre-school education. These have been provided to ensure that the preschool curriculum covers the major areas of development, that developmentally appropriate pedagogical practices are used, and that specified early learning standards are attained. Further, in Hong Kong, as in many other countries, preschool teachers have lower academic and professional qual-ifications than teachers in primary and secondary schools, and therefore guidelines are considered important.

The 1996 Guide to Pre-Primary Curriculum published by Hong Kong's Curriculum Development Institute followed a child-centered approach and stressed all-round development. It espoused contemporary views on effective early teaching and learning, and provided suggestions for facilitating intellectual, communicative, personal, physical and aesthetic development. In January 2006, the Curriculum Development Council released a Consultation Document containing a revised guide to the Pre-Primary Curriculum (Curriculum Development Council, 2006).

The Hong Kong government was concerned that some kinder-gartens went too far in presenting formal academic curricula, using in-appropriate teaching methods for children below the age of six. Hence, in 1999, the Hong Kong government (Education Department, 1999) published a list of 'Dos and Don'ts' for kindergartens. The list of 'Dos' included: having a curriculum that covered moral, cognitive, physical, social, and aesthetic aspects of development by organizing activities that promote all-round development; organizing various child-centered learning activities; using the mother-tongue as the language of instruction; and respecting individual differences. Good programs in any country include all these goals, but some are especially pertinent to Hong Kong idio-syncrasies. For example, Chinese culture emphasizes moral development, and it is recommended that the curriculum attends to this perspective.

The vast majority of Hong Kong's population speaks Cantonese as a first language, but parents also want their children to learn English. A common practice for teachers in Hong Kong is to use a mixed-code that combines Cantonese and English, but this presently results in poor standards in both languages. The document pointed out that a focus on separate language development can help to improve the situation. The list of 'Don'ts' also reflected the Hong Kong context: don't ask children in Nursery Class (aged three to four years) to write; don't ask children to do mechanical copying exercises; don't adopt a one-way, lecturing form of teaching; and don't design a curriculum which is too difficult. Yet while all kindergartens and child-care centers had access to the Guide, not all of them implemented its recommendations: less than satisfactory practices were evident in a small proportion of kindergartens (Rao, 2002).

*Educational reforms.* In the mid-1990s, the Hong Kong government undertook a comprehensive review of the education system with the intention of enhancing the overall quality of education services delivered. The first stage of this review, conducted in 1999, focused on the aims of education. The consultation document (Education Commission, 1999) stated that the aims of early childhood education should include helping children to (i) enjoy schooling and learning, and foster a sense of curiosity and interest in learning; (ii) experience a rich and pleasurable group life; (iii) achieve all-round child development; and (iv) develop self-confidence. After public consultation, these aims were adopted. The second stage of the review examined how the existing academic structure, the curricula, and the assessment mechanisms could be improved to meet the aims of education. The third stage culminated in the reform proposals issued by the Education Commission in September 2000. The proposals embraced the notions that early childhood education lays the foundation for lifelong learning and all-round development. The Commission put forward proposals to enhance the professional competence of early childhood educators, improve quality assurance, reform the monitoring mechanism, enhance the links between early childhood and primary education, and promote home-preschool co-operation (Education Commission, 2000). These reforms have either directly or indirectly positively affected preschool pedagogy in Hong Kong (Rao & Li, 2009).

The government appears to have focused largely on management in its identification of areas that are in need of reform. However, the role of teachers in implementing and sustaining these reforms is critical. Indeed, this government-initiated impetus for improvement at all levels of education has led to a widespread analysis of Hong Kong teachers and the extent to which the proposed reforms clash with their beliefs about education and classroom practices (Pearson & Rao, 2006). Teachers' culturally-defined beliefs about children's education may be equally (or more) potent in shaping children's educational experiences as educational policy (Pearson & Rao, 2004). The implications of this are significant with regard to evaluating implementation of the reforms, and whether or not the reforms are intended to change the culture of teaching and learning, or simply learning outcomes (Pearson & Rao, 2006). The following section discusses Chinese cultural beliefs about learning, and the section after that analyses the extent to which these and reform proposals relevant to early pedagogy are evident in classroom practice.

## Traditional Cultural Beliefs about Early Learning and Development

Of particular relevance to early pedagogy are cultural beliefs about learning as we assume that teachers' cultural beliefs (ethnotheories) about early development and learning will be reflected in their interactions with children. Research is increasingly describing children's learning and development through the lens of sociocultural theory which, as Robert Serpell (2002, p. 290) explains, offers an understanding of children and their learning based on a view of context as central to development, "as an incorporating system of social activities and cultural meanings, rather than an external physical world impacting the behavior and mental process of individuals". Each of the stakeholders involved in children's learning (teachers, parents and peers, to name but a few) will have experienced their own unique "developmental niche" (Harkness & Super, 1996), and those experiences, in turn, shape their approach to raising, teaching and socializing the children with whom they interact.

Sociocultural theory has contributed significantly to our understanding of the importance of social context and related implications for importing educational ideologies that do not fit with local cultures (Serpell, 2002). For example, Prochner (2002) has critiqued the adoption, in non-Western contexts, of approaches to early childhood education based on Western concepts, which tend to emphasize the development of children's autonomy and independence and may not reflect priorities of local parents and/or teachers. In Hong Kong, Chan and Chan's (2003) discussion of recent educational reforms examines childhood educators' tendency to resist downward pressure to reform, instead adopting the teacher-centered, academically oriented methods that are associated with primary schooling and that parents in this Confucian-heritage tend to feel more comfortable with.

The following section summarizes widely acknowledged characteristics of teaching and learning that reflect Chinese cultural beliefs. We then discuss four studies that have highlighted the implications of these characteristics in the light of recent educational reforms in Hong Kong.

*Teacher authority, training and discipline.* Kindergartens tend to have highly structured days. This is partly due to the children's age, but also a reflection of Chinese cultural beliefs about the early years being a time for training young children to be disciplined and to behave properly (Rao & Li, 2008; Rao, McHale, & Pearson, 2003). Chinese classrooms have been described as authoritarian (Biggs, 1996) and teachers typically maintain good classroom discipline (Cheng, 1996). Primary school children in Hong Kong have been described as being passive, dependent and obedient students, who conform to group norms and complete assigned tasks (Biggs, 1996; Ho, 1994). This characterization is also true of preschools in Hong Kong although there have been many child-friendly changes in the past decade (Rao, 2002).

Children are expected to be silent during large group teaching and individual work. Young students in Hong Kong are also required to keep the noise level at a minimum when they interact with one another during group work. Teachers' voices are typically clearly heard and classrooms are seldom "too noisy" (Ng, 2005).

*Emphasis on the acquisition of knowledge through memorization.* Children from Confucian-heritage cultures have been encouraged to memorize and practice cognitive skills (Liu, 1986). The traditional Chinese education and examination systems stressed the recitation of classical books and poems (Chan, 1996; Cheng, 1996), and traditional learning for beginners emphasized recounting the three classical texts[2]. Memorization is unavoidable in the learning of Chinese characters hence the habit is inculcated at an early age. As mentioned earlier (Rao & Chan, chap. 1, this volume), Western educators assume that rehearsal and repetition are less desirable than metacognitive strategies in promoting effective academic learning, but researchers working with East Asian learners have argued that the memorization shown by these learners is qualitatively different from mechanical or rote memorization, which is considered to be a lower level cognitive strategy (Gow, Balla, Kember, & Hau, 1996; Marton, Watkins, & Tang, 1997). This assertion is nicely illustrated by the popular Confucian proverb, "Read it one hundred times, and understanding will follow spontaneously" (cited in Hess & Azuma, 1991, p. 6) and supported by empirical research.

*Emphasis on effort.* Chinese tend to hold an incremental view of ability, believing that intelligence is not relatively fixed but can be improved by hard work (Cheng, 1996; Lee, 1996; Rao, McHale, & Pearson, 2003). A person has to be determined, persistent, humble, and be prepared to endure hardship. The exertion of effort and memorization are both considered precursors to success. In her interviews with Chinese kindergarten teachers in Hong Kong, Ng (2005) found that the teachers acknowledged the influence of intelligence on the speed of learning new mathematical concepts, but also stressed practice and diligence as the means to success in learning.

The following popular Chinese proverbs and idioms nicely illustrate cultural notions about child-rearing, discipline, early education and training. For example, these excerpts from the Three Character Classics [三字經] reflect the emphasis on shaping children and their behavior through formal education:

> *"Jade that has not been polished cannot be used. A person that has not studied cannot know righteousness."*

> *"Learn and constantly review/practice what you have learned.*
> *Recite it verbally; examine it with your heart. Do this in the morning; do this in the evening."*

Maintaining good classroom discipline has long been seen as a basic skill for Chinese teachers. Teachers represent authority and are expected to act as models of morality. They are assumed to be more knowledgeable than students and thus responsible for transmitting knowledge. More than that, strict teachers are praised because discipline is viewed as important in producing capable students:

> *"Though you have taught me for only one day, you will be my mentor all my life."*

> *"Capable students are brought up by strict teachers."*

# Current and Emerging Pedagogical
# Practices in Kindergartens

Using examples from four studies, the following section considers early childhood pedagogy in Hong Kong kindergartens, focusing on language and literacy, early number concepts and social development. It should be noted that kindergartens in Hong Kong have a highly structured schedule and children move from activity to activity according to a fairly rigidly followed timetable. This, along with the fact that children typically attend half-day sessions, limits time available for free play activities.

*Language and literacy*. As part of a larger study on early Chinese literacy development, Li and Rao (2005) observed classes for 3 and 4-year olds in three kindergartens and one child care centre in Hong Kong. The focus of the observation was the instructional strategies used by the teacher, and a running record was made of classroom events. An excerpt from the observations is presented below.

> *Teacher B3: Please put your hands on your knees and keep quiet. Look at the whiteboard.*
> *[The children became quiet and turned to the whiteboard. Some boys in the rear of the classroom were still chatting, and the teacher paused for several seconds to wait for them. They stopped talking and looked at the teacher.]*
>
> *Teacher B3: Look at this character, what is it? It is "faa1" [1] (flower).*
> *[The teacher read this new character and showed how to write it and directed children's attention to the placement and order of strokes. The teacher told a story about this character to make it memorable.]*
>
> *Teacher B3: Follow me, read it aloud, "faa1 (flower)! faa1 (flower)! faa1 (flower)!" [The students read it repeatedly, the whole class reading, alternating with individual turns. The reading was followed by a 15-minute period for writing the new characters they had just learned in the group session.]*
>
> (Li & Rao, 2005)

Several aspects of the above observation reflect the influence of traditional Chinese beliefs on both children's behavior and the method of instruction. Children were expected to sit properly, keep silent and behave well. Indeed, early behavioral and emotional control are considered prerequisites for learning in Chinese culture (Ho, 1994).

Children in this study were taught how to recognize and write Chinese characters, and, as is typical in Hong Kong, the teachers used explicit instruction. After instruction, the children had to practice writing what they had learned in class on worksheets (and they also had to copy characters for homework). This traditional drill-and-practice approach is typically used for the teaching of Chinese characters in primary schools in China (Wu, Li, & Anderson, 1999). However, it should be pointed out that, unlike in Hong Kong, the teaching of reading and writing is prohibited in kindergartens in Mainland China. This suggests that attempts can be made to adjust traditional practices through legislation and education.

Observations also suggest that research conducted in other parts of the world and teacher preparation have had an influence on early language teaching and learning in Hong Kong. For example, the concept of emergent literacy has had an important influence on pedagogy in kindergartens involved in this study. Early childhood centers were focused on providing literacy-rich environments and embracing "informal" skills that helped promote the more formal abilities of reading and writing commonly associated with literacy. In what is a significant shift for these kindergartens, children were read to, and encouraged to interact with books, and to share stories with their teachers. Enquiry-based approaches such as the Project Approach were also observed, and language and literacy activities were an important component of project work.

*Early mathematics instruction.* Ng's (2005) study investigated early mathematics teaching and learning at a time when educational reforms were starting to be implemented. She observed 6 preschool classes and 3 primary schools, each for 3 consecutive days, and interviewed teachers on their beliefs about mathematics teaching. She observed classes for 4-year-olds and classes for 5-year-olds in three different kindergartens, and because kindergartens teach "children" and not "subjects," she video-taped the full 3-hour-session in kindergartens. Mathematics was not taught as a distinct subject, but permeated through the curriculum.

Results indicated that mathematics instruction in kindergartens was integrated with various activities throughout the day, and addition concepts were taught through whole-class teaching, small-group teaching and daily routines. A new concept was usually introduced during whole-class or small-group teaching, and was related to themes or daily life experiences. Teachers used a variety of resources to enhance children's participation and to help them learn through direct manipulation of physical objects.

Children were encouraged to be active participants in the learning process, and continually interpret their own experiences through new information and hands-on and minds-on activities. However, at the same time, teachers emphasized proper procedures, and the importance of obtaining the correct answer. Paper-and-pencil exercises still formed an important part of the learning process. Teachers were not ready to develop a more flexible form of assessment in evaluating children's progress (Ng & Rao, 2005). In interviews, teachers reported that they had memorized facts as students, but they did not focus on mathematics facts in their own teaching. This suggests that contemporary views and reforms are influencing teaching. Teachers emphasized speed in calculation, effort, perseverance, proper behavior, self-control, and classroom discipline.

The results obtained from the study revealed a dynamic situation within teachers' mental constructs during the years of education reforms. Teachers, profoundly influenced by their own Chinese cultural ideas and their perception of parental expectations, were at the same time exposed to Western views through education reform propaganda or teacher-training courses. The convergence of Chinese cultural views and Euro-American views on learning was evident, as observed from both teachers' beliefs and practices. Chinese cultural influences were implicit, but Euro-American cultural influences were explicit and prevailing. Figure 9.2 presents the tensions between the two cultures. In recent years, teachers have been frequently exposed to new approaches to early childhood education as part of the educational reforms. Therefore, they were knowledgeable about the reform and they seemed to have a grasp of the basic tenets behind the early childhood reforms. These ideas were identifiable in interviews and in observations of classroom practice. However, there appeared to be a discrepancy between teachers' knowledge about how best to support early learning, and what was actually observed in the classroom. Their implicit cultural values and assessment methods resulted in teachers often using instructivist methods, and pushing children to practice mathematical concepts. At the same time, they were making efforts to espouse new Western pedagogies.

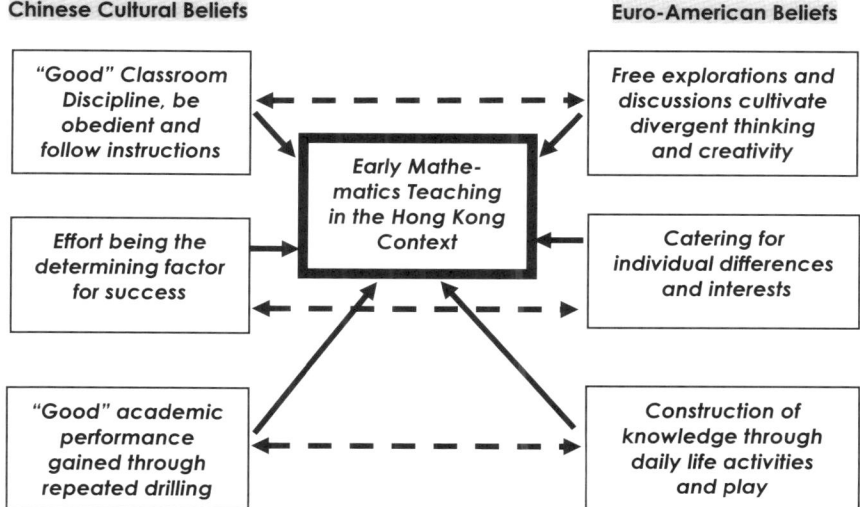

**Chinese Cultural Beliefs**

**Euro-American Beliefs**

"Good" Classroom Discipline, be obedient and follow instructions

Free explorations and discussions cultivate divergent thinking and creativity

Early Mathematics Teaching in the Hong Kong Context

Effort being the determining factor for success

Catering for individual differences and interests

"Good" academic performance gained through repeated drilling

Construction of knowledge through daily life activities and play

*Figure 9.2.* **The interplay of Chinese and Euro-American beliefs about teaching**

Observations suggested that teachers in some preschools are moving, albeit slowly, from an instructivist to a constructivist approach to teaching. Children are actively engaged in the learning process and meaning-making is encouraged. However, teachers' behaviors also reflected traditional beliefs. For example, they emphasized speed in calculation, effort, perseverance, proper behavior, self-control and classroom discipline.

*Social development.* As part of a wider study of cultural patterns of socialization, Pearson (2000) observed the influence of culturally-based socialization goals on the daily routines that exist in formal settings, catering to 4-6 year old children across cultures. She observed children in 3 classrooms in different preschools in Hong Kong. Her observations indicated widespread use of formal teaching strategies, with written and number work largely centered on worksheets. Most classroom activities were carried out in large groups, with all children involved in the same activity. In whole-class sessions, teachers introduced tasks, and children then sat down to work around their desks. Although children were focused and on-task, there was little further discussion of topics or tasks, and children were encouraged to produce a polished end-product, supervised by teachers, who pointed out mistakes to be erased and corrected. In one of the classrooms, children who completed their worksheet quickly were permitted to start their homework, reflecting an emphasis on "work" over "play." Children became active and chatted with each other once their work was complete (Pearson & Rao, 2004).

The teachers in Hong Kong involved in Pearson's study held professional views reflecting a child-centered approach towards children's education and development that is commonly associated with Western teaching ideals. Teacher-child interactions, teachers' choice of learning activities and the wider socialization experiences that children encountered daily however reflected values that are widely described as analogous with Chinese culture. Development of positive self-concept among children was associated with an orientation towards group identity as opposed to individuality, and establishment of a strong sense of identity with the school. For example, all children wore school-issued uniforms (including bag and snack utensils for children and teachers) as part of elaborate preparations for the school's annual musical performance, held in a local stadium. As Pearson and Rao (2004) suggest, although teachers' personal beliefs about children, their learning and development (in particular, beliefs related to cultural values) are more often than not implicit, their influence in shaping early childhood learning environments is pervasive.

Chen (2004) observed 40 children (including 21 girls), with a mean age of 52 months, enrolled in four kindergartens in Hong Kong. She based her conclusions on 235 hours of observations in preschools and 90 hours of individual interviews with children, conducted over a 10-month period. Her main finding was related to the role of peer group and teachers in the gender socialization process. During free play, girls tended to congregate in relatively stable, same-gender groups. Consistent with previous research, children showed preference for same gender play-mates and "gender-appropriate" toys by the end of the school year. However, teachers repeatedly enforced gender segregation. They asked boys and girls to line-up separately during transition times and often formed groups based on gender. Teachers behaved in ways that condoned certain behaviors in boys and not in girls. They also perpetuated gender stereotypes; for example, in role-play, boys were invited to be the doctor or fireman. In interviews, teachers revealed traditional Chinese beliefs about the roles of men and women in society.

Wu and Rao (2008) examined the role of free-play in early childhood programs in Hong Kong and found that children have relatively little time for free-play. She finds that play is a reward for finishing work sheets, and teachers do not guide children during free-play.

## Is There a Distinct Hong Kong Chinese Early Childhood Pedagogy?

What is reflected in classroom practice? Do observations reveal the influence of Chinese cultural belief systems, Educational Reforms, or the beliefs of Early Childhood professionals? Figure 9.1 shows some of the factors which affect pedagogy in kindergarten classes in Hong Kong. Research has influenced educational policy, curriculum guidelines, structural quality, and the beliefs of early childhood educators, while educational policy and cultural beliefs directly or indirectly influence kindergarten pedagogy. At the same time, the primary school curriculum and parent expectations for preschool education influence pedagogy.

*Classroom social environment.* Observations suggest that Chinese cultural beliefs are reflected in classroom practice in Hong Kong kindergartens. Classrooms in Confucian-heritage cultures emphasize conformity, discipline, behavioral control and academic achievement, and these characteristics were evident in teacher-child interactions (Ng & Rao, 2005; Pearson & Rao, 2004). An emphasis on practicing newly acquired skills was seen in language and mathematics classes.

Although it is important to note that all the children involved in the studies reported above (Chen, 2004; Li & Rao, 2005; Ng & Rao, 2005; Pearson & Rao, 2004) appeared to be happy in their kindergarten environment and enjoyed their experiences, the preschool classrooms described are very structured, with a clear emphasis on discipline and propriety. Nonetheless, there are claims that the emphasis on discipline and proper behavior based on the Confucian doctrine hampers the cultivation of independence and development of creativity (Murphy, 1987). There are also suggestions that teachers should not help children just to get the right answers, but rather should scaffold their learning, helping them to make progress by developing problem-solving strategies (Hatch, 1999). In the studies reported here, teachers' reflections on discussion, free explorations and inventing strategies did not appear to be reflected in their traditional classroom practices. A possible reason might be that teachers had their own image of a "desirable" classroom. The traditional Chinese classroom is well disciplined and children learn from teachers and get the "right" answer in prescribed ways. Teachers are responsible for imparting "correct knowledge" and children are expected to "receive" it without question (Ho, 1994). They do not appear actively to promote creativity, or innovative and independent thinking. This is consistent with findings in Hong Kong on the learning attitudes of students in the senior school years, who were perceived as passive (Curriculum Development Council, 1999), and tended to accept knowledge from the teacher without questioning (Murphy, 1987).

*Instructional approaches.* As mentioned above, research on early childhood teaching and learning has influenced educational policy, views of early childhood professionals, curriculum guidelines and, in turn, pedagogical practices. We see the influence of the educational re-form on classroom practice, in, for example, how teachers in Hong Kong do their best to get children actively involved in the learning process, and encourage children to construct meaning and knowledge. Pedagogical models developed in the West are commonly applied in preschools in Hong Kong, and instructional approaches based on the High Scope or Reggio Emilia[3] models have become very popular in Hong Kong in recent years (Rao, 2005). Over the past decade, there has been strong enthusiasm in Hong Kong for the Project Approach, a hallmark of the Reggio Emilia model, and it has the support of many preschool heads. However, observations of preschools indicate that in many classrooms, the Project Approach is used in a teacher-centered, rather than a child-centered way. This suggests that there can be a discrepancy between the tenets of an approach to education and the way in which that approach is actually implemented in preschools. The philosophical beliefs under-pinning these approaches or programs are quite different from the implicit traditional beliefs of Chinese culture, especially in aspects such as the roles, responsibilities and expectations of teachers and students (Wang & Mao, 1996).

Although kindergartens should not go beyond what is expected in the kindergarten curriculum guidelines, our observations and other research conducted in Hong Kong have identified a clear push-down effect of the primary school curriculum in the upper kindergarten classes. More formal and didactic methods are used to help children master more advanced concepts. Further, stakeholders such as parents often regard preschool as a preparation for primary schools, and often welcome an academic focus in kindergartens.

*Confluence of professional and cultural beliefs and practices.* Beliefs of early childhood professionals, such as notions of developmentally appropriate practice, child-centered curricula, and play-based learning, have affected the classroom behaviors of kindergarten teachers all over the world. The beliefs of early childhood educators in Hong Kong are greatly influenced by teacher-training. In 1994, the Hong Kong government took a major step by allocating HK$163 million exclusively to preschool teacher-training. Compared to 1994-1995, when only 23.6% of teachers had attained Qualified Kindergarten Teacher (QKT) status, 92.8% had QKT status by 2004-2005, indicating the government's commitment to improve the quality of preschool education. The Qualified Kindergarten Teacher (QKT) course is the benchmark for teacher-training in Hong Kong and is below the Certificate level. The Certificate in Kindergarten Education Course launched in 1995 is a benchmark only for kindergarten principals and since 2005, all newly appointed principals have a Certificate in Education.

Since teacher-training programs in Hong Kong reflect Western emphases upon child individuality, child-centeredness and learning through play, this has clearly affected teachers' professional beliefs about the form and goals of early childhood education. Kindergarten teachers in Hong Kong have expressed their concern over the conflict between primary school entry requirements and the desire to become more child-centered in their teaching, but their actual behaviors often reflect Chinese traditional values and norms (Ng & Rao, 2008; Pearson & Rao, 2004).

The findings reported here suggest that the concept of child-centered learning constitutes a major part of teachers' reflections on children's learning, and that attempts are being made to implement recommendations made in official document guides. However, it appears that this approach is being implemented in an environment that reflects traditional Chinese beliefs about children and their education. For example, much of the time of the children involved in these studies was spent engaging in activities that were arranged by the teacher, who was often an active participant. There was less time allocated to free play, where children could pursue their own interests. The highly structured day is partly due to the children's age, but also a reflection of Chinese cultural beliefs about the early years being a time for training young children (Rao, McHale, & Pearson, 2003).

In the teaching of literacy and numeracy, preschool teachers were using both instructivist and constructivist approaches. In mathematics, there was a focus on computing with real objects, drawing pictures, and relating mathematics concepts to children's daily lives. Observations also showed that many preschools subscribed to an emergent literacy approach as opposed to reading readiness.

Not surprisingly, Chinese classrooms have been changing and they appear to be less authoritarian and more student-centered than in the past (Biggs, 1994). Preschool classrooms have also changed over recent decades. Children are still expected to be obedient, quiet and complete all assigned tasks, but the nature of their learning tasks is different. Children are now engaged in activities and projects that are more enjoyable and engaging for them. Children seem motivated to engage in such learning activities. Despite the emphasis on discipline, the classroom atmosphere tends to be friendly and warm, with numerous interactions between teachers and children, and among children.

Early childhood education in China has been characterized as a hybrid of traditional Chinese, Western and communist cultures (Wang & Spodek, 2000). Is there a distinct Hong Kong Chinese early childhood pedagogy? It appears so. Western educational reform ideas are evident in pedagogy, while characteristics of Confucian-heritage cultures continue to dominate the social milieu of the classroom, therein interweaving Chinese traditional views and Western ideas about early learning. Hong Kong is currently in a transition phase in terms of early teaching and learning approaches. Kindergartens are certainly more child-centered now than they were a decade ago. Teachers also wish to be more child-centered in their teaching. However, limitations in teachers' professional qualifications, and pressure from parents' expectations, as well as difficulties in reconciling Western theories with inherent cultural beliefs about children's behavior, have hampered the speed at which they can move towards even more child-friendly practices. Given the highly structured preschool environment in Hong Kong, moving toward child-friendly pedagogy needs continued efforts in supporting teachers through this transition, and informing stakeholders through provision of preschool curriculum guidelines and effective school management committees.

# REFERENCES

Biggs, J. B. (1994). Student learning research and theory – where do we currently stand? In G. Gibbs (Ed.), *Improving student learning: Theory and practice* (pp. 1-19). Oxford, U.K.: Oxford Centre for Staff Development.

Biggs, J. B. (1996). Learning, schooling, and socialization: A Chinese solution to a western problem. In S. Lau (Ed.), *Growing up the Chinese way: Chinese child and adolescent development* (pp. 147-167). Hong Kong: The Chinese University Press.

Biggs, J. B., & Watkins, D. A. (1996). The Chinese Learner in retrospect. In D. A. Watkins & J. B. Biggs (Eds.), *The Chinese Learner: Cultural, psychological and contextual influences* (pp. 269-285). Hong Kong/Melbourne: Comparative Education Research Centre, The University of Hong Kong/Australian Council for Educational Research.

Chan, J. (1996). Chinese intelligence. In M. H. Bond (Ed.). *The handbook of Chinese psychology* (pp. 93-108). Hong Kong: Oxford University Press.

Chan, L. K. S., & Chan, L. (2002). Reforming early childhood education in Hong Kong: Meeting the challenges. In L. K. S. Chan & Mellor, E. J. (Eds.), *International developments in early childhood services* (pp. 81-117). New York: Peter Lang Publishing, Inc.

Chan, L. K. S., & Chan, L. (2003). Early childhood education in Hong Kong and its challenges. *Early Child Development and Care, 173,* 7-17.

Chen, E. S. L. (2004, July). *Gender socialization of preschool children: Observations from kindergartens.* Poster presented at the 18th biennial meeting of the International Society for the Study of Behavioral Development (ISSBD), Ghent, Belgium.

Cheng, K. M. (1996). *The quality of primary education: A case study of Zhejiang Province, China.* Paris: International Institute for Educational Planning.

Curriculum Development Council. (1999). *Report on holistic review of the mathematics curriculum.* Retrieved November 2, 1999, from http://cd.ed.gov.hk/kla/kla.asp?subject=math

Curriculum Development Council. (2006). *Guide to the pre-primary curriculum (Consultation).* Retrieved April 10, 2006 from http://www.emb.gov.hk/FileManager/EN/Content_4728/ guide_pre-primary_curriculum.pdf

Curriculum Development Institute. (1996). *Guide to the pre-primary curriculum.* Hong Kong: Author.

Education Bureau. (2008). *Kindergarten Education.* Retrieved January 22, 2009 from http://www.edb.gov.hk/index.aspx?langno=1&nodeID=1037

Education Commission. (1999). *Education blueprint for the 21st century – Review of academic system: Aims of education.* Hong Kong: Author.

Education Commission. (2000). *Learning for life learning through life: Reform proposals for the education system in Hong Kong.* Hong Kong: Author.

Education Department (1999). *List of Do's and Don'ts for Kindergartens* (Schools Curriculum Circular No. 4/99). Hong Kong: Author.

Gow, L., Balla, J., Kember, D., & Hau, K. T. (1996). The learning approaches of Chinese people: A function of socialization processes and the context of learning? In M. H. Bond (Ed.), *The handbook of Chinese psychology* (pp. 109-123). Hong Kong: Oxford University Press.

Harkness, S., & Super, C. M. (1996). *Parents' cultural belief systems: Their origins, expressions and consequences.* New York: The Guilford Press.

Hatch, G. (1999). Maximizing energy in the learning of mathematics. In C. Hoyles, C. Morgan & G. Woodhouse (Eds.), *Rethinking the mathematics curriculum* (pp. 104-117). London: Falmer Press.

Heckman, J. J. (2004). Invest in the very young. In R. E. Tremblay, R. G. Barr & R. DeV. Peters (Eds.), *Encyclopedia on early child development* [Electronic version]. Montreal, Quebec: Centre for Excellence for Early Child Development. Retrieved November 11, 2005 from http://www.excellence-earlychildhood.ca/documents/HeckmanANG.pdf

Hess, R. D., & Azuma, H. (1991). Cultural support for schooling: Contrasts between Japan and the United States. *Educational Researcher, 20*(9), 2-12.

Ho, D. Y. F. (1994). Cognitive Socialization in Confucian-heritage cultures. In P. Greenfield & R. Cocking (Eds.), *Cross cultural roots of minority child development.* Hillsdale, NJ: Lawrence Erlbaum Associates.

Lee, W. O. (1996). The culture context for Chinese Learners: Conceptions of learning in the Confucian tradition. In D. A. Watkins & J. B. Biggs (Eds.), *The Chinese Learners: Cultural psychological and contextual influences* (pp. 25-41). Hong Kong/Melbourne: Comparative Education Research Centre, The University of Hong Kong/Australian Council for Educational Research.

Li, H., & Rao, N. (2005). Influences on early literacy attainment: Evidence from Beijing, Hong Kong and Singapore. *International Journal of Early Years Education, 13*, 235-253.

Liu, I. M. (1986). Chinese cognition. In M. H. Bond (Ed.), *The psychology of the Chinese people.* Hong Kong: Oxford University Press.

Lynch, R. (2004). *Exceptional returns: Economic, fiscal and social benefits of investment in early childhood development.* Washington, DC: Economic Policy Institute.

Marton, F., Watkins, D. A., & Tang, C. (1997). Discontinuities and continuities in the experience of learning: An interview study of high-school students in Hong Kong. *Learning and Instruction, 7*, 21-48.

Murphy, D. (1987). Offshore education: A Hong Kong perspective. *Australian Universities Review, 30*(2), 43-44. London: Falmer Press.

Ng, S. S. N. (2005). *Early mathematics teaching and learning: Contextual differences in the pre-primary and early primary years*. Unpublished doctoral dissertation, The University of Hong Kong, Hong Kong.

Ng, S. S. N., & Rao, N. (2005). Teaching mathematics in Hong Kong: A comparison between the pre-primary and early primary years. *Hong Kong Journal of Early Childhood*, 4(1), 30-36.

Ng, S. S. N., & Rao, N. (2008). Mathematics teaching during the early years in Hong Kong: A reflection of constructivism with Chinese characteristics? *Early Years: An International Journal of Research and Development, 28*, 159-172.

Opper, S. (1992). *Hong Kong's young children: Their preschools and families*. Hong Kong: Hong Kong University Press.

Opper, S. (1996). *Hong Kong's young children: Their early development and learning*. Hong Kong: Hong Kong University Press.

Pearson, E. C. (2000). *Cultural antecedents of peer competence in preschoolers: A study of the "custom complexes" of teachers and parents in Hong Kong and the United Kingdom*. Unpublished doctoral dissertation, The University of Hong Kong, Hong Kong.

Pearson, E. C., & Rao, N. (2004, July). *An observational study of custom complexes among preschool teachers in Hong Kong and the UK*. Paper presented at the 18th biennial meeting of the International Society for the Study of Behavioral Development (ISSBD), Ghent, Belgium.

Pearson, E. C., & Rao, N. (2006). Early childhood education policy reform in Hong Kong: Challenges in effecting change in practices. *Childhood Education, 82*, 363-368.

Prochner, L. (2002). Preschool and playway in India. *Childhood, 9*, 435-453.

Rao, N. (2002). Early childhood education in Hong Kong: Moving towards child-friendly policies, curricula and practices. In V. Sollars (Ed.), *Curricula, policies & practices in early childhood education services* (pp. 76-88). Malta: P.E.G.

Rao, N. (2005). *Factors influencing kindergarten pedagogy in Hong Kong*. Unpublished Manuscript, The University of Hong Kong.

Rao, N. (2006). SARS, preschool routines and children's behavior: A survey of preschools in Hong Kong. *International Journal of Early Childhood, 38*(2), 11-22.

Rao, N., & Koong M. (2000). Enhancing preschool education in Hong Kong. *International Journal of Early Childhood, 32*(2), 1-11.

Rao, N., & Koong, M., Kwong, M., & Wong, M. (2003). Predictors of preschool process quality in a Chinese context. *Early Childhood Research Quarterly, 18*, 331-350.

Rao, N., & Li, H. (2008). "Eduplay": Beliefs and practices related to play and learning in Chinese kindergartens. In I. Pramling Samuelsson & M. Fleer,

(Eds.), Play and learning in early childhood settings: International perspectives (pp. 73-92). Dordrecht, London: Springer Academic Publishers.

Rao, N., & Li, H. (2009). Quality matters: Early childhood education policy in Hong Kong. *Early Child Development and Care, 179,* 233-245.

Rao, N., McHale, J. P., & Pearson, E. C. (2003). Links between socialization goals and child-rearing practices in Chinese and Indian mothers. *Infant and Child Development, 12,* 475-492.

Serpell, R. (2002). The embeddedness of human development within sociocultural context: Pedagogical and political implications. *Social Development, 11,* 290-295.

Shonkoff, J. P., & Phillips, D. A. (2000). *From neurons to neighborhoods: The science of early childhood development.* Washington, DC: National Academy Press.

Sweeting, T., & Ching, S. (1988). *The marriage of Chinese cultural tradition with modern kindergarten practice in Hong Kong: A question of compatibility* (Occasional paper). Hong Kong: The University of Hong Kong.

Trawick-Smith, J. (2006). *Early childhood development: A multicultural perspective* (4th ed.). Upper Saddle River, NJ: Pearson Prentice Hall.

Wang, J., & Mao, S. (1996). Culture and kindergarten curriculum in the People's Republic of China. *Early Development and Care, 123,* 143-156

Wang, X. C., & Spodek, B. (2000). *Early childhood education in China: A hybrid of traditional, communist, and western culture.* Paper presented at the annual meeting of the National Association of Young Children, Atlanta. GA.

Wong, N. C. M., & Rao, N. (2004). Preschool education. In M. Bray & R. Koo (Eds.), *Education and society in Hong Kong and Macau: Comparative perspectives on continuity and change* (pp. 15-34). Hong Kong/ Dordrecht, The Netherlands: The University of Hong Kong, Comparative Education Research Centre/Kluwer Academic Publishers.

Wu, S. C., & Rao, N. (2008, July). *Play and learning in Hong Kong and German kindergartens.* Poster presented at the 20th biennial meeting of the International Society for the Study of Behavioral Development (ISSBD), Wurzburg, Germany.

Wu, X. C., Li, W. L., & Anderson, R. C. (1999). Reading instruction in China. *Curriculum Studies, 31,* 571-586.

## Endnotes

[1] Since September 2007, the government has been operating a preschool voucher scheme.

<sup>2</sup> The three classic books are the "Three Character Classics"[三字經], "Book of One Hundred Surnames"[百家姓] and "Essay of a Thousand Characters" [千字文].

<sup>3</sup> Reggio Emilia is a town in Northern Italy which has gained international recognition for its early childhood programs. High Scope is a preschool curriculum approach initially developed for Head Start children in the United States.

## *Author's Note*

This chapter is based on a keynote presentation made at the OMEP China International Conference, Chinese Culture and Early Childhood Education, September, 2005, Hang Zhou, China by the first author. A Chinese version of that presentation was published as a book chapter in 2007.

# 10

# In Search of a Third Space: Teacher Development in Mainland China

*Amy B.M. Tsui and Jocelyn L.N. Wong*

## Introduction

The system and structure of teacher education in Mainland China (hereafter referred to as China) were modeled on those of the former Soviet Union. The Soviet system was based on the commune model with an emphasis on collective effort in enhancing school-based teachers' professional development (Yang & Wu, 1999). The Soviet model was adopted by China in the early 1950s to deal with the large number of untrained teachers who had been recruited to teach in schools due to a serious shortage of teachers (Xie, 2001). Teaching and Research Groups were set up in schools with two major tasks: to learn how to conduct a good lesson and to learn the educational theory expounded by Ivan Andreyevich Kairov, the then Deputy Minister of Education of the former Soviet Union. Every teacher was required to teach a good lesson and to demonstrate an understanding of the theoretical underpinnings of good instruction. This then became the patterned practice of the teaching profession in China.

The powerful learning that took place when teachers' learning was situated in the contexts of their work led to the continuation of the model. Consequently, schools have become the prime site of professional learning for teachers in China (Lin & Cheng, 2004; Ma, 1992; Paine & Ma, 1993). As Ma (1992) has observed, obtaining a professional qualification from a teacher education institution (referred to as "normal colleges" or "universities" in China) is only the beginning of a teacher's professional development; much of the learning about the work of a teacher takes place in the workplace. Hence, participating in learning activities has become an integral part of the daily practice of teachers. This distinguishes teachers' professional development (TPD) activities in China from those found in most other parts of world.

Over the years, a number of teacher development practices have emerged in China, many of which have become standard practice, for example, "lesson research" (*keyan*) [課研], which includes collective lesson preparation, lesson observation, and post-observation conferencing; "open lessons" (*gongkaike*) [公開課], which are demonstration lessons; and one-on-one "the old guiding the young" mentoring practice (*lao dai qing*) [老帶青]. Since the implementation of the economic "open door" policy in the early 1980s, Chinese education has been receptive to Western influences. However, rather than simply grafting Western strategies onto Chinese practices, some educational leaders in China have emphasized that ideas borrowed from the West must be firmly rooted in Chinese educational traditions and philosophies and in the situated experience of teachers. Gu Ling Yuan, a renowned professor of mathematics education and teacher education, uses the metaphor of "middle ground" (*zhongjian didai*) [中間地帶] to refer to the space in which East meets West (see Gu, Nie, & Yi, 2002), and suggests that it is a space in which rich mutual learning takes place and a space that needs to be created.

This chapter analyzes data collected from a study of TPD activities conducted by the Shanghai Academy of Educational Sciences in collaboration with the district Teaching Research Office (TRO) of Shanghai and a number of schools. It adopts the concept of the "third space" (Bhabha, 1994, p. 53; Gutiérrez, Baquedano-López, & Tejeda, 1999), also referred to by activity theorists as the "boundary zone," that can be found when two activity systems interact (Konkola, 2001, cited in Tuomi-Gröhn, Engeström, & Young, 2003). The TRO in Shanghai was chosen as a case study because of its outstanding work with teachers, which has made an impact on a number of schools in Shanghai. Successful experiences of this work in schools have been widely reported and acclaimed in China, and have led to the publication of two books and journal articles by a number of the teachers and TRO personnel involved (Gu, 2003; Gu et al., 2002). This chapter explores how, in the third space, Chinese conceptions of teaching and learning have guided educational leaders and practitioners as they encounter ideas and practices from the West, and how new forms of TPD have been created as they reconceptualize Western practices for the enhancement of teaching and learning in Chinese classrooms.

The data used in this chapter consist of four narrative interviews, totaling 7.5 hours, with Gu Ling Yuan, Deputy Director of the Shanghai Academy of Educational Sciences and the winner of numerous Outstanding Teacher Awards. Gu and his philosophy of teaching were selected for study because he has been one of the most influential figures in teacher education and mathematics education in China in the last few decades. His proposed "action education" (*xingdong jiaoyu*) [行動教育], (enactment-based learning) discussed in this chapter has been promulgated by the Ministry of Education and widely adopted in China. In recognition of his contribution to education, he was awarded the National Award in Education in China in 2006. This is a prestigious award given to the most outstanding professional in each of eight professions.

The interviews with Gu focused on the following: 1) The prevalent teachers' professional development (TPD) activities and models in China and their underlying philosophies, 2) Aspects of these activities and models that have undergone changes and why, and 3) What and how research in the West or other parts of world has been drawn on by him and his team. On the basis of the interviews with Gu, interviews with teachers working under his guidance were also conducted. Gu's explication of the TPD activities and the rationale for and implementation of enactment-based education, *xingdong jiaoyu* [行動教育] was triangulated with the teachers' understanding of these activities and their classroom implementation. Three group interviews of five hours in total were conducted with seven teachers working in five different schools in the outskirts of Shanghai under the guidance of Gu (the aspects covered in the interview questions are presented in a later section).

In the ensuing discussion, we briefly introduce the concept of the "third space" in which the TPD work conducted by Gu is framed and outline the professional learning of teachers in China, focusing on the organization of TPD activities and the philosophies of education that underpin these activities. This is followed by a discussion of the recent development in teacher learning modes referred to as *xingdong jiaoyu* [行動教育] (literally translated as "action education" and semantically translated is "enactment-based education"). *Xingdong jiaoyu* was adapted from a case-based methodology of teacher education developed in the United States but given local meaning and vitality as it was enacted among Chinese teachers and theorized within the framework of Chinese educational philosophy.

# The Third Space

The notion of the "third space" was proposed by Homi Bhabha in his work on culture and identity. According to Bhabha, third spaces are "discursive sites or conditions that ensure that the meaning and symbols of culture have no primordial unity or fixity; that even the same signs can be appropriated, translated, and re-historicized anew" (Bhabha, 1994, p. 37). This notion has been adopted in diverse contexts and assigned different meanings. Nonetheless, there is a common understanding that it involves an encounter of two or more perspectives, often entailing conflicts and debates, which opens up a third space in which new ways of thinking, being, and acting are conceived. This conception of the third space resonates with social theories of learning that point out that the interaction between communities of practice can be a source of deep learning because it compels participants to take a fresh look at their long-standing practices and assumptions. Wenger, McDermott, and Snyder (2002) note that "while the core of a practice is a locus of expertise, radically new insights and developments often arise at the boundaries between communities" (p. 153). Similarly, activity theorists observe that when two activity systems interact, the shared space has the richest potential for generating new activities that can lead to a transformation of the activity system itself (Engeström, 2001; Engeström, Engeström, & Kärkkäinen, 1995; Konkola, 2001, cited in Tuomi-Gröhn et al., 2003). The term "boundary zone" has been proposed to describe a place where elements from both activity systems are present (Konkola, 2001, cited in Tuomi-Gröhn et al., 2003). As such, a boundary zone is characterized by alternative or competing discourses and points of view that afford opportunities for the transformation of conflicts and tensions into rich zones of learning (Engeström, 1999, 2001).

It must be pointed out, however, that the opening up of a rich zone of learning in a third space when communities or activity systems interact is not something that can be assumed. This is because the interaction could lead to the domination of one perspective or activity system over another. Such domination could be externally or internally driven, or both. This space is something that needs to be searched for.

# Teachers' Professional Learning in China

*Enabling Structures: Jiaoyanshi, Jiaoyanzu, and Jiaoyanyuan [教研室、教研組及教研員]*

In China, TPD activities are organized systematically through the support of Teaching and Research Groups (TRGs, *jiaoyanzu*) [教研組] in schools. Within these groups are collective Lesson Preparation Groups (LPGs, *beikezu*) [備課組]. Both TRGs and LPGs are subject based, and are in turn supported by Teaching Research Officers (TR Officers, *jiaoyanyuan*) [教研員] for each subject area from the Teaching Research Offices (TROs, *jiaoyanshi*) [教研室]. TROs are established under government education departments at the district/county and provincial/municipal levels. The key functions of these bodies are to help teachers to understand the standardized curriculum framework and materials, and to provide pedagogical support to school teachers through the school TRGs in their respective districts or counties (Guo, 2005). TROs liaise with other educational institutions to organize in-service TPD activities for subject teachers. In recent years, TROs have set up learning networks to enable TRGs from a number of schools to collaborate on the improvement of teaching and learning. Running parallel with the TROs are the Academies of Educational Sciences, which also come under the Education Departments at various levels. These Academies focus on teaching and educational research, whereas the TROs focus on classroom teaching. As can be seen from the work of Gu reported in this chapter, there are synergies between these bodies. Figure 10.1 shows the hierarchical structure of the teaching research bodies in China.

TRGs organize activities relating to aspects of the subject curriculum, that is, content, pedagogy and assessment, including collective lesson preparation, lesson observations and post-observation conferencing, curriculum planning, and Open Lessons. These groups are also responsible for mentoring novice teachers. In each TRG, there are "backbone" (*gugan*) [骨幹] teachers whose professional authority is not based on their official positions in their schools but on their teaching expertise; they are models of excellent teaching.

The activities organized by TRGs provide a platform for teachers to discuss and reflect on their teaching and to learn from good practices in their subject area. Given that teachers may not have an adequate under-

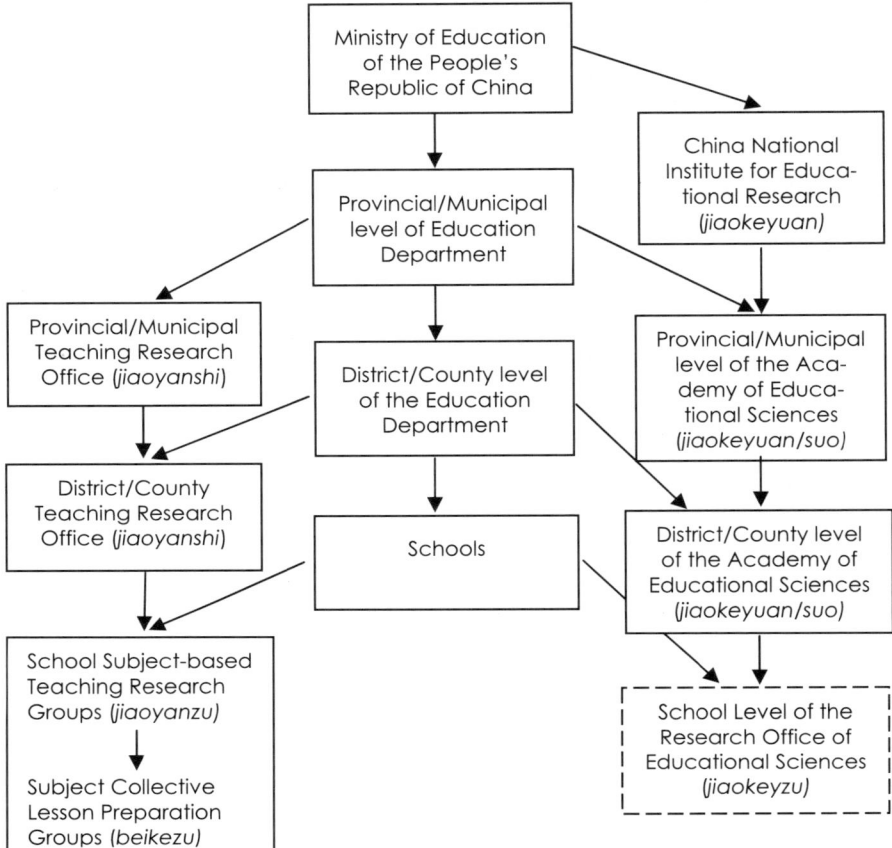

⟶ Denotes the bureaucratic structure of the teaching research bodies.

⌐ ⌐ Denotes a non-regular office in schools found in some key point
⌐ ⌐ schools.

*Figure 10.1.* **Hierarchical structure of the teaching research bodies
in China**

standing of the theoretical motivation behind their classroom instruction,
TR Officers are attached to schools and they participate regularly in TRG
learning activities. These Officers are recruited from among backbone
teachers in schools who have achieved outstanding performance in Open
Lessons or teaching competitions, have conducted research on teaching,

and have published research papers. In recent years, the number of TR Officers who have obtained doctoral degrees has steadily increased. TR Officers play a key role in providing leadership through regular participation in TPD activities in schools, and especially in lesson preparation, lesson observation, and post-lesson conferencing. They also offer Open Lessons to demonstrate effective pedagogical practices. In other words, their work is deeply rooted in classroom practices.

Apart from that, they also conduct research on issues that are directly related to teachers' needs, such as action research on specific learner difficulties (Dai, 2005). As such, they are not outside experts, but rather members of the communities of practice in their respective schools. At the same time, they also bring new ideas and practices to these communities. They are, in Wenger's term, "boundary brokers" (Wenger, 1998). It is significant that although TRGs are not administrative structures and do not have decision-making powers in relation to school management and policy, they play a critical role in transforming pedagogical practices in schools.

## The Apprenticeship Model

In China, the model adopted for TPD has been referred to as "the old guiding the young" (*lao dai qing*) [老帶青]. "Old" and "young" refer to experience rather than age, although the two are not unrelated. Each new teacher is assigned a mentor who is a backbone teacher in the school within the same lesson preparation group in order to provide daily support to him or her in terms of pedagogical skills and subject matter knowledge. In addition, the whole TRG to which he or she is assigned provides support through a series of regular learning activities. The performance of a subject teacher is often attributed to the support given by his or her TRG (Guo, 1999, 2005; Hu, 2005; Ma, 1992).

The word *"dai"* [帶] (guide) connotes an apprenticeship model in which novice teachers receive close guidance from their mentors on a one-to-one basis on all aspects of their work as a teacher. They observe their mentors in action in the classroom and are in turn observed by their mentors, from whom they receive critical feedback and specific suggestions for improvement. Mentoring practice in China is rooted in subject matter knowledge and pedagogical content knowledge. Compared with their counterparts in the United States and the United Kingdom, mentors in China are more concerned about scaffolding novice teachers' development of a deep understanding of subject matter knowledge and instructional strategies. The aim is to better help students understand the main ideas and concepts and the linkages between the key concepts in a particular subject domain (Wang, 2001). Novice teachers also receive more specific, critical, and subject-focused feedback from their mentors than their U.S. counterparts (Wang, Strong, & Odell, 2004). These scaffolding mechanisms help novice teachers to resolve the problems of having insufficient knowledge about "how" to teach, "what" to teach, and "why" (Ma, 1992, p. 13). Typically, novice teachers are given a lighter teaching load and limited responsibilities to ensure that there is room for them to learn the ropes.

This model of TPD resonates with the apprenticeship model expounded by Lave and Wenger (1991), which provides for "legitimate peripheral participation." As Lave and Wenger point out, it is a powerful form of learning because the participation in practice by novices whose performance necessarily falls short of the competence expected of "old-timers" is legitimated through an official reduction in their teaching load, membership of the TRGs, and the authority of the mentor assigned to them. The limited allocation of responsibilities to novice teachers allows them time to reflect on and make sense of practice through interacting with other members of the learning community.

## The Virtuoso Model

As mentioned in the preceding discussion, teachers' professional learning in China gives central importance to subject matter knowledge and pedagogical content knowledge (Shulman, 1986). Having in-depth disciplinary knowledge is perceived as the foundation of good teaching: teachers are expected to possess a deep understanding of the subjects that they teach and to perform as experts in the classroom. A commonly cited saying among teachers in China is "to give your students a glass of water, you need to have a pail of water."

The model of teaching that is advocated in China is described by Gu as *"you ceng ci tui jin"* [有層次推進] meaning "moving forward with well-sequenced guidance." A great deal of importance is attached to the careful planning of the scaffolding to be provided to students, on the basis of a deep understanding of the subject matter. Hence, in collective lesson preparation, the first and foremost task for teachers is to identify three elements of a topic: the knowledge point (*zhishi dian*) [知識點], the key point (*zhong dian*) [重點], and the difficult point (*nan dian*) [難點]. This means that teachers need to explicitly spell out the aspects of the topic or concepts that students need to learn, the key aspects or concepts in the topic, and the aspects or concepts that students find most difficult. Once these have been established, the lesson is carefully planned, with every step choreographed under the guidance of mentors, TR Officers, and master teachers. The lesson will be taught numerous times, critiqued, and modified until it becomes almost like a standard piece in a performance that will be practiced and rehearsed again and again until the teaching becomes automatic (see also Paine, 1990). Some topics, such as the teaching of Pythagoras' Theorem (referred to as *gougu dinglu*, [勾股定律]) in mathematics, have undergone as long as twenty years of choreographing.

To help teachers to attain an expert level of performance, teaching demonstrations and competitions are held at the school, district, provincial, and national levels. These teaching demonstrations are referred to as Open Lessons, meaning that the lessons are open to a wider audience than just teachers of the same subject or from the same school. In general, each teacher is required to conduct at least one school-level Open Lesson a year. Each Open Lesson is organized by the individual TRG in a school, and is guided by the TRO(s) attached to it. Open Lessons are organized around specific topics or issues in teaching. In nearly all schools, there are one or more special classrooms for conducting these lessons that are bigger than a normal classroom and have rows of seats at the back to accommodate up to 100 observers. After each Open Lesson, a post-observation discussion is conducted. In recent years, a new element has been added to the Open Lesson procedures, with teachers also being required to talk about the lesson first (referred to as *shuoke* [說課]) before they start the lesson. The aim of this element was initially technical in nature; to help the audience better understand the context of the lesson and the rationale behind the strategies adopted in the Open Lesson. However, the interviews with the teachers in this study revealed that in the course of preparing for *shuoke*, they clarified their thinking about their pedagogical actions. In other words, it helped them to make their tacit knowledge of teaching explicit.

This model of teacher learning, which is practiced in all schools, has proved to be very effective. As noted in Chapter 1, Ma's (1999) comparative study of mathematics teaching in schools in China and the United States shows that the quality of learning in the former is considerably higher because the Chinese teachers have a profound understanding of mathematics knowledge. This is achieved through intensive study of the teaching materials, including the curriculum framework, textbooks and teachers' manuals, in order to understand the "what" and the "how" of teaching. It is also achieved through the careful choreographing of lessons, which enhances the teachers' own understanding of the subject matter as well as how best to help students to engage in deep learning. The sharing among teachers during the collective lesson preparation, lesson observations, and Open Lessons provides a reflective and inspiring context for learning for both novice and experienced teachers (Wang & Paine, 2003).

## Chinese Philosophies of Education in Models of Teachers' Professional Development

In the preceding discussion, we outlined the characteristics of the primary models of teachers' professional learning in China, namely the apprenticeship model and the virtuoso model. In this section, we report on the Chinese philosophies of teaching and learning that underlie these models and that have shaped the conceptions of teacher learning, as revealed in our interviews with Gu and to a lesser extent with the teachers.

### Dialectics of Learning and Doing

Learning (*xue*) [學] is given centre stage in Confucian thinking. Love of learning distinguishes the superior man (*junzi*) [君子] from the small man (*xiaoren*) [小人]. The word "learn" in Chinese consists of two characters, [學] (*xue*) "learn" and [習] (*xi*) "trying it out." In our interviews with Gu, he presented the following diagram (Figure 10.2) that shows the classical written form of the two characters (Gu, 2003, p. 276).

   The first character is made up of two constituent components. The upper component [ʡ×ʡ] signifies two hands on each side holding two crosses in the middle. These two crosses stand for documentation, or the straws used for calculation, and signify knowledge that has been documented. Taken together, this constituent component therefore means that knowledge will be passed down from generation to generation. The lower constituent component [⌐||⌐] symbolizes a roof supported by two pillars, which stands for a building where knowledge is passed on. The other character [習] (*xi*) means to try things out, to experience. The meaning of this character, as explained in the "Classical Poetics" (*Shijing*) [詩經], also consists of two constituent components. The lower component [⊌] signifies a bird's nest. The upper constituent [ヲヲ] symbolizes a pair of wings of a newborn eagle. The two components taken together signify a baby eagle trying to fly away from the nest on its own (cf. *Zhu Xi*'s reading in Gardner, 2003, p. 31). Hence, there are two parts to learning. One is to receive knowledge that is passed down, and the other is to be able to experience it and to put it into action (Gu, 2003, p. 276). The meaning of *xue xi* is elaborated in *The Analects of Confucius* (*Lunyu*) [論語], in which Confucius said, "Is it not a pleasure, having learned something, to try it out at due intervals?"[1] (Confucius, translated by Lau, 1979, p. 3).

*Figure 10.2.* Ancient Chinese characters for "learn" (xue xi)

From this exposition by Gu, we can see that there are two parts to learning. One part is to acquire declarative or "formal knowledge" (Bereiter & Scardamalia, 1993) and the other part is to enact and to experience "formal knowledge." In other words, both "knowing-that" and "knowing-how" (Ryle, 1949) are given equal emphasis. The relationship between knowing and doing is perceived as dialectical. In our interviews with Gu, he pointed out that action that is not guided by theory is "blind," but theory that is not enacted is "empty." This can also be gleaned from the following quotation from the Chinese philosopher *Zhu Xi (Chu Hsi)* [朱熹] who pointed out that doing transforms knowing.

When you know something but don't act on it, your knowledge of it is still superficial. After you've personally experienced it, your knowledge of it will be much clearer and its significance will be different from what it used to be (*Chu Hsi*, [*Zhu Xi*], Chapter 9, 9.1a:6/148:5, translated by Gardner, 1990, p. 116)[2].

Apart from Zhu Xi, Gu also referred to the debate among Chinese philosophers about whether knowing or doing comes first. He cited the work of another Chinese philosopher, *Wang Yang Ming* [王陽明], who pointed out that "knowing and doing are one" (*zhixing heyi*) [知行合一] and further commented that assuming one comes after the other is a linear view of learning.

## *The Reflexivity of Teaching and Learning and the Centrality of Enactment*

In Chinese, the word teaching *jiaoxue* [教學] is made up of two characters, "teach" and "learn," indicating that learning is an integral part of teaching. Gu cited the following from *Xueji* [學記] (Han Dynasty, around 70-50 BC), which is considered one of the earliest works on education in China.

> Learn and you know your own deficiencies.
> Teach and you know the difficulties [in teaching].
> You know your own deficiencies and you are able to improve yourself.
> You know the difficulties [in teaching] and you are able to strengthen yourself.
> Therefore it is said that teaching and learning are mutually strengthening (*Xueji*, in Gao, 2005, p. 1)[3].

Embedded in this saying are two major conceptions. The first is the importance of participating in the act of learning and in the act of teaching. The second is the reflexive processes of learning and teaching. Learning makes one more knowledgeable, but also makes one realize one's own ignorance; an awareness of what one does not know is the impetus for learning more. Hence, knowing and not knowing are mutually constitutive. Similarly, it is only through teaching that one understands the difficulties of teaching; an awareness of what is difficult prompts one to be reflective about one's own teaching. Knowing how to teach and knowing what is difficult to teach are also mutually constitutive. Teaching and learning therefore go hand in hand. Again, we see the emphasis of enactment in teaching and learning: it is only through the process of participating in teaching and learning that one becomes a better teacher and a better learner.

In all schools in China, lesson observation is practiced within the same lesson preparation group or TRG. It consists of three components: observing the lesson, post-observation conference, and the subsequent enactment of ideas for improving teaching as discussed in the conference. Gu explained that the term "observation" (*guan mo*) [觀摩] was expounded by *Zhu Xi* as "Observe each other and improve [on one's weaknesses]." Therefore central to lesson observation is the act of improving one's teaching. This resonates with Schön's (1983) concept of reflection-in-action, a process in which professionals are engaged when they encounter unique and problematic situations in which they cannot depend on established theory and technique. Under such circumstances, according to Schön, professionals may reframe their understanding of the problem and experiment with different options to achieve the desired outcome. Their thinking is not separate from doing, and experimentation, as a kind of action, is built into the inquiry. Schön, however, considers reflection-in-action "an extraordinary process" although it is not rare and can even be the core practice of some practitioners (1983, p. 69).

## Expert Guidance and Peer Learning

Peer learning is much celebrated in the research literature in the West as a powerful way to help teachers learn about teaching. For example, Korthagen, Loughran, and Russell (2006) list peer learning as one of the fundamental principles for student teacher learning (see also McIntyre & Hagger, 1992; Putnam & Borko, 1997). In China, student teacher or novice teacher learning typically involves TR Officers or backbone teachers who provide guidance. Gu pointed out that peer learning is valuable in terms of stimulating discussion, promoting collaboration, and enhancing solidarity among teachers. However, from his experience in Shanghai, he found that peer learning tended to succeed in places where there was expert guidance realized by the participation of backbone teachers, expert teachers, or external specialists. In Gu's view, without guidance from specialists or expert teachers, teacher learning would be limited. A common saying that he cited to capture the situation was "cooking radish with radish" (*luobo shao luobo*) [蘿蔔燒蘿蔔], meaning that there is little added value in the work done.

He cited a survey that he conducted of 311 teachers in Qingpu [青浦]

District in Shanghai in which the teachers were asked to indicate what they considered to be the most helpful forms of learning in curriculum reform and TPD activities. The results showed that over 70% of the respondents rated classroom teaching guided by experts and experienced teachers, and guidance from experienced colleagues on teaching materials and teaching methods as most helpful. Only slightly over 20% of the teachers rated discussions of classroom practices among peers as most helpful. The teachers were also asked to indicate the forms of lesson observation and lesson critique that they found most helpful. Nearly 50% of the teachers indicated that preparing lessons together with specialists and master teachers was most helpful, followed by lesson observation and post-lesson conferencing on how to improve on the lesson observed. Almost 25% of the teachers chose observing lessons taught by master teachers and participating in post-observation conferencing related to their own classroom realities. Only 0.7% of the respondents considered lesson observation by and post-observation conferences with peers as most helpful (Gu, 2003, pp. 428-429). The results highlighted two important elements in teacher learning. First, in Chinese culture, teachers learn best when they participate in discussions of actual classroom teaching and are able to relate the discussion to their own experiences. Second, they learn best when the discussion is scaffolded by more capable members of the community of practice. Gu proposed that "peer learning also requires expert guidance" as one of the guiding principles for teacher learning. He cited the following excerpt from *Xueji* as the principles of teaching that have guided him and many master teachers in China.

> Teach without dragging [your students] by the nose.
> Demand a high level of performance [from your students] without discouragement.
> Open the door without taking [your students] to the destination (*Xueji*, translated by Gao, 2005, p. 2)[4].

The above principles emphasize the importance attached to providing guidance and direction, setting high standards and giving encouragement, while at the same time allowing room for individual effort.

## *Learning from the West and "The Theory of the Mean"(zhongyong zhi dao) [中庸之道]*

The apprenticeship and virtuoso models of teacher learning have been criticized by scholars of teacher education in the West as encouraging the reproduction of teaching styles, hence contributing to a conservative orientation in teacher development. For example, Paine (1992, 1995) maintains that the virtuoso model suggests that good teaching is to reproduce the appropriate behavior, styles, and knowledge in the classroom. The apprenticeship model is considered to reinforce the hierarchical structure in schools, the importance attached to seniority, and the neglect of individual differences. Similarly, the emphasis on expert guidance has been criticized for allowing little room for creative pedagogy (Fraser-Abder & Chen, 2002; Guo, 2005).

We interviewed Gu about his views on the characteristics of Chinese pedagogy, including those related to teacher education, how they differed from the pedagogies of the West, and what they had learnt from the West. He pointed out that China must learn from the West without uncritical adoption of ideas and practices. He related the following observation made by a visiting American scholar regarding the differences in the way teaching and learning is managed in American and Chinese classrooms.

She [referring to the U.S. scholar] used the analogy of the teacher as a swimming coach. In her view, in the United States, a coach will take the children to the sea to teach them to swim. She will ask the children to jump into the water and try swimming on their own. Before they do that, she might remind them that they need to struggle a bit to stay afloat. Out of 30 children who jump into the water, 10 will survive but 20 will drown. According to her, those who survive are great children because in the course of struggling on their own to stay afloat, they develop creativity and endurance. But this is achieved at the price of 20 children failing miserably. In China, the coach will teach swimming in stages with close guidance. The coach will teach the children the strokes first and the children will imitate those strokes in the classroom, which is very safe because there is no water. After that, he or she will take them to the shallow end of the swimming pool to try out the strokes. For those who are not able to do it, the coach will support their tummies so that they can stay afloat and practice moving their arms and legs. The third step will be similar to what the U.S. coach will do. The coach will take them to the sea, but this time all 30 children will manage to stay afloat. However, according to the U.S. scholar, this is also achieved at a price. Out of the 30 children, 10 could have done that by themselves through their own efforts. By giving them very close guidance, the children's potential for creativity is stifled.

Gu reflected on the analogy and observed that what they had learnt from the West was that if students are able to learn on their own, then they should be given the opportunity to do so. He was keen to redress the balance between the prevailing emphasis in China on the passing down of received knowledge and the relative neglect of providing room for students to explore the answer for themselves in "learning through doing" (*zuozhong xue)* [做中學]. He noted, however, that teachers in China must not lose sight of the importance of timely intervention from the teacher in student-oriented pedagogy. In his view, the provision of appropriate scaffolding by the teacher is crucial to effective learning (see also *Xueji*, in Gao, 2005, p. 2). He concluded that China must learn from the West, but must be judicious in adapting new ideas to the realities of the local context. He cited the "Theory of the Mean" (*zhongyong zhi dao)* [中庸之道] of the Chinese philosopher *Zhu Xi*, which he expounded as taking the two extremes of anything and drawing on their strengths but avoiding their weaknesses in practice. He said, "In theorizing, you can afford to take an extreme position but in practice, you must not forget the Theory of the Mean . . . The Theory of the Mean is a key to success in practice." This point was also emphasized by a number of the teachers that we interviewed.

## From Case Methods to Enactment-based Teacher Learning

In this section, we focus specifically on a model of teacher learning, termed *"xingdong jiaoyu"* [行動教育] (enactment-based learning)[5], developed by Gu and his team to help teachers address the problem outlined in the preceding section. This model emerged as a result of interaction between teacher educators in the United States and Gu's team.

### Bridging the Theory-Praxis Gap

In light of the criticism of Chinese approaches to student learning as stifling creativity and initiative, Gu was keen to help teachers adopt a student-centered pedagogy that would provide ample opportunities for students to explore the answers for themselves without relinquishing the important role of the teacher in systematically scaffolding the learning process. Similarly, he felt that the apprenticeship model should allow room for teachers to explore for themselves ways to address the pedagogical issues that emerge in their own classrooms. The gap between theory and practice, in his view, was still a major problem that had not been adequately addressed by existing TPD activities in China. He looked for answers in teacher education practices in other parts of the world, and was excited by the case methods in teacher education advocated by L. Shulman (1992). He was attracted by the conception of cases as embodiments (*zaiti*) [載體] of theories to which teachers could relate, and felt that teachers should engage with cases with a view to improving their own classroom practices.

In the following section, we provide some brief background information on the use of case methods in teacher education in the United States.

## Case Methods in Teacher Education

The use of "cases" in teacher education, which was borrowed from the use of cases in professional schools such as law, medicine, and business, was proposed in the mid-1980s (see Carnegie Task Force on Teaching as a Profession, 1986). It has been suggested that cases of teaching are powerful mediating tools for teacher learning because they capture the complexities of teaching that cannot be articulated as prescriptive principles and rules. L. Shulman (1986) observes that it is essential for teacher education to confront "principles with cases, and general rules with concrete documented events – a dialectic between the general and the particular in which the limits of the former and the boundaries of the latter are explored" (p. 13). Case-based teaching, "provides teachers with opportunities to analyze situations and make judgments in the messy world of practice, where principles often appear to conflict with one another and no simple solution is possible" (J. H. Shulman, 1992, p. xiv).

L. Shulman advocates the use of cases as catalysts for stimulating teachers' reflections and pedagogical conversations in order to enhance the quality of teaching. Because cases are congruent with the forms of practical knowledge that underlie practice, and have more credibility and relevance for professional practice, they are powerful tools for helping teachers to understand the complexity of teachers' practical knowledge, for inducting novices to "think like a teacher" (L. Shulman, 1992, p. 1), and for bridging the gap between theory and practice. L. Shulman further points out that the case method is "a strategy for overcoming many of the most serious deficiencies in the education of teachers. Because they are contextual, local, and situated – as are all narratives – cases integrate what otherwise remains separated. Content and process, thought and feeling, and teaching and learning are not addressed theoretically as distinct constructs. They occur simultaneously as they do in real life, posing problems, issues, and challenges for new teachers that their knowledge and experiences can be used to discern" (p. 28).

Notwithstanding the clear advantages of case methods in teacher education, L. Shulman (1992) has cautioned that because of the situated nature of cases and the particularities of the narratives of cases, learners may find it difficult to see the generalizations and principles that underlie these cases. Moreover, they may also tend to over-generalize a single powerful case to other situations. In view of this, he has called for the judicious use of a combination of expository teaching and case-based teaching. Similarly, Grossman (1992) has drawn attention to the fact that the quality of the discussion of cases is critical to their full exploitation for teacher learning. In her view, restrictive discussions can lead to over-simplification. She has argued that "for teachers to see relationships between the events of a case and the subsequent classroom experiences will require a broad understanding of the initial case, as the specific details of the two are likely to differ significantly" (p. 237). To address this problem, Grossman has proposed that the curriculum should allow for multiple readings of a single case over time, and that subsequent readings should enable teachers to develop multiple perspectives on a single case and a more elaborate understanding of the complexities involved.

To gain a better understanding of case methods in teacher education, Gu led a delegation to the United States and, among other activities, observed case-based teaching in action at the Institute for Case Development at the Far West Laboratory for Educational Research and Development, which is directed by Judith Shulman. He was very impressed by the richness of the cases presented and the heated discussion among the teachers. However, his reservations about the case-based approach were different from those expressed by L. Shulman and Grossman. Although he concurred strongly with them that the quality of the discussion of the cases was highly important, he nevertheless felt that the crux of bridging the theory-praxis gap lay in teachers relating these cases to their own classrooms through the enactment of the ideas, strategies, and principles embedded in the cases. He pointed out that discussions of the cases must be followed up by classroom enactment, which in turn must also be followed up by reflection and discussion in a recursive manner.

## Re-interpreting Case Methods

During his visit to the Institute for Case Development, he asked for a definition of a case and was given two succinct and brief statements: "Cases are stories" and "Cases must have problems that need to be addressed" (L. Shulman, 1992)[6]. Gu puzzled long and hard over these two statements. He related them to the Chinese philosophy of learning arriving at the following elucidation.

> The statements captured two essential elements of a story. What is a story? A story has a plot that is "within reason but out of one's expectation."[7] In other words, if it is something that teachers are expected to do everyday, then it is not a story. If something unexpected happens and there are alternative ways of dealing with it, then we may have a story here. The other element is that there are difficulties. In *Xueji*, it says, "Learn and you know your own deficiencies; teach and you know the difficulties [in teaching]." When teachers encounter difficulties (and they address these difficulties), they can develop professionally.

Based on this re-interpretation, he proposed an alternative model that uses lesson cases as the mediating tool for the enactment of theoretically motivated teaching. He coined the term *xingdong jiaoyu* (action education) [行動教育] as an abbreviated reference to the model. Incorporating the idea of case methods and Chinese philosophies of teaching and learning, Gu outlined three major elements of this model. First, it is case-based or lesson-based; second, it is a collaborative effort between front-line teachers, master teachers, and TR Officers; and third, it integrates discussions of a lesson-based case with the subsequent enactment of the theories of teaching and learning embedded in the case and reflections on the enactment. The entire process involves what has been referred to as "three phases of focusing" and "two phases of reflection" (see Figure 10.3).

At the first stage, teachers focus on their existing practices and on their conceptions of teaching and learning. This is followed by a process of collaborative reflection, guided by master teachers and TR Officers, in which teachers evaluate their existing practices and try to discern the gap between their existing practices and new practices that are informed by theory and reported in the research literature. In particular, attention is

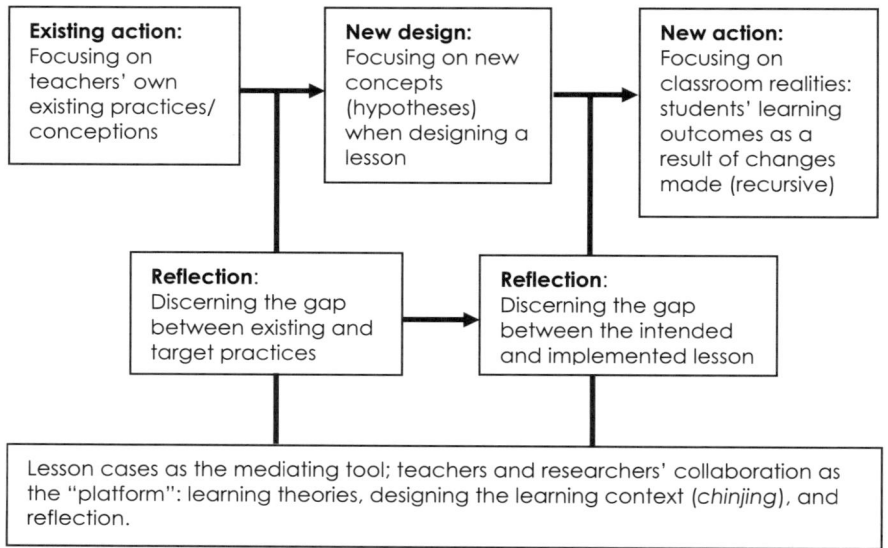

Source: Gu, L. Y. (2003). *Jiaoxue Gaige de Xingdong yu Quanshi* 《教學改革的行動與詮釋》 [Education Reform – Action and Interpretation] (p. 430). Beijing: People's Education Press.

### *Figure 10.3.* **Xingdong jiaoyu (enactment-based learning)**

paid to practices that are mentioned in the literature but are missing from the teachers' repertoire and those that are peculiar to the teachers' existing practices but not mentioned in the research literature. According to Gu, this process allows teachers to reconceptualize their practice in a theoretically motivated manner without losing their own personal style of teaching.

Based on the reflections, at the second stage, teachers focus on re-designing and re-enacting the lesson, drawing on new theories and conceptions. They collaboratively reflect once again on the classroom enactment, and try to discern the gap between the intended lesson and the implemented lesson, making modifications of their pedagogical actions to bridge the gap discerned.

At the third stage, teachers focus on the student learning outcomes that result from the modified strategies and try to discern the gap between the intended and the actual learning outcomes. The second and third stages are recursive until the team is satisfied with the learning outcomes achieved (cf. Schön's model of reflection-in-action). This model takes teachers beyond using cases for understanding and discussing theory. It emphasizes connecting theory with praxis and the bringing about of conceptual change in teachers through the enactment of lessons informed by theory.

Gu and his team spent a whole year trying out "case-based learning" in six secondary and primary schools, focusing on four subjects: mathematics and physics at the secondary level and mathematics and general science at the primary level. They observed the existing class-room practices of teachers and interviewed them on their thinking behind their lesson designs and classroom implementation. This was followed by the second stage, which was the re-design stage. Data were collected on teachers' discussions about how to improve their current practices and how the re-designed lessons might address the problems identified. At the last stage, the classroom implementations of the new lesson designs were observed, and the teachers and researchers were interviewed regarding the student learning outcomes achieved. The second and third stages, as mentioned, were recursive. If the new design did not lead to positive student learning outcomes, then it would be modified. The changes in teacher cognition and classroom practice and the possible relationships between them were also studied.

## *Making Sense of Enactment-based Learning: Perspectives from Teachers*

As mentioned, we conducted in-depth group interviews with seven teachers with teaching experience ranging from two years to nearly twenty years. Some of them were master teachers who had won teaching awards at the national level or at the municipal or district levels. All of them had conducted Open Lessons, and had been directly involved in Gu's "enactment-based learning" and had worked on lesson cases. In the interviews, all of the teachers were asked to talk about (a) their under-standing of the model, (b) a specific case of "enactment-based learning" that they had experienced, and (c) what they had gained most from participating in this model of learning. For example, a chemistry teacher provided an account of his own lesson case on how to conduct revision lessons during an examination preparation period, a mathematics teacher talked about her own lesson case on the teaching of Pythagoras' Theorem, another mathematics teacher related a lesson case on teaching similar geometric figures, and a Chinese language teacher talked about how to teach a piece of narrative text on cultural understanding.

*Teachers' awareness of xingdong jiaoyu.* The interview data revealed that the teachers had different levels of awareness of the term *xingdong jiaoyu* (enactment-based learning) proposed by Gu. For example, some teachers simply referred to it as "three stages [of implementation] and two reflections [processes]". There were also variations in the implementation. In some cases, the same teacher went through all of the processes (see, for example, Teacher Ha below), whereas in other cases the lessons were re-taught by different teachers in the same team due to practical constraints. Nevertheless, all of the teachers were able to demonstrate an awareness of the rationale behind the model when recounting their own lesson cases. They pointed out that bringing about change in pedagogy requires recursive implementation and reflection to identify the problems that contribute to unsatisfactory student learning outcomes and to design pedagogical strategies to address these problems.

For example, one general (mathematics) science primary teacher, Teacher Ha, recounted that the second stage of implementation when she tried to introduce new pedagogical elements was disastrous. She had tried to adopt a student-centered exploratory approach to teach symmetrical geometrical figures, but the activities that she designed were too complex for Primary Two children. The lesson was chaotic and the children were confused. She invited other teachers and the TR Officers to her classroom as she re-taught the lesson twice to different classes. They helped her to identify the problems and together they fine-tuned the lesson. When she taught the lesson for a fourth time, the student learning outcomes were markedly different from those at the first stage when she had adopted a transmission pedagogical approach. The students were motivated to learn, and were able to apply the principles to other geometrical shapes that they came across in their daily lives.

The teachers were also able to formulate general guiding principles which emerged from their own specific lesson cases. For example,

Teacher Ha concluded that the following factors must be considered when introducing student-centered exploratory teaching. First, the design of the activities and their objectives are critical. For example, trying to get Primary Two children to distinguish between symmetrical geometrical shapes and patterns in a single activity is beyond their reach when both concepts are new to them. Second, different kinds of scaffolding must be provided for students of different ability levels. Third, students must be coached to conduct exploratory group work. Fourth, sufficient time must be provided for exploration. Finally, not all topics lend themselves to exploratory group work; the teacher should choose topics judiciously for this kind of pedagogy.

*Theory and enactment-based learning.* All of the teachers interviewed were unanimous about the importance of understanding theory through enactment. For example, one physics teacher, Teacher Chan, drew an analogy between enactment-based learning with teaching Newton's Third Law of Action and Reaction. He explained that just telling the students about the relationship between the two forces would not lead to real understanding; it was only when students were involved in experimentation and activities that they were able to fully understand what the Law really meant. According to him, "theory is internalized through putting it in practice." He went on to state that "young teachers especially, because they are inexperienced, often just listen and say very little. Now through enacting a lesson, the teacher forms his own views about what should be taught and how the lesson should be taught. He is now a participant of a lesson. He can engage in a dialogue with you and even challenge you. When he is able to challenge you, he is engaged in critical thinking." He further added that it is only when one has actually gone through an experience that one has the right to express one's own opinion (*fayanquan*) [發言權].

*Lesson cases: focus on "knowledge points."* All of the teachers interviewed found writing lesson cases very demanding. A number of them compared writing lesson cases with *shuoke* [說課] (explaining what is to be taught in a lesson and why) and pointed out that the former was much more difficult because most lesson cases needed to address students' conceptual difficulties. For example, Teacher Li, a mathematics teacher with seven years of teaching experience who has won numerous teaching awards at different levels, explained that in writing lesson cases, she had to identify a specific topic and to be clear what conceptual problems or issues she wanted to address in the lesson. She also had to evaluate the students' learning outcomes by looking at the work the students produced, the interactions in the lesson, and the student interview data. She had to discuss whether the new pedagogical strategies were better than existing practices, whether there were remaining questions to be addressed, and what the alternative views were.

She compared the lesson cases in China and those from overseas that she had read. She said,

> I felt that the [overseas] cases [that I had read] were like stories . . . In the mathematics discipline, one must master some "knowledge points" and this is a serious matter. I can't write about teaching them in the form of stories . . . The overseas cases that I have read talked a lot about practical things, like the games and the activities conducted. In mathematics lessons in China, of course we try to make the lessons lively, but we focus more on conceptual matters and the "knowledge points" figure more prominently.

*Expert guidance and the "color blending board."* The input and guidance from experts and master teachers was another point of convergence among all teachers we interviewed. It was unanimously felt that without the guidance of more capable members, it would not be possible to engage in enactment-based learning in a meaningful way, and thus the learning would not be as effective. One teacher pointed out that without the guidance of an expert or a master teacher, peers tended to make superficial supportive comments to maintain a harmonious working relationship. Expert or master teachers were usually more direct and open with their criticisms, which had a positive effect on the quality of the discussion. Initially, the teachers were not used to having their own lessons criticized by experts, but they got used to it as time went by. They observed that only when one knew what one's shortcomings were could one improve. They also pointed out, however, that the participation of front-line teachers, master teachers, and researchers was essential to achieve a meaningful discussion, because they were able to bring different expertise and perspectives to bear in making sense of classroom realities. A metaphor that was commonly used by the teachers to refer to the collaboration between the three parties was a "color-blending board" on which different colors are blended until the right color tone is achieved.

# Discussion

As pointed out at the beginning of this chapter, the "third space" is not something that can be taken for granted when communities of practice interact, for such interaction could result in one community dominating another. Gu observed in the interviews that since China has opened up to the West, there has been a tendency, both internally and externally driven, to graft foreign practices onto local practices with little regard for historical roots and sociocultural traditions. Citing the *Theory of the Mean*, one of the Chinese classics written by the Chinese philosopher *Zhu Xi*, Gu pointed out that "the truth is often in the middle of the two extremes".

From the data presented, we can see that the enactment-based learning model that has emerged contains two critical elements that are underpinned by Chinese philosophies of teaching and learning. The first is the enactment of ideas or theories in practice, and the second is the guidance provided by more capable members of the community (Gu, 2003, p. 448). As the preceding sections show, the dialectical relationship between learning and doing is central to the Chinese conception of learning. Case method of teaching, expounded in the United States by L. Shulman (1992) and J. H. Shulman (1992), are not necessarily authentic cases of teaching, but may be cases re-written for pedagogical purposes which are based on authentic cases, and they serve to stimulate discussions about pedagogical issues.

In the "enactment-based" model, in contrast, the lesson cases are authentic, and serve not only to stimulate discussion but as references for practice. More importantly, it is through the process of enactment that teachers make sense of and re-interpret the lesson cases in light of their own classroom realities. The importance attached to understanding subject matter knowledge in China means that each case is clearly focused on how the lesson could be designed in a way that will help students to gain a thorough understanding of the key concepts and the interrelationship between them. Therefore, while teachers try to move away from teacher-centered, transmitted teaching and introduce activities that encourage students to "learn through doing" and to explore the answers for themselves, they do not lose sight of the object of learning in each lesson.

The second critical point is the importance of expert guidance. Instead of just relying on peer support, the reflections and subsequent enactments involve front-line teachers, master teachers, and TR Officers. Teachers are confronted with moment-by-moment pedagogical decisions in response to the immensely complex and ill-defined problems in the classroom. Master teachers and researchers, on the other hand, are able to make sense of classroom events in a theoretically motivated fashion. Both perspectives are brought to bear in making sense of the same lesson and the ensuing conversations about the lesson become highly meaningful.

When we asked Gu to elaborate on the three stages of focusing and the two reflective processes, he explained that in the first reflective process, teachers had to discern the variation between their own current understanding of how a concept or topic should be taught and what has been advocated either by other teachers or in the research literature. In the second reflective process, teachers had to discern the variation between the newly designed lesson and the implemented lesson. Subsequently, they also had to discern the variation between the intended and the achieved student learning outcomes. He pointed out that unless teachers are able to discern these differences, they would not be able to improve their teaching. He also emphasized that teacher discernment is greatly facilitated by the assistance of master teachers and researchers. As we can see from the interviews with the teachers, the guidance from the experts is crucial in raising the quality of the enactment and the reflections.

What distinguishes enactment-based learning from the traditional lesson research that has been in place since the 1950s is that the former is less directive. The master teachers and TR Officers do not participate in the reflective processes from the very beginning. Rather, teachers are given the opportunity to reflect on their own teaching first and to discern for themselves the gap between their existing practices and the target practices. They are given room to explore for themselves the aspects of their teaching that they wish to work on. In particular, the attention that is paid to individual teaching style is noteworthy. The recursive cycle of classroom enactment and reflection provides opportunities for teachers to make sense of the complex interplay between the multifarious dimensions of teaching and student learning outcomes. As shown by the interview data, this proved to be crucial in helping teachers to assign meaning to what seemed to be remote theoretical knowledge in the context of their own classrooms, and to formulate pedagogical principles which guided their future actions.

As all teachers interviewed pointed out, the enactment-based learning process is a "painful" process, because it challenges their existing conceptions of teaching and learning, and generates "contradictions" (in activity theory terms) as new practices are brought in. For example, the introduction of student-centered exploratory pedagogy has generated conflict between the time allocated to student activities and content coverage. It has also generated conflict over the extent to which students should be allowed to make sense of the knowledge points (*zhishi dian*) and key points (*zhung dian*) through activities and the extent to which the relationships between these aspects are made explicit by the teacher. Resolving these contradictions is something that is highly situational and must be grappled with by teachers themselves. The teacher interviews illustrate that the enactment-based model afforded opportunities for them to do so.

## Conclusion

In this chapter, we have outlined the models of teachers' professional development adopted in China and discussed the Chinese philosophies of teaching and learning that underlie these models. Drawing on the concept of the "third space," also known as the "boundary zone" or "boundary crossing," we have examined how the adoption of case methods in teacher education has been brokered by an influential teacher educator in China, Gu Ling Yuan, and his colleagues as they looked for ways to help teachers to move away from teacher-centered to student-centered pedagogies. As Wenger points out, "The learning and innovative potential of a social learning system lies in its configuration of strong core practices and active boundary processes" (Wenger, 2003, p. 85). We have seen how in the process of appropriating the boundary object, that is, the case methods that originated in the United States, Gu and the teachers in a number of schools in Shanghai re-interpreted case methods in the context of Chinese education, guided by the Chinese philosophies of education that underlie their core practices. We have seen that case methods have been reconceptualized as lesson cases, assigned new meanings, and given new elements and vitality by the teachers. The enactment-based teacher-learning model does not consist of foreign prac tices grafted onto local ones with little regard for Chinese cultural tradi-tions, educational beliefs and practices. Rather, Gu and his colleagues, as boundary brokers, have been able to fully exploit the potential for rich learning in the boundary zone. Enactment-based teacher learning con-sists of multiple perspectives embedded in practices from other parts of the world together with those from China. It contains a multiplicity of voices, including those of front-line teachers, experts, master teachers, and researchers, and the wisdom derived from the sustained interaction among them. All of this has resulted in the construction of a powerful model of teacher learning that has made a strong impact on teacher development in China, resulting in the model being widely promoted by the Ministry of Education.

# REFERENCES

Bereiter, C., & Scardamalia, M. (1993). *Surpassing ourselves: An inquiry into the nature and implications of expertise.* Illinois: Open Court.

Bhabha, H. K. (1994). *The location of culture.* London/New York: Routledge.

Carnegie Task Force on Teaching as a Profession. (1986). *A nation prepared: Teachers for the 21st century.* New York: Carnegie Forum on Education and the Economy, Carnegie Corporation.

Chu, Hsi. (1990). *Learning to be a sage: Selections from the conversations of Master Chu, arranged topically* (D. K. Gardner, Trans. with a commentary). Berkeley and Los Angeles: University of California Press.

Confucius. (1979). *The analects* (D. C. Lau, Trans.). Hong Kong: The Chinese University Press.

Dai, J. P. (2005). Lun xueke jiaoyanyuan zhi yanjiu [Discuss subject-based teaching consultants' research]. Retrieved from January 27, 2007, from http://www.jxjy.com.cn/2004/xk/shownews.asp?newsid=4116

Engeström, Y. (1999). Innovative learning in work teams: Analyzing cycles of knowledge creation in practice. In Y. Engeström, R. Miettinen & R. L. Punamäki (Eds.), *Perspectives on activity theory* (pp. 371-405). Cambridge: Cambridge University Press.

Engeström, Y. (2001). Expansive learning at work. *Journal of Education and Work, 14,* 133-156.

Engeström, Y., Engeström, R., & Kärkkäinen, M. (1995). Polycontextuality and boundary crossing in expert cognition: Learning and problem solving in complex work activities. *Learning and Instruction, 5,* 319-336.

Fraser-Abder, P., & Chen, S. L. (2002). Professional development in Japan and China: Issues and challenges. In P. Fraser-Abder (Ed.), *Professional development of science teachers: Local insights with lessons for the global community* (pp. 38-55). New York: Routledge.

Gao, S. L. (2005). *Xueji yanjiu* 《學記研究》 [Research on Xueji]. Beijing: People's Education Press.

Gardner, D. K. (2003). *Zhu Xi's reading of the analects*. New York: Columbia University Press.

Grossman, P. L. (1992). Teaching and learning with cases: Unanswered questions. In J. H. Shulman (Ed.), *Case methods in teacher education* (pp. 227-239). New York: Teachers College Press.

Gu, L. Y. (2003). *Jiaoxue gaige de xingdong yu quanshi* 《教學改革的行動與詮釋》 [Education reform — action and interpretation]. Beijing: People's Education Press.

Gu, L. Y., Nie, B. H., & Yi, L. F. (2002). *Xunzhao zhongjian didai* 《尋找中間地帶》 [Searching for the middle ground]. Shanghai: Shanghai Education Press.

Guo, S. B. (1999). *Current issues in teacher education in China*. Paper presented at the annual meeting of the Comparative and International Education Society, Toronto, Canada. (ERIC Document Reproduction Service No. 436493).

Guo, S. B. (2005). Exploring current issues in teacher education in China. *The Alberta Journal of Educational Research, 51,* 69-84.

Gutiérrez, K. D., Baquedano-López, P., & Tejeda, C. (1999). Rethinking diversity: Hybridity and hybrid language practices in the third space. *Mind, Culture and Activity, 6,* 286-303.

Hu, H. M. (2005). Jiaoyan zuzhi jianshe ji huodong kazhan [Structure and functions of teaching research group]. In X. F. Wang (Ed.), *Xin ke cheng xia bei jingxia de jiao shi zhuan ye fazhan* (pp. 185-198). Shanghai: Huadong shida.

Konkola, R. (2001). Harjoittelun kehittämisprosessi ammattikorkeakoulussa ja rajavyöhyketoiminta uudenlaisena toimintamallina [Developmental process of internship at polytechnic and boundary-zone activity as a new model for activity]. In T. Tuomi-Gröhn & Y. Engeström (Eds.), *Koulun ja työn rajavyöhykkeellä — uusia työssäoppimisen mahdollisuuksia* [At the boundary-zone between school and work — new possibilities of work-based learning] (pp. 148-186). Helsinki: University Press.

Korthagen, F., Loughran, J., & Russell, T. (2006). Developing fundamental principles for teacher education programs and practices. *Teaching and Teacher Education, 22,* 1020-1041.

Lave, J., & Wenger, E. (1991). *Situated learning: Legitimate peripheral participation*. Cambridge: Cambridge University Press.

Lin, Y. W., & Cheng, T. J. (2004). Jiao ben jiao shi pei xun de he li xing zhui jiu [An investigation of rationales of school-based teacher training ]. *Jiao Yu Yan Jiu, 6,* 77-83.

Ma, L. (1992). *Discussing teacher induction in China and relevant debates in the United States with a Chinese teacher: A conversation with Yu Yi.* (Research Report No. Craft Paper 92-2). Michigan: The National Center for Research on Teacher Learning.

Ma, L. (1999). *Knowing and teaching elementary mathematics: Teachers' understanding of fundamental mathematics in China and the United States*. Mahwah, NJ: Lawrence Erlbaum Associates.

McIntyre, D., & Hagger, H. (1992). Professional development through the Oxford internship model. *British Journal of Educational Studies, 40,* 264-283.

Paine, L. W. (1990). The teacher as virtuoso: A Chinese model for teaching. *Teachers College Record, 92,* 49-81.

Paine, L. W. (1992). Teaching and modernization in contemporary China. In R. Hayhoe (Ed.), *Education and modernization: The Chinese experience* (pp. 183-210). Oxford: Pergamon.

Paine, L. W. (1995). Teacher education in search of a metaphor: Defining the relationship between teachers, teaching and the state in China. In M. B. Ginsburg & B. Lindsay (Eds.), *The political dimension in teacher education: Comparative perspectives on policy formation, socialization and society* (pp. 76-98). London: Falmer Press.

Paine, L. W., & Ma, L. P. (1993). Teachers working together: A dialogue on organizational and cultural perspectives of Chinese teachers. *International Journal of Educational Research, 19,* 675-697.

Putnam, R. T., & Borko, H. (1997). Teacher learning: Implications of new views of cognition. In B. J. Biddle, T. L. Good & I. Goodson (Eds.), *International handbook of teachers and teaching* (Vol. 2, pp. 1223-1296). Dordrecht, The Netherlands: Kluwer Academic Publishers.

Ryle, G. (1949). *The concept of mind*. London: Hutchinson.

Schön, D. (1983). *The reflective practitioner*. London: Basic Books Ltd.

Shulman, J. H. (1992). Introduction. In J. H. Shulman (Ed.), *Case methods in teacher education* (pp. xiii-xvii). New York: Teachers College Press.

Shulman, L. (1986). Those who understand knowledge growth in teaching. *Educational Researcher, 15*(2), 4-14.

Shulman, L. (1992). Towards a pedagogy of cases. In J. Shulman, H. (Ed.), *Case methods in teacher education* (pp. 1-30). New York: Teachers College Press.

Tuomi-Gröhn, T., Engeström, Y., & Young, M. (2003). From transfer to boundary-crossing between school and work as a tool for developing vocational education: An introduction. In T. Tuomi-Gröhn & Y. Engeström (Eds.), *Between school and work: New perspectives on transfer and boundary-crossing* (pp. 1-15). Amsterdam: Pergamon.

Wang, J. (2001). Contexts of mentoring and opportunities for learning to teach: A comparative study of mentoring practice. *Teaching and Teacher Education, 17,* 51-73.

Wang, J., & Paine, L. W. (2003). Learning to each with mandated curriculum and public examination of teaching as contexts. *Teaching and Teacher Education, 19*, 75-94.

Wang, J., Strong, M., & Odell, S. J. (2004). Mentor-novice conversations about teaching: A comparison of two U. S. and two Chinese cases. *Teachers College Record, 106*, 775-813.

Wenger, E. (1998). *Communities of practice: Learning, meaning and identity.* Cambridge: Cambridge University Press.

Wenger, E. (2003). Communities of practice and social learning systems. In D. Nicolini, S. Gherardi & D. Yanow (Eds.), *Knowing in organizations: A practice-based approach* (pp. 76-99). Armonk, NY: M.E. Sharpe.

Wenger, E., McDermott, R., & Snyder, W. M. (2002). *Cultivating communities of practice.* Boston, Mass.: Harvard Business School Press.

Xie, A. B. (2001). The development and reform of teacher education in China: Theoretical issues. *Asia-Pacific Journal of Teacher Education and Development, 4*(2), 41-59.

Yang, D. P., & Wu, J. Q. (1999). Some issues in the reform and development of teacher education and training in China. *Teacher Development, 3*, 157-172.

## Endnotes

[1] The Chinese version is "學而時習之，不亦說乎。"

[2] *Chu Hsi* is a variation of the romanization of *Zhu Xi*.

[3] The Chinese version is "學然後知不足，教然後知困。知不足，然後能自反也。知困，然後能自強也。"

[4] The Chinese version is "道而弗牽，強而弗抑，開而弗達。"

[5] The literal translation of *xingdong ziaoyu* is "action education". However, in this chapter this literal translation is not adopted to avoid confusing it with "action research," which has become widely adopted in teacher education programs in the West since the 1980s. Instead, the term "enactment-based learning" is used as it better reflects the essence of the model and its underlying philosophy of learning.

[6] L. Shulman (1992) points out that "a case has a narrative, a story, a set of events that unfolds over time in a particular place." Teaching narratives have a plot and dramatic tension that needs to be resolved. They are situated and as such they reflect the sociocultural contexts in which the events take place.

[7] The Chinese expression is "情理之中，意料之外。" It is commonly used to describe events, stories, and melodrama. Events that are not within reason are unconvincing, and those that are not out of one's expectation are not worth writing about.

# CONCLUSION

# 11

# The Paradoxes Revisited: The Chinese Learner in Changing Educational Contexts

*Carol K.K. CHAN and Nirmala RAO*

## Introduction

In the introduction to this volume, we highlighted the need to revisit the Chinese learner against the background of socioeconomic and technological changes, shifts in learning paradigms, new educational policies and widespread curriculum reforms. This volume has examined the contemporary Chinese learner of the 21st century considering the changing nature of learning and epistemology, emerging pedagogy and classroom practice, and recent teacher professional development. We also focused on continuity and change in student and teacher learning in the light of traditional cultural beliefs and changing educational contexts.

This volume has extended previous research on the Chinese learner by addressing emerging issues and new developments in research in several ways. First, while earlier research has examined the paradox of the Chinese learner by taking into account cultural beliefs and contextual influences on school learning and performance, the chapters in this volume have gone further by incorporating recent research on Chinese cultural models of learning. We have also extended analyses of school learning and academic achievements to consider how Chinese learners have adapted to new educational goals in 21st century education, such as learning how to learn. Second, this volume has also extended earlier research on how teacher beliefs have influenced teaching practices and teacher change, by focusing on how Chinese teachers have addressed changes brought about by educational and curriculum reforms, and by analyzing how teachers have transformed their pedagogical practices for the Chinese learner of tomorrow. Third, teachers' professional development in the Chinese context has been considered by examining how teacher educators integrate traditional and Western concepts for teachers in professional learning.

This chapter synthesizes the following key themes:

- Characterizing the Chinese learner by highlighting the need to consider the learner in context rather than either the learner or the context in isolation
- Revisiting the paradoxes of the Chinese learner and the Chinese teacher by examining emerging themes in student learning, classroom practice, and teacher development and their interactions in the light of changing educational contexts
- Considering contributions of *Revisiting the Chinese Learner* to theories of learning, educational change, learning and innovation, and teaching and learning across cultural contexts

## Characterizing the Chinese Learner

*The Chinese Learner in Retrospect*

Research on Chinese students illustrates divergent views. From one perspective, some research has characterized Chinese students as quiet, passive learners, who are prone to rote learning (Hu, 2002; Bradley & Bradley, 1984; Samuelowicz, 1987). The other view, which started with the paradox of the Chinese learner (Biggs, 1996; Watkins & Biggs, 1996), posits that Chinese students are successful learners, who exhibit various characteristics and patterns that lead them to excel in both academic performance and cross-national achievement tests. There are also some problems with the term "Chinese learner" as it seems to invite certain biases focusing on homogenous differences among ethnic groupings.

In the first chapter, we briefly traced the development of research on the Chinese learner. Traditionally, there has been a commonly held belief among educators, some of whom have worked with overseas Chinese students studying in Western countries, that Chinese students are passive, surface-level rote learners, who rely on repetition; that they do not learn for understanding and merely reproduce information to fulfill examination requirements (Hu, 2002; Bradley & Bradley, 1984). This apparent passivity on the part of Chinese students has been attributed to the influence of the Confucian tradition, whereby obedient learners and those who comply with authority are valued.

Major insights into the Chinese learner, starting with research by Watkins and Biggs (1996, 2001), have been provided by various researchers, including Marton, Dall'Alba and Tse (1996), Kember (2000), Wong (2004), and Lee and Mok (2008), all of whom have refuted the view that Chinese learners are passive, by analyzing student learning from cultural, contextual and systems perspectives. Biggs (1996) identified different areas of problems arising from the use of a purely Western lens to interpret phenomena associated with teaching and learning in different cultural contexts (see Rao & Chan, chap. 1, this volume). Lee (1996) and Wong (2004) argued that there are different interpretations of Confucian-heritage culture and noted that Chinese students have historically been encouraged to think, reflect, and engage in discourse. Marton and colleagues identified a memorization-understanding pattern, illustrating how Chinese learners use a different approach to learning (Marton et al., 1996; Marton, Wen & Wong, 2005). Clark and Gieve (2006) coined the term "deficit model," noting that it is simplistic to describe Chinese students as passive learners.

## Learner or Learner in Context

Who is the Chinese learner? How can he or she simultaneously be a passive student and an active, reflective learner? This volume builds on earlier work (Watkins & Biggs, 1996, 2001) and puts forward the thesis that we need to examine learning in situ to address this paradox in changing educational contexts. A renowned systems theory in developmental psychology (Bronfenbrenner, 1979, 1989) has emphasized the role of the social environment in human development and considered the influences of nested macro-, meso- and micro-systems and interactions between elements of these various systems on the developing person. Such an emphasis on moving beyond the individual to focus on a broader social perspective also resonates with the current theoretical focus on situated cognition in analyzing how learning takes place (Bransford et al., 2006; Brown, Collins, & Duguid, 1989; Greeno, Collins, & Resnick, 1996; Lave & Wenger, 1991; Sfard, 1998). This volume maintains this emphasis on the need to examine cultural and contextual influences to understand the Chinese learner.

Although this volume refers to the Chinese learner, we note that it is not helpful to focus on a binary distinction between Chinese and Western students, as this may lead to the polarization of learners, or to a comparison between one kind of learner and another, as if there were an "ideal" type of student. As noted in earlier volumes (Watkins & Biggs, 1996, 2001) and the introduction of this volume (Rao & Chan, chap. 1), the Chinese learner is defined as one who studies in a classroom in a Confucian-heritage culture. Recently, new understanding has been put forward about Confucian-heritage culture (Wong, 2004) and the congruence between Confucianism and contemporary learning is receiving an increasing amount of attention (Law et al., chap. 4, this volume; Lee, 1996; Shi, 2006). It is important not to take a broad-brush approach to depict the Confucian-heritage culture or to assume the homogeneity of the Chinese people. Indeed, students vary across national and regional boundaries and socioeconomic backgrounds (e.g. urban versus rural settings), and this may influence how they approach task demands and learning situations.

Although we use the Chinese learner as the starting point, we do not focus on the learner per se; culture is not static. We also emphasize other parts of the system, for example, the background and characteristics of the learner, learning goals, learning environment, and the nature of interactions. We take a process and system approach to examine the issue. We agree with the view that Chinese learners may have certain identifiable characteristics, some of which may be related to culture, but they may also learn and behave differently in different situations, according to personal needs and situational demands (Gu & Schweisfurth, 2006). Both the "deficit" and "optimistic" views need to be examined more closely by drawing on new research based on changing cultural and educational contexts and new kinds of task demands.

We provide a framework examining the paradox considering various components and their interactions that influence 21st century Chinese learners (Figure 11.1). First, we revisit the Chinese learner through examining the influence of traditional beliefs including Confucian-heritage culture, historical background, philosophies and beliefs, along with the contemporary changes of socioeconomic development, technological advances, shifts in learning paradigms and educational policies and reforms. Second, we discuss how the impact of traditional and

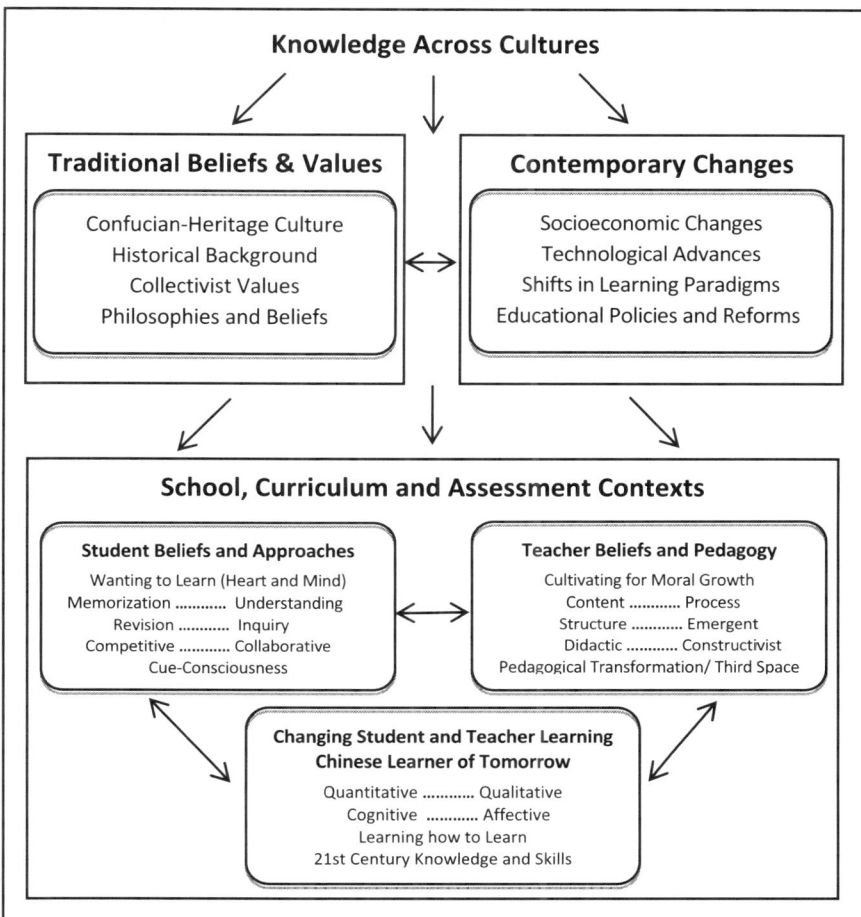

*Figure 11. 1.* **Teaching and learning for the Chinese learner in changing educational contexts**

changing forces on student and teacher learning in the Chinese context is mediated through changing school, curriculum and assessment contexts. Third, we examine student beliefs, student approaches, student learning and their characteristics and dialectics in the changing Chinese classroom context. Fourth, we examine the Chinese teacher, considering teacher beliefs, classroom pedagogy, teacher learning and professional development and how teachers respond to changing educational demands. Fifth, we examine student and teacher learning, focusing on new educational goals for the Chinese learners of tomorrow, such as learning how to learn. Finally, our analyses of 21st century Chinese learners are set against the background of a changing global context, in which different cultures are interacting with evolving knowledge and learning across cultures.

# Revisiting the Paradoxes of the Chinese Learner and the Chinese Teacher

## *Student Beliefs, Student Approaches and Student Learning*

Student approaches to learning and student beliefs about learning and knowledge have been major research themes in educational psychology over the past few decades (Alexander & Winne, 2006; Bransford, Brown, & Cocking, 1999; Hofer & Pintrich, 2002; Schommer, 2004). Research on approaches to learning has identified distinctions between deep and surface approaches from both quantitative (Biggs, 1987, 1993; Entwistle & Ramsden, 1983; Biggs, Kember, & Leung, 2001) and qualitative traditions (Marton & Säljö, 1976; Marton & Booth, 1997). Research on student epistemology has examined the nature and development of knowing and knowledge (Hofer & Pintrich, 2002; Schommer, 2004). Across these different research strands, distinctive and polarized differences in the conceptualization of learning processes have been identified. Furthermore, this research, which has mostly been Western-based, has tended to focus on cognitive and epistemological aspects of learning.

What do Chinese students believe about learning? How do they approach learning? Research on Chinese students' approaches to learning has shown that while they employ both deep and surface approaches to learning, as do their Western counterparts, they also display some distinctive patterns, including those which are ascribed to Confucian-heritage culture (Marton et al., 1996; Marton et al., 2005; Watkins, 1996; Watkins & Biggs, 1996). This volume furthers our understanding of Chinese students' beliefs and approaches, which are influenced by traditional beliefs and changing sociocultural and educational contexts.

## Traditional Beliefs and Cultural Values: Chinese Conceptualization of Learning

The first theme emphasizes the role of cultural beliefs in understanding Chinese learners. Li's study (chap. 2, this volume), which is based on her investigation of a Chinese cultural model of learning (Li, 2001, 2003), argues that Chinese students' learning goes beyond Western-based constructs. The model of Chinese learning she posits is based on an epistemology that defines what knowledge is, why people want to learn, and how knowledge is acquired. Learning, as described in the model, is seen as a necessary pathway towards moral goals and striving for self-perfection. Li uses the notion "heart and mind for wanting to learn" (*hao xue xin*) [好學心], to describe learning in the Chinese context, and notes that it is a lifelong orientation. This notion, while somewhat similar to the concept of "agency" in a Western sense (Zimmerman, 1995), also has its own characteristics: it is not dependent on others; it involves diligence and persistence; it is self-motivated and may contribute to an understanding of learning how to learn.

Li argues for a broadening of models of learning to incorporate the affective constructs of diligence, endurance of hardship, and persistence, and empirically demonstrates that these components are more common among Chinese students than among English-speaking students. Li's model of learning, highlighting personal, social and moral purposes, provides important insights into the roles of cultural beliefs and their influences on how Chinese students learn. Her findings are aligned with the role of the Confucian-heritage tradition (Lee, 1996; Wong, 2004) and interpretations of how Confucian beliefs influence learning in the Chinese context (Law et al., this volume; Shi, 2006).

In relation to ongoing changes within the educational context, Li's cultural model of self-perfection may have implications for lifelong learning. Given that self-perfection is a never-ending process, learning can be a lifelong commitment, and to accomplish lifelong learning goals, Chinese learners may exhibit heart and mind for wanting to learn (*hao xue xin*). We can see how cultural elements may be taken into account in examining and fostering agency in the Chinese context. The cultural explanation of learning may provide a useful perspective for addressing the paradox of the Chinese learner in changing contexts.

## Contemporary Changes: Educational Reform and Student Learning

The second theme examines Chinese learners in the light of changing educational contexts. Law and colleagues (chap. 4, this volume) examine the influences of educational reform and new pedagogy. They investigated students' preferred ways of learning and found that Chinese students, who are usually perceived as passive, teacher-dependent rote-learners, embraced and welcomed new pedagogical goals and approaches. They were found to value and cherish learning experiences that involved constructivist elements such as an authentic context, discourse involving diverse viewpoints, and collaborative inquiry.

Earlier research on Chinese learners' conceptions of, and approaches to, learning focused on school learning and studying (Marton, Watkins, & Tang, 1997; Watkins, 1996). Law et al.'s chapter examined what Chinese learners in the reform era, who experienced new pedagogy, thought about new modes of learning such as learning how to learn. The Chinese students who were experiencing this new pedagogy were found to hold rather sophisticated beliefs about learning that were aligned with new educational goals. In addition, students' views of their ideal teacher demonstrated that while they would like teachers to have a guiding role, they also wanted teachers to provide them with space to let them grow and develop their own views.

Similarly, other studies in this volume, conducted in the context of reform, show that students respond well to new educational pedagogy. Chan (chap. 6, this volume) discussed the role of computer-supported collaborative knowledge building in developing 21st century learning goals. Marton et al. (chap. 5, this volume) examined the *Chinese learner of tomorrow*, emphasizing the need to develop reading to learn using the variation approach. Their results demonstrate that students experiencing new pedagogy change towards new ways of thinking and learning. Analyses of students' beliefs in the context of contemporary educational reform show that students value both authentic learning and learning together. These findings about the adaptability and expectations of contemporary Chinese learners parallel the notion of cue-consciousness (Biggs, 1996) and recent research on overseas Chinese students in higher education (Jin & Cortazzi, 2006; Rastall, 2006; Shi, 2006). These chapters, which draw from the context of educational reforms, add to research on the use of new classroom pedagogy (Chan, 2001; Ho, Watkins, & Kelly, 2001; Wong & Lam, 2007; Stokes, 2001; van Aalst & Chan, 2007) and contradict earlier assumptions that Chinese students are passive rote learners.

It should be noted that we are not making a simplistic statement arguing that Chinese students are inherently active, inquisitive, lifelong learners. Examining how students respond to educational change can shed light on the paradox of the Chinese learner. In addition, we note the possibility that cultural beliefs and contemporary changes may provide the conditions necessary for Chinese students to become the Chinese learners of tomorrow. Cultural characteristics such as "heart and mind for wanting to learn" (Li, chap. 2, this volume) may provide a basis for Chinese students to continue to strive to perfect themselves and adapt to new goals and changes. In accordance with the systems perspective, when certain system components change, such as when classroom pedagogy is appropriately gauged to students' levels, Chinese learners can respond in deep ways by developing deep goals and strategies for meaningful learning. Nevertheless, if there are too many tensions between new goals and public examination, change is difficult to effect. Psychological, contextual and cultural influences interact in dynamic ways to influence learning and teaching in the changing Chinese classroom.

## Traditional and Contemporary: Integrating Dichotomies

The third theme examines the notion of moving beyond dichotomies to understand the Chinese learner. Watkins (chap. 3, this volume) analyzes students' views on learning with regard to motivation and competition and considers the educational reforms made by the Education Bureau (EDB, Hong Kong Government) to reduce competition among students. While the educational policy of reducing competition seems reasonable, his findings caution against a simple interpretation of competition versus collaboration. Written responses show that Chinese students' views on competition may be different from the assumed polarized views of competition versus collaboration; students hold positive views about competition and regard it as conducive to learning. These different interpretations of competition can be explained by collectivist values; students do not necessarily see competition as an opposing force to collaboration. Chinese students' views about competition are also described in another chapter (Law et al., chap. 4, this volume), in which students discuss how they use competition in science projects to help them collaborate and as a source of learning motivation.

A major advance in research on the paradox of the Chinese learner is the identification of the memorization-understanding process (Marton et al., 1996; Marton et al., 2005). Chinese students intertwine memorization and understanding to learn; they employ meaningful memorization and repetition to understand (Dahlin & Watkins, 2000). This characteristic *intertwining of contradictory approaches* used by Chinese learners is even more salient when Chinese students respond to new pedagogy. Chan (chap. 6, this volume) examined high school students collaborating with each other in knowledge building mediated by a computer forum. In response to the new pedagogy, the Chinese students integrated collaborative inquiry with examination preparations. They discussed how the new pedagogy of working together on the forum helped them to "gather more points" in preparing for their examination, and how discussing the materials helped them to "understand the materials" so that they revised their work regularly. In their interviews, they indicated how they valued collaborative inquiry, while also emphasizing the need to do well in the examination. They also made insightful comments about the kinds of metacognitive processes that helped them to do well in learning. Within their context, they developed a *deep* approach for their learning needs given the school and system constraints.

It may also be useful to consider *school, curriculum and assessment contexts* to explain the beliefs and approaches of the Chinese learner. Traditionally, examinations have played a key role in the Chinese context, and the importance of examinations in China has greatly influenced students' learning and shaped their thinking. Many *surface* responses exhibited by Chinese learners may exist because of the emphasis on examinations. The current change in educational requirements to focus on both examinations and learning how to learn has led students to adopt strategies relevant to the context, such as "memorization-understanding" and "revision through collaboration" to meet the demands of both new and old tasks.

The paradox of the Chinese learner may be addressed through an understanding of learning in situ and by interpreting the relevant constructs from a systems perspective. While surface and deep approaches, memorization and understanding, and individualism and collaboration, are generally considered dichotomies in the West, among Chinese learners they are more in the nature of intertwined processes. Students are attuned to contextual demands, and new demands have now been created due to educational reforms. Changing educational goals and contexts provide important opportunities for expanding the nature and dynamics of learning for the Chinese learner.

## *Teacher Beliefs, Changing Pedagogy and Teacher Learning*

Research on teacher conceptions in Western countries encompasses a broad range of issues; some key research strands examine conceptions of teaching that can be categorized as either knowledge transmission or knowledge transformation (Gow & Kember, 1993; Pratt, 1992; Prosser & Trigwell, 1998). Previous research has shown that in common with their Western counterparts, the beliefs of Chinese teachers include these dimensions (So & Watkins, 2005; Tang, 2001). At the same time, studies have shown that Chinese teachers hold certain distinctive conceptions of teaching that include moral guidance and examination preparation (Gao & Watkins, 2002), and that they believe they play a role in cultivating and nurturing students' moral development (Watkins & Biggs, 2001). This volume addresses the paradox of the Chinese teacher by examining three key themes relating to teacher beliefs, changing pedagogy and teacher development, taking into account the impact of the confluence of traditional cultural beliefs and contemporary forces on teaching and learning.

### *Teacher Beliefs of Cultivating Role and Moral Guidance*

Teachers' beliefs are important as they influence what teachers think a subject is about, how students best learn, and what the role of the teacher is in the classroom. Teachers' beliefs encompass a broad set of dimensions; we focus on how Chinese teachers' beliefs about their *cultivating role* mediate teaching practice in a changing context. As noted by Lee (1996), while great Western teachers, in historical times, have tended to focus on epistemology, great Chinese teachers seem to have been more concerned with teaching students how to live for moral purposes. The Imperial Examination in ancient China tested candidates on their ability to memorize Chinese classics and develop schemes to govern the country. Successful scholars became officials entrusted with the responsibility of governing their subjects; they were esteemed and honored as "parental officials" [父母官]. Under such historical and cultural influences, Chinese teachers see their role as not simply to help students to acquire knowledge, but also to help children observe moral codes and develop moral perfection.

As Li's research (chap. 2, this volume) shows, Chinese students have developed a view of learning as the pursuit of self-perfection as one works towards moral goals. The teacher's role, accordingly, is to support students in acquiring moral values. Western teachers are also concerned with helping children to learn how to live, but the focus is generally placed on actualizing a child's potential for all-round personal development. Chinese teachers, however, focus on ensuring that students follow the "right" paths and develop values and conduct deemed acceptable for them to grow into moral, upright persons.

How do such beliefs about teachers' nurturing and cultivating roles influence educational policy and pedagogical practice in the changing Chinese educational context? At the macro level of education policy in Hong Kong, Liberal Studies was added to Chinese, English and Mathematics in 2009 as a new compulsory subject for all senior high school students as part of the recent large-scale educational and curriculum reforms. The Liberal Studies curriculum includes 21st century educational goals of developing students' critical thinking, problem solving and inquiry skills. As discussed earlier, we observe that one of the characteristics of Chinese education is an emphasis on affective aspects, and another major impetus and educational goal of the new curriculum is to help students acquire appropriate values deemed important for them to develop into responsible citizens. The proposed assessment questions of Liberal Studies are replete with examples in which students are asked to solve practical and social problems in daily life. Whereas curriculum reform is widespread around the world, Liberal Studies is quite a unique new curriculum possibly reflecting the underlying values of the cultivating and guidance roles of the Chinese teachers.

Chan (chap. 6, this volume) describes a case study that shows how teachers' cultivating beliefs can be useful for the promotion of classroom innovation. Interview excerpts from her computer forum-based study show that the classroom teacher considered the new pedagogical approach to be helpful not only for cognitive growth, but also in contributing to students' acquisition of the positive value of interacting with others harmoniously. The teacher also interpreted the knowledge-building approach as something akin to Chinese history, alluding to the importance of spreading the ideas and wisdom of schools of philosophy for the betterment of society. The Western-based knowledge-building approach emphasizing collective learning was interpreted by the teacher as similar to collectivist values emphasized in the Chinese context. With the belief that the new pedagogical approach may contribute to students' cognitive, social and moral growth, teachers may be more inclined to engage in new pedagogical practices.

Teacher beliefs are very complex. The emphasis on the teacher as a nurturer and moral guide in the Chinese context may help to address the paradox of the Chinese teacher. With the perceived utility of new forms of education such as lifelong learning, and with China opening up to the world, Chinese teachers may adapt new pedagogy to their own settings in interesting ways through combinations of old and new beliefs. The implication is that for change and innovation to be adopted in different cultural contexts, it is useful to understand teacher beliefs and take into account what teachers consider to be valuable to their students.

## Changing Pedagogy and Pedagogical Transformation

We start with what we have learned about classroom practice in the Chinese context. What is the paradox of the Chinese teacher? Is there a Chinese pedagogy? What are some of the specific cultural patterns of Chinese pedagogical practice? Researchers have argued that teaching is primarily a cultural activity; there are "cultural scripts" of teaching that influence how teachers approach classroom practice, and these different practices influence student learning (Stigler & Hiebert, 1999). Gardner (1989) discussed how Chinese teachers first focused on drilling skills and competence before allowing students to proceed on their own; teachers in Western countries, however, generally allow students more scope to explore their environment. Paine (1990) put forward a Chinese model for teaching in which the teacher is viewed as a virtuoso playing the role of a performer. She noted that teachers stand at the center of the stage as far as Chinese school activities are concerned. Such pedagogy is based on teachers' conceptions of learning as a systematic process that involves predetermined stages. The role of the teacher is to use purposeful and planned approaches to lead students to the mastery of knowledge (Paine, 1990).

Various researchers have observed that apparently teacher-centered classrooms and large classes may not necessarily translate into passive learning. Chinese students may not be expressive, but they can be actively listening and responding in their own ways (Cortazzi & Jin, 2001). In paradoxical ways, such as through the use of variation, Chinese teachers have been shown to engage students even where the relevant activities did not appear to Western researchers to involve the use of student-centered approaches (Mok et al., 2001; Marton & Tsui, 2004). Teachers are considered to be knowledgeable experts, who provide models and examples to guide students. Authoritarian and teacher-dominated styles need to be interpreted in the light of teachers' beliefs about their guidance and parental roles.

With the changes brought about by globalization and the socio-economic changes that have occurred around the world, various forces are influencing pedagogical practice. Educational reforms are being undertaken in various Asian countries and in mainland China. Rao, Chi and Cheng (chap. 7, this volume) note that educational policies and directives such as "giving back time to students" provide an impetus for Chinese teachers to move towards more student-centered activities. For example, Siegel and colleagues (chap. 8, this volume) show the increasing need for English language education in mainland China and how teachers have successfully used immersion approaches to teach English to primary students. Marton and colleagues from the Education Bureau (EDB) (chap 5, this volume) describe a new pedagogical approach based on the use of variation to develop Chinese students' capacity to read to learn through reading argumentative text. There is a growing emphasis not just on teaching subject matter, but also on developing new goals and new forms of learning for the Chinese learners of tomorrow. We should note that these pedagogical changes are recent and have only been implemented in a small number of classrooms. Nevertheless, they are major policy developments that can be expected to prompt more changes at the classroom level.

In the different chapters of this volume, we have observed some distinctive patterns in how Chinese teachers have designed the new pedagogy, synergizing the old and the new by using a *transformed pedagogy*. A common theme emerges in that these teachers have not just copied or added certain elements, but have reflected on their existing practices and transformed the new pedagogy in ways that align student cognition and task demands with contextual and cultural dynamics, with an emphasis on deeper notions of learning.

Rao, Ng and Pearson's study (chap. 9, this volume) shows that kindergarten teachers are moving away from a traditional, didactic, drill-and-practice approach to a more activity-based one which suggests the influence of Western notions about early education, at least at policy level. However, characteristics of Confucian-heritage culture continue to dominate the social milieu of the classroom via the beliefs and practices of the teachers, thereby interweaving Chinese traditional views and current ideas about the goals and nature of early education (Ng & Rao, 2008). Observations show the teachers often ask children to chant in unison when they are engaged in play activities, which is an effective practice in that context. Law and colleagues (chap. 4, this volume) show that some teachers use competitive activities and extrinsic forms of motivation such as an award system to foster collaboration and inquiry, using seemingly contradictory and opposing approaches. In the eyes of Western researchers, these activities may not be entirely student-centered. However, we need to be mindful that notions such as teacher-centered and student-centered may have different meanings in different contexts. We need to look at how teachers engage students cognitively in deep learning in a manner relevant to the context.

Chan's study (chap. 6, this volume) shows how the typical patterns of *structure* and systematic teaching (Paine, 1990) in Chinese pedagogy have been integrated with the use of *emergent* inquiry in the Western approach. Although the contemporary expert teachers involved developed classroom routines in ways that addressed the new educational goal of learning to learn, they did not give up the traditional goal of knowledge consolidation for examinations. These teachers used well-crafted and structured approaches, including both collaborative inquiry and drilling of exam questions, to cater to students' needs. They reasoned that both approaches are important to help students to gain a better understanding and develop motivation, and thus help them to learn more productively.

Paradoxically, these expert teachers *structure* their teaching environments to engage students to help them grow as *independent* learners; they foster students to achieve high levels of cognitive engagement; they are both *didactic* and *constructivist.* As one student remarked, "My teacher 'forced' us to think." The teacher believed that he had succeeded because he is a strict (*yan*) [嚴] teacher; the Chinese concept of *yan* denotes a serious teacher with high expectations of students so that they will strive hard and follow the desired path. This concept is aligned with teacher beliefs about their cultivating role and conduct guidance, in that they see themselves as parents charged with the duties of bringing up children for both academic and moral purposes. Higher-order thinking normally implies student-centered activity; here, the Chinese teachers designed their environments using highly-structured approaches that required their students to learn and think. The expert teachers used approaches that seemed contradictory as they transformed the pedagogy to meet contextual demands.

In line with the mastery and virtuoso practices of the Chinese teachers described in Paine's analyses, the master Chinese teachers of the contemporary era use a synthesized form of structured constructivist teaching that transcends both teacher and student-centered teaching. The teachers observed in the various studies in this volume direct and choreograph deep learning in Chinese classrooms to achieve new educational goals that incorporate both knowledge transmission and knowledge transformation perspectives. While Western researchers tend to dichotomize these approaches, we observe that Chinese teachers blend or synergize them; they attend to both *the heart and the mind* of teaching.

## Teacher Professional Development and the Third Space

Another theme centres on teacher learning and professional development in the changing Chinese context. Research has shown that Chinese teachers have changed and learned by using new pedagogies such as the conceptual change approach (Ho et al., 2001), action learning (Gow, Kember, & McKay, 1996), and knowledge building (Chan & van Aalst, 2006). So and Watkins (2005) and Tang (2001) showed how teacher education programs influenced pre-service teachers to change their beliefs from transmission to constructivist views. In light of the trend of internationalization and educational reforms, teachers in different parts of the world all face major challenges in developing new ways of teaching. They are expected to help students develop learning how to learn, adopt the use of technology, and pursue various other new educational goals (Chan & Pang, 2006; Darling-Hammond, Bransford, LePage, Hammerless, & Duffy, 2005).

One characteristic model of teacher professional development in East Asia is the well-known "Lesson Study" approach practiced in Japan and China. Teachers work together as they reflect on their teaching, re-fine their pedagogical practices, and engage in collective learning for continual improvement. The idea of East Asian teachers working together has attracted much interest in Western countries (Stigler & Hiebert, 1999). The case of China is of particular interest because of the possible conflict between local cultural beliefs and values and Western innovations.

Tsui and Wong's study (chap. 10, this volume) on teacher professional development in mainland China incorporates two major themes: (1) the collective nature of teacher development; and (2) how teachers in mainland China incorporate changes based on Western innovations. The first theme relates to features of teacher professional development which are consistent with earlier descriptions of teacher professional development in China (Cortazzi & Jin, 2001; Paine, 1990). These characteristics include: (i) an emphasis on discipline-based knowledge, whereby teachers are expected to have a strong foundation in terms of subject matter knowledge and pedagogical content knowledge; (b) mentorship – the Chinese system has an elaborate system of mentorship of "the old leading the young" (*lao dai qing*) [老帶青], and a career path for expert teachers; (c) a well-developed teacher professional development system in schools, in which teachers are continually involved in group preparations for lessons, demonstration classes and peer evaluation; and (d) a well-established organizational structure that features hierarchical responsibilities and government support for schools.

As we examine these characteristics, it is possible to see how they may provide advantages for teacher learning and professional development. While Western systems tend to focus on student-centered pedagogy, the mainland Chinese system focuses more on preparing teachers for subject-matter teaching; this may be due to cultural and teaching beliefs in which the ideal teacher is regarded as an expert in knowledge. We now understand the pivotal role of domain knowledge in how people learn (Bransford et al., 1999; Bransford et al., 2006). While focusing solely on content is not sufficient, it is now recognized that a deep understanding of subject matter and pedagogical content knowledge is a foundation for good teaching (Bereiter, 2002; Shulman, 1986).

While there may be concerns over the weakness of the virtuoso model, Paine (1990) has argued that the Chinese model that focuses on mastery, demonstration, and perfecting teaching may have advantages for teacher learning. Among mainland Chinese teachers, the crafting of lessons for others to observe is a practice commonly used in schools that can contribute to teacher learning. Although mentorship may have different meanings for different people, the emphasis on this practice provides other key opportunities for growth. The teacher professional development model in mainland China is aligned with the Chinese conceptualization of learning (Li, chap. 2, this volume) that focuses on mastery and striving for perfection, illustrating how cultural beliefs mediate learning, teaching and teacher professional development.

Tsui and Wong (chap. 10, this volume) discuss the strengths of this practice, but also note its possible weaknesses and gaps. With the emphasis on crafting the *perfect* script, there are concerns about whether individual differences and creativity can be adequately catered for. In particular, such an approach may fall short of the need to adopt peda-gogical approaches for educational reforms designed to develop 21st century knowledge and skills. Tsui and Wong describe an exemplary project in which, against the background of change, a master Chinese teacher educator works with teachers to develop an approach called "action education" that fuses traditional and Western ideas. The teachers do not simply graft Western concepts onto Chinese soil – they work with new ideas and practices, and the authors invoke the "third space" construct to explain how the Chinese teachers make innovations relevant to their context. There is an emphasis on action that integrates the notions underlying Chinese beliefs, with a focus on pragmatic goals and actions. The notion of the "third space" accords with the idea of "transformed pedagogy"; this can be observed in classrooms as teachers integrate and synergize contradictory goals and processes. Teaching and teacher development must be seen in terms of the totality of cultures and contextual influences.

Across different strands of teacher beliefs, teacher pedagogy and teacher learning, there are *distinctive* patterns of beliefs and pedagogy, as well as *common* principles of good teaching mediated by contextual con-straints and influences. In the face of reforms, the Chinese teacher can be both didactic and constructivist. The transformed pedagogy, understood from the perspective of the third space notion, is not simply a combi-nation or 'add-on' of different tactics, but is one in which teachers take into careful consideration student cognition, classroom structure and contextual demands. Good teaching, as shown by these accounts of Chi-nese teachers, involves teachers integrating tensions as they develop and deepen student learning, all the time working with system constraints.

## Contributions, Implications and Further Issues

Following the discussion of emerging themes in previous sections, we now discuss how *Revisiting the Chinese Learner* contributes to theories and research on learning and development, innovation for educational change, and teaching and learning in cross-cultural studies. We also examine the implications for classroom pedagogy and discuss issues that require further research.

## Learning and Development – Broadening Western Interpretations

*Affective and social processes.* The chapters in this volume, in conjunction with earlier volumes, provide insights for enriching current psychological theories developed primarily within the English-speaking world. Research on the Chinese learner may extend our understanding and broaden our inquiry of human development and behavior. Li's Chinese model of learning illuminates learning constructs that go beyond those commonly used in the West, which tend to focus on the cognitive constructs of intelligence, ability, attribution and strategy deployment (Sternberg & Zhang, 2001; Winne, 1996; Zimmerman & Schunk, 2001). Li's model, which incorporates affective, social, cultural and moral dimensions, contributes to new approaches for examining child development in different cultures. Her studies challenge the limits of trying to transplant Western interpretations into the Chinese context and shed light on the possibility of considering a broader range of constructs and exploring alternative approaches that use more holistic learning embedded in Chinese cultural beliefs and values.

*Cognitive and sociocognitive processes.* Research on memorization-understanding has sparked considerable interest in understanding the Chinese learner (Marton et al., 1996; Marton et al., 2005). This volume further supports this notion using studies that examine new cognitive and learning demands using computer-based pedagogy. Chan's study (chap. 6, this volume) which investigates student collaboration and inquiry in computer forums to help with their examination preparations, is another manifestation of the memorization-understanding approach. Her findings also reflect elements of collective memorization and collective metacognition that may shed light on the relationship between individual and collective learning, a key emerging theme in contemporary learning research (Sawyer, 2006) and computer-supported collaborative learning (Stahl, 2006). While metacognition is considered to be an individual cognitive process, Chinese students work on "thinking together" in pursuing both inquiry and pragmatic goals (Chan, 2008). While these social and collective metacognitive processes are present among other learners, they may be more prevalent in Chinese societies. Further research into how Chinese learners engage in new forms of learning may shed light on new lines of inquiry for cognitive and collaborative processing.

*Beyond dichotomies and dialectics.* While researchers tend to use dichotomized constructs such as collaborative versus competitive, didactic versus constructivist or individual versus collectivist to examine learning (Biggs, 1996), Chinese learners and teachers intertwine and synergize these processes to adapt to changing contextual demands. Various chapters show how students adopt both traditional and new goals and strategies, teachers fuse cultural and contemporary beliefs in classroom pedagogy, and teacher educators adopt Western innovations while retaining traditional goals and practices. Such findings also parallel recent research about Chinese thinking in mathematics education – Chinese teachers merge *content* with *process* rather than emphasizing the distinction between the two (Fan, Wong, Cai, & Li, 2004; Leung, 2001).

Continuing with earlier volumes, we agree that we should be cautious about using a Western lens to interpret phenomena in Chinese societies (Biggs, 1996). Furthermore, we posit that Chinese learners may have a greater propensity to *integrate* contradictory processes. Such phenomena may be explained by the notion of the "Doctrine of the Mean" [中庸之道] in Chinese philosophy. Chinese people are more likely to find a middle way among different approaches and ways of living in search of harmony (Lee, 1996). Such an interpretation may draw support from research on philosophies of science and Chinese culture; the researchers contend that the Chinese take a more diffused approach (Needham, 1959). Contemporary psychological research on culture and cognition has provided some empirical data suggesting that Asians emphasize relationships and contexts; they tend to integrate contradictory processes to a greater extent than their Western counterparts (Nisbett, 2003). These assumptions about the differences between Eastern and Western thinking certainly need further research investigation.

The dialectics of integrating contradictory processes may be important in addressing the paradox of the Chinese learner. We suggest that Chinese learners and teachers do not merely juxtapose contradictory processes and add some elements, but view such contradictions relationally and dialectically. For example, they see competition as a means of encouraging collaboration; effort is seen to improve ability; thus, engaging in collaborative inquiry in a computer-mediated environment can help students to consolidate their knowledge in preparation for examinations. Psychological research in the West also considers the overlapping relationships between distinctive processes (e.g. intrinsic and extrinsic processes) and dialectical processes in adult development (Basseches, 1980, 2005) Examining the Chinese learner provides a rich context for understanding these dialectical processes, thereby deepening theories of thinking and learning.

## Educational Change – Innovation and Education Reform

*Educational change and reforms.* In the various contributions to this volume, the authors have gone beyond focusing on the teacher or learner and included processes and dynamic analyses of the interaction of learner and teacher with the learning environment. We emphasize both cultural characteristics and individuals' responses to different tasks in relation to system demands. Such an emphasis on a systems approach mirrors the shift in the emphasis of Western theories from the individual to situated cognition (Brown et al., 1989), participation (Lave & Wenger, 1991; Sfard, 1998), activity theory (Engeström, Miettinen, & Punamäki, 1999), and the emerging field of Learning Sciences that focus on the interfaces of cognition, design and context (Sawyer, 2006). The paradox of the changing Chinese learner provides another strong argument for theorizing and examining learning in context.

This volume also uses the systems perspective to shed light on how educational reform may be facilitated or constrained. Stigler and Hiebert (1999) argued that merely looking to model Western success stories in the East Asian context and vice versa does not help, because pedagogy is related to beliefs as cultural activity. For example, the mere adoption of memorization-understanding would not work in the Western context because of different cultural beliefs and contextual background. For educational change and innovations to take place, there needs to be a careful consideration of the sociocultural context and how classroom, school and system cultures can be changed or aligned with other components.

When certain components of the system change, student and teacher changes may also be possible (Biggs, 2001). As studies in this volume show, there are now changing educational policies that may initiate and foster change in the classroom (Rao et al., chap. 7, this volume). With the adoption of new pedagogies, we find that Chinese learners cherish new goals and employ new approaches (Chan, chap. 6; Law et al., chap. 4; Marton et al., chap. 5, this volume). Chinese learners are 'cue-conscious' (Biggs, 1996) and can develop new approaches they perceive to be appropriate for meeting new task demands in changing educational contexts. Presumably, positive changes among students provide positive feedback to teachers, thereby sustaining the process of change.

Given an appropriate learning environment, Chinese learners may begin to adopt a deeper approach aligned with other components of the system. However, if the focus is on isolated components, or if there are too many tensions, change will be difficult to take place. Policy changes must be accompanied by changes at the classroom level, together with shifts in teacher and student beliefs and approaches. The study of the changing Chinese learner suggests that further research is needed to explore the dynamic interaction among different components of education systems as educational changes take place.

*Classroom innovation and pedagogical transformation.* As various studies reported in this volume indicate, teachers change their approaches using *pedagogical transformations* in which new models are fused with old; they make changes that align student cognition with contextual and systems demands. While the possibility provided by pedagogical transformation is recognized, it needs to be pointed out that problems may also exist when teachers adopting a new pedagogy use 'add-on' strategies that copy surface forms in a way that distorts deeper meanings (Brown & Campione, 1996). Research on how teachers implement a new pedagogy in a different cultural context provides a useful context for understanding how evolutionary practices and pedagogical transformation may take place.

Teachers do not just change their teaching methods; they have beliefs about student learning and beliefs about the system, and they work together to bring about changes. Recent research has examined how social infrastructure affects the way in which changes take place (Bielaczyc, 2006) and the emerging relationships between culture and technology (Zhang, 2007). This volume examining the Chinese learner may help towards developing a better understanding of educational change in different cultural contexts. Different systems may have different embedded cultures and constraints, and theories of change and innovation need to tackle the problem of changing cultures and beliefs.

## Teaching and Learning in Cross-Cultural Studies

*Distinct and common principles.* While this volume contributes to identifying distinctive cultural patterns, the studies described in it also reveal general principles of good teaching and learning. Good teaching in the 21st century is about understanding student cognition and designing pedagogy and innovation that align with sociocultural contexts and dynamics. While the various accounts in this volume have different manifestations, they all show that new learning and innovation can take place in different systems, and how resourceful teachers make use of social infrastructures and contextual dynamics to work within constraints and facilitate new learning. With knowledge across cultures, globalization and reforms, many changes are now taking place. The insights these studies give into how Chinese teachers and teacher educators adapt to new innovations may have implications for supporting teachers in different parts of the world.

*Cultural frames of mind.* We have noted previously that teaching and learning are deeply embedded cultural activities and social practices. In considering educational reform and change, it is important to be aware of the cultural values and *cultural scripts* which underlie various activities. This requires a comparison of different patterns and scripts. Revisiting the Chinese Learner will contribute to such understanding. It is important not just to improve knowledge and skills, but also to improve general beliefs, scripts and conceptions. It is only through examining others' scripts that one is able to reflect more critically on one's own system.

We have revisited the Chinese learner from both insider and outsider perspectives (the editors of this volume grew up in Asia, but completed their higher education in Western countries). Just as researchers critique Western perceptions of learning in the Chinese context, bias may also appear when we use another cultural framework to interpret phenomena. Hence, it has been possible for the pendulum to swing from the earlier assumption that Chinese learners are passive learners to the current view held since the 1990s of a different, perhaps glamorized image of Chinese learners as competent, active and successful. Such polarized stereotypes should be treated with caution.

Throughout this volume, we often refer to Chinese and Western views. We need to be cautious in using such generalized distinctions, as cultures evolve and become intertwined. We have used these terms primarily for convenience of descriptions. We need to be aware of possible biases when interpreting phenomena using cultural frames of mind, whatever perspective is employed. Perhaps the focus is not on some specific qualities of Chinese learner, but rather on how the context can have a powerful influence on teaching and learning. While recognizing cultural values and patterns, we need to consider the system perspectives not only in examining the Chinese learner, but also in understanding learning and teaching in different cultural contexts.

## Classroom Implications for Teaching the Chinese Learners of the 21st Century

*Understanding student beliefs and cultural patterns.* This volume further contributes to debunking the myth that Chinese learners are passive rote-learners. When working with Chinese learners in their own countries and overseas, educators need to develop an understanding of their learners relating to both cultural beliefs and contextual influences. Teachers of Chinese students may refer to different cultural patterns and various meanings of attribution, effort versus ability, memorization-understanding and competition-collaboration in seeking to understand how Chinese students perceive learning. This volume contributes further to the characterization of the Chinese learner, such as in its reference to the Chinese cultural model of learning involving elements of self-perfection, diligence, and persistence, and the tendency amongst Chinese students and teachers to integrate and synergize contradictory approaches. Recognizing these beliefs and approaches may help teachers of Chinese learners to avoid misperceptions, build on students' strengths, and develop ways to scaffold deeper learning among Chinese students.

*Considering situational responses and emergent goals.* In addition to emphasizing cultural beliefs and traditional values in student learning, this volume also shows the influence of a changing educational context. There is now knowledge across cultures, and Chinese learners are ready to adopt new goals and new approaches to meet new demands. Apart from recognizing traditional cultural beliefs, educators need to go beyond fixed patterns and examine the needs, aspirations, and situational responses of these learners given new educational demands. Educational change and innovation need to be considered in the context of students' cultural beliefs and practices, as well as their emerging goals.

We have observed the ingenious ways in which some Chinese students and teachers respond to new task demands. They also tend to retain their traditional beliefs while developing new goals and approaches. Educators need to understand and consider these complex and varied patterns and help students reflect and develop culturally and contextually relevant approaches as they transform their learning.

Educational reforms have spurred a general move in the Asian region to adopt new goals such as the development of critical thinking and problem solving skills and learning how to learn. While incorporating these new educational goals, educators would do well to emphasize the positive characteristics that the Chinese learner exhibits, such as persistence, diligence, and effort, as these traits can serve as useful resources. The Chinese learners of tomorrow will be willing to adapt and persist, and will be cue-conscious. Changing task requirements and assessment demands may provide useful opportunities for them to consider new ways of and approaches to learning.

*Transcending dichotomies and transforming learning.* Teachers around the world are now facing the challenge of educational reform and the adoption of new pedagogies. This volume shows that it would be useful to consider the beliefs and conceptions of teachers and students when implementing new pedagogy. For Chinese teachers, many Western-based innovations may appear to be foreign; it may be useful for them to *reflect* on their beliefs and practices considering how these innovations relate to their experiences rather than just following the procedures. The preceding chapters on how Chinese teachers adapt to reform illustrate the process of *pedagogical transformation,* that is, how they adapt their practices for scaffolding student learning in the light of the curriculum and school context. Teachers can be encouraged to see that they can integrate, appropriate and transform new practices in relation to student understanding within the contextually-based constraints in the system. While there are general principles of good learning, their manifestation may vary across cultures and contexts.

*Integrating cognitive and affective goals.* In addition to cognitive dimensions, socio-affective-moral components of the innovation can be highlighted thus addressing teacher beliefs and the cultivating role of Chinese teachers. Teachers would be more likely to adopt the innovation as they see how these new classroom pedagogy can be valuable to their students. As innovations are introduced, we can capitalize on teachers' beliefs, intentions and values, as well as their common pragmatic goal of helping develop students into capable and educated 21st century citizens.

*Teacher collaboration and working together.* In the face of educational reforms, teachers need to be supported in ways that they can develop new understanding and practice as they respond to change. In the area of teacher learning and professional development, the examples provided from mainland Chinese teachers in this volume illustrate the possibilities of teachers learning together. Although the patterns are different, the emphasis of *teacher collaboration* is aligned with current work in the West emphasizing communities of practice among teachers. The insights on teacher collaboration would be important for teacher learning and innovation in the changing education era. Educators should perhaps explore ways of how we can work together across cultures to build new knowledge and practice for 21st century learning.

## Summary and Conclusion

This volume, which revisits the Chinese learner, is framed around changing education and changing contexts. The analyses of learning in contemporary Chinese classroom settings and education reforms provide a powerful context for examining how traditional Chinese cultural beliefs and values interact with contemporary forces to mediate teaching and learning. We conclude by synthesizing the main themes in this volume for addressing the paradoxes and depicting the Chinese learner of the 21st century. Figure 11.1 shows a framework for understanding the Chinese learner in changing educational contexts.

*Traditional beliefs and values.* Analyses of Confucian-heritage culture, historical background, collectivist values and philosophical beliefs (Lee, 1996; Wong, 2004) are supported by empirical research on the Chinese conceptualization of learning highlighting the roles of socio-affective-moral variables, heart and mind for wanting to learn [好學心], in pursuit of self-perfection among Chinese learners (Li, chap. 2, this volume). This volume also considers historical changes in Confucian beliefs, examining their parallels with contemporary learning goals for Chinese learners (Law et al., chap. 4, this volume). These analyses highlight the role of cultural beliefs and indicate the importance of reexamining common beliefs about Confucianism in understanding Chinese learners.

*Contemporary changes.* Technological advances, socioeconomic changes, shifts in learning paradigms, and the adoption of new educational policies and reforms have led to the use of new technologies and pedagogies that have affected teaching and learning in Confucian-heritage-culture classrooms. These changing patterns of beliefs and practice, though emerging very slowly, provide insights into and raise questions about 21st century learning, as well as further refuting the myth that Chinese students are passive, rote learners. As with other discussions of how overseas Chinese learners favour new forms of learning (Rastall, 2006; Shi, 2006), we found that Chinese learners in Chinese societies also have new aspirations and competencies when provided with new pedagogical experiences (Chan, chap. 6; Law et al., chap. 4; Marton et al., chap. 5, this volume). Changes in educational policies are bringing about new ways of teaching in Chinese classrooms (Rao, et al., chap. 7; Rao, et al., chap. 9; Siegel et al., chap. 8, this volume). Chinese learners are not predisposed to passive learning and cramming for examination; they are highly adaptive, and they develop appropriate approaches and responses to perceived task demands, constraints and 21st century learning opportunities.

*Student beliefs and approaches.* When examining how the contemporary Chinese learners respond to change, we found the theme of going beyond dichotomies to be even more distinct (Biggs, 1996). Consistent with studies of the intertwined relationship between memorization and understanding (Marton et al., 1996; Marton et al., 2005), various studies show that Chinese learners *transcend dichotomies*; they fuse competition with collaboration, viewing competition as a form of learning motivation (Watkins, chap. 3, this volume). Chinese learners also integrate inquiry with revision and interweave cognitive with affective goals (Chan, chap. 6; Law et al., chap. 4, this volume) as they respond to new perceived task demands. While these strategies may not be unique to Chinese learners, they are more likely to be used by them. Chinese learners are cue-conscious. These *relational* and *dialectical* strategies, made salient as they are affected by cultural beliefs and contextual demands, need to be investigated further both to shed light on the paradox of the Chinese learner and to enrich our understanding of the complexity of learning.

*Teacher beliefs and pedagogy.* In this volume, the paradox of the Chinese teacher has been addressed through considering new pedagogical practice. We found that teacher- and student-centred learning have different meanings in different cultural contexts. Using the background of changing educational contexts, this volume shows that Chinese teachers consider the "heart and mind" in cultivating moral growth as well as developing students to meet new educational goals. A similar theme we examine is transcending dichotomies when examining Chinese pedagogy. With the advent of curriculum reform, Chinese teachers believe that content and process need to be merged (Leung, 2001; Wong, 2004); they intertwine structure with emergent processes; they fuse traditional beliefs with new practices (Rao et al., chap. 9; Siegel et al., chap. 8, this volume); and they can be both didactic and constructivist (Chan, chap. 6, this volume; Ng & Rao, 2008). Expert teachers and teacher educators use *pedagogical transformation* (Chan, chap. 6, this volume), negotiating tensions in the *third space* to synergize their beliefs and practices to enhance teaching and learning (Tsui & Wong, chap. 10, this volume).

*Changing student and teacher learning.* With the advent of 21st century education, student and teacher learning includes, but also moves beyond, quantitative and qualitative learning in developing new goals for lifelong learning. Various chapters in this volume examine these new goals and tasks, such as learning how to learn, collaboration, technology-enhanced learning (Chan, chap. 6, this volume; Law et al., chap. 4, this volume), reading to learn (Marton et al., chap. 5, this volume) and English learning (Siegel et al., chap. 8, this volume), with an emphasis on how we can characterize and foster learning for the Chinese learner of tomorrow. While developing new expectations, teaching and learning approaches used in the Chinese context have retained traditional goals and existing standards, with an emphasis on examinations. These conflicts and tensions provide some of the most interesting contexts for examining system dynamics and how changes may be possible.

This volume sheds light on the paradox of the Chinese learner with theoretical and educational implications for 21st century learning. Our analyses of the Chinese learner may enrich conceptualization and processes of learning that draw on cross-cultural phenomena. With the advent of the knowledge era, teachers all over the world need to understand and adopt new forms of learning and pedagogy as they are required to undergo change themselves. Although there may be variations for teachers in different parts of the world, a common issue they face is that their classroom innovations must *integrate* and *transform* existing cultures into new cultures in the classroom. It is important for teachers not merely to follow tactics or *procedures*; they need to consider deep *principles* as well as the social infrastructure of the classroom, and they need to reflect on their beliefs and practices. Policy-level systemic changes need to be aligned with changes made at other levels, such as in schools and classrooms. The various paradoxes associated with the Chinese learner and the Chinese teacher can shed light on how educational changes may be possible in different cultural contexts.

Just as there can be Western misperceptions, we need to exercise caution against moving from one extreme to the other. Comparing cultural scripts and being *aware* of one's own mindset can help to enlighten our understanding. While cultural patterns influence behaviour and expectations about learning, there are also general principles that underlie learning, even though their manifestations are different. Although this volume focuses on the Chinese learner, we do not seek to emphasize homogenous ethnic groupings; the focus is not on some inherent characteristics of the learner, but on the learner in context and learning in situ. We need to consider cultural norms, as well as variations in individual factors and their interaction with contextual factors; culture is not static, and its changing characteristics need to be investigated further.

In the light of educational changes and reforms, teachers and educators may consider distinctive patterns and common principles, as well as cultural and situational influences, and reflect on their beliefs and practices, rather than assuming such influences, or simply grafting new approaches onto old ones. As many reforms take place in different countries around the world, we hope that *Revisiting the Chinese Learner* in changing educational contexts will continue to raise important questions on how best to understand and enhance the quality of teaching and learning in the 21st century.

# REFERENCES

Alexander, P. A., & Winne, P. H. (2006). *Handbook of educational psychology* (2nd ed.). Mahwah, NJ: Lawrence Erlbaum Associates.

Basseches, M. (1980). Dialectical schemata: A framework for the empirical study of the development of dialectical thinking. *Human Development, 23*, 400-421.

Basseches, M. (2005). The development of dialectical thinking as an approach to integration. *Integral Review: A Transdisciplinary and Transcultural Journal for New Thought, Research, and Praxis, 1,* 47-63.

Bereiter, C. (2002). *Education and mind in the knowledge age.* Mahwah, NJ: Lawrence Erlbaum Associates.

Bielaczyc, K. (2006). Designing social infrastructure: Critical issues in creating learning environments with technology. *Journal of the Learning Sciences, 15,* 301-329.

Biggs, J. B. (1987). *Student approaches to learning and studying.* Hawthorn, Vic: Australian Council for Educational Research.

Biggs, J. B. (1993). What do inventories of students' learning processes really measure? A theoretical review and clarification. *British Journal of Educational Psychology, 63,* 3-19.

Biggs, J. B. (1996). Western misperceptions of the Confucian-heritage learning culture. In D. A. Watkins & J. B. Biggs (Eds.), *The Chinese Learner: Cultural, psychological and contextual influences* (pp. 45-67). Hong Kong/Melbourne: Comparative Education Research Centre, The University of Hong Kong/ Australian Council for Educational Research.

Biggs, J. B., Kember, D., & Leung, D. Y. P. (2001). The revised two-factor study process questionnaire: R-SPQ-2F. *British Journal of Educational Psychology, 71,* 133-149.

Biggs, J. B., & Watkins, D. A. (2001). Insights into teaching the Chinese Learner. In D. A. Watkins & J. B. Biggs (Eds.), *Teaching the Chinese Learner: Psychological and pedagogical perspectives* (pp. 277-300). Hong Kong/Melbourne: Comparative Education Research Centre, The University of Hong Kong/Australian Council for Educational Research.

Bradley, D., & Bradley, M. (1984). *Problems of Asian students in Australia: Language, culture and education.* Canberra: Australian Government Printing Service.

Bransford, J., Brown, A., & Cocking, R. (1999). *How people learn: Brain, mind, experience and school.* Washington, DC: National Academy Press, National Research Council.

Bransford, J., Stevens, R., Schwartz, D., Meltzoff, A., Pea, R., Roschelle, J., et al. (2006). Learning theories and education: Toward a decade of synergy. In P. A. Alexander & P. H. Winne (Eds.), *Handbook of educational psychology* (2nd ed., pp. 209-244). Mahwah, NJ: Lawrence Erlbaum Associates.

Bronfenbrenner, U. (1979). *The ecology of human development.* Cambridge, MA: Harvard University Press.

Bronfenbrenner, U. (1989). Ecological systems theory. In R. Vasta (Ed.), *Annals of Child Development: Vol. 6. Six theories of child development: Revised formulations and current issues* (pp. 185-246). Greenwich, CT: JAI Press.

Brown, A. L., & Campione J. C. (1996). Psychological theory and the design of innovative learning environments: On procedures, principles, and systems. In L. Schuable & R. Glaser (Eds.), *Innovations in learning: New environments for education* (pp. 289-325). Mahwah, NJ: Lawrence Erlbaum Associates.

Brown, J. S., Collins, A., & Duguid, P. (1989). Situated cognition and the culture of learning. *Educational Researcher, 18*(1), 32-42.

Chan, C. K. K. (2001). Promoting learning and understanding through constructivist approaches for Chinese learners. In D. A. Watkins & J. B. Biggs (Eds.), *Teaching the Chinese Leaner: Psychological and pedagogical perspectives* (pp. 181-203). Hong Kong/Melbourne: Comparative Education Research Centre, The University of Hong Kong/Australian Council for Educational Research.

Chan, C. K. K., & Pang, M. F. (Eds.). (2006). Teacher collaboration in learning communities [Special Issue]. *Teaching Education, 17*(1).

Chan, C. K. K., & van Aalst, J. (2006). Teacher development through computer-supported knowledge building: Experience from Hong Kong and Canadian teachers. *Teaching Education, 17*, 7-27.

Chan, C.K. K. (2008). Pedagogical transformation and knowledge building for the Chinese learner. *Evaluation and Research in Education, 21*, 235-251.

Clark, R., & Gieve, S. N. (2006). On the discursive construction of "the Chinese Learner". *Language, Culture and Curriculum, 19*, 54-73.

Cortazzi, M., & Jin, L. (2001). Large classes in China: "Good" teachers and interaction. In D. A. Watkins & J. B. Biggs (Eds.), *Teaching the Chinese Leaner: Psychological and pedagogical perspectives* (pp. 115-134). Hong Kong/Melbourne: Comparative Education Research Centre, The University of Hong Kong/Australian Council for Educational Research.

Dahlin, B., & Watkins, D. A. (2000). The role of repetition in the processes of memorizing and understanding: A comparison of the views of German and Chinese secondary school students in Hong Kong. *British Journal of Educational Psychology, 70*, 65-84.

Darling-Hammond, L., Bransford, J., LePage, P., Hammerness, K., & Duffy, H. (Eds.). (2005). *Preparing teachers for a changing world: What teachers should learn and be able to do*. San Francisco, California: Jossey-Bass.

Engeström, Y., Miettinen, R., & Punamäki, R. L. (Ed.). (1999). *Perspectives on activity theory*. Cambridge: Cambridge University Press.

Entwistle, N., & Ramsden, P. (1983). *Understanding student learning*. London: Croom Helm.

Fan, L. H., Wong, N. Y., Cai, J. F., & Li, S. Q. (2004). *How Chinese learn mathematics: Perspectives from insiders*. Singapore: World Scientific.

Gao, L., & Watkins, D. A. (2002). Conceptions of teaching held by school science teachers in P.R. China: Identification and cross-cultural comparisons. *International Journal of Science Education, 24*, 61-79.

Gardner, H. (1989). *To open minds: Chinese clues to the dilemma of contemporary education.* New York: Basic Books.

Gow, L., & Kember, D. (1993). Conceptions of teaching and their relationship to student learning. *British Journal of Educational Psychology, 63,* 20-33.

Gow, L., Kember, D., & McKay, J. (1996). Improving student learning through action research into teaching. In D. A. Watkins & J. B. Biggs (Eds.), *The Chinese Learner: Cultural, psychological and contextual influences* (pp. 243-265). Hong Kong/Melbourne: Comparative Education Research Centre, The University of Hong Kong/Australian Council for Educational Research.

Greeno, J. G., Collins, A. M., & Resnick, L. B. (1996). Cognition and learning. In D. Berliner & R. Calfee (Eds.), *Handbook of educational psychology* (pp. 15-46). New York: Macmillan.

Gu, Q., & Schweisfurth, M. (2006). Who adapts? Beyond cultural models of 'the' Chinese learner. *Language, Culture and Curriculum, 19,* 74-89.

Ho, A. S. P., Watkins, D. A., & Kelly, M. (2001). The conceptual change approach to improving teaching and learning: An evaluation of a Hong Kong staff development programme. *Higher Education, 42,* 143-169.

Hofer, B. K., & Pintrich, P. R. (Eds.) (2002). *Personal epistemology: The psychology of beliefs about knowledge and knowing.* Mahwah, NJ: Lawrence Erlbaum Associates.

Hu, G. (2002). Potential cultural resistance to pedagogical imports: The case of communicative language teaching in China. *Language, Culture and Curriculum, 15,* 93-105.

Jin, L., & Cortazzi, M. (2006). Changing practices in Chinese cultures of learning. *Language, Culture and Curriculum, 19,* 5-20.

Kember, D. (2000). Misconceptions about the learning approaches, motivation and study practices of the Asian students. *Higher Education, 40,* 99-121.

Lave, J., & Wenger, E. (1991). *Situated learning: Legitimate peripheral participation.* Cambridge: Cambridge University Press.

Lee, W. O. (1996). The cultural context for Chinese Learners: Conceptions of learning in the Confucian tradition. In D. A. Watkins & J. B. Biggs (Eds.), *The Chinese Learner: Cultural, psychological, and cultural influences* (pp. 25-41). Hong Kong/Melbourne: Comparative Education Research Centre, The University of Hong Kong/Australian Council for Educational Research.

Lee, W. O., & Mok, M. M. C. (Eds.). (2008). The construction and deconstruction of the Chinese Learner: Implications for learning theories [Special issue]. *Evaluation and Research in Education, 21*(3).

Leung, F. K. S. (2001). In search of an East Asian identity in mathematics education. *Educational Studies in Mathematics, 47,* 35-51.

Li, J. (2001). Chinese conceptualization of learning. *Ethos, 29,* 111-137.

Li, J. (2003). US and Chinese cultural beliefs about learning. *Journal of Educational Psychology, 95,* 258-267.

Marton, F., & Booth, S. (1997). *Learning and awareness.* Mahwah, NJ: Lawrence Erlbaum Associates.

Marton, F., Dall'Alba, G. A., & Tse, L. K. (1996). Memorizing and understanding: The keys to the paradox? In D. A. Watkins & J. B. Biggs (Eds.), *The Chinese Learner* (pp. 69-83). Hong Kong/Melbourne: Comparative Education Research Centre, The University of Hong Kong/Australian Council for Educational Research.

Marton, F., & Säljö, R. (1976). On qualitative differences in learning: 1-Outcome and process. *British Journal of Educational Psychology, 46,* 4-11.

Marton, F., & Tsui, A. B. M. (2004). *Classroom discourse and the space of learning.* Mahwah, NJ: Lawrence Erlbaum Associates.

Marton, F., Watkins, D. A., & Tang, C. (1997). Discontinuities and continuities in the experience of learning: An interview study of high-school students in Hong Kong. *Learning and Instruction, 7,* 21-48.

Marton, F., Wen, Q. F., & Wong, K. C. (2005). Read a hundred times and the meaning will appear: Changes in Chinese university students' views of the temporal structure of learning. *Higher Education, 49,* 291-318.

Mok, I., Chik, P. M., Ko, P. Y., Kwan, T., Lo, M. L., Marton, F., et al. (2001). Solving the paradox of the Chinese teacher? In D. A. Watkins & J. B. Biggs (Eds.), *Teaching the Chinese Learner: Psychological and pedagogical perspectives* (pp. 161-179). Hong Kong/Melbourne: Comparative Education Research Centre, The University of Hong Kong/Australian Council for Educational Research.

Needham, J. (1959). *Science and civilization in China.* Cambridge: Cambridge University Press.

Ng, S. S. N., & Rao, N. (2008). Mathematics teaching during the early years in Hong Kong: A reflection of constructivism with Chinese characteristics? *Early Years: An International Journal of Research and Development, 28,* 159-172.

Nisbett, R. (2003). *The geography of thought: How Asians and Westerners think differently and why.* New York: Free Press.

Paine, L. (1990). The teacher as virtuoso: A Chinese model for teaching. *Teachers College Record, 92,* 49-81.

Pratt, D. (1992). Conceptions of teaching. *Adult Education Quarterly, 42,* 203-220.

Prosser, M., & Trigwell, K. (1998). *Understanding learning and teaching: The experience in higher education.* Milton Keynes: Open University Press.

Rastall, P. (2006). The Chinese Learner in higher education: Transition and quality issues [Special Issue]. *Language, Culture and Curriculum, 19*(1).

Samuelowicz, K. (1987). Learning problems of overseas students: Two sides of a story. *Higher Education Research and Development, 6,* 121-134.

Sawyer, R. K. (Ed.). (2006). *The Cambridge handbook of the learning sciences.* New York: Cambridge University Press.

Schommer, M. (2004). Explaining the epistemological belief system: Introducing the embedded systemic model and coordinated research approach. *Educational Psychologist, 39,* 19-29.

Sfard, A. (1998). On two metaphors for learning and the dangers of choosing just one. *Educational Researcher, 27(2),* 4-13.

Shi, L. (2006). The successors to Confucianism or a new generation? A questionnaire study on Chinese students' culture of learning English. *Language, Culture and Curriculum, 19,* 122-147.

Shulman, L. (1986). Those who understand knowledge growth in teaching. *Educational Researcher, 15*(2), 4-14.

So, W. M., & Watkins, D. A. (2005). From beginning teacher education to professional teaching: A study of the thinking of Hong Kong primary science teachers. *Teaching and Teacher Education, 21,* 525-541.

Stahl, G. (2006). *Group cognition: Computer support for building collaborative knowledge.* Cambridge, Mass: MIT Press.

Sternberg, R. J., & Zhang, L. F. (2001). *Perspectives on thinking, learning, and cognitive styles.* The educational psychology series. Mahwah, NJ: Lawrence Erlbaum Associates.

Stigler, J. W., & Hiebert, J. (1999). *The teaching gap: Best ideas from the world's teachers for improving education in the classroom.* New York: Free Press.

Stokes, S. F. (2001). Problem-based learning in a Chinese context: Faculty perceptions. In D. A. Watkins & J. B. Biggs (Eds.), *Teaching the Chinese Learner: Psychological and pedagogical perspectives* (pp. 205-218). Hong Kong/Melbourne: Comparative Education Research Centre, The University of Hong Kong/Australian Council for Educational Research.

Tang, T. K. W. (2001). The influence of teacher education on conceptions of teaching and learning. In D. A. Watkins & J. B. Biggs (Eds.), *Teaching the Chinese Learner: Psychological and pedagogical perspectives* (pp. 221-238). Hong Kong/Melbourne: Comparative Education Research Centre, The University of Hong Kong/Australian Council for Educational Research.

van Aalst, J., & Chan, C. K. K. (2007). Student-directed assessment of knowledge building using electronic portfolios. *Journal of the Learning Sciences, 16,* 175-220.

Watkins, D. A. (1996). Learning theories and approaches to research: A cross-cultural perspective. In D. A. Watkins & J. B. Biggs (Eds.), *The Chinese Learner: Cultural, psychological and contextual influences* (pp. 3-24). Hong

Kong/Melbourne: Comparative Education Research Centre, The University of Hong Kong/Australian Council for Educational Research.

Watkins, D. A., & Biggs, J. B. (Eds.). (1996). *The Chinese Learner: Cultural, psychological and contextual influences.* Hong Kong/Melbourne: Comparative Education Research Centre, The University of Hong Kong/Australian Council for Educational Research.

Watkins, D. A., & Biggs, J. B. (Eds.). (2001). *Teaching the Chinese Learner: Psychological and pedagogical perspectives.* Hong Kong/Melbourne: Comparative Education Research Centre, The University of Hong Kong/Australian Council for Educational Research.

Winne, P. H. (1996). A metacognitive view of individual differences in self-regulated learning. *Learning and Individual Differences, 8,* 327-353.

Wong, D. K. P., & Lam, D. O. B. (2007). Problem-based learning in social work: A study of student learning outcomes. *Research on Social Work Practice, 17,* 55-65.

Wong, N. Y. (2004). The CHC learner's phenomenon: Its implications on mathematics education. In L. H. Fan, N. Y. Wong, J. F. Cai & S. Q. Li (Eds.), *How Chinese learn mathematics: Perspectives from insiders,* (pp. 503-533). Singapore: World Scientific.

Zhang, J. (2007). A cultural look at information and communication technologies in Eastern education. *Educational Technology Research and Development, 55,* 301-314.

Zimmerman, B. J. (1995). Self-regulation involves more than metacognition: A social cognitive perspective. *Educational Psychologist, 30,* 217-221.

Zimmerman, B. J., & Schunk, D. H. (2001). *Self-regulated learning and academic achievement: Theoretical perspectives.* Mahwah, NJ: Lawrence Erlbaum Associates.

# Notes on the Authors

Carol K.K. CHAN is Associate Professor, Faculty of Education, The University of Hong Kong. Her research areas include learning, cognition and instruction, computer-supported knowledge building and teacher communities for classroom innovation. She has published widely in these areas and won international research awards on knowledge building conducted in Chinese classrooms. She also serves on the editorial boards of several leading journals and is actively involved in international organizations that contribute to the field of learning sciences. Dr Chan has received Outstanding Teaching Awards from both her Faculty and University. She is currently Co-Director of a Strategic Research Theme on Sciences of Learning at The University of Hong Kong. E-mail: ckkchan@ hkucc.hku.hk

Kai-ming CHENG is Chair Professor of Education and Senior Advisor to the Vice-Chancellor at The University of Hong Kong. His research concentrates on education policies and his recent projects include analyses of reform policies in various countries in Asia and Africa. He co-directs a cross-disciplinary Strategic Research Theme on Sciences of Learning at The University of Hong Kong. E-mail: kmcheng@hku.hk

Jin CHI is Associate Professor, Faculty of Education, China Women's University in Beijing. Her research areas include child development, educational psychology, and preschool education. She is currently conducting research on the education of "left-behind children," preschool curriculum, and children's understanding of the world. E-mail: xuchi@yahoo.com

EDB (Education Bureau) Chinese Language Research Team has members including curriculum officers, research assistants and seconded teachers from secondary schools (2004-2007), at the Curriculum Development Institute, Government of Hong Kong.

Ellen KNELL is completing her PhD at the University of Utah where she teaches international students and trains pre-service teachers. Ellen continues to be interested in second language reading research and is currently in the process of doing a follow-up study with students from the same school in Xian, China. E-mail: ellenknell@msn.com

Ming LAI is a Ph.D. candidate, Faculty of Education, The University of Hong Kong. His current research examines the relationship between argumentation and knowledge building in a computer-supported collaborative learning (CSCL) context. E-mail: minglai@hkucc.hku.hk

Nancy W.Y. LAW is Professor and Director of the Centre for Information Technology in Education, and Head of the Division of Information and Technology Studies, Faculty of Education, The University of Hong Kong. Her main research interests include the evaluation and comparative studies of ICT policies and implementation for educational innovation as well as the design, development and use of digital technology to support knowledge building and modeling. E-mail: nlaw@hku.hk

Venus S.L. LEE is Assistant Professor, Division of Psychology, Nanyang Technological University, Singapore Her current research focuses on the social, cognitive and motivational process that mediate the construction and propagation of social consensus. E-mail: slleeh@ntu.edu.sg

Jin LI is Associate Professor, Brown University, USA. She studies how children develop learning beliefs across cultures and related home socialization. She is also interested in how children across cultures develop self-conscious emotions such as shame, pride, and respect, particularly as they relate to learning and achievement. E-mail: Jin_Li@brown.edu

Ference MARTON is Professor Emeritus, University of Gothenburg, Sweden; Advisory Professor, Hong Kong Institute of Education and Honorary Professor, Faculty of Education, The University of Hong Kong. He is probably best known for his descriptions of different approaches to learning and for the introduction of the qualitative research area of Phenomenography. He is currently working on books on the Variation Theory of Learning and on Chinese Pedagogy. E-mail: ference.marton@ped.gu.se

Sharon S.N. NG is Assistant Professor, Department of Early Childhood, Hong Kong Institute of Education. Her research area and interests are in early childhood mathematics teaching and learning and early childhood education in Chinese contexts. E-mail: suinng@ied.edu.hk

Miao PEI is Lecturer, State Key Laboratory of Cognitive Neuroscience and Learning, Beijing Normal University. Her research areas are second language learning, teacher cognition, and teacher development. She is currently working on a large-scale project which aims to support the learning of English by elementary school students from rural areas of the PRC. E-mail: peimiao@bnu.edu.cn

Nicol F.C. PAN is a Ph.D. candidate, Faculty of Education, The University of Hong Kong, where she also works on a research project in the Faculty of Engineering. Her research areas are educational technologies, interdisciplinary studies, critical pedagogy and discourse analysis, with a special focus on culture and identities in education. She is involved in interdisciplinary research projects in e-learning. E-mail: pannicol@gmail.com

Emma PEARSON is Lecturer, School of Early Childhood, Macquarie University, Sydney, where she teaches classes on development and diversity. Her research activities reflect a broad interest in social and cultural diversity. She is currently engaged in work with families from culturally diverse backgrounds who are caring for a child with a disability. E-mail: Emma.Pearson@aces.mq.edu.au

Nirmala RAO is Professor, Faculty of Education, The University of Hong Kong. She is a Developmental and Educational Psychologist whose research focuses on early child development and education. She has published widely in these areas and has engaged in policy relevant child development research in several Asian countries in the region. She has also been actively involved, at the international level, in several professional organizations concerned both with the well-being of young children and research on early child development. While she has lived and worked in many different countries, she has worked in Hong Kong for most of her life. Her forthcoming book with Kai-ming Cheng and Emma Pearson is entitled, *Contexts of Learning: Teaching in Primary Schools in China and India*. E-mail: nrao@.hku.hk

Linda SIEGEL is Professor, Educational and Counseling Psychology and Special Education and holds the Dorothy C. Lam Chair in Special Education at the University of British Columbia, Canada. Her research interests include the early identification of children at risk for learning disorders, dyslexia, mathematics learning disabilities, and teaching English as a second language. She has worked in Hong Kong, Mainland China, Argentina and Spain on English language teaching. E-mail: linda.siegel@ubc.ca

Amy B.M. Tsui is Pro-Vice-Chancellor and Vice President as well as Chair Professor of Language and Education at The University of Hong Kong. Her research areas include teacher development, classroom-centered research, and language policy. Her most recent book, as lead author, is *Learning in School-University Partnership: Sociocultural Perspectives* (2008), published by Routledge/Taylor & Francis. E-mail: bmtsui@hkucc.hku.hk

David A. Watkins is Professor, Faculty of Education, The University of Hong Kong where he has taught for twenty years. He received his PhD from the Australian National University and has conducted extensive cross-cultural research in areas such as student learning, conceptions of teaching, and self-concept. He was a co-editor of the first two books in this series on the Chinese learner. E-mail: hrfewda@hkucc.hku.hk

Jocelyn L.N. Wong is Assistant Professor, Department of Educational Administration and Policy, Faculty of Education, Chinese University of Hong Kong. Her research interests are decentralization policy and teacher education in China. Her current research is on teachers' school-based professional learning activities in Mainland China. E-mail: jlnwong@cuhk.edu.hk

Haiyan Qiang is Professor of Comparative Education, Faculty of Education, South China Normal University (SCNU), Guangzhou, China. Professor Qiang studied at the University of Massachusetts and is a widely travelled Chinese scholar. She is a visiting academic fellow at The Institute of Education, University of London, and The Ontario Institute for Studies in Education of University of Toronto. She is a leading scholar of English immersion education in China. E-mail: zhugin@pub.guangxzhou.gd.cn

Allan H.K. Yuen is Associate Professor and Associate Dean (Learning and Teaching), Faculty of Education, The University of Hong Kong. His research activities focus on technology acceptance and educational change, evaluative and comparative studies on information technology in education, and e-learning and community building. E-mail: hkyuen@hku.hk

Johnny K.L. YUEN is a PhD candidate, Faculty of Education, The University of Hong Kong. His main research interests include personal epistemology in collaborative knowledge building, and data mining in knowledge building discourses. E-mail: johnny. yuen@gmail.com

Lin ZHAO is Associate Professor of Education, Shaanxi Normal University, China. Her research focuses on second language acquisition for children, early English immersion teaching models, and early literacy. She is a key researcher for the English Immersion Program for Children which commenced in 1997 and has published widely and produced curriculum materials in this area. E-mail: zhaotlin@hotmail.com

Wei ZHAO is Professor and Vice Dean, School of Education, Shaanxi Normal University, China. His research focuses on Learning Disabilities specifically on learning problems related to Chinese language learning and the learning of English as a second language. He has been a lead researcher for five national level research programs in recent years and has published over 30 research papers. E-mail: wzhao100@yahoo.com.cn

# Index